Beginning Windows Phone App Development

Henry Lee
Eugene Chuvyrov

Apress®

Beginning Windows Phone App Development

ISBN-13 (pbk): 978-1-4302-4134-8

ISBN-13 (electronic): 978-1-4302-4135-5

President and Publisher: Paul Manning
Lead Editor: Gary Schwartz
Technical Reviewer: Robert Garrett
Editorial Board: Steve Anglin, Ewan Buckingham, Gary Cornell, Louise Corrigan, Morgan Ertel, Jonathan Gennick, Jonathan Hassell, Robert Hutchinson, Michelle Lowman, James Markham, Matthew Moodie, Jeff Olson, Jeffrey Pepper, Douglas Pundick, Ben Renow-Clarke, Dominic Shakeshaft, Gwenan Spearing, Matt Wade, Tom Welsh
Coordinating Editor: Tracy Brown
Copy Editors: Damon Larson, Tiffany Taylor
Compositor: Bytheway Publishing Services
Indexer: SPi Global
Artist: SPi Global
Cover Designer: Anna Ishchenko

Distributed to the book trade worldwide by Springer Science+Business Media New York, 233 Spring Street, 6th Floor, New York, NY 10013. Phone 1-800-SPRINGER, fax (201) 348-4505, e-mail orders-ny@springer-sbm.com, or visit www.springeronline.com.

For information on translations, please e-mail rights@apress.com, or visit www.apress.com.

Apress and friends of ED books may be purchased in bulk for academic, corporate, or promotional use. eBook versions and licenses are also available for most titles. For more information, reference our Special Bulk Sales–eBook Licensing web page at www.apress.com/bulk-sales.

Any source code or other supplementary materials referenced by the author in this text is available to readers at www.apress.com. For detailed information about how to locate your book's source code, go to www.apress.com/source-code/.

To Erica, my beautiful wife, for her love and support. Thank you for always being there for me.

—Henry Lee

To Marianna—my friend, my wife, my muse—and to my parents for their gift of unconditional love.

—Eugene Chuvyrov

Contents at a Glance

■ About the Authors.. xviii

■ About the Technical Reviewer xix

■ Acknowledgments xx

■ Introduction xxi

■ Chapter 1: Introducing Windows Phone and the Windows Phone Platform 1

■ Chapter 2: Building Windows Phone Applications.....................................15

■ Chapter 3: Building Windows Phone 7 Applications Using Cloud Services
As Data Stores 37

■ Chapter 4: Catching and Debugging Errors 103

■ Chapter 5: Packaging, Publishing, and Managing Applications...............129

■ Chapter 6: Working with the Accelerometer..151

■ Chapter 7: Application Bar...171

■ Chapter 8: The WebBrowser Control..193

■ Chapter 9: Working with Controls and Themes 213

■ Chapter 10: Integrating Applications with the Windows Phone OS 235

■ Chapter 11: Creating Trial Applications...265

■ Chapter 12: Internationalization 287

■ Chapter 13: Isolated Storage 311

■ Chapter 14: Using Location Services 329

■ Chapter 15: Media..357

Chapter 16: Working with the Camera and Photos..............................379

Chapter 17: Push Notifications 405

Chapter 18: Reactive Extensions for .NET...445

Chapter 19: Security 479

Index 513

Contents

▨ **About the Authors** xviii

▨ **About the Technical Reviewer** xix

▨ **Acknowledgments** xx

▨ **Introduction** xxi

▨ **Chapter 1: Introducing Windows Phone and the Windows Phone Platform** 1

Windows Phone Overview 4

Windows Phone Hardware Specifications 4

Windows Phone Application Platform 6

    Silverlight for Windows Phone 6

    XNA for Windows Phone 7

    Tools 7

    Cloud Services 11

    Metro Design 11

Application Development Life Cycle 12

Summary 13

▨ **Chapter 2: Building Windows Phone Applications** 15

Preparing Your Development Machine 15

Building Your First Windows Phone Application 15

    Creating a Windows Phone Project 16

    Using the Windows Phone Silverlight Controls 18

    Writing the Windows Phone Code 22

Running the Silverlight Windows Phone Application 23

Customizing the Windows Phone Application 25

Styling Your Application 28

Summary 34

■ **Chapter 3: Building Windows Phone 7 Applications Using Cloud Services As Data Stores** **37**

Introducing the MVVM Pattern 38

Introducing Microsoft Azure and SQL Azure 39

Creating a Cloud Database 39

The Entity Framework 40

Creating an SQL Azure Database 40

Creating a Database in SQL Azure 51

Creating a Cloud Service to Access the Cloud Database 55

Creating a Windows Azure Project 56

Generating an Object Model to Access the Cloud Database 57

Implementing a WCF Service to Access the SQL Azure Database 63

Building a Phone Client to Access a Cloud Service 70

Creating a Windows Phone Project 70

Building the UI 71

Coding MainPage 77

Coding BoolToVisibilityConvert 79

Adding a Reference to NotepadService 81

Coding NotepadViewModel 82

Testing the Application Against NotepadService Deployed Locally 89

Deploying the Service to Windows Azure 90

Testing the Notepad Application Against the NotepadService Azure Service 99

Summary 100

■ Chapter 4: Catching and Debugging Errors 103

Debugging Application Exceptions 103

Debugging Page Load Exceptions 104

Debugging a Web Service Exception 109

Testing the Application 115

Registering a Windows Phone Device for Debugging 115

Handling Device Exceptions 121

Creating the CatchDeviceExceptionDemo Project 122

Building the User Interface 123

Coding the Application 125

Testing the Finished Application 127

Summary 127

■ Chapter 5: Packaging, Publishing, and Managing Applications 129

Windows Phone Application Publishing Life Cycle 129

Windows Phone Application Certification Requirements 131

Application Policies 131

Content Policies 133

Application Submission Validation Requirements 133

Application Certification Requirements 135

Submitting Your First Windows Phone Application to the Windows Phone Marketplace 136

Packaging the Application 136

Submitting the Application 138

Updating Your Application 146

Finding Your Application in the Marketplace 148

Summary 149

■ Chapter 6: Working with the Accelerometer 151

Understanding Orientation and Movement 151

Calculating Distance 154

Calculating Pitch, Roll, and Yaw 154

Introducing SDK Support for Accelerometers 155

Retrieving Accelerometer Data 156

Creating the CaptureAccelerometerData Project 157

Building the UI 158

Coding the Application 160

Testing the Finished Application 163

Using Accelerometer Data to Move a Ball 163

Creating the MoveBall Project 164

Building the UI 165

Coding the Application 167

Testing the Finished Application 169

Summary 169

Chapter 7: Application Bar 171

Introducing the Application Bar 173

Adding an Application Bar to a Windows Phone Application 175

Adding Images for Use with Application Bar Buttons 175

Adding a Global Application Bar Using XAML 177

Adding a Local Application Bar Using XAML 178

Adding Menu Items 179

Adding an Application Bar Using Managed Code 181

Wiring Up Events to an Application Bar 183

Adding Glue Code and a Worker Function to the Add Button 183

Reacting to Add Button Events 184

Reacting to Save Button Events 188

Reacting to Menu Events 188

Adding Event Handlers with XAML 189

Using the ApplicationBar Class to Glue XAML and Managed Code..190

Summary 191

■ **Chapter 8: The WebBrowser Control**..**193**

Introducing the WebBrowser Control..193

Adding a WebBrowser Control...194

Using a WebBrowser Control to Display Web Content...195

Using a WebBrowser Control to Display Local HTML Content 198

Using a WebBrowser Control to Display Dynamic Content...200

Saving Web Pages Locally 201

Choosing Display and Security Settings 204

Viewport...204

    CSS.. 204

    Security 205

A Brief Introduction to HTML5 Features...206

    HTML5 Features 206

    Testing HTML5 Features on Windows Phone 208

Summary 212

■ **Chapter 9: Working with Controls and Themes** **213**

Introducing the Metro Design System 213

    Windows Phone Chrome.. 214

    Screen Orientations 216

Themes on Windows Phone Devices 216

    Applying a Theme 217

    Changing the Theme... 219

    Detecting the Currently Selected Theme... 221

Panorama and Pivot Controls 222

   Using the Panorama Control 223

   Using the Pivot Control 226

Understanding Frame and Page Navigation 228

   Creating a UI for the NavigationTest Project.. 229

   Adding Navigation Code 230

   Adding Code to Pass Parameters Between Pages... 230

Adding Transition Effects..231

   Creating a UI 231

   Downloading TiltEffect.cs and Applying Dependency Properties 233

Summary 234

■ **Chapter 10: Integrating Applications with the Windows Phone OS 235**

Introducing Windows Phone Launchers and Choosers.................................235

   Launchers.. 236

   Choosers.. 237

Working with Launchers and Choosers 238

   Creating the User Interface... 238

   Coding Application Logic 238

Working with the Windows Phone Application Life Cycle.............................241

   Observing Application Life Cycle Events 242

   Managing Application State.. 246

   Best Practices for Managing the Application Life Cycle on the Windows Phone OS 252

Integrating with Facebook 252

   A Few Words about OAuth.. 253

Integrating into Windows Phone Hubs 259

   Integrating Your Application with the Music and Video Hub 260

   Integration with SharePoint... 263

Summary 263

Chapter 11: Creating Trial Applications 265

Understanding Trial and Full Modes 265

Using the IsTrial Method 267

Using the Marketplace APIs 269

Building a Trial Application 271

Building the UI 272

Connecting to a Web Service 277

Adding Page-to-Page Navigation 279

Verifying Trial and Full Modes 281

Adding the Finishing Touches 282

Summary 284

Chapter 12: Internationalization 287

Understanding Internationalization 287

Using Culture Settings with ToString to Display Dates, Times, and Text 289

Using the .NET Culture Hierarchy to Ensure Culture Neutrality 292

Storing and Retrieving Current Culture Settings 293

Using Resource Files to Localize Content 298

Localizing the Application Title and Tile 305

Creating an Application Resource File 305

Using Resource DLL from the Windows Phone Project 308

Creating Culture-Specific Resource DLLs 309

Summary 310

Chapter 13: Isolated Storage 311

Working with Isolated Directory Storage 312

Creating the IsolatedStorageStoreImageDemo Project 313

Coding the UI 314

Coding the Application.. 316

Working with Isolated Storage Settings 320

Creating a New Project.. 321

Building the Application UI (XAML) 322

Coding Application Behavior (C#) 324

Summary 327

Chapter 14: Using Location Services 329

Understanding Windows Phone Location 329

Services Architecture 329

Introducing the Windows Phone Location Service 330

and Mapping APIs 330

Simulating the Location Service 330

Creating the GeoCoordinateWatcherDemo Project.. 331

Coding the UI 332

Coding the Application.. 334

Testing the Finished Application 336

Using GeoCoordinateWatcher and the Bing Maps Control to Track Your Movements...337

Registering with the Bing Maps Service Portal and Installing the Bing Maps SDK 338

Creating the BingMapDemo Project 339

Coding the UI 340

Coding the Application.. 343

Testing the Finished Application 347

Plotting an Address on a Bing Maps Map and Working with the Bing Maps Service....347

Creating the AddressPlottingDemo Application... 348

Adding a Service Reference to the Bing Maps GeoCodeService 348

Coding the UI 350

Coding the Application.. 352

Testing the Finished Application 354

Summary 354

Chapter 15: Media...357

Introducing MediaElement...357

Working with Video..358

Creating the MediaPlayerDemo Project 359

Building the UI 360

Coding the Application... 363

Adding Sounds to an Application 370

Creating the RobotSoundDemo Project 371

Building the UI 372

Coding the Application... 375

Summary 377

Chapter 16: Working with the Camera and Photos..379

Introducing Windows Phone Photo Features 379

Using a Chooser to Take Photos.. 381

Using a Chooser to Open Photos 385

Saving Photos to the Phone.. 386

Integrating Your Application with Windows Phone 388

Using the Apps Link to Launch an Application 389

Using Share to Upload PhotoCapture Snapshots to TwitPic.. 391

Manipulating Live Photo Feeds..398

Summary 404

Chapter 17: Push Notifications 405

Understanding Push Notifications 405

Toast Notifications... 405

Tile Notifications.. 406

Raw Notifications 407

Introducing the Push Notifications Architecture 408

The Life Cycle of a Notification 409

The Push Notification Framework 410

Implementing Toast Notifications 411

Creating a Client Application 413

Creating an Application to Send Notifications 418

Implementing Tile Notifications 424

Creating a Client Application 425

Creating an Application to Send Notifications 425

Implementing Raw Notifications 429

Creating a Client Application 429

Creating an Application to Send Notifications 432

Testing Delivery of Raw Notifications 433

Implementing a Cloud Service to Track Push Notifications 434

Creating a WCF Service to Track Notification Recipients 434

Modifying the Client to Call the WCF Service 439

Verifying Automated Push Notification Subscriber Tracking 441

Using Push Notifications in the Real World.. 442

Setting Up Secure Web Services for Push Notifications 443

Summary 443

Chapter 18: Reactive Extensions for .NET... 445

Introducing Reactive Programming 446

Rx.NET Subscription Pipeline.. 447

Implementing the Observer Pattern with Rx.NET 448

Creating a Windows Phone Project 448

Adding Code to Create and Read Observable Collections 449

Using Rx.NET Event Handling to Search for Flickr Photographs..................................452

    Creating a Windows Phone Project 452

    Adding a User Interface 453

    Adding Logic to Search Flickr for Images.. 454

    Enhancing a Flickr Search with Throttling.. 455

    Adding an Animation that Plays as Flickr Images Load.. 458

Rx.NET Design Guidelines..462

    Consider Drawing a Marble Diagram... 463

    Consider Passing a Specific Scheduler to Concurrency-Introducing Operators................... 463

Using Rx.NET with Web Services to Retrieve Weather Data Asynchronously...............464

    Creating a Windows Phone Project 465

    Creating a User Interface... 466

    Adding Logic to Get Weather Information... 468

Handling Errors in Rx.NET...471

Handling Data-Connection Issues with Rx.NET 472

Revising WeatherRx to Manage Slow Data Connections 473

Handling Multiple Concurrent Requests with Rx.NET....................................475

Summary 478

Chapter 19: Security **479**

Understanding Application Security 479

    The Windows Phone Marketplace 479

    Submitting an Application to the Windows Phone Marketplace... 481

    Sandboxed Execution and the Execution Manager 483

    Private Application Distribution Options 484

Implementing Network Security 484

    Securing Connections with SSL... 484

    Testing and Opening an SSL Connection.. 485

Creating a Self-Signed Certificate 486

Exporting a Self-Signed Certificate 492

Installing a Self-Signed Certificate on Windows Phone 494

Implementing Data Security **495**

Using HMACSHA1 and HMACHSHA256... 496

Using Rfc2898DeriveBytes and AES to Encrypt Data 500

Information Rights Management 504

Understanding Device Physical Security **504**

Meeting Certification Requirements **505**

Applications Must Implement MSIL Code.. 505

Applications Must Not Implement Any Security-Critical Code............................. 506

Capability List 507

Obfuscating Your Application Code **508**

Summary **512**

▓ Index **513**

About the Authors

■ **Henry Lee** is the founder of ToeTapz (`www.toetapz.com`) and New Age Solution (`http://newagesolution.net`), and is passionate about technology. He works with various Fortune 500 companies delivering mobile applications and rich Internet applications (RIAs). He is focusing his energy on delivering mobile applications on Windows Phone 7, Android, and iPhone. In his spare time, he helps his communities by delivering sessions at technology events. He enjoys discussing current trends in technology with other technologists and sharing business insights with fellow colleagues. You will often find Henry at a local cigar bar, enjoying a cigar and a drink while trying to come up with the next big mobile application.

■ **Eugene Chuvyrov** is an independent .NET consultant in beautiful Jacksonville, Florida. He was lucky enough to start working with Microsoft technologies when he graduated from college in 1998 and has been consistently delivering a positive return on investment to the clients that engage him. His most recent venture is an online event marketing startup, Packed House Events (`http://packedhouseevents.com`), which extends event creation, marketing, and electronic payments to anybody with Internet access. Eugene also facilitates the meetings of the Jacksonville Software Architecture Group, where he enjoys networking and learning from smart people.

As soon as Eugene heard the news that a new mobile platform (Windows Phone 7) was being released by Microsoft, he was intrigued. It was hard to resist the temptation of wide-open possibilities to create smartphone applications using his favorite IDE and all the latest cloud- and functional programming–based technologies. This passion, discussed over a cigar with Henry at a local cigar bar, resulted in the book you now hold in your hands. He sincerely hopes you find it useful!

About the Technical Reviewer

Rob Garrett has worked with SharePoint since the early beta version of Microsoft Office SharePoint Server 2007 and has leveraged his talents for SharePoint architecture and design with Portal Solutions—a SharePoint consultant company in Rockville, Maryland. Rob has extensive background in .NET technologies and has developed software for Microsoft frameworks since the early days of C++ and MFC. In pursuit of his career dreams, Rob left his birthplace in England for a journey to the United States on Thanksgiving Day, 1999, and enjoyed his first American meal from a gas station.

Acknowledgments

We would like to express our love and gratitude to our wives for encouraging us to finish this book. We are also grateful to Apress for giving us the opportunity to write this book on Windows Phone development. The staff at Apress made this book possible by spending many days and nights reviewing and editing the book to meet the tight deadline. Jon Hassell provided us with this unique opportunity to share our knowledge. Thank you, Jon, for believing in us. Also, we would like to show our appreciation to the coordinating editor, Tracy Brown, and our extremely diligent reviewers, Gary Schwartz and Rob Garrett. When the first and second edition were published, we also realized that there were many Apress staff members in the marketing department promoting the book; we would like to thank Lisa Lau and the marketing department, and Simon Yu for helping us get in contact with user groups for speaking engagements.

We would also like to thank those who sent us e-mail with comments and those who blogged about our books on the Web with kind remarks. Many community members helped us improve upon our first and second editions by offering valuable feedback. We used that feedback to make this edition better and included a lot of information about new features of the latest release of the Windows Phone OS.

Introduction

This is the third edition of this book. We wanted to improve upon the first two editions and update the book with new features of the Windows Phone OS, as well as provide hands-on knowledge on how to program the plethora of features offered by Windows Phone devices.

While the second edition was being written, Microsoft and Nokia formally announced their partnership and signed an agreement to seal their commitment. While we were writing the third edition, Nokia phones were being released to the European markets, and they should be coming to the United States in days. We hope that this book will provide developers with the practical knowledge that we gained by developing real-world applications; we also hope it will inspire developers to create many cool applications for the Windows Phone platform.

Who This Book Is For

This book assumes that you have basic C# and .NET knowledge. This book will provide you with basic fundamentals and skills that you need to be successful in developing Windows Phone applications. You don't need previous experience developing mobile applications—the only thing you need is a desire to learn new technology.

What You Need to Use This Book

In order to write Windows Phone applications and test out the examples in this book, you'll need to download the tools listed here. All of these are available at no charge from Microsoft. You'll find additional information on how to install and use these tools in Part 1 of this book.

- *Windows Phone Developer Tools RTW*: http://download.microsoft.com/download/1/7/7/177D6AF8-17FA-40E7-AB53-00B7CED31729/vm_web.exe

- *Zune software*: www.zune.net/en-us/products/software/download/

- *User Experience Design Guidelines for Windows Phone*: http://go.microsoft.com/fwlink/?LinkID=183218

- *Windows Phone 7 Marketplace Certification Requirements*: http://go.microsoft.com/?linkid=9730558

- *Microsoft SQL Server 2008 R2 Express*: www.microsoft.com/express/Database/

- *Azure Tools for Visual Studio 1.2 June 2010*: http://download.microsoft.com/DOWNLOAD/1/F/9/1F96D6OF-EBE9-44CB-BD58-88C2EC14929E/VSCLOUDSERVICE.EXE

- *Azure SDK (June 2010)*: http://www.microsoft.com/windowsazure/sdk/

- *Windows Azure Platform Training Kit*: http://www.microsoft.com/downloads/en/details.aspx?familyid=413e88f8-5966-4a83-b309-53b7b77edf78

How This Book Is Organized

This book contains 19 chapters, broken into 2 major parts. In Part 1, we will walk you through the development life cycle of the application. You will go from coding the simplest possible Hello World–style Windows Phone 7 application to building a full-blown, modern n-tier application that uses both the Windows Phone development platform and the unique cloud services that support it. The section concludes with step-by-step instructions on how to gain certification from Microsoft and offer an application to the public through the Windows Phone Marketplace.

In Part 2, you will learn how to use specific features of Windows Phone devices in your applications, including the accelerometer, location services, the Application Bar, reactive extensions, application hub integration, application life cycle events, Isolated Storage, Silverlight, XAML, skinning controls, web browser controls, media elements, photos, push notifications, internalization, and security. While each of its chapters is a tutorial, you can also use Part 2 as a reference. Each chapter focuses on a single phone feature and provides step-by-step instructions on how to incorporate it into your application.

Where to Find Sources for the Examples

The source code of all of the examples is available at www.apress.com/ or http://wp7apress.codeplex.com.

Send Us Your Comments

We value your input. We'd like to know what you like about the book and what you don't like about it. When providing feedback, please make sure you include the title of the book in your note to us.

We've tried to make this book as error-free as possible. However, mistakes happen. If you find any type of error in this book, whether it is a typo or an erroneous command, please let us know about it. Visit the book's web page at www.apress.com/9781430235965 and click the Errata tab. Your information will be validated and posted on the errata page to be used in subsequent editions of the book.

Contacting the Authors

You can contact us directly at the following e-mail addresses:

Henry Lee: Henry.Lee@NewAgeSolution.net

Eugene Chuvyrov: echuvyrov@msn.com

CHAPTER 1

Introducing Windows Phone and the Windows Phone Platform

This is an exciting time for mobile app developers as the smartphone race heats up between the major players: Microsoft Windows Phone, Apple iPhone, and Google Android. As a developer, you are faced with an amazing opportunity to develop a mobile application that can be sold to millions of consumers worldwide using any of these platforms. Gartner predicts that by 2014 the smartphone market will boom, and there will be billions of dollars at stake.

Recently, Nokia, one of the largest mobile phone makers in the world, announced that it will replace its Symbian-based operating system with the Windows Phone OS. The partnership between Microsoft and Nokia will potentially boost Windows Phone's global market share to 30 percent, making it even more attractive for Windows Phone developers.

The Windows Phone *Marketplace*, where consumers can purchase applications, opened in November 2010. You might consider downloading Zune software from www.zune.net/en-US/products/software/download/downloadsoftware.htm to view the current Marketplace, or you can navigate on your browser to www.windowsphone.com/en-US/marketplace. Once you have downloaded the Zune software and fired it up, click the Marketplace APPS links, and you will be able to see all the Windows Phone applications currently published, as shown in Figure 1-1. You will learn more about the Marketplace in Chapter 5.

1

Figure 1-1. Windows Phone Marketplace

There are hundreds of ideas for applications waiting to be discovered and developed by people like you. Take a look at Simply Solitaire, QuotedSuccess, DuckCaller, and the mobile baseball game shown in Figure 1-2. Which of these will be among the first Windows Phone hits to catch fire with consumers and sell millions of units?

Figure 1-2. Windows Phone applications

What application will you be developing? We've written this book to guide you through the steps it takes to write and launch a successful application to the Windows Phone Marketplace. So what are you waiting for? Let's get started by diving into what Windows Phone offers to developers like you.

Windows Phone Overview

Microsoft Windows Phone is a great mobile platform because it offers all of the modern smartphone features, including GPS, e-mail, SMS, a camera, and a music player, and it also provides an easy-to-use development framework that allows millions of .NET developers to learn and develop on Windows Phone quickly. Also, Windows Phone offers multitouch screen capability, a beautiful user interface (UI) that implements a new modern design called Metro, social networking services such as Facebook, and support for popular e-mail services such as Yahoo, Hotmail, Gmail, and AOL (and, if you're a corporate user, Microsoft Exchange). Moreover, the platform ships with a version of Microsoft Office—a unique feature of Windows Phone. You can use this version of Office to read, edit, save, and sync Word, Excel, and other Office files. This makes Windows Phone a great mobile platform for those who use Office at home or at work. Windows Phone can also integrate with Xbox LIVE, making it a great choice for gamers.

Microsoft Windows Phone uses the Zune software to sync installed applications, pictures, and music, and back up and flash OS updates. As a developer, you'll also use Zune in conjunction with Visual Studio to debug your applications on a real device; more on that in Chapter 4.

Microsoft also introduces the concept of a *hub* with the Windows Phone—a *People* hub where users can store all of their contacts and social networking connections; a *Music* hub where consumers can listen to, download, and purchase music; and an *App* hub, also known as the Marketplace, where you will publish the applications you create.

Having a smartphone that's a hit with consumers is important because the consumer marketplace is where the greatest opportunities lie. One of the great things about Windows Phone is that Microsoft imposes the hardware specifications on the phone manufacturer, making it easy for you to develop an application without worrying about writing device-specific code. For any future release of Windows Phone, you are guaranteed that the application you write today will work regardless of the brand of the mobile device, as long as it runs Microsoft Windows Phone.

Naturally, you want to know what language you'll need to master for your work. For Windows Phone, the languages of choice today are C# and Visual Basic—the primary .NET languages. As for an application development framework, you have two choices: Silverlight or XNA. Silverlight and XNA both use the core .NET Framework. You will learn more about the two frameworks later in this chapter, but first let's take a closer look at the hardware features you can expect on a Windows Phone device.

Windows Phone Hardware Specifications

Knowing what's included in the Microsoft Windows Phone hardware specifications will help you prepare for the special needs of the projects you will undertake. Table 1-1 lists the minimum hardware requirements that any Windows Phone manufacturer must meet, and it also includes suggestions as to how they can impact developers like you.

Table 1-1. *Windows Phone Minimum Hardware Requirements*

Hardware Feature	Description
Must display at WVGA (800×480)	You only need to worry about one screen resolution. This makes it easy to develop an application.
Four-point, multitouch capable	This is unique to Windows Phone, and you can use this feature to create four-player games. There is definitely room for innovation using this particular feature.
DirectX 9 hardware acceleration	This means the phone will have a graphical processing unit (GPU), allowing graphically intense tasks to be offloaded to the graphics chips of the particular mobile device. This will help you create very smooth and responsive applications and games. This also means that 3D games are possible.
GPS	With this feature, you'll be able to create location-aware applications. See Chapter 14 to learn about location services, how to use Bing Maps, and how to plot GPS data on a map.
Accelerometer	This feature will measure the change in the acceleration in the mobile device. The accelerometer is popular in games, but is also useful in applications, such as spirit-level applications. See Chapter 6 to learn more about this feature.
Compass	With this, you can find north, south, east, and west.
Light	This feature can be used as a flash for the camera.
Digital camera	This allows you to take pictures and share them on Facebook and other social networking sites. Learn more about this feature in Chapter 16.
Hardware controls: Back, Start, and Search buttons	Every Windows phone will have three buttons on the front of the phone. Keep in mind that you will be required to use the Back button for going backward in your application, because having a separate Back button in the application might confuse the user. You will learn more about integrating the hardware buttons into an application in Chapter 10.
Data connection support: Cellular network and Wi-Fi	This feature allows you to connect to the Internet. You can create Web services and subscribe to them from your applications, or you can subscribe to third-party APIs such as Twitter or Facebook in your application.

Hardware Feature	Description
256MB of RAM and 8GB of flash storage	Keep in mind that your application can use only 90MB of memory unless the device has more than 256MB of memory. If your application does not respect this requirement, it will not pass the Marketplace certification process. See Chapter 5 for more details.
	Also, the 8GB of flash memory used for storage is shared among other applications, so if you are saving any kind of static data into the Isolated Storage, you must check if the space is available and handle the exception appropriately. For more details on this, see Chapter 13.

AT&T will carry Samsung's Focus, LG's Quantum, and HTC's Surround. T-Mobile has announced that it will carry HTC's HD7, and Verizon will carry the HTC Trophy. Also, Sprint will carry the HTC Arrive. You will find that all major providers will be carrying one or more Windows Phone devices. You can find more information on the release of new Windows phones at www.microsoft.com/windowsphone/en-us/buy/7/phones.aspx.

In the next section, you will learn how the software behind these powerful consumer smartphones provides a great platform for developers.

Windows Phone Application Platform

Microsoft did not invent any new languages or frameworks for the Windows Phone application platform. The company simply adapted its existing frameworks. This means that you will be able to program using C# and Visual Basic with the .NET Framework. .NET provides a common base-class library with which every Microsoft .NET programmer will be familiar; it includes support for multithreading, XML, LINQ, collections, events, data, exceptions, input/output (I/O), service model, networking, text, location, reflection, globalization, resources, runtime, security, and diagnostics, among many other features.

On top of the core .NET Framework, the Windows Phone application platform consists of two major frameworks: Silverlight and XNA. You'll use Silverlight primarily for business applications and simple 2D games. Silverlight uses the Extensible Application Markup Language (XAML), a declarative markup language for creating compelling UIs. Designers will have tremendous flexibility in creating UIs for Windows Phone: by using familiar tools like Adobe Illustrator, Photoshop, and Microsoft Expression Design, they can create a vector-based UI that can be easily exported to XAML. XNA is primarily used for creating games. The framework comes with a game engine that allows you to create loop-based games and a 3D engine that allows you to create 3D games.

In the following sections, you will learn more details about the main components of the Windows Phone application platform: Silverlight, XNA, tools, and cloud services.

Silverlight for Windows Phone

Silverlight has historically been a web-based technology, and it operates within a web browser plug-in. Silverlight provides you with a sandboxed experience that abides by the rules of the web browsers; in other words, within a Silverlight application, you can't access the native OS unless you have the necessary APIs. This architecture makes Silverlight very compelling for use in Windows Phone from a security standpoint, because Windows Phone provides the same restriction of providing APIs only to developers and limiting access to the native OS.

Another benefit is that Silverlight uses XAML, which can be used to declare vector-based graphics and create animations. Any designer familiar with vector-based applications, such as Adobe Illustrator and Microsoft Expression Design, can easily create highly visual elements in vector-based format that can be exported to XAML. This means that designers have full control over the layout, look and feel, and graphical assets, making Silverlight an extremely powerful choice for creating consumer-oriented applications. Also, XAML provides a powerful data-binding feature to the controls, making it ideal for creating business-oriented applications.

XNA for Windows Phone

Like Silverlight, XNA is not a new technology. XNA is used in creating Xbox games via managed code. It is a natural choice for creating games since Windows Phone has Xbox LIVE integration, allowing XNA-based Xbox games to be easily ported over to Windows Phone. The only thing Xbox game developers have to worry about is the screen resolution, which can easily be adjusted and fixed.

XNA provides a rich framework for game development, including a game loop engine, 2D and 3D engines, and the ability to manage game assets like models, meshes, sprites, textures, effects, terrains, and animations.

Tools

You can download the tools you'll need for developing Windows Phone applications from http://create.msdn.com/en-us/home/getting_started. The Getting Started page also features rich documentation and tutorials. You should also consider downloading the UI Design and Interaction Guide to understand the Metro design guidelines that Microsoft recommends as best practices when developing applications.

Visual Studio

If you don't have a purchased version of Visual Studio 2010 on your development machine, then the development tool that you download from Microsoft will install a free version of Visual Studio 2010 Express for Windows Phone, as shown in Figure 1-3. Visual Studio is absolutely necessary because it can be used to design, debug, create, and package projects, and automatically generate package manifests. It also includes a phone emulator upon which you may test your results. In Chapter 5, you will learn to debug and run the emulator from Visual Studio. You will also use Visual Studio to create a package for publication to the App hub.

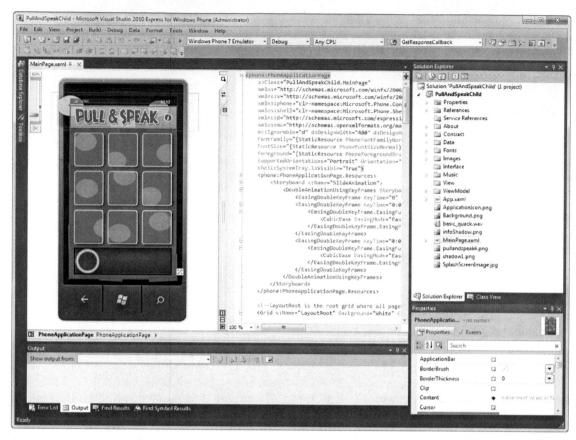

Figure 1-3. Microsoft Visual Studio 2010 Express for Windows Phone

Expression Blend

You will need Expression Blend (shown in Figure 1-4) if you want to develop compelling applications using Silverlight for Windows Phone. Typically Expression Blend is used by designers, and many of the Expression Blend functionalities are similar to those found in Adobe Illustrator, Photoshop, or Expression Design. Note that you can import any Illustrator or Photoshop files into Expression Blend; if you are using Expression Design, you can export Expression Design files directly to a XAML file.

Expression Blend also provides a way to create animation sequences. Although you can create animation in Visual Studio using XAML, it would be very difficult to write complex XAML code to represent complex graphics or animation sequences. It is best to leave complex graphics and animations to Expression Blend.

Figure 1-4. Microsoft Expression Blend 4 for Windows Phone

Windows Phone Emulator

The Windows Phone emulator, shown in Figure 1-5, is integrated with Visual Studio, and it simulates a real Windows Phone device. However, there are things that you can't do in the emulator. For instance, you can't test any features that require a physical device, such as the accelerometer, the GPS, the compass, the FM radio, SMS, e-mail, phone calling, the contact list, or the camera.

However, you can use what are called *reactive extensions* to simulate the data feed from a real phone. In Chapter 18, you'll learn how to use reactive extensions to simulate the accelerometer and GPS readings so that you can work with the emulator without having the actual device itself.

Figure 1-5. Windows Phone emulator

Documentation and Support

There are many ways to get help if you get stuck on a problem while developing your application. The Windows Phone Training Kit, at http://create.msdn.com/en-us/home/getting_started, contains how-tos on specific technology. You can go to http://forums.silverlight.net/forums/63.aspx to ask questions related to Silverlight for Windows Phone. If you have other Windows Phone–related questions, you can visit http://social.msdn.microsoft.com/Forums/en-US/windowsphone7series. The Windows Phone development team puts out many useful blogs that you can follow at http://windowsteamblog.com/windows_phone/b/wpdev/. Of course, there is Windows Phone documentation at MSDN; go to http://msdn.microsoft.com/en-us/library/ff402535(VS.92).aspx. Also, you can use this book as a reference, and feel free to reach out to its authors at this blog: http://blog.ToeTapz.com.

Cloud Services

Working with a Windows Phone application that requires saving data to an online database is tricky. The first big problem is that you don't know in advance how popular your application will wind up being. If it becomes popular, you might suddenly find millions of people using your application and saving the data to its database at a rate that would require an enterprise-level solution. You'll also need to find a Web service to provide APIs to your application to allow for the saving of data to the database because Windows Phone applications can't directly connect to the database.

This is where the Microsoft Azure cloud comes in. Microsoft Azure provides Windows Azure services for deploying services (WCF, Windows service), and it also provides SQL Azure, which allows you to scale up the database infinitely as your demand grows. You will learn more about the Microsoft Azure cloud in Chapter 3.

Microsoft also provides Bing Maps services, which you can use freely if you are developing a Windows Phone application. Along with Bing Maps services, Microsoft provides Bing Maps controls in Silverlight, which you can use in Windows Phone. You will learn about Bing Maps and location services in Chapter 14.

Push notification services are hosted in the cloud as well. These allow you to push messages to the phone—a very powerful messaging mechanism. You will learn more about this in Chapter 17. Xbox LIVE services also reside in the cloud. You can take advantage of these services in your applications as well; however, this topic is beyond the scope of this book.

You learned a bit about Windows Phone and the Windows Phone platform in the previous sections. In the following sections and in the rest of this book, you will learn about Windows Phone application development.

Metro Design

Microsoft is targeting Windows Phone toward busy professionals. In order to provide a compelling UI, Microsoft came up with the Metro design, which is derived from transportation industry typography, and puts heavy emphasis on simple and clean design elements. The Metro design follows five principles:

- An emphasis on clean, light, open, and clutter-free design and simple-to-read typography, because consumers will use their Windows Phone devices for e-mail, SMS, Facebook, and Twitter while on the go

- A focus on content, where the design premise is geared toward how the content is presented

- A focus on the seamless integration of hardware and software

- An emphasis on gestures, where the design enables a world-class multitouch user experience

- A focus on making applications soulful and alive, where the information that matters most to the user is presented in a way that is easily accessible by a single touch

You can find out more about the Metro design by downloading the document provided by Microsoft at http://go.microsoft.com/fwlink/?LinkID=183218.

Application Development Life Cycle

It's important to understand the application development life cycle helps you prepare for it. In-depth discussion of the application development life cycle, including the certification process, is provided in Chapter 5. Figure 1-6 shows a high-level view of the development life cycle of a Windows Phone application.

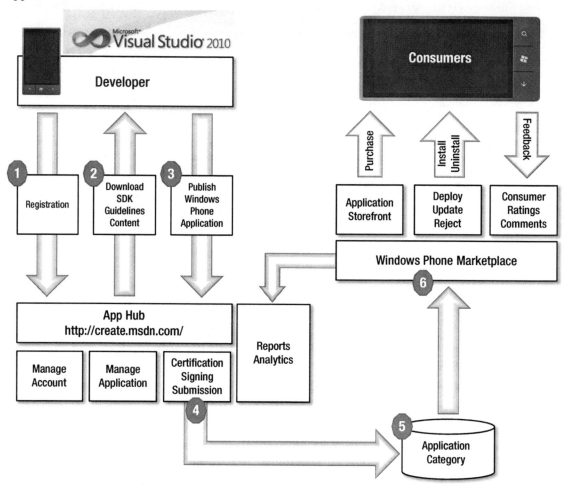

Figure 1-6. Application development life cycle

As a developer, you will start out at the App hub and register your Windows Live ID. (If you don't have a Windows Live ID, you'll be provided with the opportunity to create one.) Once you've signed up at the App hub, you register your physical device so that you can debug on the real device. Keep in mind that you can add up to three devices. Using Visual Studio and/or Expression Blend, you will be creating your application and debugging using the emulator or the device you registered. Once the application is created, you need to submit the application for the certification process.

In order to ensure that your application will pass the Marketplace certification process, it's a good idea to read and understand the application certification document found at http://msdn.microsoft.com/en-us/library/hh184843%28v=VS.92%29.aspx. As part of the certification process, your application will go through a series of validation steps that check the application and content policies, and the packaging, code, phone feature disclosure, language, and image requirements. Your application will also be tested on reliability, performance, resource management, phone functionality, and security. The certification process is in place to help promote quality applications to consumers, protect consumers from malware, and protect Microsoft services.

Once the application passes the certification process, it will be deployed to the Marketplace and then downloaded and used by consumers. The consumers who use your application will provide ratings and comments. The App hub is used to generate reports on how your application is performing in the Marketplace. Based on the feedback you receive, you can choose to deploy an updated version with bug fixes and new features. Your ultimate goal is to create a compelling application that you know consumers will use and to publish this application to the Marketplace.

There is an annual subscription fee of $99 for deploying applications to the Marketplace. This fee gives you access to the Windows Phone Marketplace and the Xbox 360 Marketplace. In the Windows Phone Marketplace, you can submit an unlimited number of paid applications and five free applications; additional submissions cost $19.99. In the Xbox 360 Marketplace, you can submit up to ten games.

You can observe Marketplace activities such as comments, ratings, and number of apps sold through the report provided so that you can effectively improve your sales and marketing efforts.

Microsoft takes 30 percent of the consumer app price; you keep 70 percent. You can choose direct deposit so that the money goes directly to your bank account; you will receive your payments on the first day of each month from Microsoft.

Summary

You are about to embark on the journey to develop applications for Windows Phone. You have a chance to develop an application that can be used by millions and become part of a billion-dollar global app market.

This chapter provided a general overview of Windows Phone features, hardware specifications, the development platform, and the Marketplace. In Chapter 2, you will build your first Windows Phone application, using Visual Studio, Expression Blend, and the Windows Phone controls.

CHAPTER 2

Building Windows Phone Applications

This chapter will prepare you with everything you need to get started with Windows Phone development. You will learn about the Windows Phone emulator, Visual Studio 2010 Express, and Microsoft Expression Blend 4. You will use these tools to create your first Windows Phone application.

Before you can write your first application, however, you need to download and install the tools. In the next section, we'll show you how.

Preparing Your Development Machine

Windows Phone developer tool version 1.0 was used in the writing of this book. The latest Windows Phone developer tools and patches can be downloaded from http://create.msdn.com/en-us/home/getting_started. The Windows Phone developer tools (vm_web.exe) will install the following:

- *The free version of Visual Studio 2010 Express for Windows Phone (the programmer's development IDE)*: If you already have a paid version of Visual Studio 2010 installed, that will work as well.

- *The Windows Phone emulator*: This is used to run and test the Windows Phone application.

- *Silverlight for Windows Phone*: This is the Silverlight framework for Windows Phone, based on Silverlight 3 technology. See Chapter 1 for a description of the subtle differences between Silverlight 3 and the Windows Phone Silverlight framework.

- *Microsoft Expression Blend for Windows Phone*: This tool can be used to design UIs.

- *XNA Game Studio 4*: This includes tools for developing games. This was originally developed for programming for Xbox, but the XNA Xbox framework was subsequently ported to Windows Phone.

Once you have installed the Windows Phone developer tools, you can start to build your first Windows Phone application.

Building Your First Windows Phone Application

In this section, you'll build a simple Hello World application using the Silverlight framework. Creating the application will provide you with an opportunity to use Visual Studio 2010 Express for Windows Phone, the Windows Phone emulator, and some Windows Phone Silverlight controls. Later in this chapter, you will use Expression Blend to design Silverlight controls. The final application is shown at the end of this chapter. A click of its OK button will display the words "Hello World" in a text box. Before you can get started, however, you must first create a Visual Studio 2010 Express project.

Creating a Windows Phone Project

To get started, fire up Visual Studio 2010 Express and create a project.

1. To launch Visual Studio 2010 Express, select Start ➤ All Programs ➤ Microsoft Visual Studio 2010 Express ➤ Microsoft Visual Studio 2010 Express for Windows Phone.

2. Create a new project by selecting File ➤ New ➤ Project on the Visual Studio 2010 Express menu, as shown in Figure 2-1.

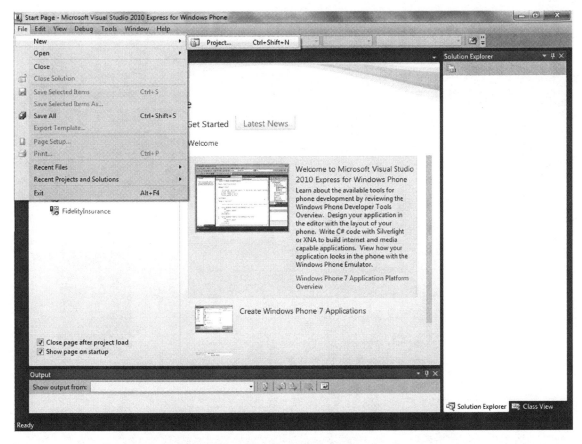

Figure 2-1. Creating a new project in Visual Studio 2010 Express

3.   From among the three C# templates that Visual Studio 2010 Express displays on its New Project dialog page, select the Windows Phone Application Visual C# template, as shown in Figure 2-2.

▓ **Note** There are three different Windows Phone Visual Studio 2010 Express project templates. The Windows Phone Application template is a template for one-page applications. The Windows Phone List Application template uses a ListBox control and page navigation framework to create applications with multiple pages. The Windows Phone Class Library template can be used to create a class library that can be referenced by other Windows Phone projects.

4. For the purposes of this exercise, change the name of the new project to HelloWorld by changing the text in the Name box, as shown in Figure 2-2. You can also change the location where the project will be saved by changing the path in the Location box.

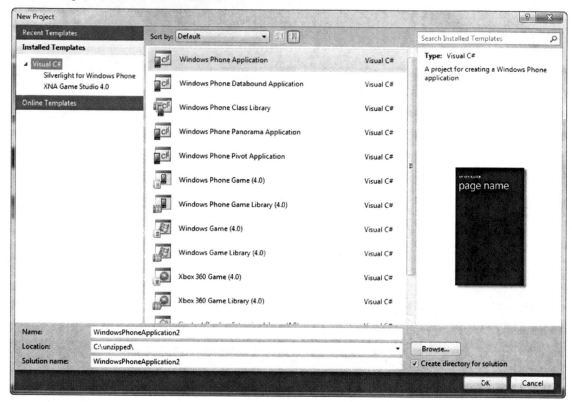

Figure 2-2. Creating a new Silverlight Windows Phone application

5. Finally, select OK in the New Project dialog, and Visual Studio 2010 Express will create your project, the elements of which are displayed in Figure 2-3.

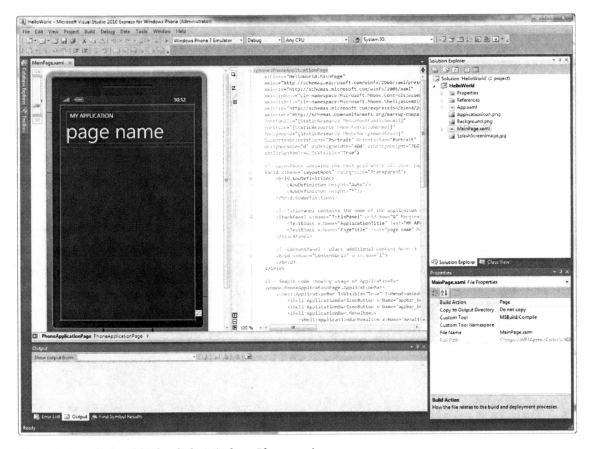

Figure 2-3. HelloWorld Silverlight Windows Phone project

By default, two TextBlock controls will be placed on the screen; you can see this in the design view at the far left in Figure 2-3.

With a phone project ready to roll, it's time to bring the application to life by adding some functionality and creating a UI. Let's start with the UI, adding some controls to its blank design surface and some areas where it can display text.

Using the Windows Phone Silverlight Controls

The next step is to add Silverlight controls to the HelloWorld Windows Phone application created in the previous steps. You'll be setting the properties of the controls so that the controls can be sized and positioned automatically in both the portrait and landscape modes of Windows Phone.

In the Windows Phone design view window, click the MY APPLICATION TextBlock. In the Properties windows in the lower-right corner of the Visual Studio IDE, change the Text property from MY APPLICATION to HelloWorld. Notice that the new text now appears on the design surface, as shown in Figure 2-4.

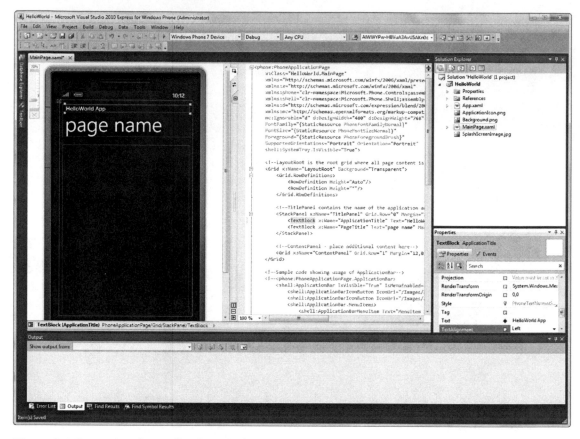

Figure 2-4. Renaming the application window title

Now open the Visual Studio 2010 Express toolbox, where you'll find some controls for the
HelloWorld UI. If you can't find the toolbox, select View Toolbox from the Visual Studio 2010 Express
menu. A list of controls will be displayed on a vertical panel on the left side of the Visual Studio IDE, as
shown in Figure 2-5.

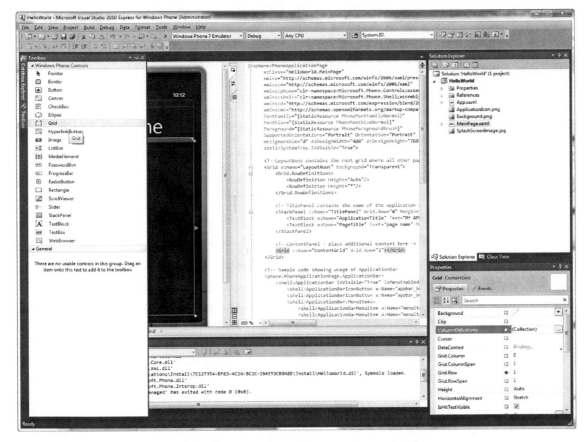

Figure 2-5. Visual Studio 2010 Express toolbox containing Windows Phone controls

The Visual Studio toolbox contains the Windows Phone controls that ship with the Windows Phone developer tools. You'll be using them throughout this book to develop increasingly sophisticated UIs. You can add any of these to your UI by dragging them to the Windows Phone design surface in Visual Studio.

To create the interface for the HelloWorld application, let's first add a TextBox to display some text. To do so, drag a TextBox control from the toolbox to the design surface directly below the page title TextBlock. When the TextBox control is successfully placed on the phone's design surface, it will be automatically selected. In the Properties window (if you can't find the Properties Window, go to View ➤ Properties Window), change the following TextBox properties:

1. Set Width and Height to Auto.

2. Set HorizontalAlignment to Stretch.

3. Set VerticalAlignment to Top.

4. Resize the TextBox width so that there is enough room to its right for an OK button.

21

5.   Set Name to txtMessage.

If you follow these steps properly, you should see the following XAML in the XAML editor area:

```
<TextBox Height="Auto" Margin="0,55,166,0" Name="txtMessage" Text="TextBlock"
VerticalAlignment="Top" HorizontalAlignment="Right" Width="290" />
```

You set HorizontalAlignment to Stretch in step 2 because you want the TextBox to stretch automatically to fill the extra space created when you rotate the phone emulator to landscape orientation. You set Width and Height to Auto because you want the TextBox to change its size automatically when the font size increases or decreases. And you set VerticalAlignment to Top so that the TextBox will always be positioned at the top. You will be able to access the TextBlock control in code by referring to its name, txtMessage.

Now let's add the application's OK button to the UI. To do so, drag and drop a Button control from the toolbox to the right of the TextBox. Change the following button properties in Properties Window:

1.   Set Button Content to OK.

2.   Set HorizontalAlignment to Right.

3.   Set VerticalAlignment to Top.

4.   Set Name to btnOk.

If you follow these steps properly, you should see the following XAML in the XAML editor area. Note that setting the button's horizontal alignment to Right will position the button at the right side.

```
<Button Content="OK" Height="72" HorizontalAlignment="Right" Margin="308,31,0,0"
Name="btnOk" VerticalAlignment="Top" Width="160" />
```

Your layout should be done. In XAML view, look for the grid containing the controls you just added. It should look similar to this:

```
<Grid x:Name="ContentGrid" Grid.Row="1">
    <TextBox Height="Auto" Margin="0,55,166,0" Name="txtMessage" Text="TextBlock"
VerticalAlignment="Top" HorizontalAlignment="Right" Width="290" />
    <Button Content="OK" Height="72" HorizontalAlignment="Right" Margin="308,31,0,0"
Name="btnOk" VerticalAlignment="Top" Width="160" />
</Grid>
```

Figure 2-6 shows the final layout after adding the TextBox and Button controls.

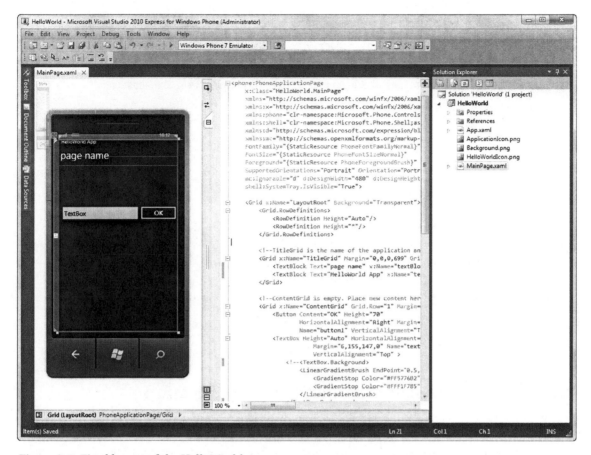

Figure 2-6. Final layout of the HelloWorld app

Writing the Windows Phone Code

In this section, you will be writing C# code that will handle the button click event that will populate the TextBlock named textBlock1 with "Hello World!"

To add behavior to the OK button, double-click the OK button on the design surface of your project. Visual Studio 2010 Express will display MainPage.xaml.cs, where you can see that the btnOk_Click method is automatically added. (You will add code later to handle the button click event.)

```csharp
using System.Windows;
using Microsoft.Phone.Controls;

namespace HelloWorld
{
    public partial class MainPage : PhoneApplicationPage
    {
        public MainPage()
        {
```

```
          InitializeComponent();
          // Setting SupportOrientations will control the behavior
          // of the page responding properly to the rotation of the
          // phone. So if you rotate the phone to the landscape
          // your page will change to landscape view.
          SupportedOrientations = SupportedPageOrientation.PortraitOrLandscape
;
      }

      private void btnOk_Click(object sender, RoutedEventArgs e)
      {

      }
   }
}
```

In MainPage.xaml, the button click event handler is automatically added to the OK button:

```
<Button Content="OK" Height="70"
        HorizontalAlignment="Right" Margin="0,155,-4,0"
        Name="button1" VerticalAlignment="Top" Width="160" Click="button1_Click" />
```

In MainPage.xaml.cs, replace the button1_click method with the following code:

```
private void button1_Click(object sender, RoutedEventArgs e)
{
    txtMessage.Text = "Hello World!";
}
```

Running the Silverlight Windows Phone Application

Your Hello World application is complete. Now it's time to build the application and run it in the Windows Phone emulator.

1. To build the solution, select Build ➤ Build Solution from the Visual Studio 2010 Express menu.

2. To run the application, select Debug ➤ Start Debugging.

3. When the emulator appears, click OK, and you will see "Hello World!" as shown in Figure 2-7.

Figure 2-7. The Hello World application in the Windows Phone emulator

4. Click the Rotate control on the Windows Phone emulator, as shown in Figure 2-8. Notice that in the landscape view, the TextBox is automatically resized—stretched out to make full use of the landscape orientation of the device, as shown in Figure 2-9.

Figure 2-8. The rotate control

Figure 2-9. The application in landscape view

5. Stop the application debugging by selecting Debug ➤ Stop Debugging.

■ **Tip** The Windows Phone emulator can take a long time to start, so you want to avoid closing it down whenever possible. If you need to stop an application in the middle of a debugging run, it's better to use the Visual Studio 2010 Express Debug ➤ Stop Debugging command than to completely close down the Windows Phone emulator. If you use this technique, the next time the application debugging starts, the project will be loaded into the emulator already.

Customizing the Windows Phone Application

In the following walkthrough, you'll learn how to customize the Windows Phone application icon that is displayed to the user and how to change the application's name.

1. In Solution Explorer, right-click the HelloWorld project and select Add ➤ Existing Item, as shown in Figure 2-10.

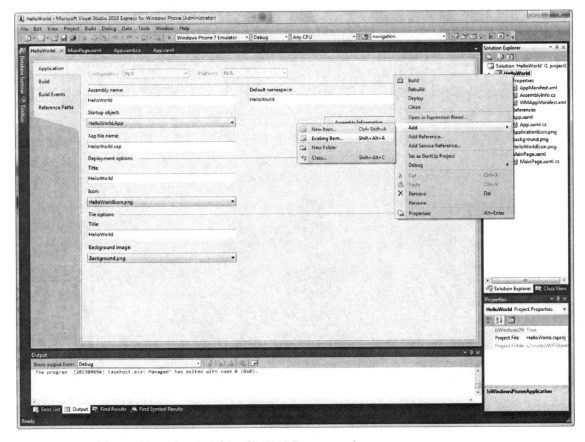

Figure 2-10. Adding a file to the Visual Studio 2010 Express project

2. Go to where you unzipped the sample code, and choose
\Codes\Ch01\Assets\HelloWorldIcon.png. The Windows Phone application
icon can be any .png file that is 62×62 pixels. By default, when the Windows
Phone application project is created, the ApplicationIcon.png file is used.

3. Right-click the HelloWorld project and choose Properties.

4. Click the Application tab.

5. In the deployment options, change the icon to HelloWorldIcon.png.

6. Change the title to HelloWorld. The changed properties are shown in
Figure 2-11.

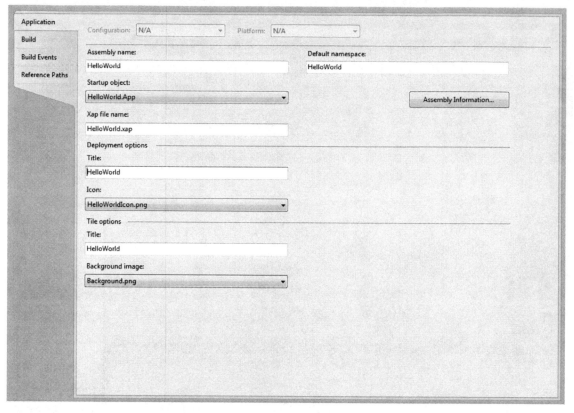

Figure 2-11. Changing the application title and icon

7. Press F5 to run the application.

8. When the application starts in the Windows Phone emulator, press the back button on the emulator, as shown in Figure 2-12.

Figure 2-12. Windows Phone back button

The list of applications installed on the emulator now includes HelloWorld with the new icon, as shown in Figure 2-13.

Figure 2-13. *Windows Phone application list*

Styling Your Application

Both Visual Studio 2010 Express and Microsoft Expression Blend 4 can be used to design XAML-based Silverlight interfaces. Expression Blend 4 provides tools for graphical manipulation and animations; thus you can create more complex controls than you can with Visual Studio 2010 Express. Let's look at the basics of Blend (see Figure 2-14) and how it makes it easy to style controls.

    1.   Open Microsoft Expression Blend 4, and select Windows Start ➤ All Programs ➤ Microsoft Expression Blend ➤ Microsoft Expression Blend 4 for Windows Phone.

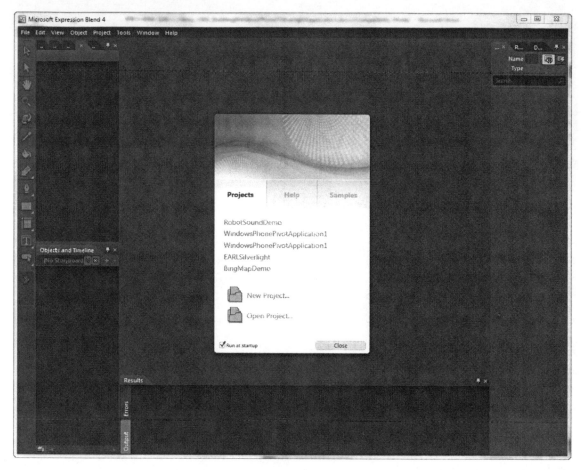

Figure 2-14. Microsoft Expression Blend 4

2. Click Close when you are prompted with the project type selector.

3. In Blend 4, go to File ➤ Open Project/Solution. Browse to the HelloWorld solution you created previously, as shown in Figure 2-15.

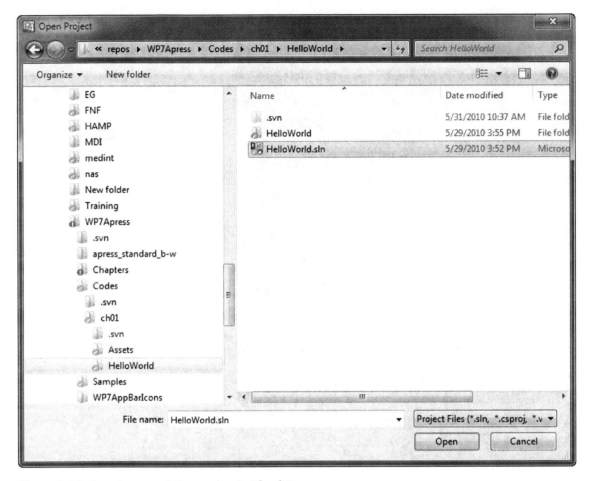

Figure 2-15. Opening an existing project in Blend 4

4.   When the project opens, click the TextBox. In the Properties window, you will
     see various properties that can be changed, as shown in Figure 2-16. (If you do
     not see the Properties window, open it by going to Window ➤ Properties from
     the main menu.)

Figure 2-16. Properties window in Blend 4 when the control is selected

5. In the Properties window's Brushes category, select Background and choose the gradient brush. Notice that the color editor now allows you to set the gradient for the TextBox's background color.

6. For the first gradient color, choose blue at 21%, and for the second color, choose yellow at 64%, as shown in Figure 2-17.

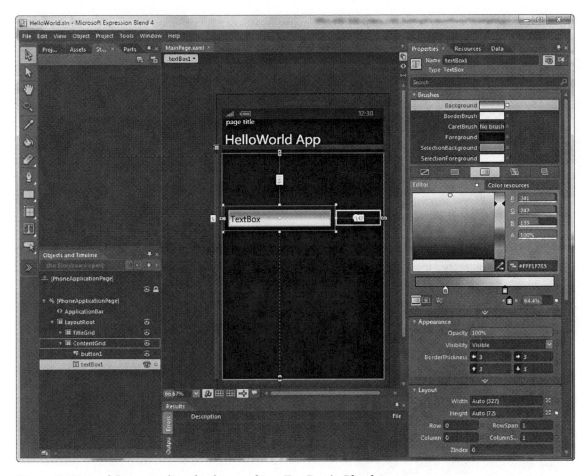

Figure 2-17. Applying a gradient background to a TextBox in Blend 4

7. From the main menu, go to Project ➤ Run Project.

8. When the Change Device Selection window appears, choose Windows Phone Emulator, as shown in Figure 2-18.

Figure 2-18. The Change Device Selection window in Blend 4

9. Click OK, and the `HelloWorld` application will start, as shown in Figure 2-19.

Figure 2-19. HelloWorld after being stylized in Blend 4

Summary

In this chapter, you learned how to set up your Windows Phone development environment. You built a simple Windows Phone application using Visual Studio 2010 Express, interacted with the phone emulator, and used Microsoft Expression Blend to style the application.

In the next chapter, you will build an application that can interact with Microsoft SQL Azure in order to store data.

CHAPTER 3

Building Windows Phone 7 Applications Using Cloud Services As Data Stores

There's lots of buzz today about cloud computing technology. By allowing you to offload infrastructure requirements, the cloud truly empowers you as a developer to focus on building an application.

Suppose you have developed an application where businesses can take pictures of invoices and then track the money they spend in a financial accounting program such as QuickBooks. In order for this application to be useful, you would need to save information from the invoices in some kind of database. With Windows Phone, you can easily use Isolated Storage (covered in Chapter 13) to support such an application. However, the problem with Isolated Storage is that the storage space is tied to the phone, which can differ from manufacturer to manufacturer; more importantly, many users will store music, videos, and other documents that consume storage space on the phone. A better solution would be to save the invoice information to a database. To do this, you would need to use a Web service that can interact with the database so that the phone can save the invoices, as shown in Figure 3-1.

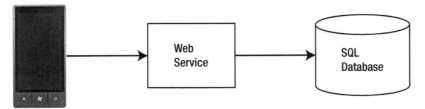

Figure 3-1. Common three-tier architecture

In order to deploy the solution depicted in Figure 3-1, you need to solve a number of problems. First, you need to consider what type of server to buy and how many of them you'll need to host the Web service and database. Once you do, you'll have to purchase and maintain them yourself or pay a hosting service to do the job for you. But this doesn't solve the problem of what you will do to scale up your application if it becomes so popular that millions of consumers want to use it, or if you experience periodic surges in use—say, at the end of each month. Finally, you will need to provide for disaster recovery and backup of the database to ensure that your service does not go down and disappoint users.

To plan ahead for the huge number of users your application might attract, a more robust architecture must be considered. One example is shown in Figure 3-2, in which a load balancer helps to accommodate massive concurrent calls to the service; this way, if any of the services go down, the load balancer will automatically point the request to an alternative available service. On the database side, you have to provide both an active and a passive database in case the main database—that is, the active one—goes down and a switch to the database that is currently passive becomes necessary. Then you have to worry about disk space, so you will need a *storage area network (SAN)*. Figure 3-2 illustrates your typical enterprise-grade deployment scenario, which provides reliability, scalability, maintenance, and performance, but is very expensive and complex.

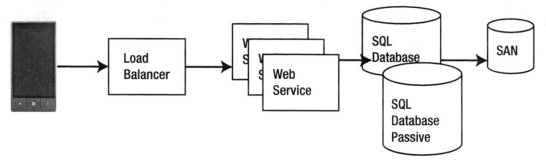

Figure 3-2. Enterprise-level n-tier deployment scenario

The architecture in Figure 3-2 might be overkill for the tiny invoice application you're creating, but you don't want to lose the potential that it might be bought by millions of adoring customers. To resolve this dilemma, Microsoft provides Azure Services to take care of hosting the infrastructure architecture in the cloud on Microsoft servers, allowing you to concentrate on developing the best app you can. Microsoft Azure provides peace of mind with a service level agreement of 99.95 percent uptime, which is equivalent to 4.38 hours downtime per year, or 43.2 minutes of downtime per month.

In the remaining sections of this chapter, you will learn how to create a simple note-taking application. The application, named Notepad, will implement the n-tier architecture described in Figure 3-2. With the Notepad application, you will be able to create, read, update, and delete notes. The application will consist of three main components: a Windows Phone client (the UI), a Web service (the middle tier) that provides the APIs the UI will use to access a central database, and the database itself, which will store the notes that the user writes.

Introducing the MVVM Pattern

In developing the Notepad phone application, you will be using the increasingly popular *Model-View-ViewModel (MVVM)* pattern. MVVM is a design pattern that provides a clear separation between the UI, the application logic, and the data of an application. The model maintains the data, the view displays the data or provides the UI for user interaction, and the view-model acts as the controller, or brain, which handles the events that affect either the data or the view. Figure 3-3 illustrates the elements of the MVVM pattern and its relationships.

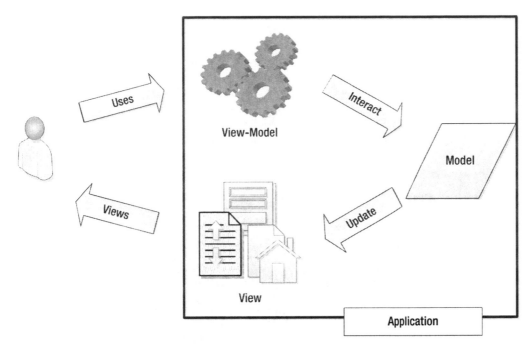

Figure 3-3. The MVVM pattern

Introducing Microsoft Azure and SQL Azure

Azure is the name of Microsoft's cloud services platform, which developers can use to deliver applications at scale for various workloads and devices. Microsoft Azure provides a runtime framework for applications that currently supports .NET 3.5 and .NET 4.0, as well as load balancers, operating systems, servers, storage, and networking that leave you free to build the application.

Microsoft Azure provides three services: Windows Azure, SQL Azure, and Windows Azure AppFabric. For building a consumer-facing Windows Phone application, you will be more interested in Windows Azure, which can host web and Web service applications, and SQL Azure for the database. Windows Azure AppFabric is more of an enterprise-level solution; it provides enterprise service bus patterns, which are popular in business process applications.

In the following section, you will first start by learning to work with SQL Azure in order to save notes to the database.

Creating a Cloud Database

The first step is to create an SQL Azure database to store the notes a user creates with this application. Think of SQL Azure as a hosted database in the cloud, where you don't have to worry about the infrastructure. If you're familiar with Microsoft SQL Server, you'll be able to work in SQL Azure. NotepadService, which you will create in the next section, will connect to this database by using the Entity Framework to create, read, and update records and delete them from the database.

The Entity Framework

The *Entity Framework* is an *object-relational mapping (ORM)* tool that allows you to generate objects based on the tables in a database; it takes care of the interaction with the database, which you would otherwise have to code yourself. Thus, the Entity Framework will save you lots of time.

Creating an SQL Azure Database

In this section, you will create a database in SQL Azure in order perform create, read, update, and delete operations for the Notepad application.

Signing Up for SQL Azure

You will create an SQL Azure account by following these steps:

1. Open your browser of choice.

2. Go to www.microsoft.com/windowsazure/ to sign up for and buy the Windows Azure service account. Follow the directions provided by Microsoft to purchase and acquire the service account. You can currently use Microsoft Azure each month for free (25 hours of computing time, 500MB storage, 10,000 storage transactions, 1GB database, and 500MB data transfer). Note that this is a promotional offer available at the time of this writing, and it could end at any time.

3. Go to https://windows.azure.com/, and sign in using the account you created in step 1.

4. Once you have signed in, click the Database menu tab on the left. You will see the subscriptions that you purchased during the registration process in step 1. Figure 3-4 corresponds to this step. Notice that you can purchase multiple subscriptions of the databases.

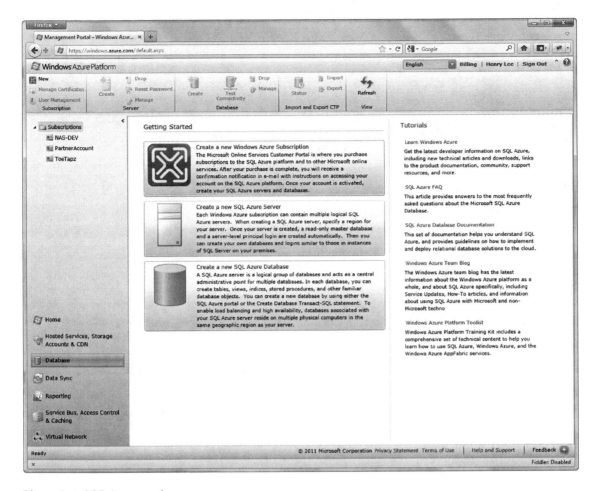

Figure 3-4. *SQL Azure main screen*

Connecting to the SQL Azure Project

After you register and purchase your Azure service account, you can log in to an SQL Azure portal.

1. Click the name of the database subscription that that you created in the "Signing up for SQL Azure" section.

2. Click the Create button, and the Create Server wizard will appear, as shown in Figure 3-5.

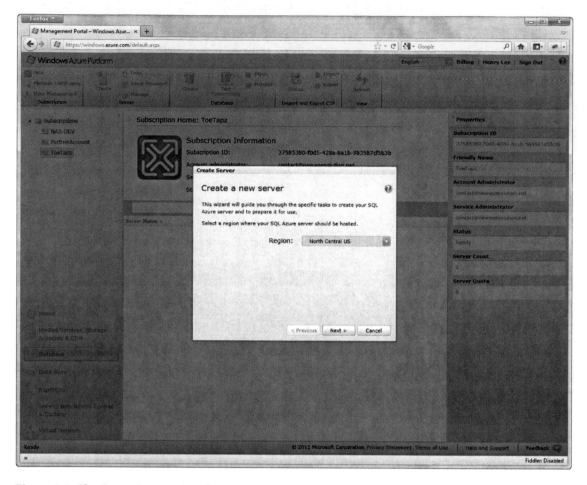

Figure 3-5. *The Create Server wizard*

Creating an SQL Azure Database

Here you will create an SQL Azure database with a username and password.

1. By now you should see the Create Server wizard screen shown in Figure 3-5. For optimal performance, choose the region that is closest to where you are located from the drop-down list. If you are planning to deploy the application to a specific region not close to your location, select the appropriate region from the drop-down list accordingly.

2. On the "Create a new server" page, enter **NotepadAdmin** as the administrator username and **P@ssword** as the administrator password. Retype the password (see Figure 3-6). Click the Next button.

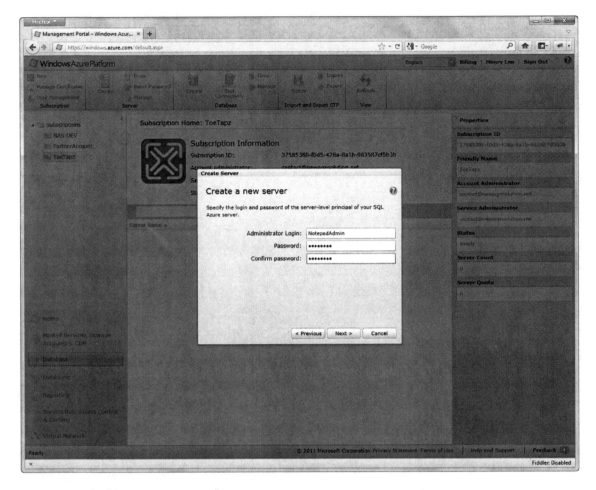

Figure 3-6. The "Create a new server" page

3. In this step, you will configure the SQL Azure firewall so that you can connect to the database. By default, SQL Azure denies all access to the database until you add a specific IP address. First, select the "Allow Microsoft Services access to this server" check box, which will allow programs such as Microsoft SQL Management consoles to connect directly to the SQL Azure database, as shown in Figure 3-7.

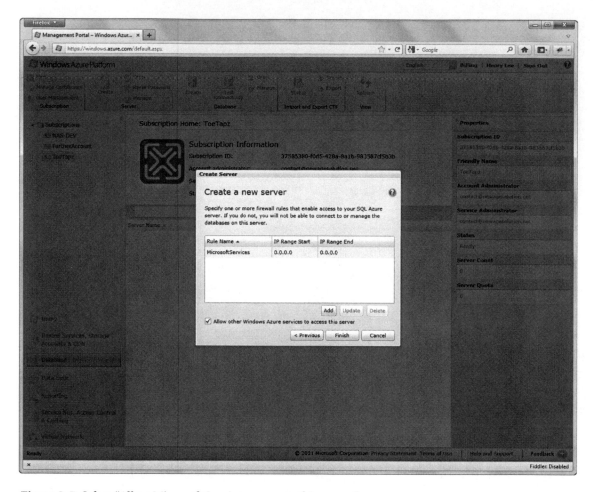

Figure 3-7. Select "Allow Microsoft Services access to this server."

4. Click the Add button to add a rule, and when the pop-up appears, enter **My IP** into the "Rule name" text box. The pop-up displays your IP address, which you should now copy and paste into the "IP range start" and "IP range end" text boxes, as shown in Figure 3-8. Click the OK button.

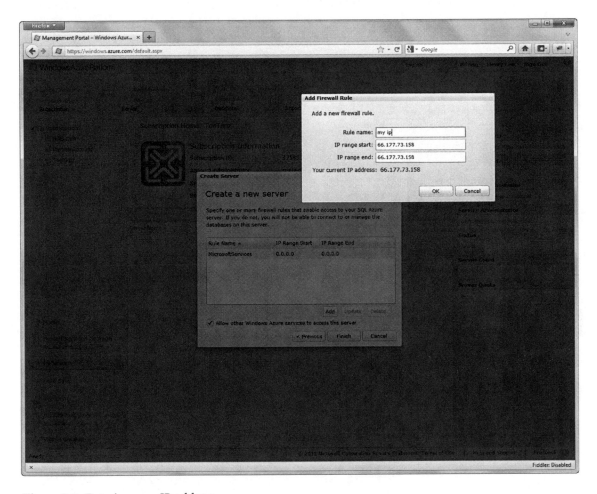

Figure 3-8. Entering your IP address

5. You will see Microsoft Services and My IP added as firewall rules, as shown in Figure 3-9. Click the Finish button to continue.

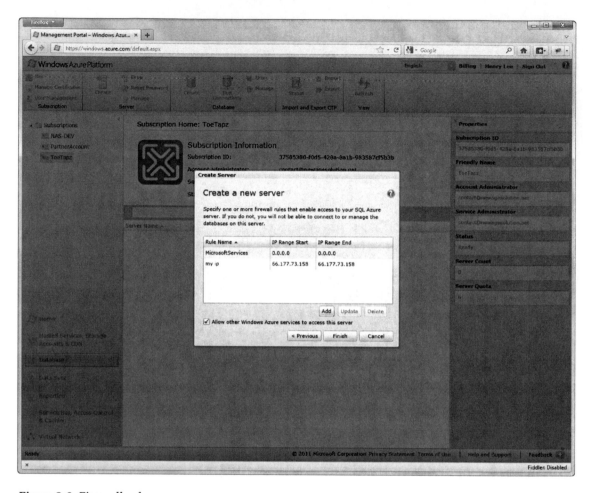

Figure 3-9. Firewall rule screen

6. It will take few minutes to create a database server instance. Once the instance has been created, you will see the database server on the list, as shown in Figure 3-10.

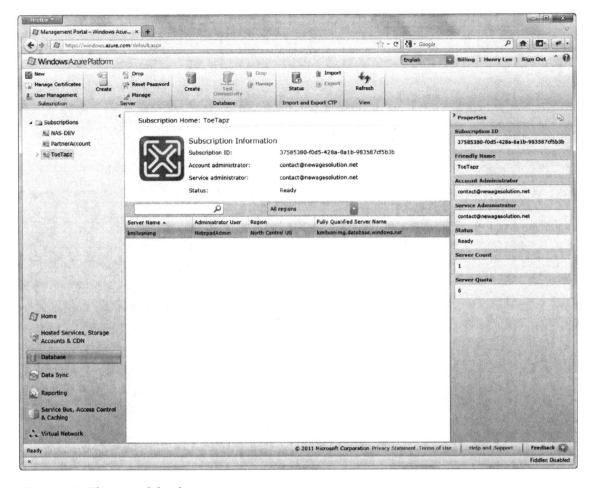

Figure 3-10. The created database server

7. Click the Create Database button. When the pop-up window appears, enter
NotepadDB as the name of your database, choose Web from the Edition drop-
down menu, and choose 1GB from the Maximum Size drop-down menu, as
shown in Figure 3-11. Then click OK.

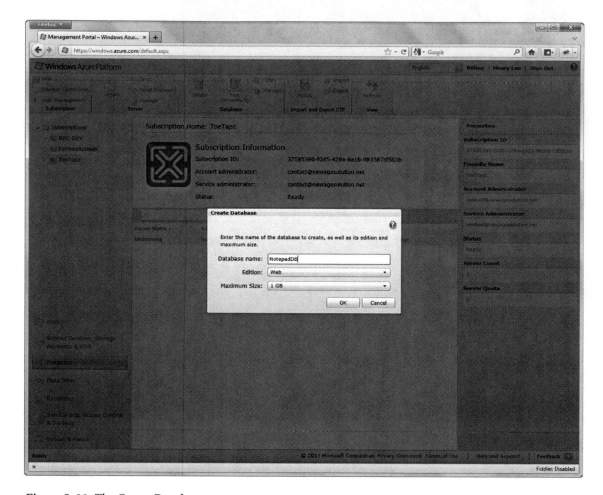

Figure 3-11. The Create Database screen

Note that on the left-hand menu, you can now drill down to your subscription to see the newly created SQL database server, as shown in Figure 3-12.

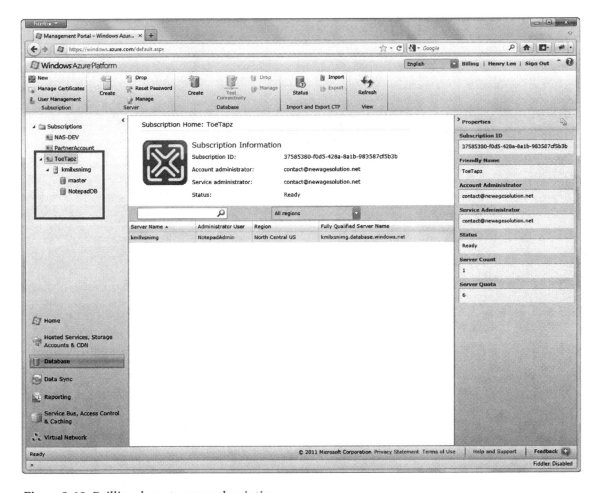

Figure 3-12. Drilling down to your subscription

Testing the SQL Azure Database Connection

In this section, you will test that all the configuration steps have been performed properly and that you can connect to the database.

1. Drill down to your database server from your subscription, and select your database, as shown in Figure 3-12. Click the Test Connectivity button.

2. Enter NotepadAdmin for the login and P@ssw0rd for the password, as shown in Figure 3-13.

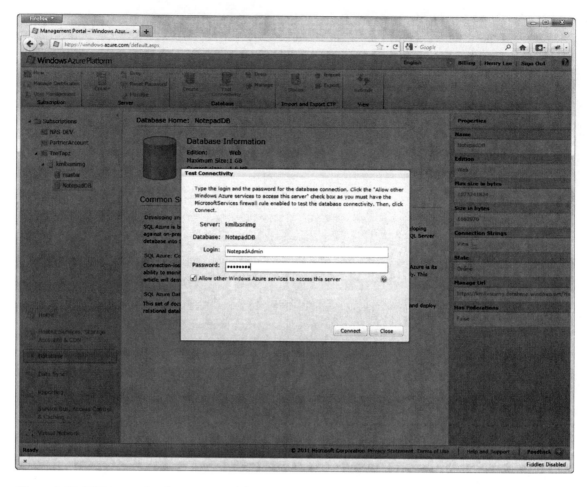

Figure 3-13. SQL Azure database connectivity test

3. Click the Connect button, and you will see a success indicator, as shown in
    Figure 3-14. Click Close to return to the main page.

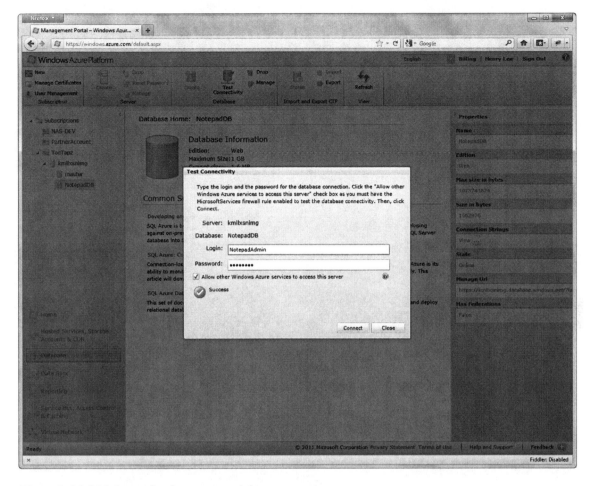

Figure 3-14. SQL Azure database connectivity test success screen

Creating a Database in SQL Azure

In the following section, you will create database tables in the NotepadDB database, which is hosted directly in SQL Azure using Microsoft SQL Server Management Studio.

Using SQL Server Management Studio to Connect to the Cloud Database

You will connect directly to the SQL Azure database you created in the previous steps using SQL Server Management Studio.

1. Make sure that you can connect to SQL Azure directly from SQL Server Management Studio, which you will need to do to perform various database operations. If you do not have SQL Server Management Studio installed, you can download the free SQL Server 2008 R2 Express version from www.microsoft.com/express/database/. Open SQL Server Management Studio by going to Start ➤ Programs ➤ Microsoft SQL Server 2008 R2, as shown in Figure 3-15.

■ **Note** You must use SQL Server Management Studio version 2008 or later.

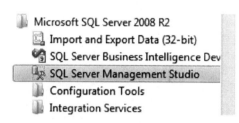

Figure 3-15. *Selecting SQL Server Management Studio from the Windows menu*

2. In the Connect to Server window, enter the server name you obtained previously in the "Server name" text box, enter **NotepadAdmin** and **P@ssword** in the Login and Password text boxes, and click the Connect button, as shown in Figure 3-16.

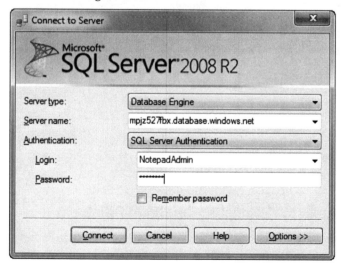

Figure 3-16. *The Connect to Server dialog*

3. Once you are connected successfully to your SQL Azure database, SQL Server Management Studio will display an Object Explorer window on the left side of its IDE, as shown in Figure 3-17. Expand the Databases folder and you will find NotepadDB there.

Figure 3-17. SQL Server Management Studio Object Explorer

Creating SQL Azure Database Tables

Once you are connected to NotepadDB, you can create the tables you'll use to store and manage the notes your users will create and save. You will create the database schema shown in Figure 3-18.

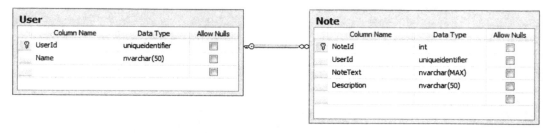

Figure 3-18. NotepadDB database schema

1. Right-click NotepadDB from the Object Explorer window. From the context menu, choose New Query.

2. You will be executing SQL scripts in the query window in order to create tables in NotepadDB.

3. In the newly opened query window, enter the following database script or cut and paste it from the files you downloaded for this book:

```
USE [NotepadDB]
GO

CREATE TABLE [dbo].[User]
(
        [UserId] [uniqueidentifier] NOT NULL,
        [Name] [nvarchar](50) NOT NULL,
    CONSTRAINT [PK_User] PRIMARY KEY ( [UserId] )
)
Go

CREATE TABLE [dbo].[Note]
(
        [NoteId] [int] IDENTITY(1,1) NOT NULL,
        [UserId] [uniqueidentifier] NOT NULL,
        [NoteText] [nvarchar](max) NOT NULL,
        [Description] [nvarchar](50) NOT NULL,
    CONSTRAINT [PK_Note] PRIMARY KEY CLUSTERED ( [NoteId] )
)
GO

ALTER TABLE [dbo].[Note]
        WITH CHECK ADD CONSTRAINT [FK_Note_User] FOREIGN KEY([UserId])
        REFERENCES [dbo].[User] ([UserId])
GO

ALTER TABLE [dbo].[Note] CHECK CONSTRAINT [FK_Note_User]
GO
```

4. After executing the script, notice that when you expand the tables from NotepadDB in Object Explorer, you will see two tables, Note and User, as shown in Figure 3-19.

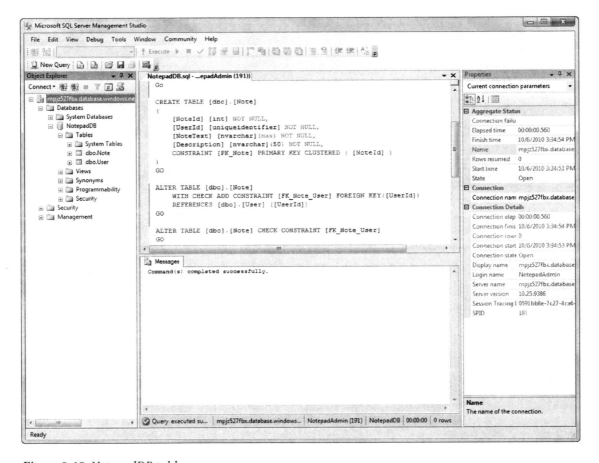

Figure 3-19. NotepadDB tables

You now have a live database in SQL Azure! In the next section, you will create a Web service using Windows Communication Foundation (WCF). The Web service layer provides managed APIs that the phone application can use to access the database.

Creating a Cloud Service to Access the Cloud Database

You will create a WCF service called NotepadService that will be consumed by the Windows Phone Notepad application. Think of NotepadService as the layer that provides managed APIs to the Notepad application. NotepadService will utilize the Entity Framework to generate object models based on the database tables (schema), and it will also generate a persistence layer that performs the database operations, which otherwise you would have to code yourself.

The following steps will provide you with instructions on creating and deploying NotepadService to Windows Azure. You will create a WCF Azure service and run it from your computer, and then you will package and deploy the project to the Azure cloud, where you will be able to configure it to run multiple services if your application demand increases.

Creating a Windows Azure Project

You will create a Windows Azure NotepadService project in Visual Studio in the following steps. In order to create Azure services, you need to download the Azure tools and SDK from www.microsoft.com/windowsazure/windowsazure/default.aspx.

1. Create a new Windows Phone Application by selecting File ➤ New Project on the Visual Studio command menu. Select the Cloud installed template on the left, and choose Windows Azure Cloud Service from the list on the left (see Figure 3-20). Name the Azure service NotepadService and click OK.

Figure 3-20. Windows Azure Cloud Service project

2. You will be prompted to select the type of role. Note here that if you want to host the web project, you need to select ASP.NET Web Role. For the Notepad WCF service, select WCF Service Web Role, as shown in Figure 3-21, and click the arrow pointing to the right. In the Cloud Service Solution dialog, you will see WCFServiceWebRole; if you hover your mouse over the item, a little pencil icon will appear. Click the pencil icon, and change the name to NotepadServiceRole (also shown in Figure 3-21).

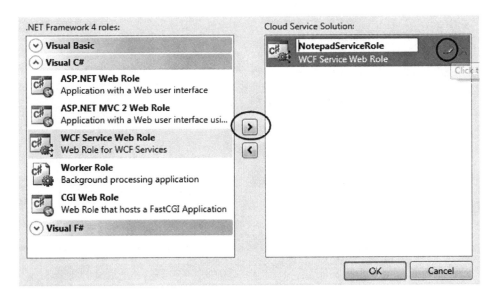

Figure 3-21. Selecting WCF Service Web Role

Generating an Object Model to Access the Cloud Database

Now that you have the basic plumbing for implementing a WCF service, it's a good time to implement a persistence layer that allows you to interact with the database. The Entity Framework will act as an ORM tool that will take database tables and create equivalent object models, and handle many of the tedious tasks of coding methods (such as add, delete, update, and search).

At the end of this section, you will have created two object models, User and Note, with which you can work directly in the code. The Entity Framework provides the ability to save these models directly back to the database.

In the following steps, you will add an Entity Framework item to the project and then connect to NotepadDB in SQL Azure and generate object models.

1. Right-click the NotepadServiceRole project found in Solution Explorer, and choose Add ➤ New Item.

2. Choose Data from the Installed Templates list on the left, choose ADO.NET Entity Data Model, and name the model NotepadService.edmx (see Figure 3-22).

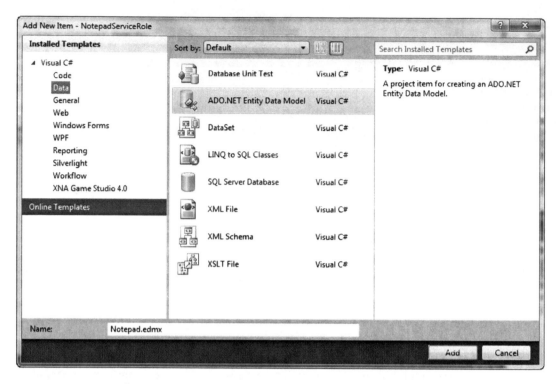

Figure 3-22. Adding an Entity Framework item

3. You will be prompted with the Entity Data Model Wizard, as shown in Figure
    3-23. Click Next.

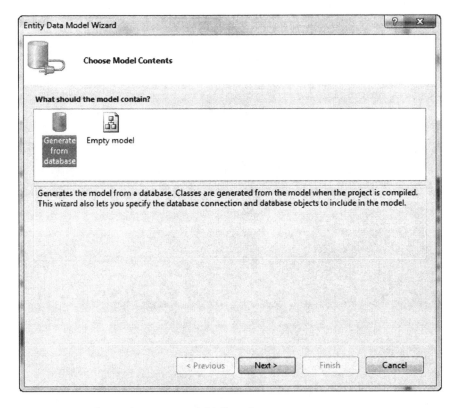

Figure 3-23. The Entity Data Model Wizard

4.   Click the New Connection button. When Choose Data Source appears, select
      Microsoft SQL Server from the list, as shown in Figure 3-24. Click Continue.

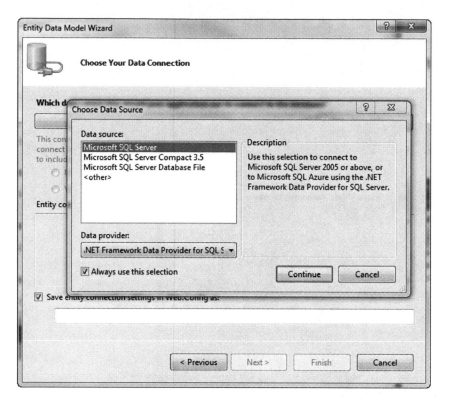

Figure 3-24. *The Choose Data Source window*

5. You will be prompted with a Connection Properties window. For the service name, enter the SQL Azure server name that you acquired from the previous steps, and enter **NotepadAdmin** and **P@ssword** as your username and password. From the "Select or enter a database name" drop-down, select NotepadDB, as shown in Figure 3-25.

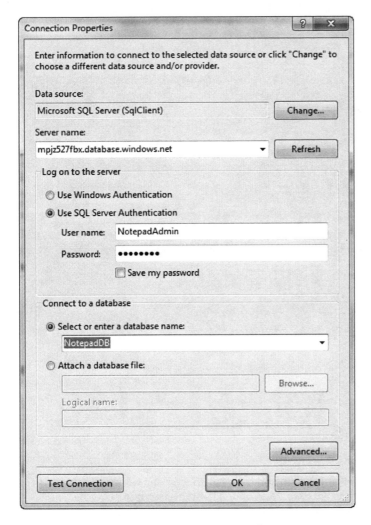

Figure 3-25. The Connection Properties window

6. Click OK, and you will return to the Entity Data Model Wizard window. Select Yes, include the sensitive data in the connection string radio button, and click Next.

7. If you expand the tables, you will see the two tables (Note and User) that you created previously. Select both of the tables, as shown in Figure 3-26.

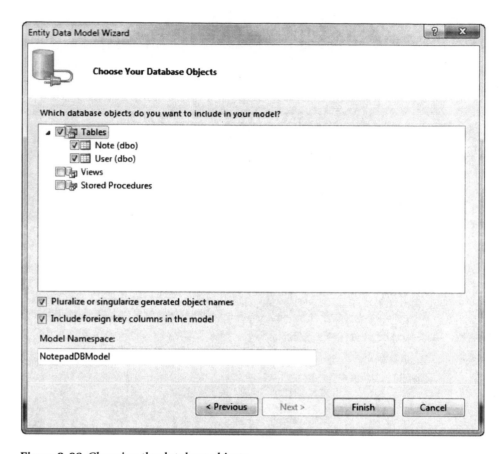

Figure 3-26. Choosing the database objects

8. Accept the default option for everything else, and click Finish. You will return to the Visual Studio project and see Notepad.edmx, which contains two object models, User and Note, as shown in Figure 3-27.

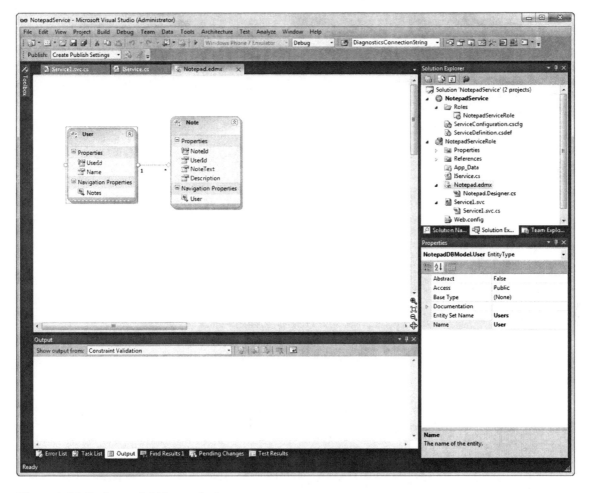

Figure 3-27. Entity model Notepad.edmx

You now have User and Note object models that you can work with in NotepadService. In the next section, you will prepare NotepadService, which will implement simple create, read, update, and delete operations using the entity model that you generated in this section.

Implementing a WCF Service to Access the SQL Azure Database

Now that you have an entity model of User and Note, you can implement NotepadService, which will add, update, delete, and search notes. In this section, you will learn to implement a WCF service. You will also learn to use the Entity Framework to interact with the SQL Azure database.

Coding the WCF Contract

In order to create a WCF service, you must first define a WCF service contract. If you have done everything successfully, Solution Explorer in Visual Studio will resemble Figure 3-28.

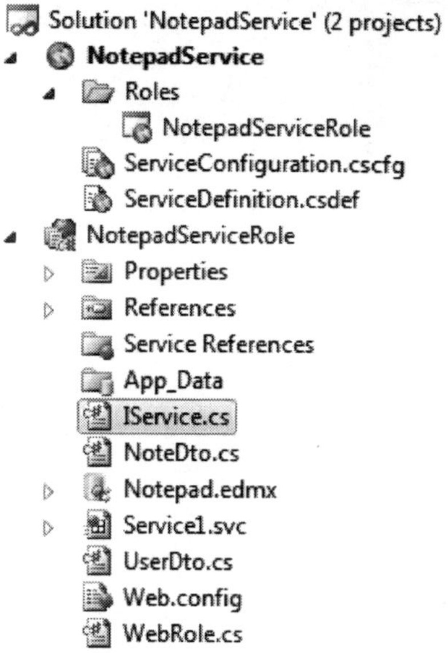

- Solution 'NotepadService' (2 projects)
  - ▲ ● **NotepadService**
    - ▲ 📁 Roles
      - 📇 NotepadServiceRole
    - 📇 ServiceConfiguration.cscfg
    - 📇 ServiceDefinition.csdef
  - ▲ 📦 NotepadServiceRole
    - ▷ 📄 Properties
    - ▷ 📄 References
    - 📁 Service References
    - 📁 App_Data
    - 📄 IService.cs
    - 📄 NoteDto.cs
    - ▷ 📄 Notepad.edmx
    - ▷ 📄 Service1.svc
    - 📄 UserDto.cs
    - 📄 Web.config
    - 📄 WebRole.cs

Figure 3-28. NotepadService project in Solution Explorer

Open IService.cs and replace the content with the code that follows. The WCF contract will contain methods to add, delete, update, and search notes in NotepadDB. The namespace System.ServiceModel allows you to add the attributes ServiceContract and OperationContract, which must be defined in order to create a WCF service.

```
using System.ServiceModel;
using System.Collections.Generic;
using System;

namespace NotepadServiceRole
{
    [ServiceContract]
    public interface IService
    {
        [OperationContract]
        Guid AddUser(Guid userId, string userName);

        [OperationContract]
        NoteDto AddNote(Guid userId, string notedescription, string noteText);

        [OperationContract]
        Void UpdateNote(int noteId, string noteText);
```

```
        [OperationContract]
        void DeleteNote(Guid userId, int noteId);

[OperationContract]
        List<NoteDto> GetNotes(Guid userId);

        [OperationContract]
        NoteDto GetNote(Guid userId, int noteId);

    }
}
```

In the next section, you will create a data contract that will be sent to the client through the service.

Coding the Data Contract

Before you implement the service contract, you will need to define two data transfer objects to map to the entity object. Although you can expose the entity generated by the Entity Framework directly to the WCF service, it is not a recommended practice because the Entity Framework exposes information not necessary for the client. For example, certain types of information, such as foreign keys, primary keys, and any Entity Framework–related information, have no meaning to the client. Also, when the Entity Framework object is serialized, it will include all this unnecessary information, causing the serialized objects coming through the Internet to become huge. Since you are working with Windows Phone over wireless or Wi-Fi transmission, you will want to keep the amount of information sent to a minimum.

1. Add the `UserDto.cs` class to `NotepadServiceRole` via the following code. The namespace you will be using, `System.Runtime.Serialization`, lets you add `DataContract` and `DataMember` attributes that allow the WCF service to serialize this object to be sent over the service to the client.

```
using System.Runtime.Serialization;

namespace NotepadServiceRole
{
    [DataContract]
    public class UserDto
    {
        [DataMember]
        public int UserId { get; set; }

        [DataMember]
        public string Name { get; set; }
    }
}
```

2. Add the `NoteDto.cs` class to `NotepadServiceRole` via the following code:

```
Using System.Runtime.Serialization;

Namespace NotepadServiceRole
{
    [DataContract]
```

```
public class NoteDto
{
    [DataMember]
    public int NoteId { get; set; }

    [DataMember]
    public string Description { get; set; }

    [DataMember]
    Public string NoteText { get; set; }

}
}
```

Coding the Service

In the following steps, you will implement the NotepadService WCF contract defined in the previous section. You will use the Entity Framework to access the SQL Azure database.

Open Service1.svc.cs in the NotepadServiceRole project, and add the code blocks presented in the following sections.

Coding the AddUser Method

AddUser will add a new user to the database. Note that you are instantiating NotepadDBEntities, which is the Entity Framework–generated context that connects to the SQL Azure NotepadDB.

```
public Guid AddUser(Guid userId, string userName)
{
    using (var context = new NotepadDBEntities())
    {
        context.AddToUsers(new User()
            {
                UserId = userId,
                Name = userName,
            });
        context.SaveChanges();

        return userId;
    }
}
```

Coding the AddNote Method

In the AddNote method, after instantiating NotepadDBEntities, you create the Note entity that you generated in the previous steps using the Entity Framework Wizard. Once the note is saved, you map it to NoteDto to be sent to the client.

```
public NoteDto AddNote(Guid userId, string notedescription, string noteText)
{
    using (var context = new NotepadDBEntities())
    {
```

```
        Note note = new Note()
            {
                Description = notedescription,
                UserId = userId,
                NoteText = noteText,
            };
        context.AddToNotes(note);
        context.SaveChanges();

        return new NoteDto()
            {
                NoteId = note.NoteId,
                Description = note.Description,
                NoteText = note.NoteText,
            };
    }
}
```

Coding the UpdateNote Method

In order to update the note, you first need to instantiate the entity context that connects to NotepadDB, and then you must query for the note that you are going to update. Once the note is retrieved, you will then update the properties and save the changes.

```
public void UpdateNote(int noteId, string noteText)
{
    using (var context = new NotepadDBEntities())
    {
        var note = context
                        .Notes
                        .Where(n => n.NoteId.Equals(noteId)
                                ).Single();
        note.NoteText = noteText;
        context.SaveChanges();
    }
}
```

Coding the DeleteNote Method

When deleting the note, you must retrieve it first, and then add it to the DeleteObject of the Notes collection. Then you will save the changes where the delete will be performed by the Entity Framework.

```
public void DeleteNote(Guid userId, int noteId)
{
    using (var context = new NotepadDBEntities())
    {
        var note = context
                        .Notes
                        .Where(n => n.NoteId.Equals(noteId)).Single();
        context.Notes.DeleteObject(note);
        context.SaveChanges();
```

```
        }
    }
```

Coding the GetNotes Method

GetNotes will bring in all the notes associated with the specific userId. You will be using *Linq to Entity*, which closely resembles the SQL statement. Inside Linq to Entity, you will be performing translation of the Note entity to NoteDto. This is a very useful technique for mapping an entity object to a data transfer object.

```
public List<NoteDto> GetNotes(Guid userId)
{
    using (var context = new NotepadDBEntities())
    {
        var notes = (
                    from eachNote in context.Notes
                    where eachNote.UserId == userId
                    orderby eachNote.Description ascending
                    select new NoteDto
                    {
                        NoteId = eachNote.NoteId,
                        Description = eachNote.Description,
                        NoteText = eachNote.NoteText,
                    }
                ).ToList();

        return notes;
    }
}
```

Coding the GetNote Method

GetNote will query a single user note from the database.

```
public NoteDto GetNote(Guid userId, int noteId)
{
    using (var context = new NotepadDBEntities())
    {
        var notes = (
                    from eachNote in context.Notes
                    where eachNote.NoteId == noteId
                          && eachNote.UserId == userId
                    select new NoteDto
                    {
                        NoteId = eachNote.NoteId,
                        Description = eachNote.Description,
                        NoteText = eachNote.NoteText,
                    }
                ).SingleOrDefault();

        return notes;
```

```
        }
    }
```

Testing the Azure WCF NotepadService on Your Machine

You will test NotepadService on your computer so that when you connect to NotepadService from the Windows Phone Notepad application, you will be able to debug and step through NotepadService when the service call is made from the Notepad application.

Press F5, and the Development Fabric window will appear in Internet Explorer. Development Fabric simulates the Azure service environment on your computer. Note that when you expand NotepadService, you'll see NotepadServiceRole, which is the WCF service that you coded in the previous steps. When NotepadService is deployed, you will see one instance of the service deployed, as shown in Figure 3-29. Don't stop the service, as you will be referencing the service from the Notepad application.

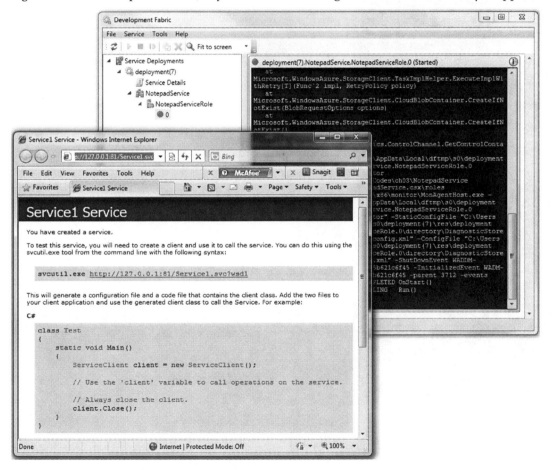

Figure 3-29. Development Fabric simulating the Azure service environment

In the previous steps, you created the NotepadDB database in SQL Azure and the NotepadService hosted locally using Development AppFabric to simulate Windows Azure. In the following section, you will consume NotepadService from the Notepad application. When the service is working properly, you will deploy NotepadService to Windows Azure.

Building a Phone Client to Access a Cloud Service

The Notepad application will allow you to add notes and retrieve the notes that will be saved to the cloud database NotepadDB. You will build the Notepad application that will consume NotepadService, the WCF Azure service that you created previously, and you will verify at the end that the notes are properly saved to SQL Azure NotepadDB. When it's finished, the UI for the Notepad application will resemble Figure 3-30.

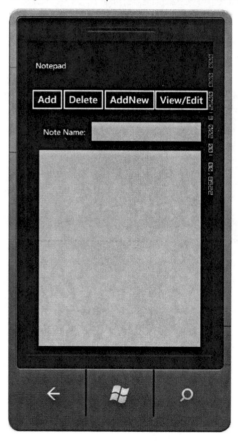

Figure 3-30. Notepad application

Creating a Windows Phone Project

To set up the Notepad project, follow the steps you've taken in previous examples in this book:

1. Open Microsoft Visual Studio 2010 on your workstation.

2. Create a new Windows Phone Application by selecting File ➤ New Project from the Visual Studio command menu. Select Silverlight for Windows Phone from Installed Templates, and then select the Windows Phone Application template on the right when the list appears, as shown in Figure 3-31. Name the application Notepad and click OK.

Figure 3-31. Creating a Windows Phone Application project

Building the UI

You will build the UI using XAML in Visual Studio. For building simple controls, it's faster to work with XAML code. First, you'll build two user controls: NoteListUserControl, which will display the list of the notes that the user can select to display and edit, and UserRegistrationUserControl, where the user can register so that the notes can be saved to NotepadDB in the cloud.

Building UserRegistrationUserControl

UserRegistrationUserControl is displayed the first time when the user starts the Notepad application. Thereafter, the user registration information will be saved to the Isolated Storage application settings. (Isolated storage will be covered in detail in Chapter 13.)

1. Right-click the Notepad project and choose Add ➤ New Item.

2. From the Add New Item window, choose Windows Phone User Control and name the control UserRegistrationUserControl.xaml, as shown in Figure 3-32. Click the Add button.

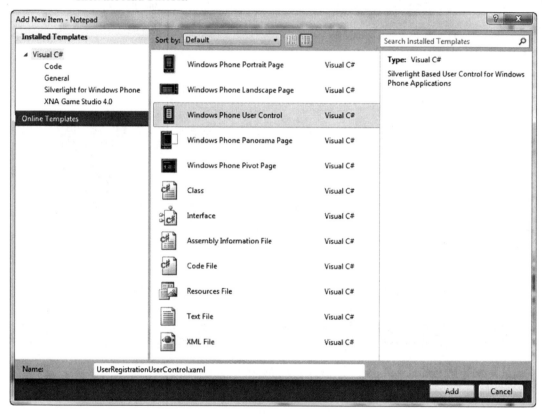

Figure 3-32. Creating UserRegistrationUserControl

3. Open UserRegistrationUserControl.xaml, which you just added from Solution Explorer. Replace the content with the following XAML code, and you will see a control resembles Figure 3-33 in Visual Studio design view.

Figure 3-33. *UserRegistrationUserControl in design view*

Declaring the UI Resources

Take the default namespaces as shown in the following code in order to use out-of-the-box controls, such as Buttons and TextBoxes:

```
<UserControl x:Class="Notepad.NoteListUserControl"
    xmlns="http://schemas.microsoft.com/winfx/2006/xaml/presentation"
    xmlns:x="http://schemas.microsoft.com/winfx/2006/xaml"
    xmlns:d="http://schemas.microsoft.com/expression/blend/2008"
    xmlns:mc="http://schemas.openxmlformats.org/markup-compatibility/2006"
    mc:Ignorable="d"
    FontFamily="{StaticResource PhoneFontFamilyNormal}"
    FontSize="{StaticResource PhoneFontSizeNormal}"
    Foreground="{StaticResource PhoneForegroundBrush}"
    d:DesignHeight="480" d:DesignWidth="480">
```

Adding Components for UserRegistrationUserControl

You will add a Register button, a UserName label, and a TextBlock to capture the username.

```
<Grid x:Name="LayoutRoot" Background="{StaticResource PhoneChromeBrush}">
        <Button Content="Register" Height="72" HorizontalAlignment="Left"
                Margin="118,260,0,0" Name="btnSave" VerticalAlignment="Top"
                Width="160" Click="btnSave_Click" />
        <TextBox Height="72" HorizontalAlignment="Left"
                Margin="118,154,0,0" Name="txtUserName" Text=""
                VerticalAlignment="Top" Width="337" />
        <TextBlock Height="30" HorizontalAlignment="Left"
                Margin="17,177,0,0" Name="textBlock1"
                Text="UserName: " VerticalAlignment="Top" />
</Grid>
```

Building NoteListUserControl

NoteListUserControl displays the list of notes that the user created. The control is prompted when the user clicks the View/Edit button from the main page.

1. Right-click the Notepad project, and choose Add ➤ New Item.

2. From the Add New Item window, choose Windows Phone User Control and name the control NoteListUserControl.xaml. Click the Add button.

3. Open NoteListUserControl.xaml, which you just added from Solution Explorer, and replace the content with the following XAML code. You will see a control that resembles Figure 3-34 in Visual Studio design view.

Figure 3-34. *NoteListUserControl in design view*

Declaring the UI Resources

Accept the default namespaces shown in the following code:

```
<UserControl x:Class="Notepad.NoteListUserControl"
    xmlns="http://schemas.microsoft.com/winfx/2006/xaml/presentation"
    xmlns:x="http://schemas.microsoft.com/winfx/2006/xaml"
    xmlns:d="http://schemas.microsoft.com/expression/blend/2008"
    xmlns:mc="http://schemas.openxmlformats.org/markup-compatibility/2006"
    mc:Ignorable="d"
    FontFamily="{StaticResource PhoneFontFamilyNormal}"
    FontSize="{StaticResource PhoneFontSizeNormal}"
    Foreground="{StaticResource PhoneForegroundBrush}"
    d:DesignHeight="480" d:DesignWidth="480">
```

Adding Components for NoteListUserControl

You will add a ListBox control that will be bound to Notes, which is a collection of NoteDto coming from the NotepadViewModel object that you will implement later. Each ListBoxItem will contain a TextBlock that is bound to NoteDto's Description property.

```
<Grid x:Name="LayoutRoot" Background="{StaticResource PhoneChromeBrush}">
    <ListBox Height="458" HorizontalAlignment="Left" Margin="10,10,0,0" Name="lstNotes"
            VerticalAlignment="Top" Width="460"
SelectionChanged="lstNotes_SelectionChanged"
            ItemsSource="{Binding Notes}">
        <ListBox.ItemTemplate>
            <DataTemplate>
                <StackPanel>
                    <TextBlock Text="{Binding Description}" />
                </StackPanel>
            </DataTemplate>
        </ListBox.ItemTemplate>
    </ListBox>
</Grid>
</UserControl>
```

Building MainPage

MainPage will contain the user controls NoteListUserControl and UserRegistrationUserControl (which you just created) and the buttons Add, AddNew, Delete, and View/Edit, which will allow the user to add, insert, delete, and edit notes.

Declaring the UI Resources

The namespaces in the following code snippet are typically declared by default when you first create a Windows Phone project. In particular, the namespaces xmlns:phone="clr-namespace:Microsoft.Phone.Controls; assembly=Microsoft.Phone" allow you to add common Windows Phone controls to the application main page.

You will also add xmlns:uc="clr-namespace:Notepad";, which allows you to add BooleanToVisibilityConverter, which implements the conversion of a value from Boolean to Visibility that is set on the controls.

```
<phone:PhoneApplicationPage
    x:Class="Notepad.MainPage"
    xmlns="http://schemas.microsoft.com/winfx/2006/xaml/presentation"
    xmlns:x="http://schemas.microsoft.com/winfx/2006/xaml"
    xmlns:phone="clr-namespace:Microsoft.Phone.Controls;assembly=Microsoft.Phone"
    xmlns:shell="clr-namespace:Microsoft.Phone.Shell;assembly=Microsoft.Phone"
    xmlns:d="http://schemas.microsoft.com/expression/blend/2008"
    xmlns:mc="http://schemas.openxmlformats.org/markup-compatibility/2006"
    xmlns:uc="clr-namespace:Notepad"
    mc:Ignorable="d" d:DesignWidth="480" d:DesignHeight="768"
    FontFamily="{StaticResource PhoneFontFamilyNormal}"
    FontSize="{StaticResource PhoneFontSizeNormal}"
    Foreground="{StaticResource PhoneForegroundBrush}"
    SupportedOrientations="Portrait" Orientation="Portrait"
    shell:SystemTray.IsVisible="True">
```

Building the Main Page and Adding Components

In MainPage, you will add Add, Delete, AddNew, and View/Edit buttons to work with the notes. Two TextBlocks—txtNote and txtNoteName—are added to display the note name and the note content. txtNote and txtNoteName are bound to SelectedNote.NoteText and SelectedNote.Description. The SelectedNote property comes from the NotepadViewModel object, which gets bound to the context of MainPage so that any control in MainPage can bind to any properties of the NotepadViewModel object.

There are two user controls that you will add; visibility of these user controls is controlled by the ShowNoteList and NeedUserId properties found in NotepadViewModel. When the user clicks the View/Edit button, ShowNoteList will be set to true, causing NoteListUserControl, bound to the ShowNoteList property, to appear to the user.

When the user first starts the application and doesn't have the user ID stored in the application settings, NeedUserId will be set to true in NotepadViewModel, causing the UserRegistrationUserControl to appear.

Adding BoolToVisibilityConvert

Note that you will be adding a custom converter that will convert the Boolean value received from NotepadViewModel to a Visibility enumeration in order to hide and unhide the controls. You will code BoolToVisibilityConvert later.

```
<UserControl.Resources>
    <uc:BoolToVisibilityConverter x:Key="BoolToVisibilityConverter" />
</UserControl.Resources>

<Grid x:Name="LayoutRoot" Background="Transparent">
    <Grid.RowDefinitions>
        <RowDefinition Height="Auto"/>
        <RowDefinition Height="*"/>
    </Grid.RowDefinitions>

    <StackPanel x:Name="TitlePanel" Grid.Row="0" Margin="12,17,0,28">
        <TextBlock x:Name="ApplicationTitle" Text="Notepad"
                   Style="{StaticResource PhoneTextNormalStyle}"
                   HorizontalAlignment="Left" Margin="12,0,0,0" Width="89"/>
    </StackPanel>

    <Grid x:Name="ContentPanel" Grid.Row="1" Margin="12,0,12,0">
        <Button Content="Add" Height="72" HorizontalAlignment="Left"
                Margin="-8,10,0,0" x:Name="btnSave" VerticalAlignment="Top" Width="99"
                Click="btnSave_Click" />
        <Button Content="Delete" Height="72" HorizontalAlignment="Left"
                Margin="71,10,0,0" x:Name="btnDelete" VerticalAlignment="Top" Width="125"
                Click="btnDelete_Click" />
        <Button Content="AddNew" Height="72"
                Margin="176,10,128,0" x:Name="btnAddNew" VerticalAlignment="Top"
                Click="btnAddNew_Click" />
        <Button Content="View/Edit" Height="72" HorizontalAlignment="Left"
                Margin="306,10,0,0" Name="btnEdit" VerticalAlignment="Top" Width="160"
                Click="btnViewEdit_Click" />
        <TextBox x:Name="txtNote" TextWrapping="Wrap"
```

```
                    Margin="10,163,8,8" AcceptsReturn="True"
                    Text="{Binding Path=SelectedNote.NoteText}"/>
            <TextBlock x:Name="lblNoteName" HorizontalAlignment="Left" TextWrapping="Wrap"
                    Text="Note Name:" VerticalAlignment="Top" Margin="32,114,0,0"/>
            <TextBox x:Name="txtNoteName" TextWrapping="Wrap"
                    VerticalAlignment="Top" Margin="143,91,8,0"
                    Text="{Binding Path=SelectedNote.Description}"/>
            <uc:NoteListUserControl x:Name="ucNoteList"
                    Visibility="{Binding ShowNoteList, Converter={StaticResource
BoolToVisibilityConverter}}" d:IsHidden="True" />
            <uc:UserRegistrationUserControl x:Name="ucUserRegistration"
                    Visibility="{Binding NeedUserId, Converter={StaticResource
BoolToVisibilityConverter}}" d:IsHidden="True"  />
        </Grid>
    </Grid>
```

In the next section, you will add events for the controls that you built in the previous steps.

Coding MainPage

In Solution Explorer, open `MainPage.xaml.cs` and replace the code there with the following C# code blocks to implement the UI that interacts with the user to add, delete, view, and edit notes, and to register the user for the first time.

Specifying the Namespaces

Begin by listing the namespaces the application will use:

```
using System.Windows;
using Microsoft.Phone.Controls;
```

The Code Constructor

In the constructor of `MainPage`, you will set the `DataContext` of the user controls to the `NotepadViewModel` instance. When the `DataContext` of `ucNoteList` and `ucUserRegistraton` is set to `NotepadViewModel`, the controls within the user controls' values will be controlled by the properties of `NotepadViewModel`.

```
        public MainPage()
        {
            InitializeComponent();

            this.DataContext = NotepadViewModel.Instance;
            ucNoteList.DataContext = NotepadViewModel.Instance;
            ucUserRegistration.DataContext = NotepadViewModel.Instance;
        }
```

Coding the Save Button Event

When the user clicks the Add button, the SaveNote method from the NotepadViewModel instance will be called. Any direct calls to NotepadService will be handled from NotepadViewModel, leaving the handling of the Web service call complexity centralized to NotepadViewModel. This is a great abstraction technique, allowing you to maintain the application easily.

```
private void btnSave_Click(object sender, RoutedEventArgs e)
{
    if (!string.IsNullOrEmpty(txtNote.Text))
    {
        NotepadViewModel.Instance.SaveNote(txtNoteName.Text, txtNote.Text);
    }
}
```

Coding the View/Edit Button Event

When the View/Edit button is clicked, the ShowNoteList property in NotepadViewModel will be set to true, which will trigger NoteListUserControl to appear. ShowNoteList will be set to true only if there are notes to be selected.

```
private void btnViewEdit_Click(object sender, RoutedEventArgs e)
{
    if (!string.IsNullOrEmpty(txtNote.Text))
    {
        NotepadViewModel.Instance.SaveNote(txtNoteName.Text, txtNote.Text);
    }
}
```

Coding the AddNew Button Event

When the AddNew button is clicked, SelectedNode in NotepadViewModel will be set to null, triggering the txtNote and txtNoteName contents to be set to empty because they are bound to SelectedNote. Although you can directly set the text fields of txtNote and txtNoteName to an empty string, you are abstracting this particular task to NotepadViewModel because, when the user selects the specific user note from NoteListUserControl, the txtNote and txtNoteName content will be automatically changed because they are bound to SelectedNote.

```
private void btnAddNew_Click(object sender, System.Windows.RoutedEventArgs e)
{
    NotepadViewModel.Instance.SelectedNote = null;
}
```

Coding the Delete Button Event

When the Delete button is clicked, the DeleteNote method from the NotepadViewModel instance will be invoked, SelectedNode will be set to null, and txtNote and txtNoteName will be set to an empty string automatically because they are bound to SelectedNode.

```
private void btnDelete_Click(object sender, System.Windows.RoutedEventArgs e)
```

```
    {
        NotepadViewModel.Instance.DeleteNote();
    }
```

Coding BoolToVisibilityConvert

You will create a custom converter that implements IValueConverter, which can be used during the
binding in the control where the bound value can be converted to any value that the control will
understand. BoolToVisibilityConvert will convert the Boolean value bound to the control Visibility to
Visibility enumeration so that the controls can be hidden and unhidden.

1. Right-click the Notepad project and choose Add ➤ Add New Item.

2. When the Add New Item window pops up, choose Class and name the class
    BoolToVisibilityConvert, as shown in Figure 3-35. Click the Add button.

Figure 3-35. Adding the BoolToVisibility class to the project

3. Open BoolToVisibilityConvert.cs and paste the code blocks in the following
    sections.

Specifying the Namespaces and Applying the IValueConverter Interface

The namespace System.Windows.Data will allow you to declare the IValueConverter interface for the BoolToVisibilityConverter class.

```
using System;
using System.Windows;
using System.Windows.Data;

namespace Notepad
{
    public class BoolToVisibilityConverter : IValueConverter
    {
```

Implementing IValueConvert

In order to convert the bound value to the control property or transform it to another value, you need to implement the Convert and ConvertBack methods.

```
        public object Convert(object value, Type targetType,
object parameter, System.Globalization.CultureInfo culture)
        {
            bool boolValue;

            if (bool.TryParse(value.ToString(), out boolValue))
            {
                return boolValue ? Visibility.Visible : Visibility.Collapsed;
            }
            else
            {
                // By default it will always return Visibility.Collapsed
                // even for the case where the value is not bool
                return Visibility.Collapsed;
            }

        }

        public object ConvertBack(object value, Type targetType,
object parameter, System.Globalization.CultureInfo culture)
        {
            Visibility visibilityValue = Visibility.Collapsed;

            try
            {
                visibilityValue = (Visibility)Enum.Parse(typeof(Visibility),
(string)value, true);
                return visibilityValue;
            }
            catch (Exception)
            {
                // if fails to conver the value to Visibility
```

```
                     // it will return Collapsed as default value
                     return visibilityValue;
                 }

             }
         }
}
```

Adding a Reference to NotepadService

Before you code NotepadViewModel, add a Web service reference to the NotepadService WCF service that will be hosted in Azure.

1. Right-click the References folder found under the Notepad project entry in Solution Explorer, and choose Add Service Reference.

2. You will be prompted with the Add Service Reference window. In the Address field, enter **http://127.0.0.1/Service.svc**, and enter **NotepadServiceProxy** in the Namespace text box. Click the Go button, and the NotepadService information will be retrieved. You will see Service1 in the Services box.

3. When you expand Service1, you will see IService. Click IService, and the Operations box will be populated with NotepadService, as shown in Figure 3-36. Click OK.

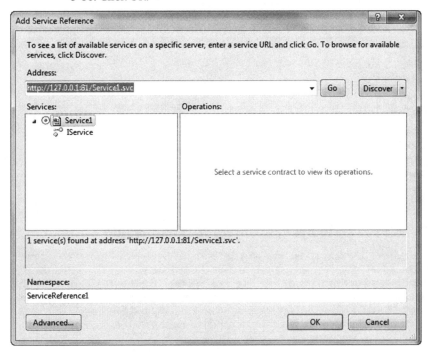

Figure 3-36. Adding a service reference to NotepadService

Coding NotepadViewModel

NotepadViewModel is considered the controller of this application, and it controls the events and the data that will manipulate the UI. You can think of it as the brain of the application.

1. Right-click the Notepad project and choose Add ➤ Add New Item.

2. When the Add New Item window pops up, choose Class; name the class NotepadViewModel. Click the Add button, and Solution Explorer should resemble Figure 3-37.

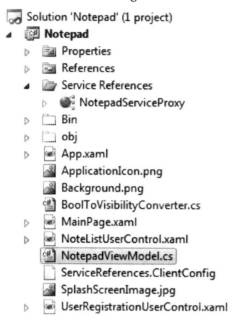

Figure 3-37. Notepad project items in Solution Explorer

3. Open NotepadViewModel.cs, found under the Notepad project, and enter the C# code that follows.

Specifying the Namespaces and Applying INotifyPropertyChanged

The namespace Notepad.NotepadServiceProxy allows you to work with the NotepadService Web service that you referenced. System.IO.IsolatedStorage allows you to save the registered user ID so that the application will know which notes to work with inside the database. System.ComponentModel allows you to implement the INotifyChanged interface, which can raise the property-changed events, allowing the controls that are bound to properties like Notes, SelectedNotes, ShowNoteList, and NeedUserId to respond to the changes. System.Linq allows you to query objects with a syntax that resembles the SQL statement.

```csharp
using System;
using System.Windows;
using System.IO.IsolatedStorage;
using System.ComponentModel;
using Notepad.NotepadServiceProxy;
using System.Collections.ObjectModel;
using System.Linq;

namespace Notepad
{
    /// <summary>
    /// Settings class is a singleton instance that will contain various application
    /// configurations that will be used by all the controls of the application.
    /// </summary>
    public sealed class NotepadViewModel : INotifyPropertyChanged
    {
```

Initializing the Variables

Many variables will be added to NotepadViewModel to control the behavior of the UI controls. Please refer to the comments in the following code for an explanation of what significance the properties have for the UI controls.

```csharp
        // For creating the singleton instance
        public static NotepadViewModel Instance = new NotepadViewModel();

// For calling the Notepad Web service
        private ServiceClient _svc;

        // Populated when the user registers for the first time
        // and the value is saved to Isolated Storage
        public Guid UserId
        {
            get
            {
                if (IsolatedStorageSettings.ApplicationSettings.Contains("UserId"))
                {
                    return (Guid)IsolatedStorageSettings.ApplicationSettings["UserId"];
                }
                else
                {
                    return Guid.Empty;
                }
            }
            set
            {
                if (IsolatedStorageSettings.ApplicationSettings.Contains("UserId"))
                {
                    IsolatedStorageSettings.ApplicationSettings["UserId"] = value;
                }
```

```
                    else
                    {
                        IsolatedStorageSettings.ApplicationSettings.Add("UserId", value);
                    }

                    // Raise-property-changed event to alert user registration control
                    // so that if the UserId is empty, the user registration screen
                    // will prompt the user to register.
                    //
                    // To see how the raise-property-changed event works with control binding,
                    // see binding attributes on the ucUserRegistration control in MainPage.xaml
                    this.RaisePropertyChanged("UserId");
                    this.RaisePropertyChanged("NeedUserId");
                }
            }
// Check to see if the UserId exists in Isolated Storage
        // and make sure the UserId is not an empty Guid
        public bool NeedUserId
        {
            get
            {
                return !IsolatedStorageSettings.ApplicationSettings.Contains("UserId")
                  || (Guid)IsolatedStorageSettings.ApplicationSettings["UserId"]
== Guid.Empty;
            }
        }

        // ShowNoteList is bound to NoteListUserControl in the MainPage
        // and it will hide if false and else unhide if true.
        private bool _showNoteList = false;
        public bool ShowNoteList
        {
            get
            {
                return _showNoteList;
            }

            set
            {
                _showNoteList = value;
                this.RaisePropertyChanged("ShowNoteList");
            }
        }

        // SelectedNote is populated from NoteListUserControl
        // when the user selects the note from the list box.
// SelectedNote is then used in MainPage by txtNote and
// txtNoteName to populate to text box content.
        private NoteDto _note;
        public NoteDto SelectedNote
        {
            get
```

```
        {
            return _note;
        }

        set
        {
            _note = value;
            this.RaisePropertyChanged("SelectedNote");
        }
    }
            // Collection of NoteDto is populated by calling GetNotes service call
// and all user notes will be contained in this collection.
        private ObservableCollection<NoteDto> _notes;
        public ObservableCollection<NoteDto> Notes
        {
            get
            {
                return _notes;
            }

            set
            {
                _notes = value;
                this.RaisePropertyChanged("Notes");
            }
        }
    }
```

Adding the Constructor

In the constructor, you will add event handlers for the service calls. GetNotesCompleted will return all the user notes. AddNote, UpdateNote, and DeleteNote will add, update, and delete the note and return successfully if no error occurs; Otherwise the error will be reported back to the callbacks. In the constructor ServiceClient, the Web service proxy will be initialized, and the RebindData method that makes the call to the GetNotes method will populate the Notes property.

```
        private NotepadViewModel()
        {
            _svc = new ServiceClient();
            _svc.GetNotesCompleted += new
EventHandler<GetNotesCompletedEventArgs>(_svc_GetNotesCompleted);
            _svc.AddNoteCompleted += new
EventHandler<AddNoteCompletedEventArgs>(_svc_AddNoteCompleted);
            _svc.UpdateNoteCompleted += new
EventHandler<AsyncCompletedEventArgs>(_svc_UpdateNoteCompleted);
            _svc.AddUserCompleted += new
EventHandler<AddUserCompletedEventArgs>(_svc_AddUserCompleted);
            _svc.DeleteNoteCompleted += new
EventHandler<AsyncCompletedEventArgs>(_svc_DeleteNoteCompleted);

            if (this.NeedUserId)
            {
```

```
            this.Notes = new ObservableCollection<NoteDto>();
        }
        else
        {
            this.RebindData();
        }
    }

    // To rebind the data, GetNotes will be called to retrieve
    // all the user notes and reset the Notes value.
    public void RebindData()
    {
        _svc.GetNotesAsync(this.UserId);
    }
```

Adding SaveNote, AddUser, and DeleteNote

Here you will be using the Linq to Object technique to query the Notes property to check if noteName exists. If the note exists, UpdateNote will be called; otherwise AddNote will be called. The AddUser method will make a service call to add the user. DeleteNote will call the DeleteNote service.

```
    public void SaveNote(string noteName, string noteText)
    {
        // Search the user notes and see if the note already exist
        var note = (from eachNote in this.Notes
                    where eachNote.NoteText.Equals(noteText,
StringComparison.InvariantCultureIgnoreCase)
                    select eachNote).SingleOrDefault();

        if (note == null)
        {
            _svc.AddNoteAsync(this.UserId, noteName, noteText);
        }
        else
        {
            _svc.UpdateNoteAsync(note.NoteId, noteText);
        }

        this.SelectedNote = note;
    }

    public void AddUser(Guid userId, string userName)
    {
        if (this.NeedUserId)
        {
            _svc.AddUserAsync(userId, userName);
        }
    }

    public void DeleteNote()
    {
```

```
        _svc.DeleteNoteAsync(this.UserId, this.SelectedNote.NoteId);
    }
```

Adding NotepadService Event Handlers

The following code will handle callbacks for NotepadService calls.

AddNoteCompleted

When the note is added successfully, SelectedNote will be set with the result returned from the call.

```
private void _svc_AddNoteCompleted(object sender, AddNoteCompletedEventArgs e)
{
    if (e.Error == null)
    {
        this.SelectedNote = e.Result;
        this.RebindData();
    }
    else
    {
        MessageBox.Show("Failed to add the note. Please try again!");
    }
}
```

GetNotesCompleted

The returned result will contain all the user notes, and it will be set to the Notes property.

```
private void _svc_GetNotesCompleted(object sender, GetNotesCompletedEventArgs e)
{
    if (e.Error == null)
    {
        this.Notes = e.Result;
    }
    else
    {
        MessageBox.Show("Failed to get the notes. Please try again!");
    }
}
```

UpdateCompleted

When the updated note is completed, RebindData is called, which will trigger the UI element txtNote, txtNoteName, to be updated in MainPage.

```
private void _svc_UpdateNoteCompleted(object sender, AsyncCompletedEventArgs e)
{
    if (e.Error == null)
    {
        this.RebindData();
```

```
        }
        else
        {
            MessageBox.Show("Failed to update the note. Please try again!");
        }
    }
```

AddUserCompleted

If the user registration is successful, the UserId property will be set with the return result, saving it to Isolated Storage.

```
private void _svc_AddUserCompleted(object sender, AddUserCompletedEventArgs e)
{
    if (e.Error == null)
    {
        // Set the UserId only when AddUser service call
        // is made successfully
        this.UserId = e.Result;
    }
    else
    {
        this.UserId = Guid.Empty;
        MessageBox.Show("Failed to add user please try again!");
    }
}
```

DeleteNoteCompleted

When the delete note call is successful, SelectedNote will be set to null so that txtNote and txtNoteName will be set with an empty string in MainPage, and RebindData will be called to update the properties.

```
private void _svc_DeleteNoteCompleted(object sender, AsyncCompletedEventArgs e)
{
    if (e.Error == null)
    {
        this.SelectedNote = null;
        this.RebindData();
    }
    else
    {
        MessageBox.Show("Failed to delete note please try again!");
    }
}
```

Coding the INotifyPropertyChanged Interface

Here you will code the implementation of the INotifyPropertyChanged event that will be called whenever the Notes, ShowNoteList, NeedUserId, and SelectedNote properties are changed.

```
    // Implement INotifyPropertyChanged interface
    public event PropertyChangedEventHandler PropertyChanged;
    private void RaisePropertyChanged(string propertyName)
    {
        PropertyChangedEventHandler propertyChanged = this.PropertyChanged;
        if ((propertyChanged != null))
        {
            propertyChanged(this, new PropertyChangedEventArgs(propertyName));
        }
    }
  }
}
```

Testing the Application Against NotepadService Deployed Locally

Before you begin, make sure that NotepadService is running Development AppFabric; if not, press F5 to start NotepadService as shown in the previous steps. Then press F5 on the Notepad Windows Phone project. You will see the application shown previously in Figure 3-30. Enter the username and register, and add some notes so that you can confirm that the notes are being saved to NotepadDB in SQL Azure.

Open up SQL Server Management Studio by following the steps provided in the previous sections, type in the following SQL statement, and press F5, and you will see the notes and the user data saved to NotepadDB.

```
select * from [User]
select * from Note
```

When the SQL statement is executed, you should see the data you added in the Results window, as shown in Figure 3-38.

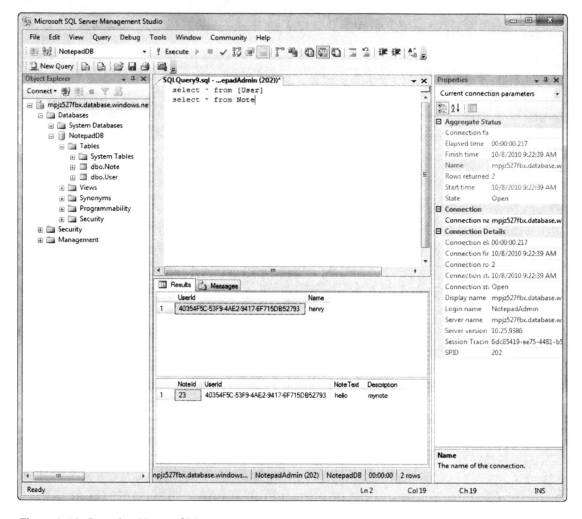

Figure 3-38. *Querying NotepadDB*

In the next section, you will deploy NotepadService directly to Windows Azure and modify the Notepad application to consume the Web service located in Windows Azure instead of from the local machine.

Deploying the Service to Windows Azure

By deploying to Windows Azure, you will have a redundant, fault-tolerant service that you can scale up if you need to meet the demands of heavy usage. You will see how simple it is to configure and deploy the service.

Preparing for Windows Azure NotepadService

You will create a Windows Azure service host in order to deploy WCF NotepadService to a Windows Azure platform.

Signing Up for Windows Azure and Creating a Project

1. Open the browser of your choice.

2. Go to www.microsoft.com/windowsazure/ to sign up for and buy the Windows Azure service account. Follow the directions provided by Microsoft in order to purchase and acquire the service account.

3. Go to https://windows.azure.com/ and sign in using the account you created in step 1.

Connecting to the Windows Azure Project

1. Once you've signed in, click the Windows Azure menu tab on the left side of the page. When the Windows Azure page loads, you will see the project that you created in step 1 of the registration process (see Figure 3-39).

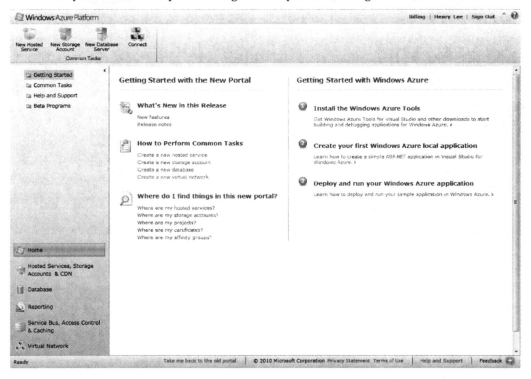

Figure 3-39. Windows Azure project list

91

2. Click the project hyperlink NAS-DEV. In your case, you should click the name of the project that corresponds to the one you created in step 1.

Creating and Configuring Windows Azure NotepadService

Now you're ready to create and configure the service.

1. Create a new service that will host your WCF service by clicking the New Hosted Service icon at the top left of the page. You will see the form shown in Figure 3-40.

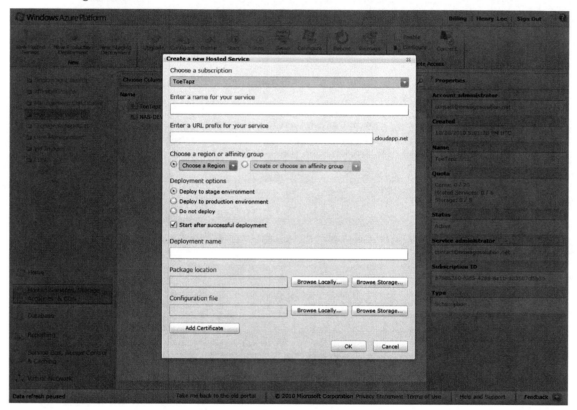

Figure 3-40. Adding a new Azure service to the project

2. In the "Enter a name for your service" box, enter **NotepadService**; in the "Enter a URL prefix for your service" text box, type **NotepadServiceDemo**. Note here that NotepadServiceDemo.cloudapp.net will become your WCF production endpoint, which you will be using later in your Windows Phone application.

3. In the "Choose a region or affinity group" section, you have two options. Typically, relating the affinity among other services allows you to run the services in the same region in order to optimize performance.

4. If you are creating multiple services that will interact with other services in the same region, select "Create a new affinity group" or choose an existing affinity group from the "Create or choose an affinity group" drop-down.

5. If you won't be creating multiple services that need to be in the same region, then select the Anywhere US option from the Choose a Region drop-down.

6. In the "Deployment options" section, select "Deploy to production environment" and make sure the "Start after successful deployment" check box is checked.

7. For the deployment name, we recommend using the version number of your NotepadService, which would be 1.0.0.0.

See Figure 3-41 for an appropriately filled-in form. Keep your browser window open, as you will be coming back here and deploying the packages.

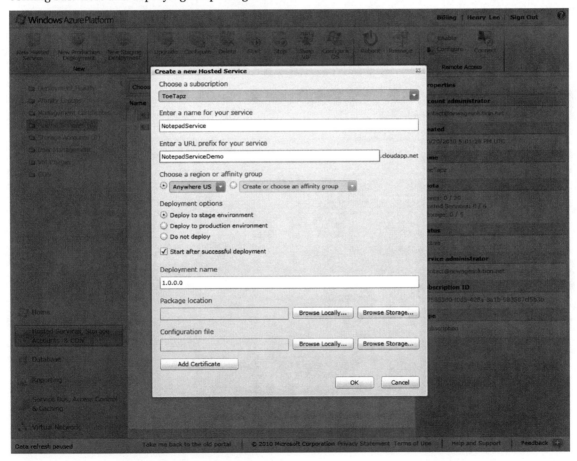

Figure 3-41. Configuring the WCF Azure service

Deploying NotepadService to Windows Azure

In the previous steps, you prepared the NotepadService host. Now it's time for you to deploy NotepadService so that you can consume the Azure service from the phone. You will deploy the service to staging first. *Staging* is where you test your service before going to production. This is a very convenient way of making sure your service works before going live.

Compiling and Publishing NotepadService

You will need a compiled binary so that you can deploy to the Windows Azure host.

1. Go to your NotepadService project, stop the project if it is running, right-click the NotepadService project, and choose Publish.

2. The Publish Cloud Service window will appear. Choose "Create Service Package Only," as shown in Figure 3-42.

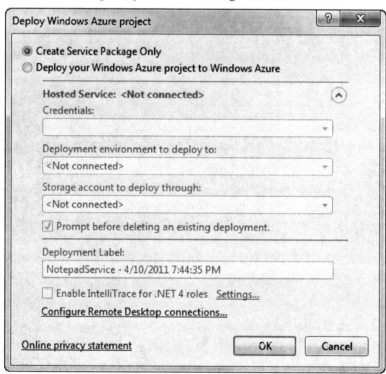

Figure 3-42. Creating a NotepadService package for Windows Azure

3. Click OK. Windows Explorer will open with a directory where you will see two files: NotepadService.cspkg and ServiceConfiguration.cscfg. NotepadService.cspkg is the compiled binary of NotepadService, and ServiceConfiguration.cscfg is the configuration file used by Windows Azure. Take note of the directory path, as you will be uploading these files to Windows Azure.

Deploying NotepadService.cspkg and ServiceConfiguration.cscfg to Windows Azure

You will deploy the packages created in the previous steps to Windows Azure.

1. Go to the "Create a new Hosted Service" screen in your browser, as shown previously in Figure 3-41.

2. Click Browse Locally in the "Package location" section. Browse to where you published the compiled NotepadService in the previous section, and choose NotepadService.cspkg.

3. In the "Configuration file" section, click the Browse Locally button. Browse to where you published NotepadService, and choose ServiceConfiguration.cscfg. You should see a screen that resembles Figure 3-43.

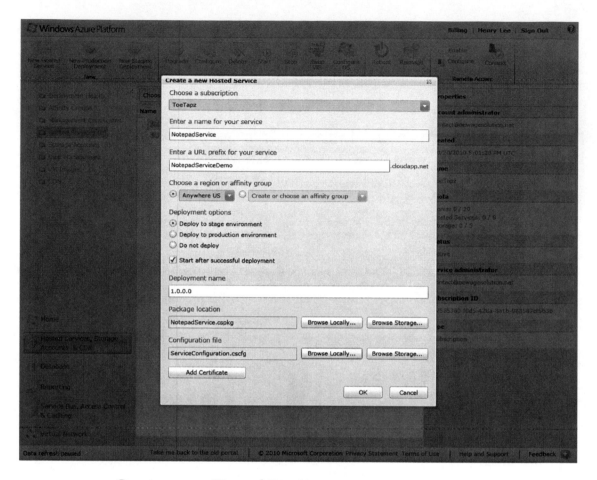

Figure 3-43. The "Create a new Hosted Service" *screen*

4. Click OK to deploy. You will see a Warning screen, as shown in Figure 3-44. Click Yes to ignore this warning.

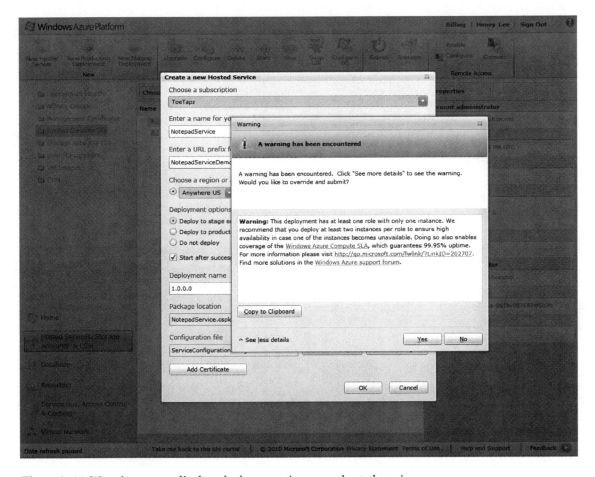

Figure 3-44. Warning screen displayed when creating a new hosted service

5. You will be returned to the main hosted-service screen. Note that
    NotepadService is being created (see Figure 3-45). You will need to wait until
    the status changes to Ready.

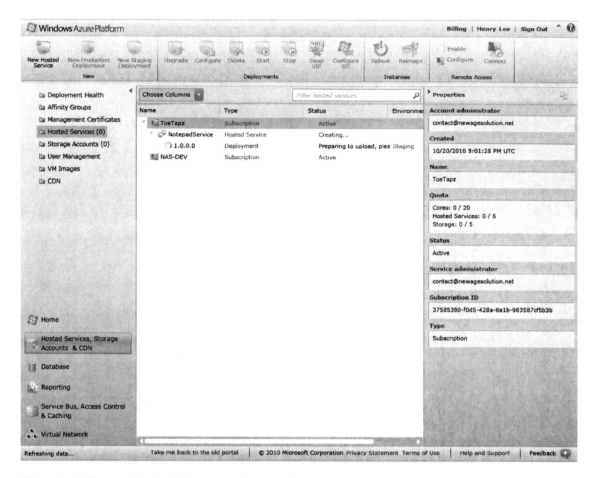

Figure 3-45. NotepadService being created in Windows Azure

6. When the status changes to Ready, select NotepadService 1.0.0.0 and note the DNS name on the right. This is the WCF end URL that you will be using. Simply append /Service.svc to this DNS name in the browser. (For a demo, see http://ef8c3aa169c04db99fbfb74616a0afd6.cloudapp.net/service1.svc). If everything was successful, you should see your NotepadService in the browser, as shown in Figure 3-46.

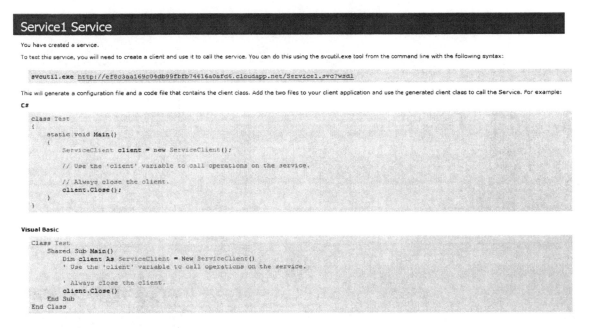

Figure 3-46. NotepadService WCF endpoint when deployed to Windows Azure staging

In the following section, you will consume the NotepadService deployed to Windows Azure staging.

Testing the Notepad Application Against the NotepadService Azure Service

In the previous steps, you deployed NotepadService to the Windows Azure host. You will change the Notepad phone configuration to point to the Web service that is hosted in Windows Azure and test it in the same way you tested the service when it was deployed locally to your computer.

1. Go to Visual Studio and open the Notepad project.

2. Under the Notepad project in Solution Explorer, open ServiceReferences.ClientConfig. Change the endpoint address from 127.0.0.1 to the URL that you received when you deployed to staging in the previous steps. See Figure 3-47 with the changed endpoint address.

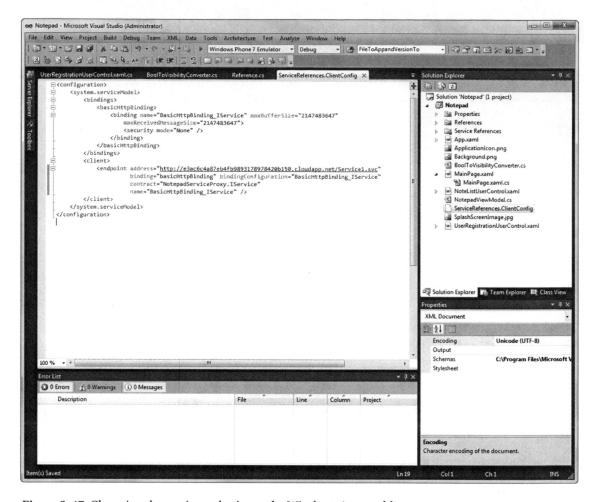

Figure 3-47. Changing the service endpoint to the Windows Azure address

3. Make sure that NotepadService has a status of Ready, and then press F5 to run your Notepad phone application in the emulator. Follow the previous steps to test the Notepad application. It should exhibit exactly the same behavior, except that now you are running your Notepad application against the Windows Azure service.

Summary

In this chapter, you built a Windows Phone application that makes use of Microsoft's Windows Azure service to store data to an SQL server in the cloud. Your application is now scalable and fault tolerant, and it can accommodate a large number of users. You learned how simple it is to create the service and the database in the Azure cloud, and how Microsoft Azure gives you the power to build an application without having to worry about creating your own complex IT infrastructure to support it.

In Chapter 4, you will learn critical skills that will help you be successful in building a Windows Phone application, including how to catch exceptions and debug and test Windows Phone applications.

CHAPTER 4

Catching and Debugging Errors

As you develop Windows Phone applications, you must learn how to equip them to handle a number of exceptions that are unique to smartphones. Unlike a desktop computer, a Windows Phone includes devices over which you have little direct control, including GPS, an accelerometer, Wi-Fi, isolated storage, and a radio. A user can decide to turn off an onboard device to save power at any time. Isolated storage can run out of space. A resource, such as a cell tower, GPS satellite, or Wi-Fi router, might not be available. To identify and fix unexpected exceptions in an application, you need to know how to use the powerful debugging facilities of Visual Studio. To be sure that you have dealt with all of the bugs in your application, you need to know how to test it on a real device.

In this chapter, you will learn to master critical debugging and troubleshooting skills using the Visual Studio IDE, which you can also use to debug any application, including Web applications (ASP.NET) and Windows applications.

The following sections are divided into three major topics. We'll walk you through a series of tutorials covering general exception handling in Windows Phone, Visual Studio debugger features, and testing using both the emulator and the real device.

Debugging Application Exceptions

In this section, you will learn how to find and deal with two exceptions that are common to Windows Phone applications. The first is the navigation failed exception, which can be thrown when a main page is loaded. The second deals with the Web service call that is consumed by the application.

The ErrorHandlingDemo application that you'll use contains two projects: a Windows Phone project and the Calculator Web service project, which has an Add method that adds two numbers and then returns the result to the caller. Being able to debug and handle Web service call exceptions will be critical, especially if you are planning to work with external services like Microsoft Bing Maps, which are covered in Chapter 14.

When you finally debug and fix all the issues in the application, you will see the result shown in Figure 4–1.

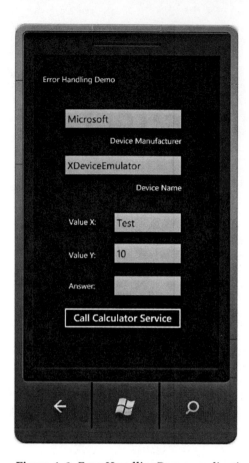

Figure 4–1. ErrorHandlingDemo application

Debugging Page Load Exceptions

The `ErrorHandlingDemo` application contains bugs that will cause exceptions to be thrown when the application's main page is loaded. In this section, you will learn how to find and fix such problems in Visual Studio.

Catching an Exception

Whenever an application throws an exception, Visual Studio will stop execution at the line where it's thrown. To observe this behavior, let's run the application and take a closer look using the Visual Studio IDE.

Fire up Visual Studio, select File ➤ Open, and browse to the following file, which you can download from the site for this book:

`{unzippeddirectory}\ch04\ErrorHandlingDemo\Start\ErrorHandlingDemo.sln.`

Once the solution file is loaded, press F5 to run it. Notice the raised exception message in Figure 4–2, which points to the code that has caused `FormatException` to be thrown. From `DeviceStatus` you can obtain Windows Phone system information like `DeviceManufacturer`, `DeviceName`, `DeviceUniqueId`, `DeviceTotalMemory`, `ApplicationCurrentMemoryUsage`, and `ApplicationPeakMemoryUsage`. When you try to write out the `DeviceName` using `string.Format` the application throws a `FormatException` error because `string.Format` is expecting {1} which is the second argument passed, but there is no second argument. The solution to fix this problem would be use {0} instead of {1}. You will go through each step to help troubleshoot this error below.

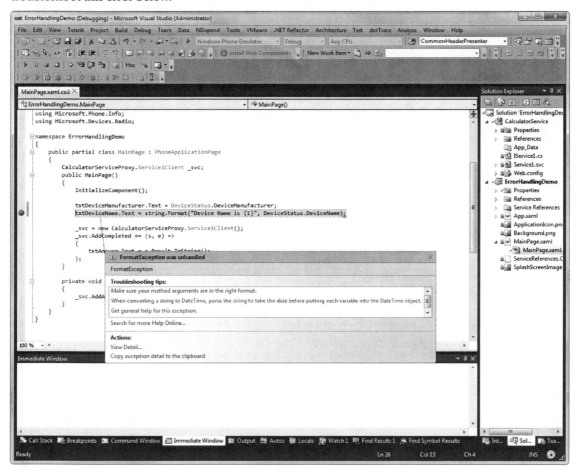

Figure 4–2. *A raised format exception in Visual Studio*

Querying Exception Object Values with Immediate Window

Whenever a Visual Studio application pauses at a line where an exception has been thrown, you have the opportunity to observe its variables in Visual Studio's Immediate Window.

Immediate Window is a very useful debugging feature because it allows you to evaluate any statement when the code execution pauses at the breakpoint. If you do not see the Immediate Window when the breakpoint is hit, you can go to Debug ➤ Windows ➤ Immediate to bring up the Immediate Window, as shown in Figure 4–3.

1. With ErrorHandlingDemo still paused in the debugger, go to the Immediate Window and type in: DeviceStatus.Devicenameto query the object value and press Enter. You will see the result printed in an Immediate Window, as shown in Figure 4–3.

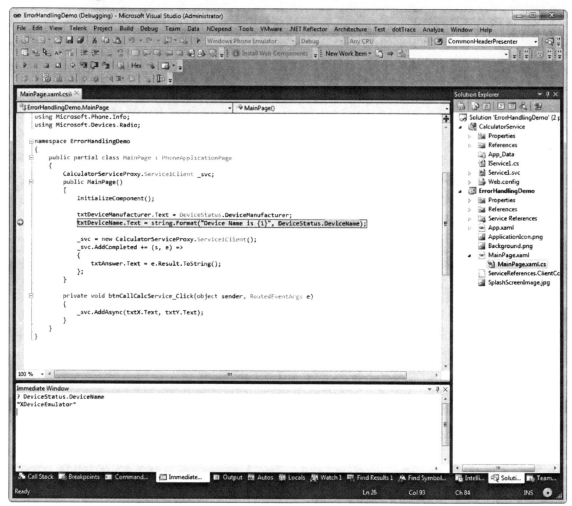

Figure 4–3. Query object value in Immediate Window

In next section, you will learn how to handle exceptions specific to Windows Phone.

Catching an Unhandled Exception in RootFrame_NavigationFailed or Application_UnhandledException

Unhandled exceptions in a Windows Phone application will be caught by one of two methods: RootFrame_NavigationFailed and Application_UnhandledException. RootFrame_NavigationFailed catches unhandled exceptions thrown while a page is being loaded while Application_UnhandledException catches exceptions thrown in all other cases.

1. Press F5 to continue debugging from the breakpoint in the previous section.

The debugger will next break inside RootFrame_NavigationFailed in App.xaml.cs, as shown in Figure 4–4. Notice that, in App.xaml.cs, you will find various Windows Phone application-related events, such as Application_Launching, Application_Activated, Application_Deactivated, Application_Closing, RootFrame_NavigationFailed, and Application_UnhandledException. As far as exceptions are concerned, only two events will be of interest. RootFrame_NavigationFailed captures unhandled exceptions when the Windows Phone page fails to load. In ErrorHandlingDemo, unhandled exceptions occur when MainPage tries to load and throws a FormatException error.

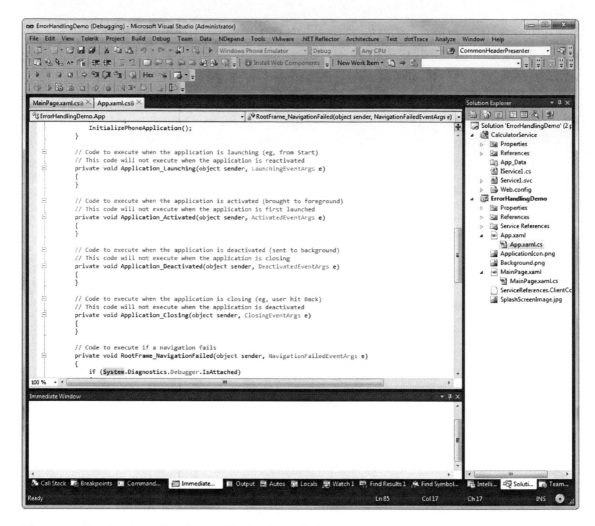

Figure 4–4. Breakpoint at RootFrame_NavigationFailed

2. With your mouse, hover over NavigationFailedEventArgs e. You will be able to drill into the object value and see the e.Uri that contains the page that caused the error during the load, as shown in Figure 4–5.

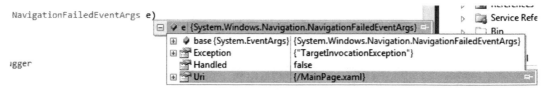

Figure 4–5. NavigationFailedEventArgs.Uri

3. Press F5 to continue debugging. You will notice that code execution next breaks in the Application_UnhandledException method. All exceptions that are not handled specifically by a try-catch-finally block will ultimately end up in this method.

Handling an Exception RootFrame_NavigationFailed

When an exception is thrown in the MainPage of an application, the exception will be caught by the RootFrame_NavigationFailed method, and this is where you want to handle it in order to stop the exception from bubbling up to the Application_UnhandledException method.

In ErrorHandlingDemo, replace the RootFrame_NavigationFailed method with following code. Notice the use of MessageBox in the code to display the proper error with stack trace, and set e.Handled to true, which will stop the breakpoint from moving to the Application_UnhandledException method.

```
// Code to execute if a navigation fails
private void RootFrame_NavigationFailed(object sender, NavigationFailedEventArgs e)
{
    if (System.Diagnostics.Debugger.IsAttached)
    {
        // A navigation has failed; break into the debugger
        System.Diagnostics.Debugger.Break();
    }

    MessageBox.Show(
string.Format("Page {0} failed to load because of with error: {1}",
e.Uri.ToString(), e.Exception.StackTrace));
    e.Handled = true;
}
```

Fixing the Error in the Code

In the previous section, you added a MessageBox display in case any other page fails to load. In the following steps, you will fix the actual cause of the exception in MainPage. But first let's fix the error in MainPage.xaml.cs.

Fix the error in MainPage.xaml.cs by replacing:

```
txtDeviceName.Text = string.Format("DeviceName is {1}", DeviceStatus.Devicename);
```

with the following:

```
txtDeviceName.Text =
string.Format("DeviceName is {0}", DeviceStatus.Devicename);
```

Debugging a Web Service Exception

ErrorHandlingDemo contains the CalculatorService Web service project where the service will be hosted locally and consumed by the demo application. The code is written so that the application will throw the exceptions that you will fix.

Catching a Web Service Exception

You will be stepping through the breakpoints in order to understand the behavior of the thrown exception. Before you begin, make sure that both the Windows Phone project and the Web service project start simultaneously when you Press F5.

1. Right-click the ErrorHandlingDemo solution in Solution Explorer, and choose the property. The solution property page window shown in Figure 4–6 will display.

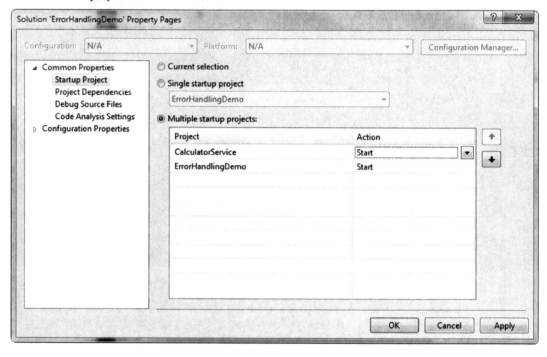

Figure 4–6. Multiple project startup option

2. Select the Multiple startup projects option, and CalculatorService and ErrorHandlingDemo projects' Actions are set to Start.

3. Also, put two breakpoints in MainPage.xaml.cs at the line txtAnswer.Text = e.Result.ToString() and _svc.AddAsync(txtX.Text, txtY.Text), as shown in Figure 4–7.

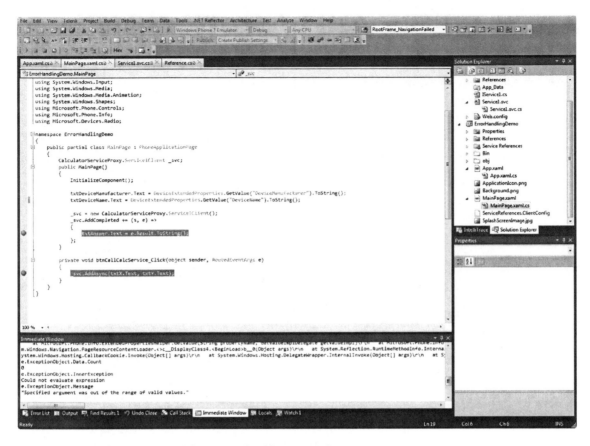

Figure 4–7. Breaking point to debug CalculatorService Web service

4. Press F5. You will see the application shown in Figure 4–1 in the emulator, and you will notice that your default browser startsnavigated to http://localhost:1599/Service1.svc, as shown in Figure 4–8. The browser will host the CalculatorService, allowing you to step into the Web service call.

CHAPTER 4 ▪ CATCHING AND DEBUGGING ERRORS

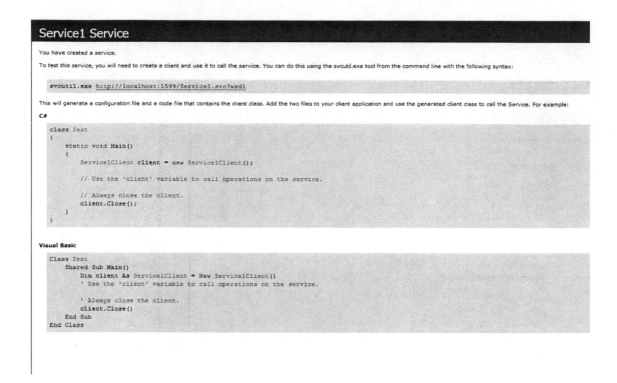

Figure 4–8. *WCF test client*

> 5. From the emulator, press the Call Calculator Service button.

Notice that Visual Studio catches `InvalidCastException` error thrown from the `CalculatorService` project, as shown in Figure 4–9.

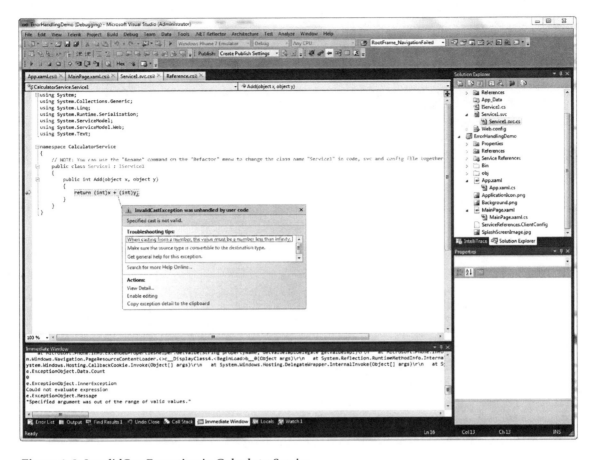

Figure 4–9. InvalidCastException in CalculatorService

6. When you hover over x value, you will notice that it contains Test, which can't be converted to integer, thus causing InvalidCastException.

7. Press F5 to continue. Visual Studio breaks at Reference.cs, which is the Web service proxy class that was generated against WSDL from Visual Studio. (See Chapter 3 for more details on how to consume Web services.)

8. Press F5 again. The execution will break on the line txtAnswer.Text = e.Result.ToString() found in MainPage.xaml.cs.

9. In Immediate Window, type in e.Error. You will notice that e.Error is not empty. When the Web service returns any kind of error, e.Error will not be empty, and when you try to access e.Result that contains the Web service call, the result will throw an exception.

10. Press F5 again. Note the exception thrown in the e.Result property, as shown in Figure 4–10.

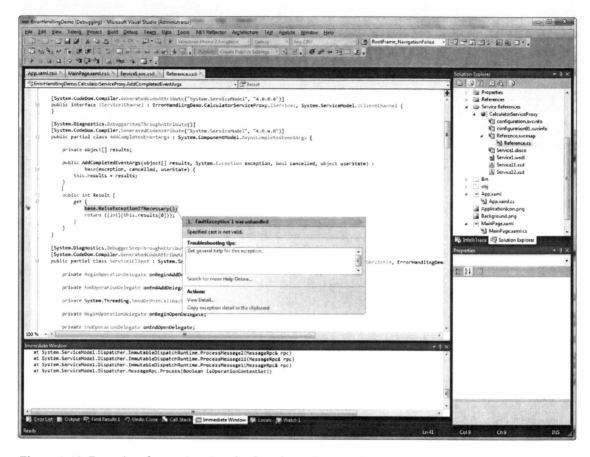

Figure 4–10. Exception thrown in e.Result when the Web service has an error

11. Press F5. The exception will be finally caught in
    `Application_UnhandledException`.

Fixing the CalculatorService Exception

After stepping through the breakpoints, you now have enough information to fix the exception.

First, let's check the values received from the caller in `CalculatorService`. Replace the `Service1.svc.cs` code with the following snippet. The `CheckValue` method will make sure that the received value is not null and convert the value to the integer.

```
public int Add(object x, object y)
{
    int xValue = CheckValue(x);
    int yValue = CheckValue(y);

    return xValue + yValue;
```

```
        }

        private int CheckValue(object value)
        {
            int convertedValue = -1;
            if (value == null)
            {
                throw new ArgumentNullException("value");
            }
            else if (!int.TryParse(value.ToString(), out convertedValue))
            {
                throw new ArgumentException(
string.Format("The value '{0}' is not an integer.", value));
            }

            return convertedValue;
        }
```

In MainPage.xaml.cs, replace the AddCompleted event delegate with following code. You will be checking to make sure that e.Error is empty before retrieving e.Result; if e.Error is not empty, you will throw the proper error message.

```
_svc.AddCompleted += (s, e) =>
            {
                if (e.Error == null)
                {
                    txtAnswer.Text = e.Result.ToString();
                }
                else
                {
                    MessageBox.Show(
string.Format("CalculatorService return an error {0}",
e.Error.Message));
                }
            };
```

Testing the Application

You've finished debugging and fixing the application exceptions, and now you'll be able to run the application and handle exceptions properly.

Press F5, and you will see the screen shown in Figure 4–1; notice now that txtDeviceManufacturer and txtDeviceName are properly populated during the MainPage load. When you change txtX to an integer and click the Call Calculator Service button, txtAnswer will be populated with the result received from the Web service.

Registering a Windows Phone Device for Debugging

Testing an application on a Windows Phone device involves a lot more work than using the Windows Phone emulator because it involves registering your device, physically connecting it to your computer via a USB cable, and running the Zune software in the background on your workstation. Here are the steps you need to follow to set up a phone as your debugging platform.

First, you must apply for a Windows Phone Marketplace account at the Windows Phone developer portal.

1. If you don't have a Windows Phone account yet, go to http://create.msdn.com/ and sign up.

2. Microsoft will review your application and activate your account. If you have not yet installed Zune software, you can download the latest Zuneversion from www.zune.net/en-us/products/software/download/default.htm.

3. Once you're approved, click the Windows Start menu on your workstation and select All Programs ➤ Zune to start the Zune software. The Welcome page is shown in Figure 4–11.

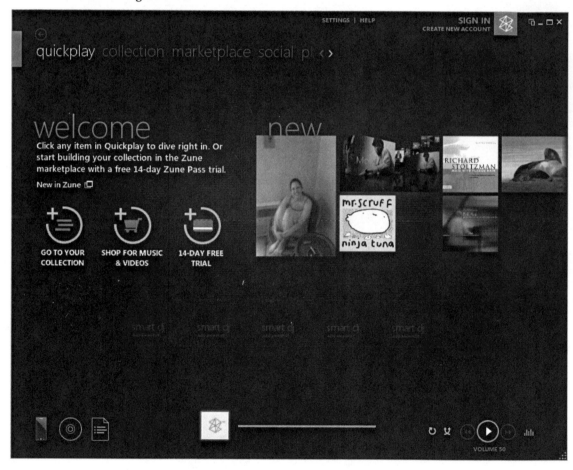

Figure 4–11. The Zune software welcome page

■ **Note** The Windows Phone device is based on the Zune, which is a Microsoft iPod competitor for playing video and audio. A Windows Phone uses the Zune software to update the Windows Phone system, and Zune must be running in order to deploy an application to a device. You can also use the Zune software to back up your device.

4. Connect your Windows Phone device to your developer workstation using a USB cable.

5. To confirm that your device is properly connected and recognized by the Zune software, click the phone icon at the bottom-left corner of the Zune Welcome screen, as indicated by the arrow in Figure 4–12.

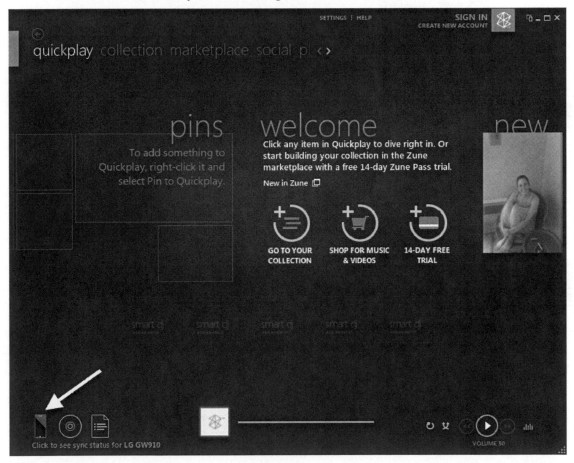

Figure 4–12. Clicking the phone icon in the Zune software

6. When you click the phone icon, the Zune software will display detailed information about your device, as shown in Figure 4–13.

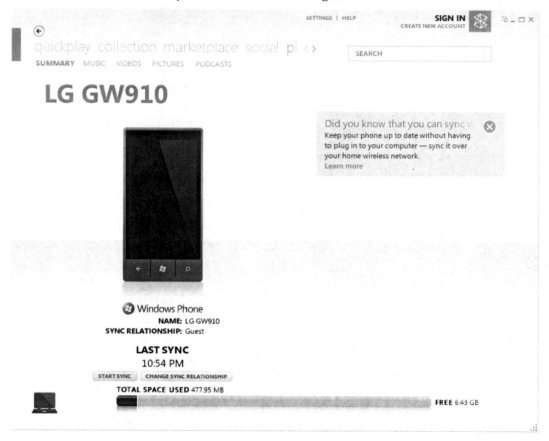

Figure 4–13. Windows Phone device detail page in Zune software

Now you are ready to register your device:

7. Go to the Windows Start menu, select All Programs ➤ Windows Phone Developer Tools, and select Windows Phone Developer Registration, as shown in Figure 4–14.

Figure 4–14. Windows Phone developer registration

A Windows Phone developer registration form will display, as shown in Figure 4–15.

8. Enter the ID and password you used to register for a Windows Phone Marketplace account in step 1.

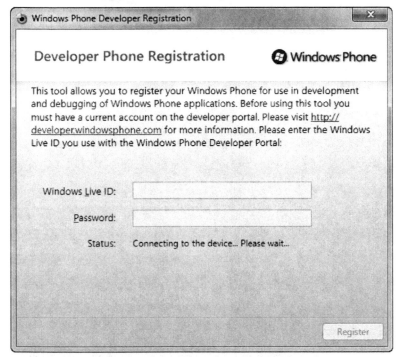

Figure 4–15. Windows Phone developer registration

To confirm that your phone is properly registered, go to `http://create.msdn.com/` and log in.

Once you have logged in, click your registered name at the top right of your Windows Phone page, as shown in Figure 4–16.

Figure 4–16. *My Windows Phone page*

In the following section, you will learn tips and tricks for making your life easier when you begin to debug and test using a real device.

TIPS AND TRICKS: DEBUGGING ON A DEVICE

Here are a few things that you should keep in mind when you're debugging an application on a live Windows Phone:

1. When debugging, it's best to disable screen time-out, especially if you are debugging through a complex program that takes a long time. On the Windows Phone device, go to Settings ➤ Lock & Wallpaper, and set the screen time-out to never. After debugging, remember to come back and reset the screen time-out to other, so that you don't waste your battery.

2. When you try to debug in the Windows Phone device, you will get the error message shown here. When you click No, you will see an "Access Denied" message in your Error List window. This is because your device is locked due to time-out. To avoid this problem during debugging, disable time-out on the device by following step 1. To resolve this issue, simply unlock your device and restart in debug mode in Visual Studio.

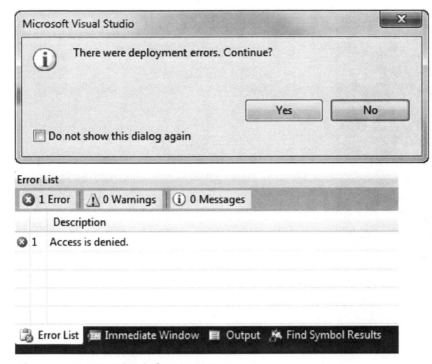

Figure 4–17. Access Denied error message

3. When the Zune application is not started, you will receive the error "Zune software is not launched. Retry after making sure that Zune software is launched" in the Visual Studio Error List Window.

Handling Device Exceptions

In the following section, you will learn to capture device-specific exceptions. You will use the accelerometer device as an example to handle unexpected exceptions properly by catching an `AccelerometerFailedException`. `AccelerometerFailedException` can occur if the accelerometer device on the phone is broken. The exception can also occur if the device throws an unexpected error caused internally by Microsoft Window Phone framework. Figure 4–18 displays the basic UI of the `CatchDeviceExceptionDemo` project that you will build.

Figure 4–18. CatchDeviceException UI

Creating the CatchDeviceExceptionDemo Project

To set up the CatchDeviceExceptionDemo project, follow the steps you've used for previous examples in this book.

1. Open Microsoft Visual Studio 2010 Express for Windows Phone on your workstation.

2. Create a new Windows Phone Application by selecting File ➤ New Project on the Visual Studio command menu. Select the Windows Phone Application template, name the application CaptureAccelerometerData, and click OK.

3. In order to use the accelerometer, add an assembly reference to Microsoft.Devices.Sensors by right-clicking the References folder in Solution Explorer, and choose Microsoft.Devices.Sensors from the Add Reference window, as shown in Figure 4–19.

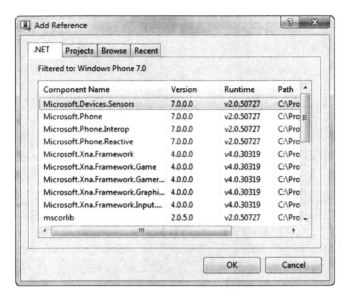

Figure 4–19. Adding reference to Microsoft.Devices.Sensors

Building the User Interface

You will build the user interface using XAML in Visual Studio. For building simple controls, it's faster to work with XAML code. Go to Solution Explorer, open MainPage.xaml, and replace the XAML code you find there with the code in the next section.

Declaring the UI Resources

The namespaces you see in the following code snippet are typically declared by default when you first create a Windows Phone project. In particular, namespaces xmlns:phone="clr-namespace:Microsoft.Phone.Controls and assembly=Microsoft.Phone" allow you to add common Windows Phone controls to the application main page.

```
<phone:PhoneApplicationPage
    x:Class="CatchingDeviceExceptionsDemo.MainPage"
    xmlns="http://schemas.microsoft.com/winfx/2006/xaml/presentation"
    xmlns:x="http://schemas.microsoft.com/winfx/2006/xaml"
    xmlns:phone="clr-namespace:Microsoft.Phone.Controls;assembly=Microsoft.Phone"
    xmlns:shell="clr-namespace:Microsoft.Phone.Shell;assembly=Microsoft.Phone"
    xmlns:d="http://schemas.microsoft.com/expression/blend/2008"
    xmlns:mc="http://schemas.openxmlformats.org/markup-compatibility/2006"
    mc:Ignorable="d" d:DesignWidth="480" d:DesignHeight="768"
    FontFamily="{StaticResource PhoneFontFamilyNormal}"
    FontSize="{StaticResource PhoneFontSizeNormal}"
    Foreground="{StaticResource PhoneForegroundBrush}"
    SupportedOrientations="Portrait" Orientation="Portrait"
    shell:SystemTray.IsVisible="True">
```

Building the Main Page and Adding Components

Create two buttons to start and stop the accelerometer.

```xml
<!--LayoutRoot is the root grid where all page content is placed-->
<Grid x:Name="LayoutRoot" Background="Transparent">
    <Grid.RowDefinitions>
        <RowDefinition Height="Auto"/>
        <RowDefinition Height="*"/>
    </Grid.RowDefinitions>

    <!--TitlePanel contains the name of the application and page title-->
    <StackPanel x:Name="TitlePanel" Grid.Row="0" Margin="12,17,0,28">
        <TextBlock x:Name="ApplicationTitle" Text="CatchingDeviceExceptionsDemo"
Style="{StaticResource PhoneTextNormalStyle}"/>
    </StackPanel>

    <!--ContentPanel - place additional content here-->
    <Grid x:Name="ContentPanel" Grid.Row="1" Margin="12,0,12,0">
        <Button Content="Start Accelerometer" Height="72" HorizontalAlignment="Left"
Margin="84,45,0,0" Name="btnStartAcc" VerticalAlignment="Top"
Width="284" Click="btnStartAcc_Click" />
        <Button Content="Stop Accelerometer" Height="72" HorizontalAlignment="Left"
Margin="84,123,0,0" Name="btnStopAcc" VerticalAlignment="Top"
Width="284" Click="btnStopAcc_Click" />
    </Grid>
</Grid>

</phone:PhoneApplicationPage>
```

Once you have loaded the XAML code, you should see the layout shown in Figure 4–20. In the next section, you will code the application.

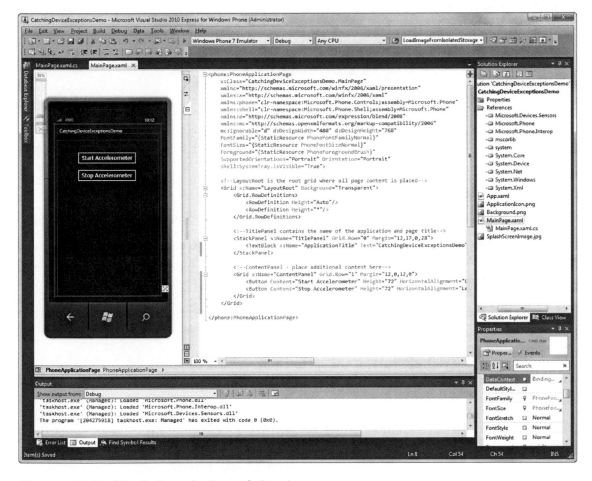

Figure 4–20. CatchDeviceExceptionDemo design view

Coding the Application

In Solution Explorer, open `MainPage.xaml.cs`, and replace the code there with the following C# code blocks.

Specifying the Namespaces

Begin by listing the namespaces the application will use. Note that the inclusion of `Microsoft.Devices.Sensors` will allow you to start and stop Windows Phone's accelerometer.

```
using System.Windows;
using Microsoft.Phone.Controls;
using Microsoft.Devices.Sensors;
```

Initializing Variables

The variable _acc, Accelerometer object, will be used to start and stop.

```
Accelerometer _acc;

    public MainPage()
    {
        InitializeComponent();
        _acc = new Accelerometer();
    }
```

Implementing Accelerometer Start and Stop Behavior

Implement a button event for stopping and starting the accelerometer. Note that you are catching AccelerometerFailedException, which can be raised during the start and stop of the accelerometer. In the exception property, you will find ErrorId and Message that contains specific error code and a description that could explain why the error was raised

```
private void btnStartAcc_Click(object sender, RoutedEventArgs e)
    {
        try
        {
            _acc.Start();

            _acc.ReadingChanged += (s1, e1) =>
                {
                    // Do something with captured accelerometer data
                };
        }
        catch (AccelerometerFailedException ex)
        {
            string errorMessage = string.Format(@"
                        Accelerometer threw an error with ErrorId {0}
    during the start operation
                        with error message {1}
                        ", ex.ErrorId, ex.Message);
            MessageBox.Show(errorMessage);
        }
    }

    private void btnStopAcc_Click(object sender, RoutedEventArgs e)
    {
        try
        {
            _acc.Stop();
        }
        catch (AccelerometerFailedException ex)
        {
            string errorMessage = string.Format(@"
                        Accelerometer threw an error with ErrorId {0}
```

```
during the stop operation
                    with error message {1}
                    ", ex.ErrorId, ex.Message);
        MessageBox.Show(errorMessage);
    }
}
```

Testing the Finished Application

To test the finished application, press F5. The result should resemble the screen shown in Figure 4–16. The only thing you will not be able to test is being able to raise the `AccelerometerFailedException`, which can be raised only if the accelerometer device fails. But the demo will give you a good idea of how you should handle the device-related exception if it ever occurs.

Summary

In this chapter, you learned how catch and handle errors in an application and how to handle unexpected errors thrown by a Windows Phone. You also learned how to use Visual Studio's powerful debugging features to troubleshoot and fix defects, regardless of whether you're running an application in the emulator or on a real device.

In Chapter 5, you will learn to package, publish, and manage a Windows Phone application for distribution through the Windows Phone Marketplace.

CHAPTER 5

Packaging, Publishing, and Managing Applications

Every developer dreams of becoming an instant millionaire by creating an application that everyone loves to use. You will have that chance when you develop your own application and then package, distribute, and sell it to millions of Windows Phone users worldwide through the Windows Phone Marketplace.

There are three options for distributing your application through the Windows Phone Marketplace.

- You can sell your application at a fixed cost that you specify and earn 70 percent on each sale.

- You can distribute your application for free. (You can distribute up to 100 applications free and then pay $19.99 each for additional applications). If you decide to distribute your application for free, consider incorporating a Windows Phone Ad SDK so that you can earn money from advertising. Using the Microsoft Advertising service, you can produce targeted advertising for your application to display. For example, if you're creating a health-related application, you might choose advertising categories from the sports, lifestyle, and/or health categories. Note that you are limited to three categories.

- You can distribute your application as a trial application using the Market Trial API so that users can download the application and try it before making a purchase decision. A trial application usually only includes a subset of your application's features.

To package and publish your application to the Windows Phone Marketplace, you must pay a yearly fee of $99.00, and your application must abide by the rules of the Windows Phone Marketplace. In the following sections, you will learn in great detail what you need to do in order to deliver your application to the Windows Phone Marketplace successfully.

Windows Phone Application Publishing Life Cycle

After you develop a Windows Phone application, you distribute it to the Windows Phone Marketplace through the Windows Phone developer portal. Figure 5-1 shows the application publishing life cycle, from the developer, to the developer portal, to the Windows Phone Marketplace, and on to consumers.

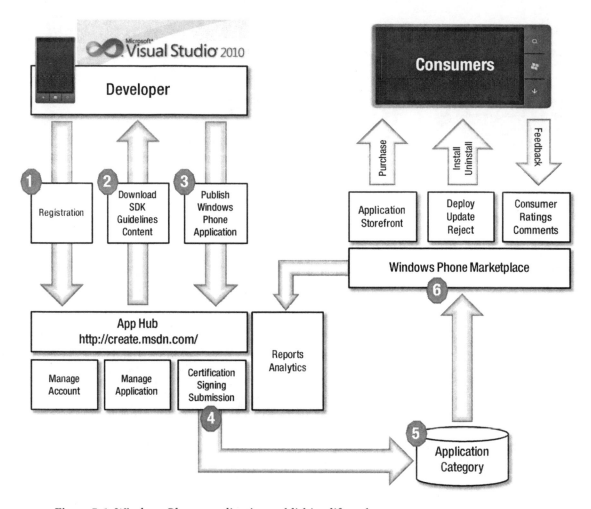

Figure 5-1. Windows Phone application publishing life cycle

To begin the process of selling your Windows Phone application, do the following:

1. First you must register as a developer with the Windows Phone portal and pay the $99.00 fee. Your identity will be verified and you will be issued a certificate that the Windows Marketplace will use to sign your application. In addition, your bank account will be verified so that your earnings can be deposited there.

2. Next, if you haven't already done so, you'll need to download the SDK tools for Visual Studio.

3. After you've created your application, you will submit it to the portal for validation and certification. There Microsoft will check that the application abides by the Windows Phone Marketplace rules.

4. Once your application becomes eligible, it will be signed using the certificate you received during the registration process.

5. Finally, your application will be published to the Windows Phone Marketplace.

Once the application is published, users will be able to buy, download, and install it from the Windows Phone Marketplace portal. There, users can also rate it and comment on its virtues and flaws, providing you with feedback that you can use to make improvements. The Marketplace will provide you with downloads and sales information as well.

In the followings sections, you will learn about the certification requirements and process so that your application can pass through and be submitted to the Windows Phone Marketplace.

Windows Phone Application Certification Requirements

In the battle between iPhone, Android, and Windows Phone, the applications available on each smartphone play a critical role in winning over consumers. The Windows Phone Marketplace puts in place the rules and process to ensure that the published applications are of high quality. You can download the Windows Phone application certification requirements from http://go.microsoft.com/?linkid=9730558. The following list describes the ideas behind the rules and the process for publishing an application to the Windows Phone Marketplace:

- *Applications must be reliable.* You will be dealing with the consumer, who will be picky. Any hint of instability in the application will reflect negatively on the application and the brand behind the phone. Thus Microsoft enforces best practices for creating reliable applications.

- *Applications must make efficient use of resources.* Your application must make efficient use of the phone resources while not adversely affecting performance. For example, the battery can be drained quickly if the location service continues to run even after the user has left your application. Your code needs to plan for such events.

- *Applications must not interfere with the phone functionality.* The user must be notified before your application modifies any phone settings or preferences.

- *Applications must be free of malicious software.* The application must be safe to install and use.

In the following sections, a summary of main points will be presented to teach you about the content of the certification documents. Remember that the descriptions of the certification requirements are based on version 1.3 of the Windows Phone application certification requirements document. Since Microsoft could modify it or release a newer version after this writing, it's a good idea to check the developer portal, at http://create.msdn.com/, frequently.

Application Policies

This section covers the policies that protect the Windows Phone Marketplace and the consumers using any Windows Phone application purchased through the Marketplace.

Windows Phone Application Binary (XAP File)

You must compile your application in release mode from Visual Studio; this will produce a file with a
.xap file extension. A *XAP file* is nothing more than a ZIP file with a different extension name. In fact, if
you change the extension name of your XAP file from .xap to .zip, you will be able to extract its file
content. You should be aware of following facts:

- For installation over the air, the XAP file must be no larger than 20MB.

- You must notify the user that there might be additional charges depending on
  how the data package is downloaded. You must disclose if an additional data
  package to be downloaded is greater than 50MB.

- The maximum size of a XAP file is 400MB; a XAP file greater than 20MB can only
  be installed through Zune or over Wi-Fi.

Things Your Application Must Not Do

Your application can't do the following:

- Your application can't sell, link to, or promote mobile voice plans.

- Your application can't distribute, link to, or direct users to an alternate
  marketplace.

- Your application can't taint the security or functionality of Windows Phone
  devices or the Windows Phone Marketplace.

Things Your Application Must Do

Your application must do the following:

- Your application must be functional.

- If submitted as a trial application, it must include a reasonable feature subset of
  the fully functional application.

- If your application includes or displays advertising, the advertising must abide by
  the rules found at http://advertising.microsoft.com/creative-specs.

- If your application enables chat, instant messaging, or person-to-person
  communication and allows the user to create accounts, the user must be verified
  as being at least 13 years of age.

- If your application sells music, the application must be included in the Windows
  Phone Music Marketplace. If the content of the music is purchased elsewhere
  instead of from the Windows Phone Music Marketplace, the application must
  include its own media player to play back the samples of the music.

Location Service (GPS)

The following requirements concern the location service (GPS):

- The location must be obtained using the Microsoft Location Service API. (Notifications are the subject of Chapter 17.)

- An application must not override, ignore, or circumvent Microsoft toast or prompts related to the Location Service API. (Location services are covered in Chapter 14.)

- An application must not override a user's choice to disable location services on the phone.

- An application must have options for enabling and disabling the location services.

- If the location data is published to other services or other people, the application must fully disclose how the location service information will be used, obtain permission to use the location information, provide the user with the option to opt in and out, and show a visual indicator whenever the information is transmitted. It must also provide a privacy policy statement regarding the location service information usage.

- Security must be in place to protect the location data obtained.

Push Notification Service (PNS)

The following points summarize the policies relating to push notifications:

- The application must provide opt-in and opt-out options to use the service.

- The application cannot use PNS excessively, thereby causing a burden to the Microsoft network or the Windows Phone device.

- PNS can't be used to send critical or life-or-death information.

Content Policies

Your application must conform to the content restrictions of the Windows Phone Marketplace. If your application already has ratings from ESRB, PEGI, and USK, you need to submit the certificates of these ratings. Be mindful of licensed materials, logos, names, and trademarks. The content must not be illegal or suggest harm. Promotion of items that are illegal under local or federal laws (such as alcohol, tobacco, weapons, and drugs) is not allowed. X-rated content, hate-related content, realistic violent content, and excessive use of profanity are not allowed.

Keep in mind that these restrictions are highly subjective, and Microsoft will make the final ruling on any such content. We suggest that you take a practical approach: ask yourself if your application can safely be used and viewed by a minor.

Application Submission Validation Requirements

In order to package and submit an application for certification, you must make sure the requirements in the following sections are met.

Packaging Requirements

When you are getting ready to create a XAP file, it's best to use Visual Studio and compile the binaries in release mode, which will produce the XAP file and take care of the many requirements identified in the certification document. The following requirements are mentioned because they are easy to overlook:

- The XAP file can't be greater than 400MB.

- The application icon must be 62×62 pixels and of PNG file type.

- The application tile image must be 173×173 pixels and of PNG file type.

- A submitted application must have a title.

Code Requirements

Your application will be subject to coding requirements. The application can use only the documented APIs found at `http://msdn.microsoft.com/en-us/library/ff626516(VS.92).aspx`. The following list describes the coding requirements:

- PInvoke and COM interoperability is not allowed.

- The application must be compiled in release mode.

- Windows Phone assemblies can't be redistributed.

- When using a method from `System.Windows.Controls`, APIs in `Microsoft.Xna.Framework.Game` or `Microsoft.Xna.Framework.Graphics` can't be called.

Using the Application Manifest File to Disclose Phone Features

When the user purchases an application from the Windows Phone Marketplace, the Marketplace will display what phone features the application will use. This is done through submission of the application manifest file for Windows Phone (`http://msdn.microsoft.com/en-us/library/ff769509(VS.92).aspx`). The phone features added to the application manifest are typically added and removed automatically by Visual Studio, so this is something with which you would not normally be concerned. However, during your packaging process, you must make sure that the features listed in the application manifest are correctly represented.

Language Validation

The languages supported are English, French, Italian, German, and Spanish. Depending on where you are submitting your application, you must properly localize your application for at least one of the supported languages.

Images for the Windows Phone Marketplace

Your application must be submitted with the images and screenshots that will be displayed in the Windows Phone Marketplace.

- Microsoft recommends that you use 262 dpi.

- The required small mobile application tile should be 99×99 (PNG). The large mobile application tile should be 173×173 (PNG).

- The required large PC application tile should be 200×200 (PNG).

- The optional background art should be 1000×800 (PNG).

- The required screenshot should be 400×800 (PNG).

Application Certification Requirements

Once the application is submitted for the certification process, it will be tested against a series of certification requirements. The following sections summarize these requirements.

Application Reliability

This section lists the certification requirements for application reliability.

- The application must run on all Windows Phone devices.

- The application must handle all raised exceptions, and it must not crash unexpectedly.

- The application must not hang and become unresponsive to user input. If the application is processing, it must show a visual element (such as a progress bar) and provide the ability to cancel the operation.

Performance and Resource Management

This section describes the requirements that deal with performance and resource management issues.

- The application must launch the first screen within 5 seconds of the application being launched. The 5-second rule also applies even after the application is closed or deactivated and then restarted.

- The application must respond to user input within 20 seconds after launch. The 20-second rule also applies even after the application is closed or deactivated and then restarted.

- When the Windows Phone back button is pressed from the first screen, the application must be exited. If the back button is pressed from any screen other than the first, the previous page must be returned to. In games, if the back button is pressed, the game should be paused with the context menu displayed; if the back button is pressed again, the game will resume.

- The application should not use more than 90MB of RAM, unless the device has more than 256MB of RAM.

Phone Functionality

The application can't prevent the use of the phone's functionalities or hang when the user is making a call, answering an incoming call, ending a call, or sending and receiving SMS or MMS messages.

Security

The application must not contain any viruses or malware. The application must implement type-safe code, as described in the document "Unsafe Code and Pointers" (http://msdn.microsoft.com/en-us/library/t2yzs44b(v=VS.80).aspx). Finally, the application must not run security-critical code, as described in the document "Security Changes in the .NET Framework 4" (http://msdn.microsoft.com/en-us/library/ dd233103(v=VS.100).aspx). Security is covered in greater detail in Chapter 19.

Technical Support Information

The application must include the application name, version, and technical support information.

Submitting Your First Windows Phone Application to the Windows Phone Marketplace

In the previous sections, you learned how to pass through the Windows Phone Marketplace's validation and certification process by understanding the rules and process set forth to protect the consumer and the Marketplace. Now you will learn to deploy your first Windows Phone application to the Marketplace so that you can start making millions. First, we'll discuss how to package the application for submission.

Packaging the Application

To package the application, you will use Visual Studio. For this demo, you will use the Notepad project that you created in Chapter 3.

1. Open the Notepad solution found in the directory where you unzipped the source code that accompanies this book. The solution is found at [*unzipped directory*]\Codes\ch03\Notepad\Notepad.sln. Double-click the solution to open it.

2. Click the Notepad solution in Solution Explorer, and then select Release from the mode drop-down menu (see Figure 5-2).

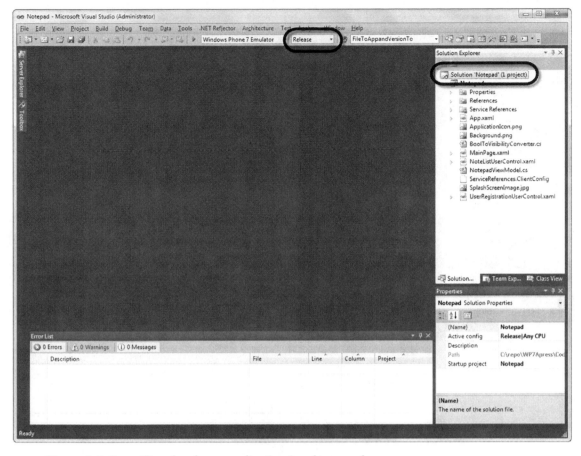

Figure 5-2. Compiling the phone application in release mode

3. Press F6 to build the solution in release mode.

4. When the build is done, you'll find the binaries within the `bin\release` directory where the project file is located. To find the location of the project file, click the Notepad project in Solution Explorer. In the Properties window, you will see the project path (see Figure 5-3).

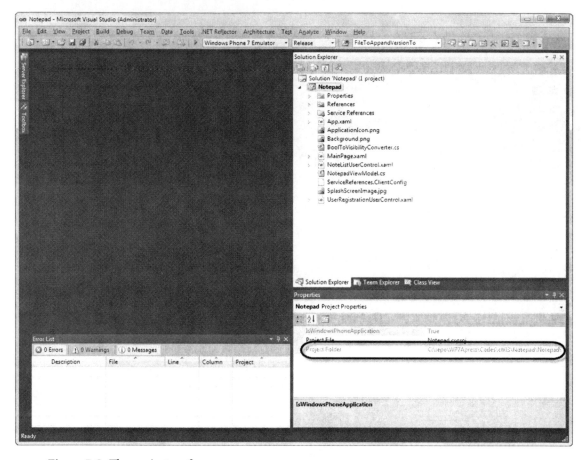

Figure 5-3. *The project path*

5. Inside of [*your project folder*]\bin\release, you will find Notepad.xap, which you will use in next section to submit to the Windows Phone Marketplace.

Submitting the Application

In the previous sections, you compiled a notepad application and created the Notepad.xap file. In this section, you will deploy the application. Open your browser of choice, go to http://create.msdn.com, and sign in to the portal.

1. From the dashboard menu, choose Windows Phone. You will see the page shown in Figure 5-4.

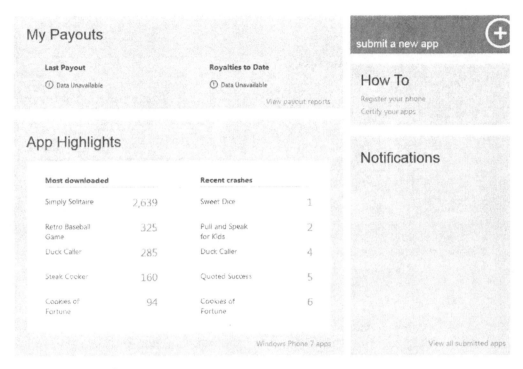

Figure 5-4. The My Apps page

2.   Click the Submit a New App button to get to the upload page shown in
     Figure 5-5.

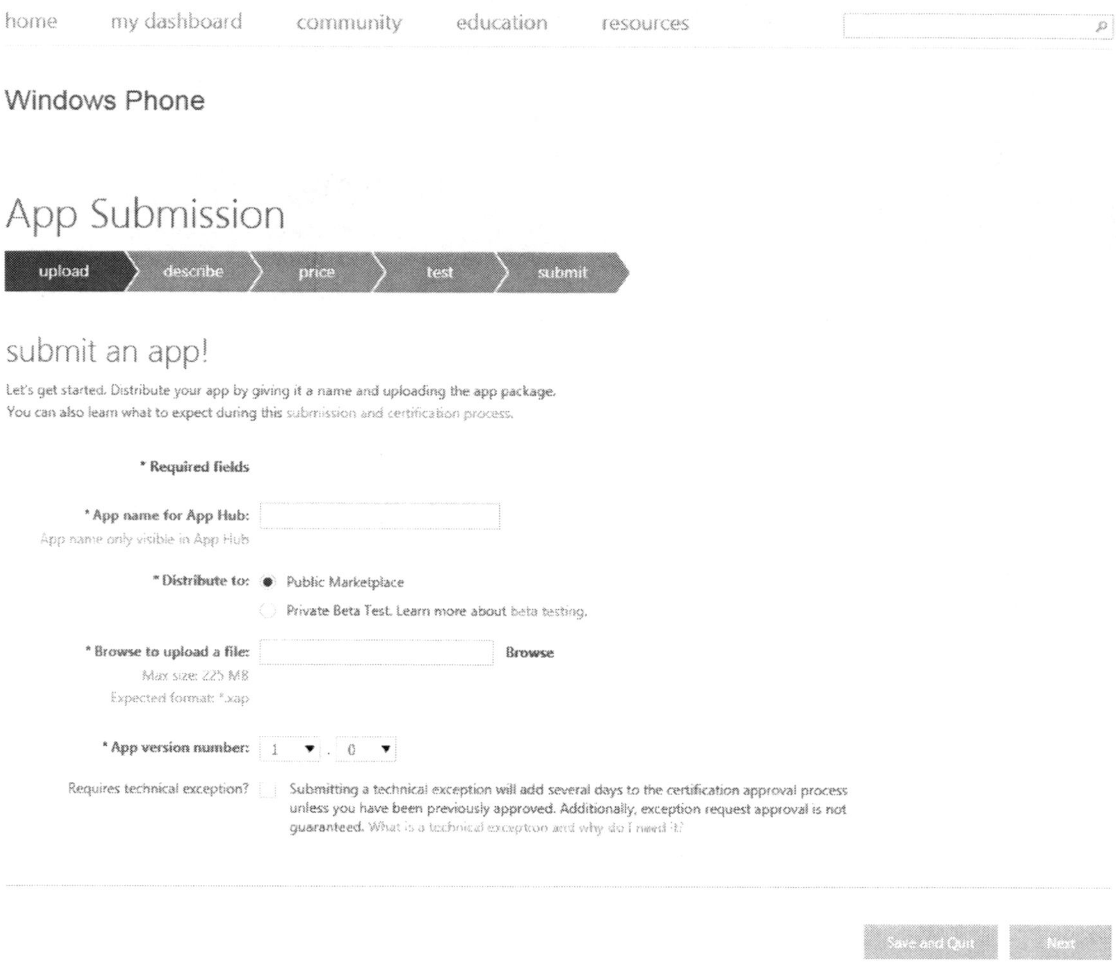

home   my dashboard   community   education   resources

Windows Phone

App Submission

upload > describe > price > test > submit

submit an app!

Let's get started. Distribute your app by giving it a name and uploading the app package.
You can also learn what to expect during this submission and certification process.

* Required fields

* App name for App Hub:

App name only visible in App Hub

* Distribute to: ● Public Marketplace

○ Private Beta Test. Learn more about beta testing.

* Browse to upload a file: **Browse**

Max size: 225 MB

Expected format: *.xap

* App version number: 1 ▼ . 0 ▼

Requires technical exception? ☐ Submitting a technical exception will add several days to the certification approval process
unless you have been previously approved. Additionally, exception request approval is not
guaranteed. What is a technical exception and why do I need it?

Save and Quit   Next

Figure 5-5. The upload page

3. From the upload page, enter the app name in the "App name for App Hub"
   field, and choose Public Marketplace as the distribution option, since you will
   want to publish the application to consumers. Next, click the Browse button
   and browse to Notepad.xap, and select this file. Select your app version number
   from the drop-down menu, and click the Next button.

4. The description page shown in Figure 5-6 will load. Fill out the description
   section by completing the following steps:

   a. From the Category drop-down menu, choose a category that is appropriate for
      your application.

   b. Choose a subcategory.

c. Add a detailed description and a featured-app description. (This should be a single sentence that will catch a user's eye in the Marketplace.)

d. Add keywords that that the user can search to find your new application easily in the Marketplace. Note here that it is good practice to use your company name in your keywords so that you can quickly search your company's applications.

e. Add a legal URL, if you have one, and a contact e-mail.

f. In the Artwork section, you will upload a large and small application tile, a large PC application tile, and screenshots. The screen resolution is defined in the certification requirements document. The images for this step can be found in [*directory where source code is unzipped*]\Codes\ch05. Click Next to continue.

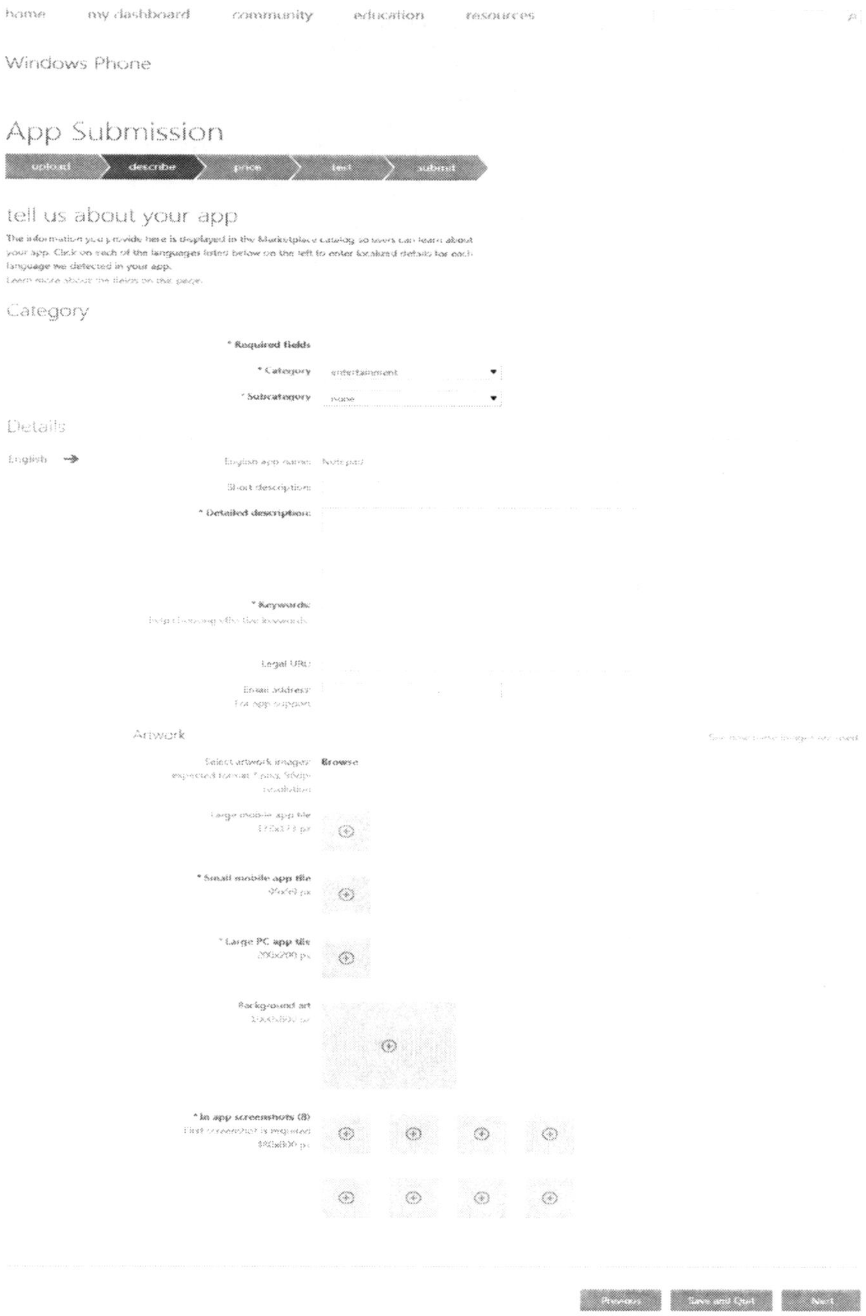

Figure 5-6. *The description page*

5.   The pricing page shown in Figure 5-7 will load. Choose a currency and select
     the application price. If you are targeting the worldwide market, select
     "Worldwide distribution." If the application is a trial application, select "Trial
     supported." Click Next to continue.

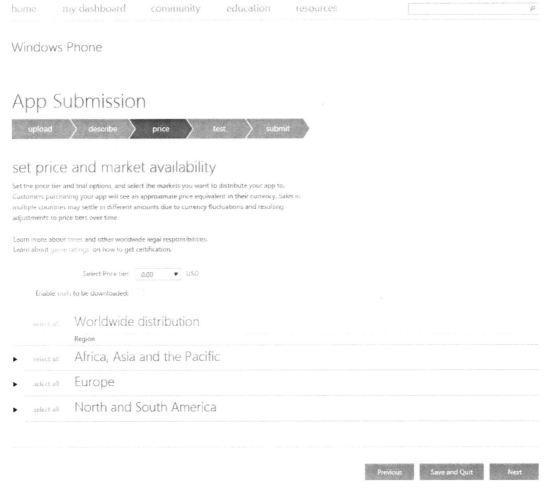

Figure 5-7. The pricing page

6.   The submit page shown in Figure 5-8 will load. Choose "As soon as it's
     certified" from the drop-down menu, and click the Submit button.

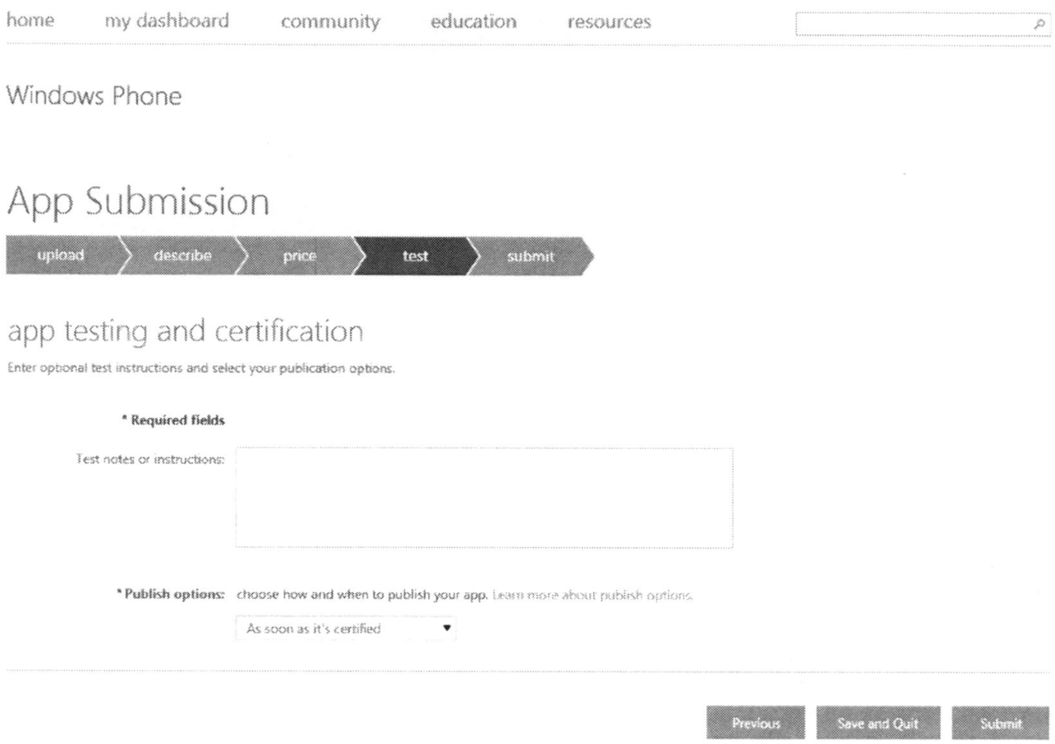

Figure 5-8. The submit page

7.   You will see a confirmation page, as shown in Figure 5-9.

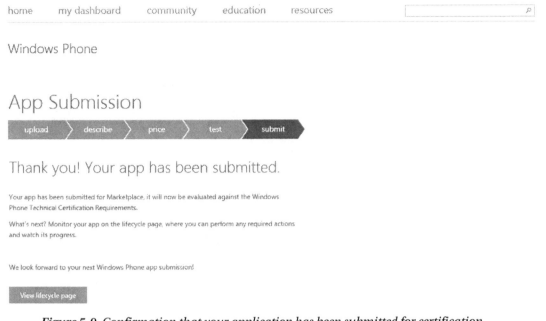

Figure 5-9. Confirmation that your application has been submitted for certification

8. From the "my dashboard" menu, choose Windows Phone, and you will be taken to the home page where you will see the status of your recently submitted application, as shown in Figure 5-10.

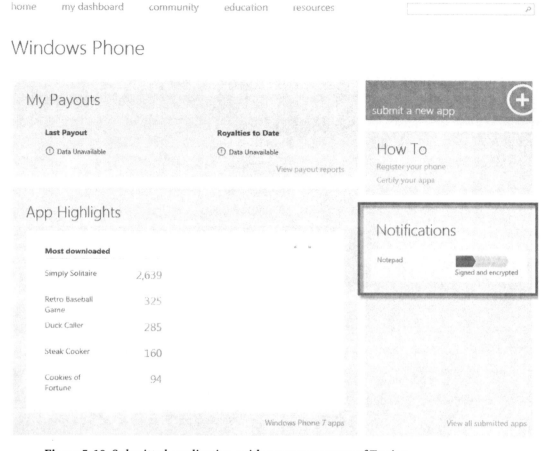

Figure 5-10. Submitted application, with a progress status of Testing

Congratulations! You have successfully submitted your Windows Phone application to the worldwide market of Windows Phone users for the price of 99 cents. If your application successfully passes through the certification process, you will be notified by e-mail. If your application fails the certification process, you will be able to see the report of why your application failed, and you will have the option to resubmit.

Updating Your Application

In this section, you will learn to redeploy your application with a revised version that might contain new features or fixes to the bugs that users have reported.

1. Sign in to your App Hub. Then, from the "my dashboard" menu, choose Windows Phone, and you will see a screen similar to Figure 5-10.

2. From the App Highlights section, click the "Windows Phone apps" link, and you will see a published-app screen, as shown in Figure 5-11.

Figure 5-11. Updating an application published to the Marketplace

3. From the application list, click the application name that you want to resubmit to the Marketplace, and you will see the application details screen, as shown in Figure 5-12.

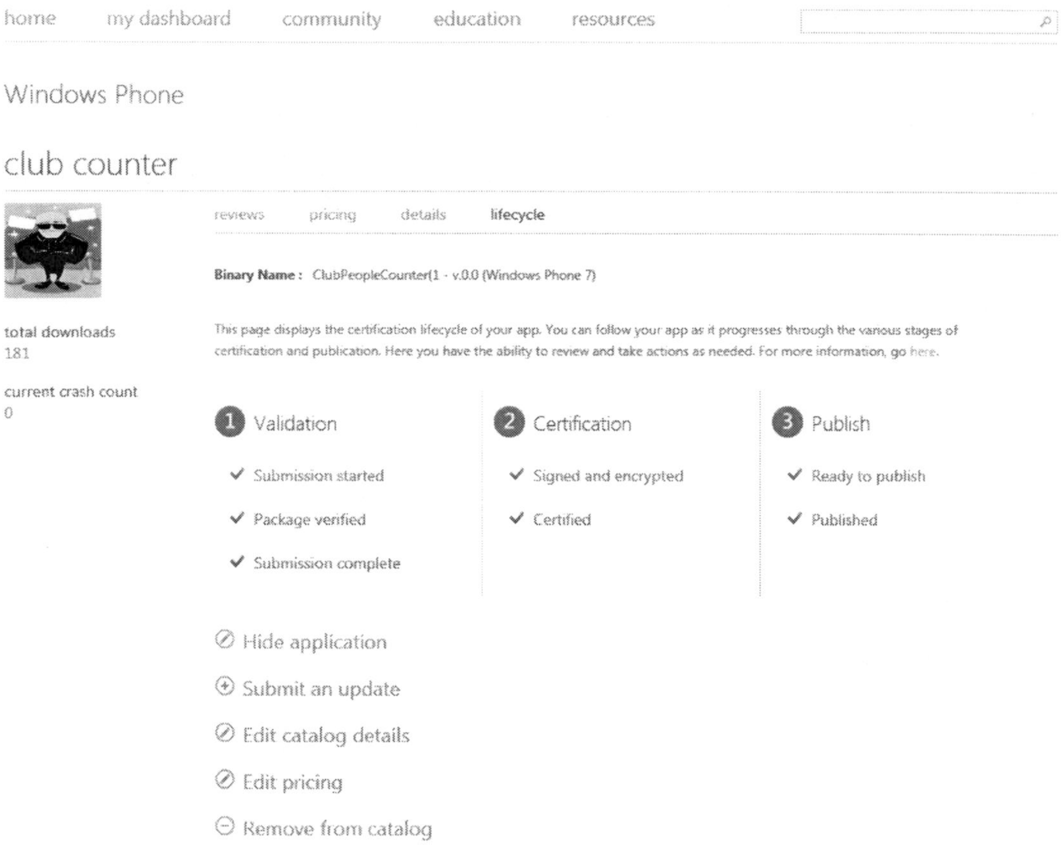

home   my dashboard   community   education   resources

Windows Phone

club counter

reviews   pricing   details   **lifecycle**

Binary Name : ClubPeopleCounter(1 - v.0.0 {Windows Phone 7}

total downloads
181

This page displays the certification lifecycle of your app. You can follow your app as it progresses through the various stages of certification and publication. Here you have the ability to review and take actions as needed. For more information, go here.

current crash count
0

1 Validation

✓ Submission started

✓ Package verified

✓ Submission complete

2 Certification

✓ Signed and encrypted

✓ Certified

3 Publish

✓ Ready to publish

✓ Published

⊘ Hide application

⊕ Submit an update

⊘ Edit catalog details

⊘ Edit pricing

⊖ Remove from catalog

Figure 5-12. The application details screen

4. Click "Edit catalog details." The remaining steps are exactly the same as those for submitting a new application to the Marketplace, as described in the previous section. An update must go through the certification process again.

Finding Your Application in the Marketplace

In this section, you will learn to find your application and view ratings and comments. You will use the Zune software that you downloaded from www.zune.net/en-US/products/software/download/downloadsoftware.htm.

1. Install your downloaded Zune software.

2. Open up your Zune software (found at Start ➤ All Programs ➤ Zune). Follow the steps to configure Zune if it's the first time you're using it.

3. Once you are on the Zune main page, click the Marketplace link, and then click the APPS link, as shown in Figure 5-13.

Figure 5-13. Finding your application in the Marketplace using Zune

4. You can either search for your application or navigate to a category to look for your application.

Summary

In this chapter you learned a great deal about the Windows Phone Marketplace's certification requirements. Then you learned how to package the application in Visual Studio to produce the XAP file and how to submit the application through the Windows Phone development portal for the certification process.

In the following chapters, you will learn about the specific features of a Windows Phone. Chapter 6 covers the accelerometer, which can be used in games—for example, to use the phone like a steering wheel. You will use the accelerometer to detect the orientation of the phone and capture phone shakes.

CHAPTER 6

Working with the Accelerometer

An accelerometer has many practical uses for applications that depend on the movement of a Windows Phone in three-dimensional space. With data from an accelerometer, you can steer a simulated car in a driving game or fly a plane in a flight simulator. You can capture motion such as a shake, punch, swing, or slash and mix this accelerometer data with a physics engine to create Wii-like games. Just for fun, you can build novelty applications to amaze your friends, such as a light saber simulation that makes Star Wars sounds as you swing your phone in the air. An accelerometer can even be used for business applications, such as a level for hanging a picture frame. Under the covers, the controller devices for games that run on consoles, such as the Wii controller, are nothing more than accelerometers wrapped in buttons and plastic.

The accelerometer in a Windows Phone measures the device's movements in space, or more precisely, its acceleration along three axes (x, y, and z) relative to the earth's gravitational pull (9.8 m/sec^2), which is perpendicular to the ground. Think of Newton's apple. When you drop an apple, it falls to the earth, and the force that pulls it down can be calculated using the formula force = mass × acceleration. Thus, in a Windows Phone, the accelerometer can tell you the orientation of the phone with respect to the earth's gravitational force.

In this chapter, you will learn how to write a Windows Phone application that takes advantage of the data the accelerometer provides. In the first example, you will capture data from the accelerometer and interpret the x, y, and z values. In the second demo, you will use readings from the accelerometer to move a ball in a 2D space.

Understanding Orientation and Movement

When you hold a Windows Phone in your hand with its display facing you, think of it as occupying the origin of a three-dimensional graph with its z-axis pointing toward you (a positive direction), its y-axis pointing downward (a negative direction), and its x-axis pointing toward the right (a positive direction). Figure 6-1 shows how these three axes are positioned relative to the device when you hold it facing toward you.

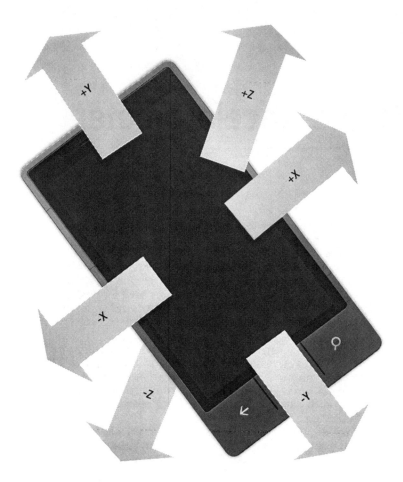

Figure 6-1. *Accelerometer axis directions when the device is facing toward you*

An accelerometer reading of (x, y, z) = (0, –1, 0) might involve standing the phone up on the table, for example, with the front of the phone facing toward you and the phone buttons facing downward, as shown in Figure 6-2.

- If you were to rotate the phone in Figure 6-2 to the right 90 degrees so that the Windows Phone control buttons were to the right, as shown in Figure 6-3, the expected accelerometer readings would be (x, y, z) = (–1, 0, 0).

- If you took the phone in Figure 6-2 and rotated it 180 degrees, (x, y, z) would be (0, 1, 0), as shown in Figure 6-4.

- If you were to rotate the phone in Figure 6-4 to the left 90 degrees, as shown in Figure 6-5, (x, y, z) would be (1, 0, 0).

- If you were to put the phone flat on the table with the phone facing up, as shown in Figure 6-6, (x, y, z) would be (0, 0, –1).

- If you put the phone facing down on the table, as shown in Figure 6-7, (x, y, z) would be (0, 0, 1).

Figure 6-2. *(x, y, z) = (0, –1, 0)*

Figure 6-3. *(x, y, z) = (–1, 0, 0)*

Figure 6-4. *(x, y, z) = (0, 1, 0)*

Figure 6-5. *(x, y, z) = (1, 0, 0)*

Figure 6-6. *(x, y, z) = (0, 0, –1)*

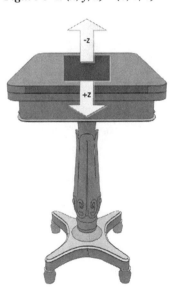

Figure 6-7. *(x, y, z) = (0, 0, 1)*

Calculating Distance

The Euclidean distance algorithm is useful for calculating a distance between two points in three-dimensional space. This equation allows you to detect sudden movements such as the shaking of the phone.

If (Ox, Oy, Oz) is a previous accelerometer value and (Nx, Ny, Nz) is a new one, you can calculate Euclidean distance as follows:

$$EuclideanDistance = \sqrt{(Nx - Ox)^2 + (Ny - Oy)^2 + (Nz - Oz)^2}$$

Calculating Pitch, Roll, and Yaw

With the accelerometer readings you obtain, you will have a pretty good understanding of the current orientation of the phone, and using the accelerometer data will tell you how far the phone is tilted on the x-, y-, and z-axes. This information can be very useful if you are planning to create airplane simulation games or racing games that use the accelerometer to control the direction of moving objects. Think of it as using a phone like a joystick by detecting the tilt motions known as pitch, roll and yaw.

When you hold the phone vertically, with the screen facing toward you, both the pitch and roll angles are 0 degrees, as shown in Figure 6-8.

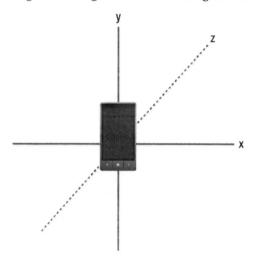

Figure 6-8. Pitch and roll angles of 0 degrees

Now, if you tilt the phone slightly to the right, you will be able to calculate the pitch (ρ) and roll (φ) angles shown in Figure 6-9. There's another angle of interest, yaw, which is the angle respective to the z-axis (not shown in Figure 6-9); think of yaw as the degree to which the phone is tilted toward or away from you into the page.

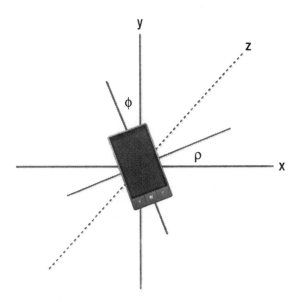

Figure 6-9. Pitch and roll angles

In order to calculate pitch (ρ), roll (φ), and yaw (θ) angles, you will need the following equations, where Ax, Ay, and Az are the accelerometer values for x, y, and z.

$$\rho = arctan\left(\frac{Ax}{\sqrt{Ay^2 + Az^2}}\right)$$

$$\varphi = arctan\left(\frac{Ay}{\sqrt{Ax^2 + Az^2}}\right)$$

$$\theta = arctan\left(\frac{\sqrt{Ax^2 + Ay^2}}{Az}\right)$$

You'll use Euclidean distance and pitch, roll, and yaw calculations in the examples that follow.

Introducing SDK Support for Accelerometers

In order to use the Windows Phone accelerometer, you'll need to reference the
Microsoft.Devices.Sensors namespace, which contains the Accelerometer class. Among its members is the ReadingChanged event, which constantly updates the x-, y-, and z-coordinates of the device as event arguments e.X, e.Y, and e.Z, with a timestamp that can be used to calculate velocity, acceleration, and other values.

There are two things that you must remember about the accelerometer device. The first is that heavy use of the accelerometer will consume battery power, and thus you must remember to turn it on only when it's needed and turn it off when it's not. Second, the accelerometer runs on a thread that is completely separate from the thread upon which the current UI runs. This means that you must use `Deployment.Current.Dispatcher.BeginInvoke` to update the UI; otherwise you will receive an invalid cross-thread exception.

Retrieving Accelerometer Data

You will begin by building a simple application that captures the accelerometer data. The accelerometer data consist of acceleration data in x, y, and z directions, plus the time in which the acceleration data was captured. Figure 6-10 displays the basic UI of the accelerometer data. In order for this demo to work, you must deploy the project to an actual Windows Phone device (please refer to Chapter 4 for deploying to the device). If you don't have a Windows Phone device, you might consider using a reactive extension to simulate the accelerometer behavior. Reactive extensions will not be covered in this chapter, but you can refer to Chapter 18 for more detail on how to create a simulation in order to work with the accelerometer in the emulator.

Figure 6-10. CaptureAccelerometerData demo

You will build the demo in three steps. First, you'll create a Visual Studio project. Next, you'll build the project's UI, and then you'll finish up by adding the code that the application needs to retrieve and display data from the accelerometer.

Creating the CaptureAccelerometerData Project

To set up the CaptureAccelerometerData project, follow the steps you've used for previous examples in this book:

1. Open Microsoft Visual Studio 2010 Express for Windows Phone on your workstation.

2. Create a new Windows Phone application by selecting File New Project on the Visual Studio command menu. Select the Windows Phone Application template, name the application CaptureAccelerometerData, and click OK.

3. In order to use the accelerometer, add an assembly reference to Microsoft.Devices.Sensors and Microsoft.Xna.Framework by right-clicking the References folder in Solution Explorer and choosing Microsoft.Devices.Sensors and Microsoft.Xna.Framework from the Add Reference window, as shown in Figure 6-11.

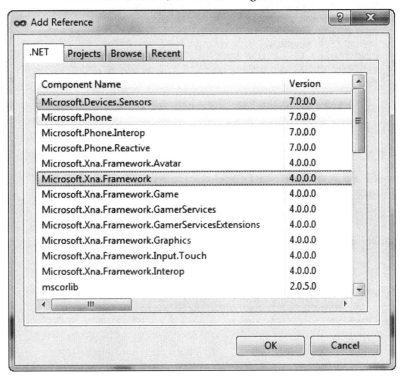

Figure 6-11. Adding a reference to Microsoft.Devices.Sensors

Building the UI

You will be building the UI using the XAML in Visual Studio (for building simple controls, it's faster to work with the XAML code). Go to Solution Explorer, open `MainPage.xaml`, and replace the XAML you find there with the code in the following sections.

Declaring the UI Resources

The namespaces you see in the following code snippet are typically declared by default when you first create a Windows Phone project. In particular, the namespace `xmlns:phone="clr-namespace: Microsoft.Phone.Controls; assembly=Microsoft.Phone"` allows you to add common Windows Phone controls to the application main page.

```
<phone:PhoneApplicationPage
    x:Class="CaptureAccelerometerData.MainPage"
    xmlns="http://schemas.microsoft.com/winfx/2006/xaml/presentation"
    xmlns:x="http://schemas.microsoft.com/winfx/2006/xaml"
    xmlns:phone="clr-namespace:Microsoft.Phone.Controls;assembly=Microsoft.Phone"
    xmlns:shell="clr-namespace:Microsoft.Phone.Shell;assembly=Microsoft.Phone"
    xmlns:d="http://schemas.microsoft.com/expression/blend/2008"
    xmlns:mc="http://schemas.openxmlformats.org/markup-compatibility/2006"
    FontFamily="{StaticResource PhoneFontFamilyNormal}"
    FontSize="{StaticResource PhoneFontSizeNormal}"
    Foreground="{StaticResource PhoneForegroundBrush}"
    SupportedOrientations="Portrait" Orientation="Portrait"
    mc:Ignorable="d" d:DesignWidth="480" d:DesignHeight="768"
    shell:SystemTray.IsVisible="True">
```

Building the Main Page and Adding Components

Now create the components you need to display the x, y, and z values plus the time reading that your application captures from the accelerometer. You'll also want to add components to display the pitch, roll, and yaw values of the device, which you will calculate and use to understand how the phone is oriented. Finally, you also need buttons to start and stop the accelerometer, which are also specified.

```
<Grid x:Name="LayoutRoot" Background="Transparent">
    <Grid.RowDefinitions>
        <RowDefinition Height="Auto"/>
        <RowDefinition Height="*"/>
    </Grid.RowDefinitions>

    <StackPanel x:Name="TitlePanel" Grid.Row="0" Margin="24,24,0,12">
        <TextBlock x:Name="ApplicationTitle" Text="CaptureAccelerometer Data"↵
Style="{StaticResource PhoneTextNormalStyle}"/>
    </StackPanel>

    <Grid x:Name="ContentGrid" Grid.Row="1">
        <TextBlock Name="txtX" Text="TextBlock"
                    Margin="160,56,12,0" FontSize="20"
                    Height="31" VerticalAlignment="Top" />
```

```xml
                <TextBlock Name="txtY" Text="TextBlock"
                        Margin="160,119,12,556" FontSize="20" />
                <TextBlock Name="txtZ" Text="TextBlock"
                        Margin="155,181,12,490" FontSize="20" />
                <TextBlock Name="txtTime" Text="TextBlock"
                        Margin="155,244,12,427" FontSize="20" />
                <Button Content="Start" Height="72"
                        Name="btnStart" Width="160"
                        Margin="36,514,284,119" Click="btnStart_Click" />
                <Button Content="Stop" Height="72"
                        Name="btnStop" Width="160"
                        Margin="207,514,113,119" Click="btnStop_Click" />
                <TextBlock FontSize="40" Margin="66,34,331,614"
                        Name="lblX" Text="X" />
                <TextBlock FontSize="40" Margin="66,97,331,552"
                        Name="lblY" Text="Y" />
                <TextBlock FontSize="40" Margin="66,159,346,489"
                        Name="lblZ" Text="Z" />
                <TextBlock FontSize="40" Margin="12,222,331,422"
                        Name="lblTime" Text="Time" />
                <TextBlock FontSize="20" Margin="160,285,7,386"
                        Name="txtPitch" Text="TextBlock" />
                <TextBlock FontSize="22" Margin="0,283,370,365"
                        Name="lblPitch" Text="Pitch" TextAlignment="Right" />
                <TextBlock FontSize="20" Margin="160,345,7,326"
                        Name="txtRoll" Text="TextBlock" />
                <TextBlock FontSize="22" Margin="0,343,370,305"
                        Name="lblRoll" Text="Roll" TextAlignment="Right" />
                <TextBlock FontSize="20" Margin="160,408,7,263"
                        Name="txtYaw" Text="TextBlock" />
                <TextBlock FontSize="22" Margin="0,406,370,242"
                        Name="lblYaw" Text="Yaw" TextAlignment="Right" />
        </Grid>

</phone:PhoneApplicationPage>
```

Once you have loaded the XAML code, you should see the layout shown in Figure 6-12. In the next section, you will be adding events to update the UI with captured accelerometer data.

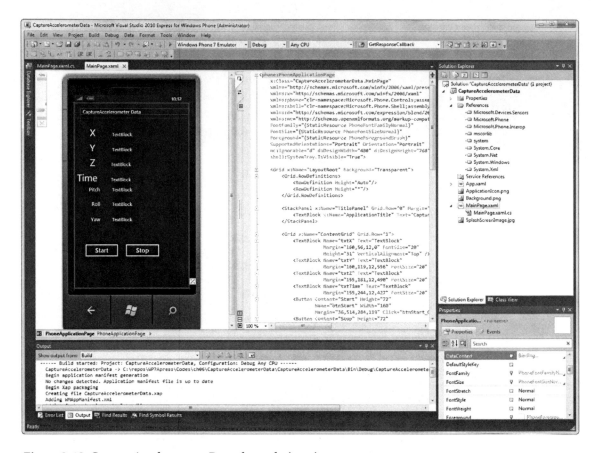

Figure 6-12. CaptureAccelerometerData demo design view

Coding the Application

In Solution Explorer, open `MainPage.xaml.cs` and replace the code there with the following C# code blocks, which will implement the UI updates using accelerometer data.

Specifying the Namespaces

Begin by listing the namespaces the application will use. The inclusion of `Microsoft.Devices.Sensors` will allow you to start and stop the Windows Phone's accelerometer.

```
using System;
using System.Windows;
using Microsoft.Phone.Controls;
using Microsoft.Devices.Sensors;
using Microsoft.Xna.Framework;
```

```
namespace CaptureAccelerometerData
{
    public partial class MainPage : PhoneApplicationPage
    {
```

Initializing Variables

The variable _ac, an Accelerometer object, will be used to start and stop the accelerometer and to retrieve x, y, z, and time. Also notice the inclusion of the ReadingChanged event, which you'll draw on to send captured accelerometer data to your UI.

```
Accelerometer _ac;

        public MainPage()
        {
            InitializeComponent();

            _ac = new Accelerometer();
            _ac.CurrentValueChanged+=new EventHandler<SensorReadingEventArgs↩
<AccelerometerReading>>(_ac_CurrentValueChanged);

        }
```

Capturing and Displaying Accelerometer Data

Note here that you can't directly change the UI elements upon receiving the accelerometer data because the accelerometer data comes from a different thread than the current UI thread. If you try to change the UI elements directly here, you'll get an invalid cross-thread access error, as shown in Figure 6-13. In order to overcome this problem, you must use the Dispatcher in the current UI thread, as shown in the following code.

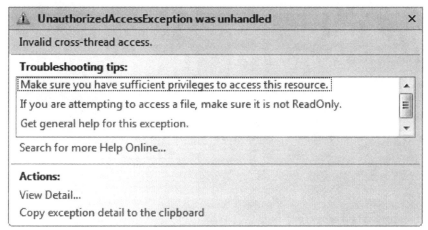

Figure 6-13. Invalid cross-thread access error

```csharp
private void _ac_CurrentValueChanged(object sender,
    SensorReadingEventArgs<AccelerometerReading> e)
{
    // Invoke accelerometer reading in current UI thread in order to be
    // able to update UIElements
    Deployment.Current.Dispatcher.BeginInvoke(() => ProcessAccelerometerReading(e));
}

private void ProcessAccelerometerReading(SensorReadingEventArgs<AccelerometerReading> e)
{
    Vector3 reading = e.SensorReading.Acceleration;

    txtTime.Text = e.SensorReading.Timestamp.ToString();
    txtX.Text = reading.X.ToString();
    txtY.Text = reading.Y.ToString();
    txtZ.Text = reading.Z.ToString();
    txtPitch.Text = RadianToDegree((Math.Atan(reading.X / Math.Sqrt(Math.Pow↵
(reading.Y, 2) + Math.Pow(reading.Z, 2))))).ToString();
    txtRoll.Text = RadianToDegree((Math.Atan(reading.Y / Math.Sqrt(Math.Pow↵
(reading.X, 2) + Math.Pow(reading.Z, 2))))).ToString();
    txtYaw.Text = RadianToDegree((Math.Atan(Math.Sqrt(Math.Pow↵
(reading.X, 2) + Math.Pow(reading.Y, 2)) / reading.Z))).ToString();
}
```

Implementing Accelerometer Start and Stop

Implement the button event for stopping and starting the accelerometer. Note here that you must anticipate an error that might occur when you are trying to start or stop the accelerometer.

```csharp
private void btnStart_Click(object sender, RoutedEventArgs e)
{
    try
    {
        _ac.Start();
    }
    catch (AccelerometerFailedException)
    {
        MessageBox.Show("Acceleromter failed to start.");
    }
}

private void btnStop_Click(object sender, RoutedEventArgs e)
{
    try
    {
        _ac.Stop();
    }
    catch (AccelerometerFailedException)
    {
        MessageBox.Show("Acceleromter failed to stop.");
    }
```

```
        }
      }
}
```

Testing the Finished Application

To test the finished application, press F5. The result should resemble the screenshot shown previously in Figure 6-10. You will see that the x, y, z, and time text blocks are updated each time you click the Start button. Remember that, to run the application on a Windows Phone 7 device, you must choose the Windows Phone 7 Device option shown in Figure 6-14.

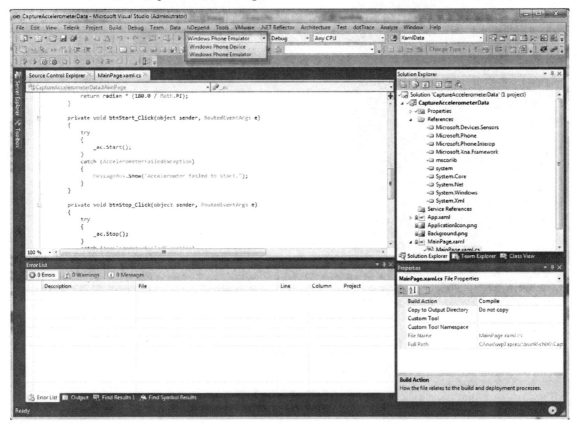

Figure 6-14. Choose Windows Phone Device before running the application.

Using Accelerometer Data to Move a Ball

In this demo, you will use the captured accelerometer data to do something more useful. You will move the image of a ball as you tilt the phone left, right, forward, and back. This demo will help you understand how to translate the user input of the accelerometer data and apply it to UI elements. Figure 6-15 displays the basic UI of the MoveBallDemo application.

Figure 6-15. *MoveBallDemo UI*

Creating the MoveBall Project

To set up the CaptureAccelerometerData project, follow the steps you've used for previous examples in this book:

1. Open Microsoft Visual Studio 2010 Express for Windows Phone on your workstation.

2. Create a new Windows Phone Application by selecting File   New Project from the Visual Studio command menu. Select the Windows Phone Application template, name the application MoveBallDemo, and click OK.

3. In order to use the accelerometer, add an assembly reference to Microsoft.Devices.Sensors and Microsoft.Xna.Framework by right-clicking the

References folder in Solution Explorer and choosing
`Microsoft.Devices.Sensors` and `Microsoft.Xna.Framework` from the Add
Reference window, as shown previously in Figure 6-11.

Building the UI

You will be building the UI using the XAML in Visual Studio (for building simple controls, it's faster to work with the XAML code). Go to Solution Explorer, open `MainPage.xaml`, and replace the XAML you find there with the code in the following sections.

Declaring the UI Resources

Again, the namespaces you see here are typically declared by default when you first create the Windows Phone project, and namespaces such as `xmlns:phone="clr-namespace:Microsoft.Phone.Controls;assembly=Microsoft.Phone"` will allow you to add common Windows Phone controls.

```
<phone:PhoneApplicationPage
    x:Class="MoveBallDemo.MainPage"
    xmlns="http://schemas.microsoft.com/winfx/2006/xaml/presentation"
    xmlns:x="http://schemas.microsoft.com/winfx/2006/xaml"
    xmlns:phone="clr-namespace:Microsoft.Phone.Controls;assembly=Microsoft.Phone"
    xmlns:shell="clr-namespace:Microsoft.Phone.Shell;assembly=Microsoft.Phone"
    xmlns:d="http://schemas.microsoft.com/expression/blend/2008"
    xmlns:mc="http://schemas.openxmlformats.org/markup-compatibility/2006"
    FontFamily="{StaticResource PhoneFontFamilyNormal}"
    FontSize="{StaticResource PhoneFontSizeNormal}"
    Foreground="{StaticResource PhoneForegroundBrush}"
    SupportedOrientations="Portrait" Orientation="Portrait"
    mc:Ignorable="d" d:DesignWidth="480" d:DesignHeight="768"
    shell:SystemTray.IsVisible="True">
```

Building the Main Page and Adding Components

The UI consists of Start and Stop buttons for starting and stopping the accelerometer and a ball that moves as the Windows Phone device is tilted left, right, forward, and backward.

```
    <Grid x:Name="LayoutRoot" Background="Transparent">
        <Grid.RowDefinitions>
            <RowDefinition Height="Auto"/>
            <RowDefinition Height="*"/>
        </Grid.RowDefinitions>

        <StackPanel x:Name="TitlePanel" Grid.Row="0" Margin="24,24,0,12">
            <TextBlock x:Name="ApplicationTitle" Text="MoveBallDemo"
Style="{StaticResource PhoneTextNormalStyle}"/>
        </StackPanel>
        <Button Content="Start" Height="72"
                HorizontalAlignment="Left" x:Name="btnStart"
                VerticalAlignment="Top" Width="160"
```

```
                Click="btnStart_Click" Margin="8,537,0,0"
                Grid.Row="1" d:LayoutOverrides="HorizontalAlignment" />
        <Button Content="Stop" Height="72"
                HorizontalAlignment="Left" x:Name="btnStop"
                VerticalAlignment="Top" Width="160"
                Click="btnStop_Click" Margin="168,537,0,0"
                Grid.Row="1" />

        <Canvas x:Name="ContentGrid" Margin="0,8,8,0"
                Grid.Row="1" HorizontalAlignment="Right"
                Width="472" Height="479" VerticalAlignment="Top">
            <Ellipse x:Name="ball" Canvas.Left="126"
                    Fill="#FF963C3C" HorizontalAlignment="Left"
                    Height="47" Stroke="Black" StrokeThickness="1"
                    VerticalAlignment="Top" Width="46"
                    Canvas.Top="222"/>
        </Canvas>
    </Grid>

</phone:PhoneApplicationPage>
```

Once you've loaded the XAML code, you should see the layout shown in Figure 6-16. Now it's time to animate the ball and add the sound effect by wiring up some events.

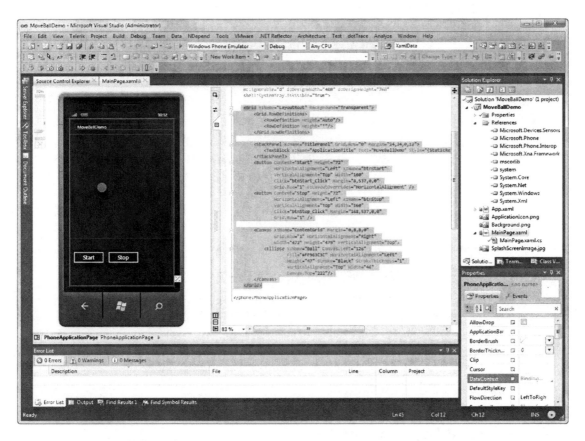

Figure 6-16. MoveBall demo design view

Coding the Application

In Solution Explorer, open `MainPage.xaml.cs` and replace the code there with the following C# code blocks.

Specifying the Namespaces

Begin by listing the namespaces that the application will use. The inclusion of `Microsoft.Devices.Sensors` will allow you to start and stop the Windows Phone accelerometer.

```
using System;
using System.Windows;
using System.Windows.Controls;
using Microsoft.Phone.Controls;
using Microsoft.Devices.Sensors;
using Microsoft.Xna.Framework;
```

```
namespace MoveBallDemo
{
    public partial class MainPage : PhoneApplicationPage
    {
```

Initializing Variables

The variable _ac, an Accelerometer object, will be used to start and stop the sensor and retrieve the x, y, z, and time values. The ReadingChanged event sends the captured accelerometer data to be displayed in the UI. Finally, the starting position of the ball is set to the center of the canvas where the ball is placed.

```
private Accelerometer _ac;

public MainPage()
{
    InitializeComponent();

    SupportedOrientations = SupportedPageOrientation.Portrait;

    ball.SetValue(Canvas.LeftProperty, ContentGrid.Width / 2);
    ball.SetValue(Canvas.TopProperty, ContentGrid.Height / 2);

    _ac = new Accelerometer();
    _ac.CurrentValueChanged +=
        new EventHandler<SensorReadingEventArgs<AccelerometerReading>>
            (_ac_CurrentValueChanged);
}
```

Handling Captured Accelerometer Data

Here, as shown in the previous demo, you can't directly change the UI elements upon receiving the accelerometer data because the data comes from a different thread than the current UI thread. If you try to change the UI elements directly here, you will get an invalid cross-thread access error, as shown previously in Figure 6-13. In order to overcome this problem, you must use the Dispatcher in the current UI thread, as shown in the following code:

```
private void _ac_CurrentValueChanged(object sender,
        SensorReadingEventArgs<AccelerometerReading> e)
{
    Deployment.Current.Dispatcher.BeginInvoke(() => MyReadingChanged(e));
}
```

Applying Captured Accelerometer Data to the Ball

The following code achieves the behavior where, if the phone is tilted vertically with the display facing toward you, based on the algorithm specified in the method, the ball will fall straight very fast. But if you tilt the phone slightly while the display is facing up, the ball will slowly slide in the direction in which the phone is tilted.

```
private void MyReadingChanged(SensorReadingEventArgs<AccelerometerReading> e)
{
    Vector3 reading = e.SensorReading.Acceleration;

    double distanceToTravel = 2;
    double accelerationFactor = Math.Abs(reading.Z) == 0 ? 0.1 : Math.Abs(reading.Z);
    double ballX = (double)ball.GetValue(Canvas.LeftProperty) + distanceToTravel *↵
reading.X / accelerationFactor;
    double ballY = (double)ball.GetValue(Canvas.TopProperty) - distanceToTravel *↵
reading.Y / accelerationFactor;

    if (ballX < 0)
    {
        ballX = 0;
    }
    else if (ballX > ContentGrid.Width)
    {
        ballX = ContentGrid.Width;
    }

    if (ballY < 0)
    {
        ballY = 0;
    }
    else if (ballY > ContentGrid.Height)
    {
        ballY = ContentGrid.Height;
    }

    ball.SetValue(Canvas.LeftProperty, ballX);
    ball.SetValue(Canvas.TopProperty, ballY);
}
```

Adding Start and Stop Button Events

Implement the button event for stopping and starting the accelerometer:

```
private void btnStart_Click(object sender, RoutedEventArgs e)
{
    if (_ac == null)
    {
        _ac = new Accelerometer();
    }
    _ac.Start();
}

private void btnStop_Click(object sender, RoutedEventArgs e)
{
    if (_ac == null)
    {
        _ac = new Accelerometer();
```

```
                }
                _ac.Stop();
            }
        }
    }
}
```

Testing the Finished Application

To test the finished application, press F5. (Remember to choose to run the application on a Windows Phone device, as shown previously in Figure 6-15.) Once the application runs on the Windows Phone, click the Start button. Tilt the phone and watch the ball move in the direction that the phone is being tilted.

Summary

In this chapter, you learned about the fundamentals of the accelerometer. In the first demo, you captured the accelerometer data and displayed it by updating UI elements on the currently executing UI thread. In the second demo, you moved a ball on the phone screen by using captured accelerometer data to calculate its speed and position.

In Chapter 7, you will create an application bar to display shortcuts for the most commonly used tasks in the application and design it to be a compelling application.

CHAPTER 7

Application Bar

When you're ready to program your Windows Phone application in Visual Studio 2010, you'll know what general features your application will provide. Each of the major application features will need to be accessible via a shortcut or some form of a navigation menu. For Windows Phone applications, Microsoft recommends that you use a standard Windows Phone Application Bar to provide shortcuts for most common tasks within the application. Metro UI design concepts for Windows Phones were covered in Part 1 of this book. The use of an Application Bar within the application helps ensure that these guidelines are properly observed.

An Application Bar is essentially a Windows Phone menu system with clickable icons that conform to the general Metro UI guidelines provided by Microsoft. For example, take a look at the Windows Phone version of the popular social networking application Foursquare (one place you can find its screenshots is http://4square.codeplex.com). At the bottom of the screen, you will see an Application Bar with shortcuts to most common features of the application. Another example is Graphic.ly (www.pcworld.com/article/191549/graphicly.html), an application that uses Deep Zoom capabilities of Silverlight to provide an immersive comic book–reading experience. On its Application Bar, Graphic.ly naturally has shortcuts to zoom into and out of the comic book contents, since those features are the most important ones for that application. The screenshots of those applications appear side by side in Figure 7-1. Note that you can also download the full source code for the Foursquare application—something that may prove to be a handy learning tool—from the preceding link.

In this chapter, you will learn how to create an Application Bar in your programs and the specifications for various elements within the Application Bar. You will also learn about the two types of Application Bars, and you will program them both. Within each Windows Phone application, two types of Application Bars can be present: a *global* Application Bar and a *local* one. A global Application Bar offers the convenience of being added to any .xaml page within the application via a single XAML statement. Alternately, a local Application Bar is local to a single application page and must be defined for each .xaml page separately. You will create both global and local Application Bars in this chapter.

Figure 7-1. Both Foursquare and Graphic.ly use the Application Bar for shortcuts to applications' main features.

The position of the Application Bar on the screen varies with the phone orientation. When the phone is in the default, portrait orientation, an Application Bar is displayed as a single row of icons at the bottom of the screen. Figure 7-2 shows an example of an Application Bar with three icons, for Add, Save, and Delete. The ellipsis to the right of the Delete button signifies the presence of additional shortcuts on the Application Bar (called menu items) that will become visible to you when you click that ellipsis button. In this chapter, you'll learn how to create visually appealing Application Bars that conform to the best practices published by Microsoft.

Figure 7-2. An Application Bar with Add (+ icon), Save (disk icon), and Delete (trash can icon) on a Windows Phone

Introducing the Application Bar

The contents of an Application Bar are limited to a maximum of four elements, which means that, at most, you can have four icons (and shortcuts associated with those icons) appear in the Application Bar. The elements are added and automatically centered on the Application Bar from left to right. Additional application shortcuts can be added to the Application Bar via text-based menu items and are hidden from view by default. The presence of an ellipsis to the right of the main Application Bar icons hints that, in addition to the main icons, there are text-based menu items in the Application Bar. These items serve as additional shortcuts and slide up as a list when the user clicks the ellipsis or the empty space right underneath the ellipsis. An example of what the phone screen looks like when there are menu items present in the application and the ellipsis is pressed is shown in Figure 7-3.

Figure 7-3. Application Bar with menu items shown. Note how menu items appear in lowercase, regardless of the letter casing when they were created, to conform to the Metro design guidelines for Windows Phone.

There is good and bad news when it comes to working with the Application Bar. The good news is that an Application Bar is easy to create and comes with a lot of built-in functionality. For example, when the phone changes orientation from portrait to landscape, the Application Bar automatically moves to the left side of the phone screen. In addition, there is a default animation for showing text-based menu items (shown in Figure 7-3) that didn't fit in the four main icon slots on the Application Bar. Finally, some minor but handy features that ensure a consistent user experience are the automatic addition of a circle around each Application Bar icon (that is, you do not have to draw it) and the conversion of textual menu items to lowercase text to conform to Metro design guidelines.

The bad news is that there is little flexibility in creating icons and menus for the Application Bar. The height of the Application Bar is fixed and can't be changed. The size of the icons on the Application Bar is 48 pixels wide and 48 pixels high (generally expressed as 48×48 pixels); icons of other sizes will be scaled to fit that size, which results in distortion, and thus you should generally avoid using them. The actual graphic within the icon has to be 26×26 pixels to fit properly within the circle that the Application Bar automatically draws for each icon. In addition, Microsoft recommends that you always try to use the default system theme colors for the Application Bar because the use of custom colors can lead to unpredictable and potentially unfavorable effects on display quality, menu animations, and power consumption. The Application Bar graphics requirements are summarized in Table 7-1.

Table 7-1. Application Bar Graphics Requirements

Graphic	Size
Full icon size	48×48 pixels
Actual graphic within the icon (without a circle)	26×26 pixels

In the following section, you will create an Application Bar that looks like the one in Figure 7-3. Later in this chapter, you will write code to react to Application Bar events to access different features of your application.

Adding an Application Bar to a Windows Phone Application

Windows Phone provides two types of Application Bars for use with phones apps: a global bar and a local bar. The only way to define a global Application Bar is inside the App.xaml. Once defined, it can be added to any page within the Windows Phone application with a single line of XAML code. On the other hand, there are two ways to define a local Application Bar and add it to a particular application page:

- Using XAML
- Using managed code (for example, C# or Visual Basic)

You'll get to try both methods in this chapter when you build an Application Bar that provides simple functionality, such as asking for a person's name and then reacting as if that name has been saved to the database or the cloud storage. Regardless of the approach you choose, and regardless of whether you are building a local or a global Application Bar, there is a preparatory step you should take before you can properly display and use it. That step involves adding images for your Application Bar buttons to project resources, which we cover in the next section.

Adding Images for Use with Application Bar Buttons

Because the maximum size of each Application Bar icon is 48×48 pixels, the size of each image you add to the Application Bar is limited to 26×26 pixels so that a circle can be properly drawn around it. Since Windows Phone OS supports the concept of themes, the background of an icon has to match the rest of the theme, and therefore it should be made transparent (for more information on working with different themes, please refer to Chapter 9). On this transparent background, the actual graphic should have a white foreground color using an alpha channel. Fortunately, in many cases, you won't have to create icons yourself, since Microsoft has released a set of commonly used images for the Windows Phone Application Bar, all properly sized and formatted in Microsoft's approved style. These icons are automatically installed for you as part of the Windows Phone Developer Tools installation, and their default location is in the %Program Files\Microsoft SDKs\Windows Phone\v7.1\Icons folder.

1. Start off by creating a new Visual Studio 2010 project and naming it ApplicationBarSample.

2. Next, organize the project for easier readability by creating a folder for the icon images you'll use in the ApplicationBarSample project. Right-click the project name in Solution Explorer, and select Add New Folder. Name it Images.

3. Next, copy the icon images to the newly created folder within your project. Using Windows Explorer, copy the image files you need to the Images folder of your project. In the example that follows, you will be using the images located in the dark subfolder of the icon archive that comes with the Windows Phone tools. Make sure to copy the *.png files only, without any folder structure.

4. Now the images are copied, but Visual Studio 2010 still needs to make them a part of the project. Right-click Solution Explorer, and then select Add Existing Item and select all images. Finally, you need to instruct Visual Studio 2010 to include new images in every build of an application. For each image, right-click the image in Solution Explorer and choose Properties. (You can also press F4 to bring up the Properties dialog.) In the Properties dialog box, set the Build action to Content and set the Copy to Output property to Copy Always, as shown in Figure 7-4.

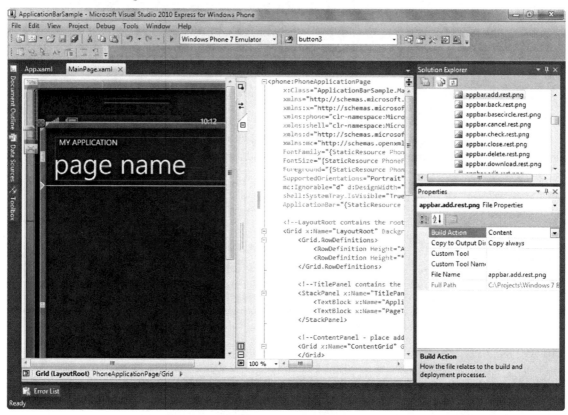

Figure 7-4. *For each image, set Build Action to Content and Copy to Output Directory to Copy Always.*

Now that the project knows where to find the icon images for an Application Bar, it's time to add code to showcase the Application Bar's features.

Adding a Global Application Bar Using XAML

A global Application Bar is created as an application resource in the App.xaml configuration file. Follow these steps to create and add a global Application Bar to the ApplicationBarSample project:

1. In Solution Explorer, right-click the App.xaml file for the ApplicationBarSample project and select Open. This action causes Visual Studio 2010 to display the XAML code for the application's resource and configuration page.

2. Next, paste the complete XAML definition of the Application Bar with three icons and two menu items into the Application Resources section. Locate the <Application.Resources> section of the App.xaml file, and paste the following code into that section. Note that setting the Text property for each control is required.

```
    <shell:ApplicationBar x:Key="GlobalAppMenuBar" Opacity="1" IsVisible="True"
IsMenuEnabled="True">
        <shell:ApplicationBar.Buttons>
            <shell:ApplicationBarIconButton IconUri="/Images/appbar.add.rest.png"
Text="add">
            </shell:ApplicationBarIconButton>
            <shell:ApplicationBarIconButton IconUri="/Images/appbar.save.rest.png"
Text="save">
            </shell:ApplicationBarIconButton>
            <shell:ApplicationBarIconButton IconUri="/Images/appbar.delete.rest.png"
Text="delete">
            </shell:ApplicationBarIconButton>
        </shell:ApplicationBar.Buttons>
        <shell:ApplicationBar.MenuItems>
            <shell:ApplicationBarMenuItem Text="Menu Item 1" IsEnabled="True">
            </shell:ApplicationBarMenuItem>
            <shell:ApplicationBarMenuItem Text="Menu Item 2" IsEnabled="True">
            </shell:ApplicationBarMenuItem>
        </shell:ApplicationBar.MenuItems>
    </shell:ApplicationBar>
```

3. With the global Application Bar defined, you are ready to add it to the pages within your application. Open MainPage.xaml, and add the following attribute within the <phone:PhoneApplicationPage> node:

    ```
    ApplicationBar="{StaticResource GlobalAppMenuBar}"
    ```

4. Press F5 to run the application. You should see an Application Bar identical to the one shown in Figure 7-3. Note that if you see gray x symbols instead of the expected Application Bar icons, the application can't locate the image files to use inside its Application Bar. Make sure the names and paths to those files are spelled correctly, that the build action of the images is set to Content, and that the Copy to Output property is set to Copy Always, as shown in Figure 7-4.

Before moving onto the next section and taking a look at a local Application Bar, let's clean up the `MainPage.xaml` code by removing the `ApplicationBar="{StaticResource GlobalAppMenuBar}"` XAML. If you don't do that, you will get an application exception in the next section after you add a local Application Bar.

Adding a Local Application Bar Using XAML

Although a global Application Bar provides an easy way to add the same Application Bar to all pages or screens within your program, sometimes you will need more flexibility than this. In such cases, where you want to make an Application Bar unique for a given page, you would need to create a local Application Bar. One of the two ways to add a local Application Bar to a Windows Phone application is to use XAML markup. Using XAML markup wherever possible is considered a best practice (over the managed-code approach demonstrated later in this chapter) since it allows for the separation of an application's design (XAML) and logic (C#). The following steps show the XAML you need to add to `ApplicationBarSample` to construct a local Application Bar for the app:

1. If you haven't done so already, remove the global Application Bar from `MainPage.xaml` by removing the following XAML fragment: `ApplicationBar="{StaticResource GlobalAppMenuBar}"`. If you don't do that, you will get an application exception after you add a local Application Bar.

2. In Solution Explorer, right-click `MainPage.xaml` and select Open. This action causes Visual Studio 2010 to display the XAML code for the application's main page. Make sure you have removed the global Application Bar reference from `MainPage.xaml`, as mentioned at the end of the previous section.

3. You must define a `PhoneNavigation` element within XAML before adding a local Application Bar. To accomplish that, inside the `phone:PhoneApplicationPage`, add a `phone:PhoneApplicationPage.ApplicationBar` element. Notice how this element is automatically available for selection via Visual Studio 2010 IntelliSense once you start typing the first few characters—an excellent way to limit typing errors. In addition, Visual Studio 2010 provides a commented-out version of an Application Bar within `MainPage.xaml`. You can overwrite that commented-out portion with the following XAML code:

    ```
    <phone:PhoneApplicationPage.ApplicationBar>
    </phone:PhoneApplicationPage.ApplicationBar>
    ```

4. It is now time to add the Application Bar XAML to the page. Inside the `phone:PhoneApplicationPage.ApplicationBar` element, add a `shell:ApplicationBar` element. Set the `IsVisible` and the `IsMenuEnabled` properties to `True`, and set the `Opacity` property to 1, like so:

    ```
    <shell:ApplicationBar Opacity="1" IsVisible="True" IsMenuEnabled="True">
    </shell:ApplicationBar>
    ```

5. Now that you have defined an Application Bar in XAML, you are ready to create buttons for it. The buttons you add are a part of the `shell:ApplicationBar.Buttons` element, so go ahead and add that element now inside the `shell:ApplicationBar` element.

    ```
    <shell:ApplicationBar.Buttons>
    </shell:ApplicationBar.Buttons>
    ```

6. Inside the shell:ApplicationBar element, you will create three
    shell:ApplicationBarIconButton XAML elements to add three button
    definitions: one each for Add, Save, and Delete action. These buttons will show
    up with images, which you will define for each button. If you had any text-
    based menu items to add to the Application Bar, the ellipsis in the right corner
    of the Application Bar would be created automatically for you by Windows
    Phone. The ellipsis is not counted as one of the buttons on the Application Bar;
    therefore you can have a maximum of four buttons plus an ellipsis. The XAML
    markup to add three buttons is shown here:

```
<shell:ApplicationBarIconButton IconUri="/Images/appbar.add.rest.png" Text="add">↩
</shell:ApplicationBarIconButton>
<shell:ApplicationBarIconButton IconUri="/Images/appbar.save.rest.png" Text="save">
</shell:ApplicationBarIconButton>
<shell:ApplicationBarIconButton IconUri="/Images/appbar.delete.rest.png"↩
Text="delete">
</shell:ApplicationBarIconButton>
```

7. Note that the IconUri properties in this code snippet refer to the default names
    of the images that come as part of the Windows Phone tools installation. If you
    have changed default names of those images, make sure to edit the reference
    used in IconUri properly as well. Also note the Text element—it's a required
    element, and it can't be an empty string. This text will be visible if you click the
    ellipsis in the right corner of the Application Bar, as shown in Figure 7-3.

8. At this point, you are done creating icon, buttons and you should be sure to
    close the shell:ApplicationBar.Buttons element with a closing tag. Press F5 to
    view the results of your work—you should see the Application Bar containing
    three items at the bottom of the phone screen.

The full XAML for a local Application Bar is shown in Listing 7-1, together with text-based menu
items for the Application Bar, which you will be adding in the next section. Since menu items are text-
based, they are useful in cases where text would convey a clearer indication of the shortcut than an icon
in the Application Bar. Of course, if you need more than four items to be present in the Application Bar,
your only choice is to resort to menu items. In the next section, you will enhance an Application Bar with
menu items.

Adding Menu Items

Let's add two menu items, Menu Item 1 and Menu Item 2, to the ApplicationBarSample app.

1. All menu items are a part of the shell:ApplicationBar.MenuItems element, so
    add that element now inside the shell:ApplicationBar element:

```
<shell:ApplicationBar.MenuItems>
</shell:ApplicationBar.MenuItems>
```

2. Finally, you will define the menu items themselves by adding
    shell:ApplicationBarMenuItems inside the shell:ApplicationBar.MenuItems
    element:

```
<shell:ApplicationBarMenuItem Text="Menu Item 1" IsEnabled="True">
</shell:ApplicationBarMenuItem>
```

```
<shell:ApplicationBarMenuItem Text="Menu Item 2" IsEnabled="True">
</shell:ApplicationBarMenuItem>
```

If you run the application now, you will see an Application Bar displayed by the Windows Phone emulator. If you click the ellipsis to the right of the icons, the application bar slides up, revealing the two menu items. The close-up of the Application Bar and the menu items is shown in Figure 7-5. Try it for yourself by pressing F5 inside Visual Studio 2010.

Figure 7-5. A close-up of the Application Bar and the menu items

Let's talk briefly about the Opacity property of an Application Bar used in this example. Even though its values can range from 0 to 1, Microsoft recommends that developers use only three values for this property: 0, 0.5, and 1. If the Opacity is set to anything less than 1, the Application Bar will overlay the displayed page of an application. In other words, the contents of that page will extend to the area underneath the Application Bar, which is desirable in cases where you want to maximize the real estate on the phone screen and not have the Application Bar consume a sizeable portion of it. If Opacity is set to 1, however, the Application Bar will have a dedicated region at the bottom of the screen and will not overlay any portion of an application.

The full XAML markup for creating an Application Bar with three main icons and two menu items is shown in Listing 7-1.

Listing 7-1. XAML Code to Implement an Application Bar

```
<phone:PhoneApplicationPage.ApplicationBar>
<shell:ApplicationBar Opacity="1" IsVisible="True" IsMenuEnabled="True">
        <shell:ApplicationBar.Buttons>
            <shell:ApplicationBarIconButton IconUri="/Images/appbar.add.rest.png"↵
  Text="add">
            </shell:ApplicationBarIconButton>
            <shell:ApplicationBarIconButton IconUri="/Images/appbar.save.rest.png"↵
  Text="save">
            </shell:ApplicationBarIconButton>
            <shell:ApplicationBarIconButton IconUri="/Images/appbar.delete.rest.png"↵
  Text="delete">
            </shell:ApplicationBarIconButton>
        </shell:ApplicationBar.Buttons>
        <shell:ApplicationBar.MenuItems>
            <shell:ApplicationBarMenuItem Text="Menu Item 1" IsEnabled="True">
            </shell:ApplicationBarMenuItem>
            <shell:ApplicationBarMenuItem Text="Menu Item 2" IsEnabled="True">
```

```
        </shell:ApplicationBarMenuItem>
      </shell:ApplicationBar.MenuItems>
    </shell:ApplicationBar>
</phone:PhoneApplicationPage.ApplicationBar>
```

Adding an Application Bar via XAML is pretty straightforward thanks to the powerful and easy-to-use tools provided by Visual Studio 2010. Using XAML allows you to separate presentation from logic, which is a very good practice. We recommend that you use XAML wherever possible. Sometimes, however, XAML alone is not sufficient for the task. Luckily, it is perhaps even easier to work with the Application Bar from managed code, especially if you have some programming experience. The next section will show you how to do that.

Adding an Application Bar Using Managed Code

The second way to create an Application Bar for a Windows Phone application is to use one of the .NET languages. It is possible to create an Application Bar in both C# and Visual Basic .NET. The steps necessary to create an Application Bar using C# are described here. But first, be sure to remove all of the Application Bar XAML code you wrote for the previous demos.

1. You will be editing the MainPage code of your application. To accomplish this, locate the MainPage.xaml.cs file by expanding the MainPage.xaml file in Solution Explorer. Right-click MainPage.xaml.cs and select View Code.

2. For easier reference to an Application Bar component inside the Microsoft.Phone assembly (for example, to avoid having to type Microsoft.Phone.Shell.ApplicationBar before each component name), add the following using directive to the top of the MainPage.xaml.cs file:

    ```
    using Microsoft.Phone.Shell;
    ```

3. Inside the constructor for the page (that is, inside the public MainPage() code block), right after InitializeComponent(), initialize the Application Bar and set its IsVisible and IsMenuEnabled properties, as shown in the following code:

    ```
    ApplicationBar = new ApplicationBar();
    ApplicationBar.IsVisible = true;
    ApplicationBar.IsMenuEnabled = true;
    ```

4. Initialize the Application Bar buttons, providing the relative URI to the image that will be used for each button. Note that you must set the Text property of each button; otherwise your code will raise an exception.

    ```
    ApplicationBarIconButton btnAdd = new ApplicationBarIconButton(new
    Uri("/Images/appbar.add.rest.png", UriKind.Relative));
    btnAdd.Text = "add";
    ApplicationBarIconButton btnSave = new ApplicationBarIconButton(new
    Uri("/Images/appbar.save.rest.png", UriKind.Relative));
    btnSave.Text = "save";
    ApplicationBarIconButton btnDelete = new ApplicationBarIconButton(new
            Uri("/Images/appbar.delete.rest.png", UriKind.Relative));
    btnDelete.Text = "delete";
    ```

5. Add the buttons to the Application Bar via the following code:

```
ApplicationBar.Buttons.Add(btnAdd);
ApplicationBar.Buttons.Add(btnSave);
ApplicationBar.Buttons.Add(btnDelete);
```

6. Next you will create two menu items that will appear as text when the ellipsis button is clicked in the Application Bar. Very similar to adding icons, there are initialization and addition steps for each menu item. The initialization code for the menu items looks like this:

```
ApplicationBarMenuItem menuItem1 = new ApplicationBarMenuItem("Menu Item 1");
ApplicationBarMenuItem menuItem2 = new ApplicationBarMenuItem("Menu Item 2");
```

7. The strings Menu Item 1 and Menu Item 2 are the text for the two menu items; you will certainly change that text to something much more meaningful in your application.

8. Add menu items to the Application Bar:

```
ApplicationBar.MenuItems.Add(menuItem1);
ApplicationBar.MenuItems.Add(menuItem2);
```

9. Finally, you are ready to test the Application Bar. Save your work, and press F5 to start debugging the application using the Windows Phone emulator. You should see an Application Bar identical to the one shown in Figure 7-5. If you click the ellipsis to the right of the icons, the Application Bar slides up, revealing two menu items identical to the ones also shown in Figure 7-5.

The full code for adding the Application Bar using managed C# code is provided in Listing 7-2. Note that the full MainPage() constructor is included for readability purposes.

Listing 7-2. C# Code to Implement an Application Bar

```
public MainPage()
{
        InitializeComponent();
        SupportedOrientations = SupportedPageOrientation.Portrait |
        SupportedPageOrientation.Landscape;

        ApplicationBar = new ApplicationBar();
        ApplicationBar.IsVisible = true;
        ApplicationBar.IsMenuEnabled = true;
        ApplicationBarIconButton btnAdd = new ApplicationBarIconButton(new
                Uri("/Images/appbar.add.rest.png", UriKind.Relative));
        btnAdd.Text = "add";
        ApplicationBarIconButton btnSave = new ApplicationBarIconButton(new
                Uri("/Images/appbar.save.rest.png", UriKind.Relative));
        btnSave.Text = "save";
        ApplicationBarIconButton btnDelete = new ApplicationBarIconButton(new
                Uri("/Images/appbar.delete.rest.png", UriKind.Relative));
        btnDelete.Text = "delete";

        ApplicationBarMenuItem menuItem1 = new ApplicationBarMenuItem("Menu Item 1");
        ApplicationBarMenuItem menuItem2 = new ApplicationBarMenuItem("Menu Item 2");
```

```
ApplicationBar.Buttons.Add(btnAdd);
ApplicationBar.Buttons.Add(btnSave);
ApplicationBar.Buttons.Add(btnDelete);

ApplicationBar.MenuItems.Add(menuItem1);
ApplicationBar.MenuItems.Add(menuItem2);
```

}

While adding the Application Bar to Windows Phone is cool in itself, you can't do much with that Application Bar right now. You can push buttons a few hundred times, but nothing changes on the phone screen or inside the application. To make the buttons react to button press events, you need to write some managed code (C# in this case), also called the *event handler code*. In the next section, you'll learn how to write code that processes and reacts to the button press events.

Wiring Up Events to an Application Bar

There are two steps to writing code that reacts to Application Bar events:

1.   Writing a small snippet of *glue code* that links an Application Bar button or menu item click to the function that does all the processing (let's call this function the *worker function*)

2.   Writing a worker function that performs all the heavy lifting, such as rearranging UI elements on the screen, saving data, prompting the user for input, or anything else that the developer decides to do in response to the button or the menu item click event

Let's start with the Add button, which you'll wire up in the next section.

Adding Glue Code and a Worker Function to the Add Button

Visual Studio 2010 has made adding both glue code and a worker function virtually a two-keystroke procedure. Let's see how easy it is to create an event handler for the Add button on your Application Bar using a couple of Visual Studio 2010 shortcuts. This demo assumes that you have already created the Application Bar via managed code (not XAML) by following the steps in the "Adding an Application Bar Using Managed Code" section earlier in this chapter.

1.   Once again, you will be editing the code of the MainPage of your application. To accomplish this, locate the MainPage.xaml.cs file by expanding the MainPage.xaml file in Solution Explorer. Right-click MainPage.xaml.cs and select View Code.

2.   At the very end of the MainPage() constructor, type the following code:

```
btnAdd.Click+=
```

3.   Notice the appearance of a small pop-up window to the right of the = sign as you type it. You should see the following message:

```
new EventHandler(btnAdd_Click); (Press TAB to insert)
```

4. Press the Tab key and notice how a line of code is automatically added after the = sign. This one line of code is the glue code you need to tie together user interaction with the Add button.

```
btnAdd.Click+=new EventHandler(btnAdd_Click);
```

5. Now press the Tab key again, and Visual Studio 2010 will automatically create a skeleton for the worker function for you. This may not seem like a big deal at first, but it's usually a challenge to remember exactly what parameter types this worker function must have. This shortcut is just one example of how Visual Studio 2010 really enhances developer productivity.

The worker code that Visual Studio 2010 adds to your application looks like this:

```
void btnAdd_Click(object sender, EventArgs e)
{
        throw new NotImplementedException();
}
```

Now you're ready to add a bit of interactivity to your Application Bar, which you'll do in the next section.

■ **Tip** You are certainly not required to use the shortcut just described to generate event handler code for the Application Bar, or for any other event for that matter. You can write all of the previous code by hand, but be very careful to pass the proper parameter types and the proper number of parameters to your event handlers.

Reacting to Add Button Events

With a skeleton of a worker function in place for the Add button, let's expand it to accommodate a simplified real-world scenario. When a user clicks the Add button (the button with the + icon on the Application Bar), you will show a text box on the screen that is ready and waiting for user input. You will also add functionality to the Save button (the button with a floppy disk icon) that will display the thank-you message and hide the text box. Of course, in the real world, you would want to store the values entered by the user and react based on the user input in some fashion, but that is beyond the scope of this chapter.

Follow these steps to add interactivity to the Application Bar events:

1. Locate MainPage.xaml in Solution Explorer, and double-click that file to bring up XAML designer. Click View Other Windows Toolbox. You should see the XAML *designer* (not code) and a toolbox side by side, as shown in Figure 7-6.

■ **Tip** If you see the toolbox, Windows Phone design surface, and XAML *code* on the screen side by side, click the Collapse button (>> icon) in the area between the design surface and XAML view to hide the XAML code, as illustrated in Figure 7-6.

■ **Tip** If you do not see the XAML view, click the Expand button (<< icon) to bring that view back, as shown in Figure 7-7.

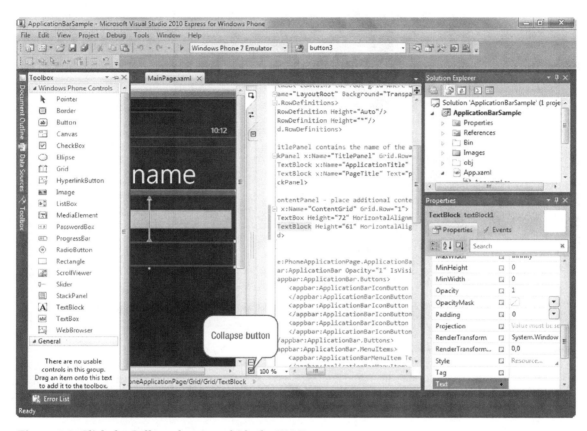

Figure 7-6. Click the Collapse button to hide the XAML.

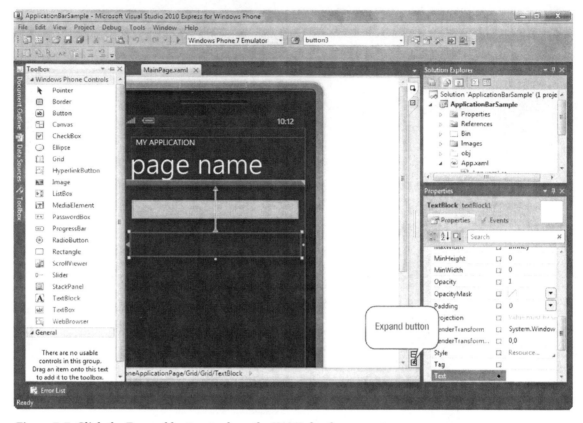

Figure 7-7. Click the Expand button to show the XAML for the current page.

    2.   From the toolbox, click and drag the text box to the Windows Phone design surface, as shown in Figure 7-8. Right-click the Text item, and select Properties to show the Properties window in the right corner of the screen.

    3.   Set the Text property to "blank," and set the Visibility property to Collapsed.

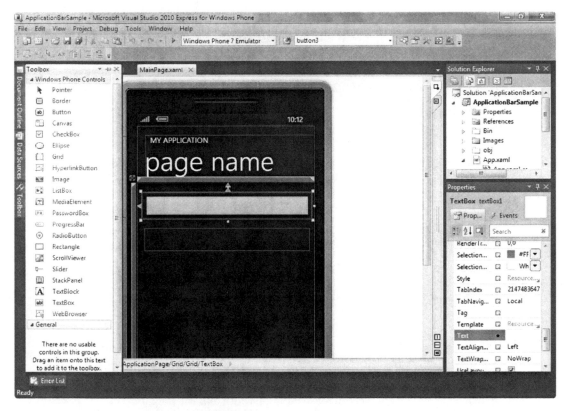

Figure 7-8. Adding a text box to the application

4. In the toolbox, click and drag the TextBlock to the Windows Phone design surface and place it right underneath the text box. Right-click the TextBlock, and select Properties to show the Properties window in the right corner of the screen.

5. Set the Text property to "Please enter your name," and set the Visibility property to Collapsed.

6. Now edit the worker function that was created for you by Visual Studio 2010 in the previous section. Right-click the MainPage.xaml.cs file, and select View Code. Remove the following line from the btnAdd_Click function:

```
throw new NotImplementedException();
```

7. Edit the btnAdd_Click function to match the following code:

```
void btnAdd_Click (object sender, EventArgs e)
{
    textBox1.Visibility = Visibility.Visible;
    textBlock1.Visibility = Visibility.Visible;
}
```

8. Press F5 to view the results of your work.

Now when you click the + icon on the Application Bar, the text box will be ready to accept user input.

Reacting to Save Button Events

Continuing the demo, let's now add an event handler to the Save button of the Application Bar. You'll write code so that, when the user clicks the Save button, the application will hide the text box and change the text of the textblock to thank the user for entering a name.

1. Locate MainPage.xaml in Solution Explorer, right-click, and select View Code. Add the following line of code to the MainPage() constructor code. Don't forget to use the Tab-Tab trick to let Visual Studio 2010 automatically generate skeleton code for you (as described in the previous section).

   ```
   btnSave.Click += new EventHandler(btnSave_Click);
   ```

2. Add the following code to the btnSave_Click function:

   ```
   void btnSave_Click(object sender, EventArgs e)
   {
       textBlock1.Text = "Thank you, "+ textBox1.Text;
       textBox1.Visibility = Visibility.Collapsed;
   }
   ```

3. Press F5 to see the results of your work. When you click the + icon, you will be prompted to enter your name. Once you enter your name and press the Save button on the Application Bar, the application will display a simple thank you message. If, for some reason, the full text of the message doesn't fit within the textblock you created, you can increase both the width and the height of the textblock by setting the TextWrapping property of the textblock to Wrap.

Now you're ready to enhance the Application Bar even further by writing code for your menu items to do some meaningful work.

Reacting to Menu Events

The code you write to react to menu click events is almost identical to the code for Application Bar button events, except that the glue code gets attached to the menu item instead of the Application Bar button. The block of code shown next displays a simple text message when the user clicks the first menu item on the Application Bar that you created previously. Note that only a portion of the MainPage() constructor is shown, since the rest of it remains unchanged from the prior demo.

```
    menuItem1.Click+=new EventHandler(menuItem1_Click);
}

void menuItem1_Click(object sender, EventArgs e)
{
    textBlock1.Visibility = Visibility.Visible;
    textBlock1.Text = "You just clicked on Menu Item 1";
}
```

Press F5 to run the application now. You should see an Application Bar with an ellipsis in the right corner. If you click the ellipsis, two menu items become visible. Once clicked, the text on the phone screen changes to reflect the name of the menu item clicked.

In a real application, you will certainly want to do something more meaningful than what you did here. For instance, you may have Help and About menu items. You could program a Web Browser control (discussed in the next chapter) to display a set of application help files if the user clicks Help. If the About menu item is clicked, you could use the Web Browser control to show your company's web page or some basic information on how to get in touch with you.

One final thing you need to examine before leaving this chapter is how to use XAML to link event handling code to XAML elements.

Adding Event Handlers with XAML

It is also possible, and in fact preferable, to write the necessary code that attaches (or glues) a certain event to managed code in XAML. In other words, using this approach, you would define an Application Bar in XAML following the guidelines in the section on creating an Application Bar with XAML, but you would write managed C# code to react to events when the user presses Application Bar buttons. For code readability and understandability purposes, this approach may be preferable to the purely managed-code approach (where you define an Application Bar from managed code) already discussed. Imagine that you are trying to maintain an application that someone else wrote. It would be easier for you to understand and trace application behavior by starting with the XAML design elements and following their glue code into the event handlers. The steps you follow to wire up events in XAML are straightforward, as illustrated here:

1. Locate MainPage.xaml in Solution Explorer, and double-click that file to bring up the XAML designer.

2. If only the Windows Phone design surface is shown and no XAML *code* is visible, click the Expand (<<) button in the lower-right portion of the screen, as shown previously in Figure 7-7.

3. Paste the following XAML code into MainPage.xaml (it's identical to the XAML code from the "Adding a Local Application Bar Using XAML" section of this chapter):

```xaml
<phone:PhoneApplicationPage.ApplicationBar>
    <shell:ApplicationBar IsVisible="True" IsMenuEnabled="True">
        <shell:ApplicationBar.Buttons>
            <shell:ApplicationBarIconButton IconUri="/Images/appbar.add.rest.png"↵
Text="add">
            </shell:ApplicationBarIconButton>
            <shell:ApplicationBarIconButton IconUri="/Images/appbar.save.rest.png"↵
Text="save">
            </shell:ApplicationBarIconButton>
            <shell:ApplicationBarIconButton IconUri="/Images/appbar.delete.rest↵
.png" Text="delete">
            </shell:ApplicationBarIconButton>
        </shell:ApplicationBar.Buttons>
        <shell:ApplicationBar.MenuItems>
            <shell:ApplicationBarMenuItem Text="Menu Item 1" IsEnabled="True">
            </shell:ApplicationBarMenuItem>
            <shell:ApplicationBarMenuItem Text="Menu Item 2" IsEnabled="True">
```

```
            </shell:ApplicationBarMenuItem>
          </shell:ApplicationBar.MenuItems>
        </shell:ApplicationBar>
    </phone:PhoneApplicationPage.ApplicationBar>
```

4. Locate the `<shell:ApplicationBarIconButton IconUri="/Images/appbar.add.rest.png" Text="add">` statement in XAML and add `Click="` to the end of that statement, so that it resembles the code here:

```
<shell:ApplicationBarIconButton IconUri="/Images/appbar.add.rest.png" Text="add"↵
    Click="">
```

Note how Visual Studio 2010 automatically shows a choice to create a new event handler right after you type the first double-quote character. If you press the Tab key now, the skeleton code for the worker function will be automatically inserted into the `MainPage.xaml.cs` file, and it will have a default name of `ApplicationBarMenuItem_Click`. To add functionality to the Application Bar button click event, open `MainPage.xaml.cs` (by right-clicking the `MainPage.xaml` file and selecting View Code), and edit that function in a similar way to what you did in the preceding "Reacting to Save Button Events" and "Reacting to Menu Events" sections.

There is also another way to glue XAML code with code-behind by using an `ApplicationBar` class, as you will see in the next section.

Using the ApplicationBar Class to Glue XAML and Managed Code

At this point, you have all the knowledge necessary to create Application Bars for your projects. There might be an occasion, however, when an Application Bar has been created in XAML, but you would like to access its elements programmatically from managed code. Once you create an Application Bar in XAML, you can use the `ApplicationBar` class and its `Buttons` and `MenuItems` properties to glue managed code to defined XAML elements within that Application Bar. The `Buttons` property provides access to all the buttons created for the application bar, in the order that they were added to the Application Bar. For example, the following code references the Add, Save, and Delete buttons created in the previous section and then programmatically disables the Delete button. Notice that, since the Add button was added first in your XAML code, it has an index of 0; and the Delete button, which was added third, has an index of 2 within the `Buttons` list.

```
        ApplicationBarIconButton btnAdd = ApplicationBar.Buttons[0] as↵
ApplicationBarIconButton;
        ApplicationBarIconButton btnSave = ApplicationBar.Buttons[1] as↵
ApplicationBarIconButton;
        ApplicationBarIconButton btnDelete = ApplicationBar.Buttons[2] as↵
ApplicationBarIconButton;

        btnDelete.IsEnabled = false;
```

Obtaining programmatic references to Application Bar buttons from code may be desirable when you want to manipulate certain properties of the buttons, such as their enabled/disabled state, in response to some event triggered by the user. As you can see, you can easily obtain those references using properties of the `ApplicationBar` class.

Summary

In this chapter, you learned how to add an Application Bar with buttons and menu items to your Windows Phone application using either XAML or managed (C#) code. You also learned basic guidelines for Application Bar development and wrote code to react to Application Bar button and menu item events. The presence of an Application Bar is certainly expected for any mobile application today, and Visual Studio 2010 has made the process of adding one easy and straightforward.

In the next chapter, you will learn about the Web Browser control on Windows Phone. The Web Browser control helps you provide professional-looking application help files and aids in navigating the Internet. In addition, the Web Browser control has been enhanced for the Windows Phone 7.5 release—it now supports HTML5 via Internet Explorer 9. You will be taking a look at the power of HTML5 in the next chapter. Finally, you will also learn how to generate HTML content dynamically and show it in a web browser.

CHAPTER 8

The WebBrowser Control

It felt like false advertising when, just ten short years ago, cellular phone companies began to promote Internet access as a feature of their devices. As customers quickly learned when they tried to get online that their phones could only display web pages properly if they were written in Wireless Markup Language (WML) and not the traditional HyperText Markup Language (HTML) used in the vast majority of web sites. Very few sites could afford to build and maintain code in two separate languages, and as a result, web browsing on mobile phones did not take off until relatively recently.

We live in much more progressive times now. The first release of the Windows Phone OS shipped with Internet Explorer 7 installed, which meant that any content that could be viewed in the desktop version of Internet Explorer 7 could also be viewed on the phone. A lot has changed in just over a year since that first release of Windows Phone devices. Windows Phone 7.5 comes with Internet Explorer 9 preinstalled. With Internet Explorer 9, you can construct very rich UIs within the browser with the help of HTML5. The Windows Phone SDK includes a WebBrowser control that you can use to embed one or more instances of a small but fully capable browser inside your applications.

In this chapter, you'll learn how and when to use the WebBrowser control. You will also become familiar with a few HTML5 concepts to help you appreciate the full potential of this promising standard. But first, let's look at three common scenarios where you would want to use the WebBrowser control.

Note The WebBrowser control in Windows Phone is very similar to the WebBrowser control you would use if you were creating a full-blown Silverlight application (not the phone version of it)—with few notable differences. Certain features, such as the ability to download and install ActiveX controls, have been disabled to prevent security risks originating from such components. Other differences, such as the ability to access local storage and the absence of cross-domain restrictions in the Windows Phone WebBrowser control, allow for more flexible browser behavior on Windows Phone as compared to Silverlight.

Introducing the WebBrowser Control

The most obvious reason to use the WebBrowser control is to display web content within the page of a Windows Phone application. For instance, if you're developing an application that shows Twitter feeds on a portion of the screen, the easiest way to do this would be to create a WebBrowser control in the application and navigate to a given Twitter page from within that control.

Another reason to use the WebBrowser control is to show HTML-formatted content that resides locally on a Windows Phone device. For example, if you decide to include help files with your application, the easiest way to create those files would be in the form of HTML web pages. Then you could load those web pages in Windows Phone and display them in the WebBrowser control.

Finally, you can use the WebBrowser control to show content that a Windows Phone application generates on the fly. That means that you can compose an HTML page dynamically in code and display it, without first writing that web page out to disk. This is certainly a handy feature that avoids the intermediate steps of first writing an HTML file to local storage and then reading it. This feature is important when the HTML pages you want to show the user are context sensitive. For example, if you are developing an application that tracks basketball teams and you want to provide links to information about each individual player on a team, you will want to build your list of players based on the name of the team the user selects. Dynamic content generation allows you to do just that.

This chapter consists of two parts. In the first part of this chapter, you'll learn how to use the capabilities of the WebBrowser control in your application by building a simple car browser that searches the Web for photos of popular car models and displays them. In the second part of this chapter, you will get a brief introduction to HTML5, since it is becoming an increasingly more popular platform for building applications both for the Web and mobile devices. HTML5 support on the Windows Phone platform is pretty big news, and in this chapter you will discover the reasons for this.

To get started experimenting with the WebBrowser control, you must first create a main page and add some UI elements, including a WebBrowser control to display web and HTML content, as illustrated in the next section.

Adding a WebBrowser Control

Before you can use the WebBrowser control to browse for the images of cars online, you need to add this control to your application. Follow these steps to place the WebBrowser control inside your application:

1. Create a new Windows Phone application project. Launch Visual Studio 2010 Express, and select the Windows Phone Application template. Then change the project name to WebBrowserSample and click OK. Visual Studio will set up a new project.

2. From the View menu select Other Windows ➤ Toolbox (alternately, you can click the toolbox icon on the Visual Studio application bar) to show the toolbox with the list of controls available for use.

3. From the toolbox window on the left, select the WebBrowser control, click it, and drag it onto the Windows Phone design surface, as shown in Figure 8-1.

4. Position and resize the control as needed. In Figure 8-1, the WebBrowser control is positioned to take the upper third of the phone screen.

5. Finally, change the name of the application from My Application to My Car Browser, and change the name of the page to Car Explorer. You can do that by double-clicking MainPage.xaml and editing the ApplicationTitle and PageTitle elements accordingly.

■ **Note** You can set the Height and the Width properties to Auto. (This is the default when the control is first dropped on the Windows Phone design surface and is not resized.) You can also set the HorizontalAlignment and VerticalAlignment properties to Stretch. All these settings combined will allow the browser window to expand as much as possible on the phone without covering other visible elements on the phone screen.

With the WebBrowser control in place, you are now ready to look at how to use this control for each of the scenarios previously described.

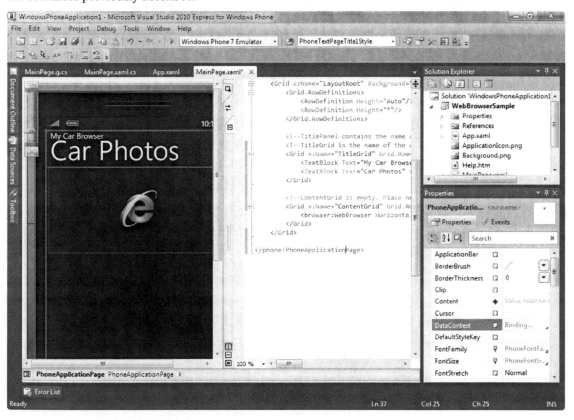

Figure 8-1. To add the WebBrowser control to the application, drag it from the toolbox and drop it onto MainPage.xaml on the Windows Phone design surface.

Using a WebBrowser Control to Display Web Content

In the first of the WebBrowser demos, you will use this control to display the contents of the web site. You will show a list of photos of one of the fastest street cars in the world—the Lamborghini Gallardo.

1. With the WebBrowser control in place, it's time to add code to initialize its content when it loads. First, right-click MainPage.xaml in Solution Explorer and select View Code (or go directly to the MainPage.xaml.cs file).

2. Whenever the My Car Browser application loads the WebBrowser control, it fires off a Loaded event. By creating a Loaded event handler, you can write code to display a web page with car photos. Add the following code to the MainPage() constructor to create the handler:

```
webBrowser1.Loaded += new RoutedEventHandler(webBrowser1_Loaded);
```

   Note how the same Visual Studio shortcuts you used for the Application Bar code in the previous chapter apply here as well; namely, right after you type +=, Visual Studio hints that, if you press the Tab key twice, it will create all of the necessary code stubs you need for a handler.

3. Next, let's code the event handler. To the webBrowser1_Loaded() function, add the following code, which will navigate to Microsoft Bing's image search page and pass the phrase "cars Lamborghini Gallardo" to it.

```
webBrowser1.Navigate(new
Uri("http://www.bing.com/images/search?q=cars+Lamborghini+Gallardo"",
UriKind.Absolute));
```

   This code creates a new Uri object and specifies that the Uri is not local to your application (that would be UriKind.Relative), but rather a location on the Internet (UriKind.Absolute).

Press F5 to debug your application and see the results so far. You should now see Lamborghini photos, courtesy of the Microsoft Bing engine. You can easily extend this example to respond to user input. For example, you could use the Bing image search to show photos of any car whose name a user enters. Here's how:

1. Add a text box to the page so that the user can change the name of the car for which Bing searches. To do that, go to MainPage.xaml and display the page in the designer (either by double-clicking MainPage.xaml or by right-clicking MainPage.xaml and selecting View Designer). If the toolbox is not visible, select Other Windows ➤ Toolbox from the View menu, or click the toolbox icon on the Visual Studio application bar. Click and drag the TextBox from the toolbox, and position it below the WebBrowser control. Next, click and drag the Button and position it next to the text box.

2. Right-click the text box and select Properties. Delete everything from the Text property. Next, right-click the button and change the value of its Content property to Show It!. The end result should resemble Figure 8-2.

Figure 8-2. Adding a text box and a button to interact with the WebBrowser control

3. It's time to add some interactivity to your application. With MainPage.xaml still open in design view, double-click the button. Notice how the method button1_Click opens by default when you do that, ready for your code. Place the following code in the body of that method:

```
webBrowser1.Navigate(new Uri ("http://www.bing.com/images/search?q=cars " +
                        textBox1.Text, UriKind.Absolute));
```

4. Press F5 to run the application. Initially, you should see the photos of the Lamborghini Gallardo added in the first part of this demo. Go ahead and type **Ford Mustang** in the text box, and click the Show It! button. In the WebBrowser control, you should now see a set of photos of this great American muscle car.

But there's more. You can also use a WebBrowser control to display HTML files—and even strings—that have been stored locally. You'll use that capability to add help functionality to the Car Browser application in the next section.

Using a WebBrowser Control to Display Local HTML Content

Frequently, you will want to include documentation with your application to advertise its features to users and answer their most common questions. Because of its simplicity and ubiquity (it's everywhere!), HTML, the same language used to create web pages, has become the default format for such documentation. In this section, you'll create a simple HTML page describing how to work with the car photo application that you created in the previous section. Follow these steps to create and show HTML content on a Windows Phone device:

1. Because adding an HTML file is currently not an option in Visual Studio Express for Windows Phone, you will need to add a new XML file to the project. XML files support automated syntax verification features, making it harder for you to make accidental mistakes than if you were creating a plain text file. Right-click the WebBrowserSample project in Solution Explorer and select Add ➤ New Item. Then select XML File from the list of available item types.

2. Type the following in the newly created file (you can also copy and paste this code from the files available for download for this chapter):

```
<html>
<title>Web Browser Help File</title>
  <body>
    <h1>Welcome to the Windows Phone Car Browser Application!
      To view the car photos, type the name of the car in the textbox and press "Show
    It!"
    <br/><br/>For example, "Ford Mustang"</h1>
  </body>
</html>
```

3. Save the file by clicking the Save button in Visual Studio. Next, right-click XMLFile1.xml in Solution Explorer and click Rename. Change the name of that file to Help.htm, and make sure that the Build action for that file is set to Content by right-clicking and selecting Properties to bring up the Properties window.

4. Now you will need to copy the Help.htm file to the storage on the Windows Phone device or the emulator. Here's why: while you would expect the Help.htm file to be available automatically to the application running inside the Windows Phone emulator since it's a part of your project, it isn't. Project files that do not become executable code need to be copied over to the local storage on the phone or the emulator before they are available for manipulation. Hence, Help.htm file created in the previous step needs to be available to your application inside the Windows Phone Isolated Storage, which you can think of as disk space reserved for use by your application on Windows Phone. There is a whole chapter (Chapter 13) dedicated to the subject of Isolated Storage. For your purposes here, however, it will be sufficient to copy Help.htm to an Isolated Storage location upon application load, and then retrieve it from there for display by the WebBrowser control. To accomplish that, simply add the following using directives to the top of the code page and then copy the SaveHelpFileToIsoStore method into your code, as shown in Listing 8-1:

```
using System.IO.IsolatedStorage;
using System.Windows.Resources;
using System.IO;
```

Listing 8-1. SaveHelpFileToIsoStore Method

```
private void SaveHelpFileToIsoStore()
    {
        string strFileName = "Help.htm";
        IsolatedStorageFile isoStore =
                        IsolatedStorageFile.GetUserStoreForApplication();

        //remove the file if it exists to allow each run to independently write to
        // the Isolated Storage
        if (isoStore.FileExists(strFileName) == true)
        {
            isoStore.DeleteFile(strFileName);
        }
        StreamResourceInfo sr = Application.GetResourceStream(new Uri(strFileName,
                        UriKind.Relative));
        using (BinaryReader br = new BinaryReader(sr.Stream))
        {
            byte[] data = br.ReadBytes((int)sr.Stream.Length);
            //save file to Isolated Storage
            using (BinaryWriter bw = new
                        BinaryWriter(isoStore.CreateFile(strFileName)))
            {
                bw.Write(data);
                bw.Close();
            }
        }
    }
```

5. Finally, you will invoke the SaveHelpFileToIsoStore method to save and then display the contents of Help.htm by navigating to it inside the web browser when the browser first loads. Add the call to SaveHelpFileToIsoStore in the WebBrowser1_Loaded method, and set the WebBrowser URL to navigate to the Help.htm file, as shown following. Note that the Uri object is of Relative type, which indicates that you are loading content from the local storage as opposed to the Internet.

```
void webBrowser1_Loaded(object sender, RoutedEventArgs e)
{
    SaveHelpFileToIsoStore();
    webBrowser1.Navigate(new Uri("Help.htm", UriKind.Relative));
}
```

6. Press F5 to run the application. You should see the HTML help page displayed inside the WebBrowser control.

In your application, you can use the technique shown previously to provide documentation or help files, as well as contact information about your company. Sometimes, however, all you want to show is a short, nicely formatted HTML message, and it's somewhat tedious to write and include all the code to save HTML files to Isolated Storage and such, as shown in the previous section. Fortunately, the WebBrowser control has a solution for scenarios like this. In the next section, you will learn how to bypass Isolated Storage and show HTML generated directly by code.

Using a WebBrowser Control to Display Dynamic Content

Suppose a user enters "Ford" in the text box of your photo-browsing application. Unless you query the user, you won't know whether the user meant to search for "Ford Mustang" or "Ford F-150." One way to find out would be to create a page with HTML markup and display it to the user, asking for more information. You could then save the generated file to Isolated Storage and load it using the technique described in the previous section. But that would certainly be a cumbersome approach for such a simple task. Luckily, there's a much easier way to show a dynamically generated HTML page, using the NavigateToString method of the WebBrowser control. This method takes a single argument—a string—that contains the complete HTML code needed to display the page in the WebBrowser control. The next demo shows just how easy it is to use this method.

1. Bring up the MainPage.xaml.cs file in the code editor, either by double-clicking it or clicking the MainPage.xaml file in Solution Explorer and choosing View Code.

2. Next you will construct the HTML code to display to the user. Make the button1_Click method look identical to the following code. Notice how NavigateToString loads up what amounts to a basic HTML page directly into the WebBrowser control, without you having to save this HTML to Isolated Storage. Also note that building an HTML string in code becomes a bit ugly very quickly, so NavigateToString should not be abused for large HTML messages or files. If you do face the possibility of constructing large chunks of HTML for use with the NavigateToString method, you may want to consider using the StringBuilder class, which will allow you to construct HTML in a stepwise manner.

```
if (textBox1.Text.ToLower() == "ford")
{
    webBrowser1.NavigateToString(@"<html><head><meta name='viewport'
      content='width=900, user-scalable=yes' /></head><body><center><div
      style='font: Arial 12px;'>
      Which Ford model would you like to see?<br><br>
      <a href='http://www.bing.com/images/search?q=cars+Ford+Mustang'>Ford
      Mustang</a> or <a
      href='http://www.bing.com/images/search?q=cars+Ford+F150'>Ford F-
      150</a></style></center></body></html>");
}
else
{
    webBrowser1.Navigate(new Uri("http://www.bing.com/images/search?q=cars " +
                            textBox1.Text, UriKind.Absolute));
}
```

3. Press F5 to run the application. If you type **Ford** in the text box and click the Show It! button, you should see a dynamically generated HTML message with

hyperlinks asking you to clarify which Ford model you would like to see, just like in Figure 8-3.

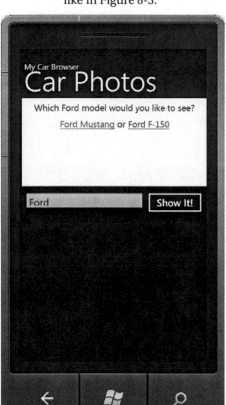

Figure 8-3. Displaying dynamically generated HMTL content

Many web-based applications have been built, from translators to elaborate e-commerce systems, and all of them are easily accessible and could even be enhanced with the use of the WebBrowser control on Windows Phone. But the WebBrowser control can do even more. In the next section, you will learn how to save the web pages locally so that, potentially, you can parse certain information or search within the pages.

Saving Web Pages Locally

You can also save the contents of web sites and web pages to Windows Phone as strings of HTML code using Isolated Storage and the SaveToString method of the WebBrowser control. This approach only saves the HTML on a page (of course, you probably already guessed that from the name of the method!) and

ignores its images and CSS files. After saving the HTML to Isolated Storage, you can load it on demand. Before doing that, however, make sure to read the security considerations at the end of this chapter.
This demo will show you how to save an HTML web page locally and then load it at a later time.

1. Open the WebBrowserSample project, and bring up MainPage.xaml in the design window.

2. Add two buttons to the Windows Phone design surface, as shown in Figure 8-4. Change the Content property of the top button to "Save to local storage." Change the Content property of the bottom button to "Load saved content."

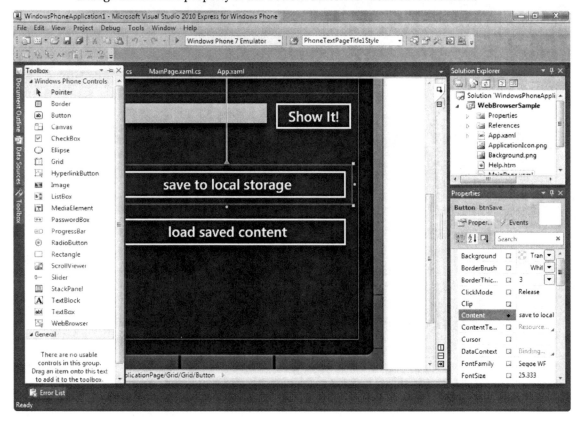

Figure 8-4. Adding the buttons to persist web content to Isolated Storage

3. Make sure to change the names of both buttons, as shown in Figure 8-4. You can change the name in the Properties window by clicking next to the Button text at the very top of the Properties window. Name the top button btnSave, and name the bottom button btnLoad.

4. Next, write the event handler code for the Save button click. Double-click the top button to bring up MainPage.xaml.cs in code view. Change the btnSave_Click method as follows:

```
private void btnSave_Click(object sender, RoutedEventArgs e)
{
    string strWebContent = webBrowser1.SaveToString();
    SaveStringToIsoStore(strWebContent);
}
```

5. Next is the event handler code to load the previously saved web page. Double-click the bottom button, and make the btnLoad_Click method look like the code block here:

```
private void btnLoad_Click(object sender, RoutedEventArgs e)
{
    webBrowser1.Navigate(new Uri("web.htm", UriKind.Relative));
}
```

6. You need to add the implementation of the SaveStringToIsoStore method, which will perform the actual save of the HTML string to a file in the local storage. The following code accomplishes just that:

```
private void SaveStringToIsoStore(string strWebContent)
{
    IsolatedStorageFile isoStore =
                        IsolatedStorageFile.GetUserStoreForApplication();

    //remove the file if it exists to allow each run to independently write to
    // the Isolated Storage
    if (isoStore.FileExists("web.htm") == true)
    {
        isoStore.DeleteFile("web.htm");
    }
    StreamResourceInfo sr = new StreamResourceInfo(new
MemoryStream(System.Text.Encoding.UTF8.GetBytes(strWebContent)), "html/text");

    using (BinaryReader br = new BinaryReader(sr.Stream))
    {
        byte[] data = br.ReadBytes((int)sr.Stream.Length);
        //save file to Isolated Storage
        using (BinaryWriter bw = new
                        BinaryWriter(isoStore.CreateFile("web.htm")))
        {
            bw.Write(data);
            bw.Close();
        }
    }
}
```

7. Make sure the button1_Click event looks identical to the one here:

```
private void button1_Click(object sender, RoutedEventArgs e)
{
    webBrowser1.Navigate(new Uri
    ("http://www.bing.com/images/search?q=cars " + textBox1.Text,UriKind.Absolute));
}
```

8. You are now ready to test the application. Press F5 to run it, type **Ford Mustang** in the text box, and click the Show It! button. Photos of the Ford Mustang should appear in the browser window. Next, click the Save Content to Isolated Storage button. Then erase the word *Mustang* from the text box, leaving only *Ford*, and click the Show It! button. A friendly reminder that you need to provide more information pops up. Finally, click Load Saved Content to show the (distorted) thumbnails of the Ford Mustang.

The content is distorted because only the HTML of the web page is saved. Many CSS style sheets that control the positioning of elements and their look are not persisted as part of the SaveToString method. Images may be missing as well, since the paths to those images may also no longer be valid.

Choosing Display and Security Settings

In quite a few cases, the web pages look the same in both the desktop version of Internet Explorer and the Windows Phone Internet Explorer Mobile browser, on which the WebBrowser control is based. There are many cases, however, where special considerations apply to the WebBrowser control running on Windows Phone. The next few sections will go over those special cases.

Viewport

In Internet Explorer Mobile, the viewport is a rectangular region that controls where text will wrap on a page. At the time of this writing, only three properties are supported for the viewport: height, width, and user-scalable. The height and width properties control the height and the width of the viewport accordingly, with values ranging between 480 and 10,000 for the height and between 320 and 10,000 for the width. The user-scalable property controls whether a user can zoom in and out within the content of the viewport. (Basically, this setting controls whether a user can zoom into the content shown inside the WebBrowser control.) This property has two possible values: yes and no. The default (and recommended) setting for this property is yes. You set the properties of the viewport inside the meta tag, as shown in the example in the next section.

CSS

There is also an Internet Explorer Mobile–specific CSS property, -ms-text-size-adjust, that controls the size of the text displayed on the screen. When the browser tries to determine the most readable format for given content within the Internet Explorer viewport, the content is zoomed in, and if text is present, the text size is adjusted according to the setting of this property. If this CSS property is set to auto for a given element, Windows Phone tries to determine the text size that will be most readable on a given screen. If that property is set to none, Windows Phone does not make any adjustments to text. There is also a third option for this property: a numeric percentage value, which will scale the text from its original size according to the percentage specified. Just like any other CSS property, -ms-text-size-adjust can be set for the whole page or any portion of the page. Let's take a look at an example that will help you visualize this property:

1. Refer to the Help.htm file you created for showing static HTML content in the WebBrowser control. Edit that file to make it look like the following HTML block.

In essence, you are simply adding a CSS <div> element and introducing -ms-text-size-adjust around one of the elements:

```html
<html>
  <head>
    <title>Web Browser Help File</title>
  </head>
  <body>
    <h1>Welcome to the Windows Phone Car Browser Application!
    To view car photos, type the name of the car in the textbox and press "Show It!"
      <br/><br/>For example, <div style= "-ms-text-size-adjust:450%">"Ford
      Mustang"</div>
    </h1>
  </body>
</html>
```

2. Press F5 to run the application. You should see the text "Ford Mustang" 250 percent larger than the rest of the text on the page (although the rest of the text content may be scaled as well to adjust to the current viewport).

Security

With phones constantly becoming "smarter and smarter," there's always the danger of mobile applications behaving badly, whether unintentionally or not. To help protect phone users from the most common types of security problems plaguing desktop computers connected to the Internet, Microsoft introduced a set of security rules for loading web content onto the phone. All Windows Phone applications must observe these rules if they are to run on Windows Phone devices.

As Windows Phone developers, we must be aware of these security restrictions to ensure the smoothest possible performance of our applications. The following list summarizes items that are either disabled or just different in the Internet Explorer Mobile version compared to its desktop counterpart:

1. Script is disabled by default in the WebBrowser control. To enable it, the developer must explicitly set the IsScriptEnabled property of the control. This setting becomes extremely important for HTML5 content, since a lot of manipulation in HTML5 is performed using JavaScript.

2. Internet Explorer Mobile does not allow users to download and install third-party plug-ins, such as ActiveX controls and Adobe Flash plug-ins. Sites that rely on such plug-ins for their functionality will not work properly on Windows Phone.

3. Within the WebBrowser control, users cannot navigate from https:// (secure) to http:// (insecure) Internet locations.

4. Applications cannot share cookies with Internet Explorer Mobile.

Table 8-1 summarizes the differences between Internet Explorer Mobile and its desktop counterpart.

Table 8-1. Internet Explorer Mobile vs. Internet Explorer Desktop

Feature	Internet Explorer Mobile	Internet Explorer Desktop
Script execution (JavaScript)	Disabled by default; set IsScriptEnabled property explicitly	Enabled by default
Downloading and installing plug-ins (ActiveX, Flash, etc.)	Not allowed	Allowed
Navigating from https:// (secure) to http:// (unsecure) Internet locations	Not allowed	Allowed
Sharing cookies between applications	Not allowed	Allowed

In addition to the differences listed in the table, there are special cross-site considerations applicable just to the WebBrowser control. When a web page loads into the Windows Phone WebBrowser control from the network location (for instance, from the Internet), it is prohibited from making Web service calls into a domain other than the one from which it has been loaded. This is done to prevent unauthorized access to sensitive information without a user's knowledge. This behavior is identical to the behavior of a standard Silverlight application restricted to Web service calls into its own domain unless a special crossdomain.xml file is present at the root of another domain, allowing remote calls.

However, on Windows Phone, content loaded from Isolated Storage or via the NavigateToString method is not subject to cross-domain restrictions. This also includes content previously loaded from the network location and saved to Isolated Storage via the SaveToString method, as you have seen in this chapter.

■ **Note** It is extremely important to consider the possible implications of relaxed cross-domain consequences of saving web pages into the local storage and then reloading them.

A Brief Introduction to HTML5 Features

Windows Phone 7.5 is a huge leap forward. One of the biggest new features of this release is the inclusion of the Internet Explorer 9 web browser. Internet Explorer 9 offers support for HTML5, which implies cross-platform mobile application development with all the major players in the mobile space supporting the HTML5 standard. But what is HTML5, and what makes it the development platform of tomorrow? In this section, you will take a brief look at some of the features of HTML5 that make this environment appealing for a large spectrum of mobile applications.

HTML5 Features

HTML5 is much more than just a new markup language. Although the exact definitions of HTML5 vary, the best way to think about it, in our opinion, is as a set of features that will make the web applications of tomorrow more local, more interactive, and easier to build. The way HTML5 accomplishes this is through a multitude of features, some of which are discussed following. It is beyond the scope of this book to provide a comprehensive overview of all HTML5 features. We recommend reading the excellent book *HTML5 Solutions* by Marco Casario (Apress, 2011). Meanwhile, the HTML5 standard continues to evolve.

New Form Fields with HTML5

All web developer, from beginners all the way to professionals, have built some form of user input validation of basic web forms. For example, if you prompt users to enter their e-mail address, you must then validate that the address is indeed valid; if you collect date information, you must verify that the input indeed contains a date value; and so on. Even though there are libraries (such as jQuery) and ASP.NET controls (Validators) that help you with the validation task, HTML5 simplifies such validation by introducing new input types, such as email or date. For example, the following input type, <input type="date">, will automatically validate the input to be formatted as a date and even show a drop-down calendar if the browser-specific implementation supports it. (Some browsers display the calendar while others present spinner controls for date values.)

```
<input type="date" id="DateOfBirth" />
```

It's important to note that new input types are not supported in Internet Explorer 9. Support for this new HTML5 feature, however, has been added to the next version of Internet Explorer, Internet Explorer 10, and it should be available on Windows Phone devices shortly.

Geolocation

Perhaps the most exciting HTML5 feature for Windows Phone and other mobile developers is support for tracking a user's current location using HTML5. This support is enabled via the geolocation object and its methods, including geolocation.getCurrentPosition(), which retrieves the current geographical position (latitude and longitude) of the user. You will observe the use of the geolocation object in the next section.

Media Playback

HTML5 makes both video and audio playback extremely simple with the new <audio> and <video> tags. A set of controls for performing media playback is automatically available within the browser. A nice bonus for Windows Phone developers is that video playback of HTML5 video elements is automatically performed in full-screen mode on Windows Phone. A full set of controls for playing video is also automatically available. A word of caution is appropriate here, however—there are currently no audio or video formats that are supported across all platforms. For instance, the H.264 video standard is supported by the Internet Explorer 9 and Safari browsers; however, Firefox and Chrome are not supporting this format. If you are going to be relying on these new media elements inside your web pages and/or applications, it would be prudent to see if your target demographic will be able to play back your video or audio files.

Canvas

The new HTML5 <canvas> element allows you to draw on a web page just like you would on a surface inside any graphics editor, such as Paint.NET or Photoshop. At the moment, with HTML5 tooling being in its infancy, this drawing has to happen by explicitly specifying what, where, and how you want the objects to be drawn. You will see an example of drawing on a canvas in the next section. In addition to drawing objects on a canvas, it is possible to animate those objects by continuously redrawing the canvas at a given frames-per-second rate and thus create the movements of those objects through the canvas.

SVG

Scalable Vector Graphics (SVG) is the standard way of encoding two-dimensional graphics and animations using XML files. Within those files, a set of tags controls what and where graphics will be drawn. Internet Explorer 9 supports SVG graphics.

The list of HTML5 features just described is far from a comprehensive treatment of HTML5. This list should, however, give you a good idea of how extensive and far-reaching the implications of this new standard are.

Testing HTML5 Features on Windows Phone

To get a feel for working with HTML5 elements on a mobile device, you will use the NavigateToString method we covered previously in this chapter. In this section, you will first use this method to get the current geographical position of the device. Next, you will use the <audio> element to control the playback of an MP3 file from the Internet. Finally, you will draw a red circle on a canvas. To get started, create a new project in Visual Studio Express for Windows Phone and change the MainPage() constructor inside the MainPage.xaml.cs to look like this:

```
public MainPage()
{
    InitializeComponent();
    webBrowser1.IsScriptEnabled = true;
    webBrowser1.IsGeolocationEnabled = true;

    webBrowser1.Loaded += webBrowser1_Loaded;
}
```

Notice how you set the IsScriptEnabled property of the WebBrowser control to true. Recall from our discussion on WebBrowser control security that, by default, script execution is disabled inside the WebBrowser control. Notice also how you set the IsGeolocationEnabled property to true to allow HTML5 to access the geographic position of the user of the application. The fact that an application tracks a user's geographic location must be documented during submission of the application to the Windows Phone Marketplace. The user then would have a choice whether to grant you permission to track his or her location or not.

Testing the Geolocation API

The simplest way to introduce HTML5 into your application is by using the `NavigateToString` method of the `WebBrowser` control. Follow these steps to test the geolocation properties of HTML5 inside your application:

1. If it's not already present, add the following shell declaration of the `webBrowser1_Loaded` method:

```
void webBrowser1_Loaded(object sender, RoutedEventArgs e)
{

}
```

2. To obtain the current latitude and longitude coordinates of the user, you will use the `navigator.geolocation.getCurrentPosition()` method, and pass it the callback function `onPositionReady`, which will print the latitude and longitude values on the screen. Inside the `webBrowser1_Loaded` method, add the following code:

```
webBrowser1.NavigateToString(@"
                            <!DOCTYPE html>
                                <html>
                                  <head>
                                    <META name='MobileOptimized' content='320' />
                                  </head>
                                  <body>

                                    <div id='message'>
                                        geolocation data will be shown here
                                    </div>

                <script type='text/javascript'>
                    navigator.geolocation.getCurrentPosition(onPositionReady);

                            function onPositionReady(position) {
                                document.getElementById('message').innerHTML = 'lat ' +
                        position.coords.latitude + ' long ' + position.coords.longitude;
                              }

                </script>
              </body>
          </html>
        ");
```

3. Press F5 to run your application. After a slight delay, you should see the latitude and longitude values displayed on your emulator screen. Note, however, that the Windows Phone emulator always returns the values for the suburbs of Seattle, Washington, the location of Microsoft headquarters.

Having access to a user's location without asking people to install an app is a truly powerful feature; it significantly lowers the barriers for users to try out your app. There are many more features in HTML5 to keep users engaged, however; and you will test a couple more of these features in the next section.

Testing Media Playback with the HTML5 <audio> Element

To test out the HTML5 <audio> tag, you will once again use the NavigateToString method of the WebBrowser object. Follow these steps to introduce an <audio> element from the Web into your app:

1. If it's not already present, add the following shell declaration of the webBrowser1_Loaded method:

```
void webBrowser1_Loaded(object sender, RoutedEventArgs e)
{

}
```

2. To play an MP3 file from the Internet, you will use the <audio> HTML5 element and set its source property to the location of that file. Here, both the media playback and the geolocation feature test are included in the document markup to allow you to build a single HTML5 document containing the features you test in this chapter. Inside the webBrowser1_Loaded method, add the following code:

```
webBrowser1.NavigateToString(@"
                            <!DOCTYPE html>
                                <html>
                                  <head>
                                    <META name='MobileOptimized' content='320' />
                                  </head>
                                  <body>

          <audio src='http://www.eugenechuvyrov.com/iheartwp/punk.mp3' controls='true'>
              Your browser does not support the audio element.
          </audio>

                                    <div id='message'>
                                        geolocation data will be shown here
                                    </div>

          <script type='text/javascript'>
              navigator.geolocation.getCurrentPosition(onPositionReady);

                      function onPositionReady(position) {

                          document.getElementById('message').innerHTML = 'lat ' +
                  position.coords.latitude + ' long ' + position.coords.longitude;
                          }

                      </script>
                  </body>
              </html>
          ");
```

3. Press F5 to run your application. After a slight delay, you should see the latitude and longitude values displayed on your emulator screen, as well as a

set of audio playback controls (Play and Pause) that should enable you to play
the tune from the Internet.

In the next section, you will draw on an HTML5 canvas to get a sense of the API available to you in
HTML5 for drawing purposes.

Drawing on an HTML5 Canvas

Although drawing shapes on an HTML canvas is an extremely tedious manual process currently, it is
certain to change in the very near future. New HTML5 automation tools are becoming widely available,
with major vendors lining up to deliver HTML5 productivity applications. For the moment, however,
here's the code to draw a circle shape on a canvas inside the web page. Note that the HTML for this
example, in addition to canvas drawing, also includes the geolocation test and the <audio> tag test from
the previous two sections. All of these features together provide a small glimpse into the power of
HTML5-enabled applications.

1. If it's not already present, add the following shell declaration of the
    webBrowser1_Loaded method:

```
void webBrowser1_Loaded(object sender, RoutedEventArgs e)
{

}
```

2. To allow drawing on a canvas inside HTML5, you must first declare a <canvas>
    element within the body of an HTML5 document. Then, from within
    JavaScript, you must get the <canvas> element using the
    document.getElementById function. Next, you get the context for the canvas
    using the getContext('2D') function. Finally, you invoke a function to begin
    the path, draw an arc, fill the path, and close the path, in that order. Here's the
    code that does all this work:

```
webBrowser1.NavigateToString(@"
                    <!DOCTYPE html>
                        <html>
                          <head>
                            <META name='MobileOptimized' content='320' />
                          </head>
                          <body>
<canvas id='myCanvas' width='200' height='100' style='border:1px solid #c3c3c3;'>
    Your browser does not support the canvas element.
</canvas>

<audio src='http://www.eugenechuvyrov.com/iheartwp/punk.mp3' controls='true'>
    Your browser does not support the audio element.
</audio>

                          <div id='message'>
                              geolocation data will be shown here
                          </div>

<script type='text/javascript'>
```

```
var c=document.getElementById('myCanvas');
var cxt=c.getContext('2d');
cxt.fillStyle='#FF0000';
cxt.beginPath();
cxt.arc(70,18,15,0,Math.PI*2,true);
cxt.closePath();
cxt.fill();

navigator.geolocation.getCurrentPosition(onPositionReady);

function onPositionReady(position) {
            document.getElementById('message').innerHTML = 'lat ' +
            position.coords.latitude + ' long ' +
            position.coords.longitude;
        }

</script>
                </body>
                </html>
        ");
```

As you can see, drawing on a canvas is a somewhat tedious process at the moment. Tools are on the way to make this task significantly easier. Coupled with canvas-based animations, canvas drawing is an extremely powerful feature of HTML5 that enjoys the support of all major browser vendors.

Summary

In this chapter, you learned to use the WebBrowser control for Windows Phone to search for and display web content in an application. You created a simple car-browser application using the WebBrowser control and displayed local static and dynamically generated HTML pages. You also learned how to store and retrieve web and HTML content from local storage on the phone itself. You'll explore local storage in greater depth in Chapter 13. Finally, you should now have a basic understanding of the viewport and custom Internet Explorer Mobile CSS elements, and you should have an appreciation of the security issues you'll encounter when you use the WebBrowser control.

You also became acquainted with the evolving HTML5 standard and its support inside Internet Explorer 9 on Windows Phone. You built several sample applications to test out a small subset of HTML5 features, which should allow you to make informative decisions in the future on whether your application can benefit from inclusion of HTML5-specific features.

In the next chapter, you'll explore what is perhaps the most important aspect of any modern application: its styling. We will go over the general principles of using appealing layouts and themes and delve into the specifics of visually engaging controls within applications.

CHAPTER 9

Working with Controls and Themes

Every time you pass through an airport or a train station, you expect to see a myriad of signs directing you to vital information such as connecting gates, the direction of baggage claim, and the location of ground transportation. While the words on these signs are certainly important, perhaps just as important are the accompanying visual symbols. Our minds become so accustomed to visual elements that we often don't need to read the words to understand a sign's meaning. Furthermore, the presence of visual elements helps tremendously when we're in another country where we don't speak the language.

This universal visual language of signs is the main idea behind the UI in Windows Phone. Microsoft designers want the elements in the Windows Phone UI to direct users to the content that they want, just as airport signs direct people where they need to go. Within Microsoft, this contemporary UI has been code-named Metro, and per the UI Design and Interaction Guide for Windows Phone, elements of the Metro UI are meant to be visually appealing and to encourage exploration of the applications that you build.

In this chapter, you will explore the most important design principles that are at the heart of the Metro UI and learn how to ensure that your applications conform to them. You will also gain an understanding of themes on Windows Phone devices and learn how to make your application theme-aware. Finally, you will take a look at the controls that are available for use in Windows Phone applications, especially the innovative Panorama and Pivot controls, which are unique to the Windows Phone platform. You have already used many of the controls within Windows Phone in the previous chapters of this book, so this chapter will recap those controls and introduce you to some of the less common ones.

Introducing the Metro Design System

The big idea behind the Windows Phone UI (Metro) is to direct users to the content they want using design elements that are both attractive and effective in conveying their message. The User Experience Guidelines for Windows Phone (available as a PDF download from http://go.microsoft.com/fwlink/?LinkID=220811) specifically states that visual elements within applications "should encourage playful exploration so that the user feels a sense of wonder and excitement" when using your application. The guidelines also advise developers to create interfaces that are responsive and perform well—also an important part of UI design. Microsoft strongly encourages all application developers to adopt the Metro design principles in their applications. Fortunately, to help those who may not be particularly strong in graphic design, Microsoft has ensured that all application controls (for example, TextBox, Button, and so on) are Metro-compliant by default. The controls that ship with the Windows Phone development tools already have the look and feel dictated by the Metro UI guidelines, so it's your job as a developer to preserve that look and feel throughout your applications.

■ **Note** An open source project, Silverlight for Windows Phone Toolkit, contains many additional controls that are ready to use inside your application and that conform to the Metro design guidelines as well. This toolkit is also constantly being updated with new controls and features, so make sure to check it out at `http://silverlight.codeplex.com/`. Perhaps it already contains that cool control that you were considering building yourself (Date or Time Picker, for example).

When you first start working with standard controls within Windows Phone applications, you may be surprised by their minimalistic, two-dimensional look. That appearance, however, emphasizes another one of the main principles of Metro UI design: "Delight through content instead of decoration." Microsoft encourages developers to reduce the complexity of visual elements that are not part of content and to communicate with users of their applications as directly as possible. According to the Metro designers, the content and functionality of the application should be the most engaging factor of the Windows Phone application.

Another pillar of the Metro UI is the use of a standard contemporary-looking font. Segoe WP is the standard system font on Windows Phone devices, and it is a Unicode font. It is available in the following five styles:

- Regular
- Bold
- Semi-bold
- Semi-light
- Black

You can also embed your own fonts in any application that you write, but they will be available for use only within your application, not outside of it. To conform to the Metro guidelines, however, it's probably wise to stick to the standard fonts that ship with the Windows Phone development tools.

Windows Phone Chrome

There are two areas on the phone screen that are reserved for special purposes on Windows Phone. Those areas are at the very top and the very bottom of the phone screen; the top area is referred to as the *System Tray* and the bottom one is the *Application Bar*. The term *Windows Phone Chrome* is sometimes used to describe those two areas of the screen, as illustrated in Figure 9-1.

The System Tray is the top portion of Windows Phone Chrome and contains several indicators that display system-level status information. The System Tray displays the following icons, left to right, in the order listed here:

- Signal strength
- Data connection

- Call forwarding

- Roaming

- Wireless network signal strength

- Bluetooth status

- Ringer mode

- Input status

- Battery power level

- System clock

■ **Note** The screen shown in Figure 9-1 is the emulator screen, and it does not include all of the items mentioned in the preceding list.

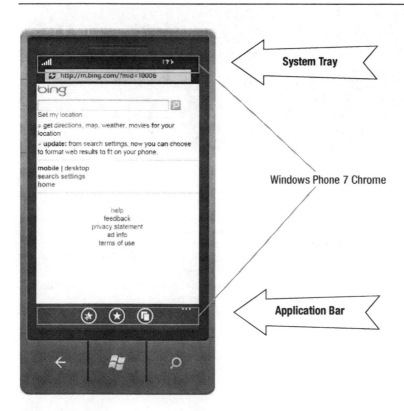

Figure 9-1. Windows Phone Chrome

By default, only the system clock is visible at all times. To make other items visible, you need to double-tap (double-click in the emulator) in the System Tray area. These indicators slide into view for approximately 8 seconds before sliding out of view. Note that, although you can programmatically hide the System Tray, it is not a recommended practice under Metro guidelines.

In Chapter 7, you learned how to work with the Application Bar, the second part of Windows Phone Chrome. To quickly recap, the Application Bar is limited to four icons; if there are more navigational items to display, they should be put inside menu items. There is a set of default Application Bar icons included with each distribution of the Windows Phone tools, and it can be used to build basic Application Bars quickly.

Screen Orientations

Windows Phone supports three screen orientations: portrait, landscape left, and landscape right. In portrait orientation, the page is vertically oriented with hardware buttons appearing at the bottom of the device. Portrait orientation is the default orientation of the device, and the Start screen is always shown in portrait orientation. In landscape left, the System Tray appears on the left of the device; and in landscape right, the System Tray appears on the right, as illustrated in Figure 9-2. You can also set the visibility of the System Tray by manipulating the IsVisible property of the SystemTray object.

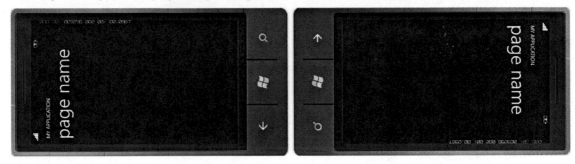

Figure 9-2. System Tray in landsape left and landscape right modes

Your application can't switch the orientation of its screen by itself, since the Orientation property is read-only. You can, however, set a fixed orientation where you disallow application support for certain screen orientations. Some system components can adjust to changes in orientation. For example, application bar icons automatically rotate when the device changes from portrait to landscape mode. Other components with similar orientation-aware behaviors include the System Tray, the Application Bar menu, the volume/ring/vibrate display, push notifications, and dialogs.

Now that we've discussed some of the principles and components of the Metro UI, it's time to turn your attention to support for themes on Windows Phone devices. Themes make the phone more personal, which goes hand in hand with the Metro guideline that the experience of using the phone should be an engaging one.

Themes on Windows Phone Devices

A Windows Phone theme is a combination of a background and an accent color. Users can select from themes that ship with the phone, developers can access them in their code, and companies can alter them to match their own branding colors. Themes are set in the Settings ➤ Themes portion of the Windows Phone device or the emulator.

You can create your own themes and apply them dynamically during the runtime of an application by overwriting or injecting the custom themes into Resources.MergedDictionaries, found in Application.Current. For example, if you have created a custom theme inside the MyStyles.xaml file in the Assets folder of an application named MyApplication, you would make your theme available as shown in the following code snippet:

```
ResourceDictionary res = new ResourceDictionary();
res.Source =
   new Uri("/MyApplication;component/Assets/MyStyles.xaml", UriKind.RelativeOrAbsolute);
Application.Current.Resources.MergedDictionaries.Add(res);
```

Currently, there are two possible background settings: Dark (default) and Light. There are ten accent colors to choose from, starting with a Microsoft-ish blue (the default) and ranging all the way to a decidedly '70s lime green.

> **Note** Microsoft recommends that you use as little background white as possible, since excessive use of white may have a negative impact on battery life.

The combination of 2 background colors and 10 accent colors provides the user with a total of 20 possible themes, delivering on the engagement and personalization promise of Metro design principles. Applications automatically adjust to the selected theme and ensure that all UI elements appear consistently across the platform. A quick walkthrough demonstrates theme-awareness of the Windows Phone controls and UI elements.

Applying a Theme

In this walkthrough, you will add a set of Windows Phone controls to an application, creating some of them with XAML and some through managed code. You will change the theme in the emulator and observe the effect this change has on the controls. Follow these steps to get a better understanding of theming support in Windows Phone.

Creating a UI

First you will add a set of standard controls to a Windows Phone application.

1. Launch Visual Studio 2010 Express and select the Windows Phone Application template. Change the project name to Theming and select OK, and Visual Studio will set up a new project.

2. Open MainPage.xaml in design mode and add a TextBox, a TextBlock, a CheckBox, a Button, and a black rectangular shape to the page. Your goal is a simple interface that resembles the one in Figure 9-3. Here's the XAML:

```
<!--LayoutRoot is the root grid where all page content is placed-->
```

```
<Grid x:Name="LayoutRoot" Background="Transparent">
    <Grid.RowDefinitions>
        <RowDefinition Height="Auto"/>
        <RowDefinition Height="*"/>
    </Grid.RowDefinitions>

    <!--TitlePanel contains the name of the application and page title-->
    <StackPanel x:Name="TitlePanel" Grid.Row="0" Margin="12,17,0,28">
        <TextBlock x:Name="ApplicationTitle" Text="THEMES AND COLORS"
    Style="{StaticResource PhoneTextNormalStyle}"/>
    <TextBlock x:Name="PageTitle" Text="THEMES" Margin="9,-7,0,0"
Style="{StaticResource PhoneTextTitle1Style}"/>
    </StackPanel>

    <!--ContentPanel - place additional content here-->
    <Grid x:Name="ContentPanel" Grid.Row="1" Margin="12,0,12,0">
        <TextBox Height="72" HorizontalAlignment="Left" Margin="-4,6,0,0"
Name="textBox1" Text="TextBox" VerticalAlignment="Top" Width="454" />
        <TextBlock Height="30" HorizontalAlignment="Left" Margin="11,80,0,0"
Name="textBlock1" Text="TextBlock" VerticalAlignment="Top" Width="329" />
        <CheckBox Content="CheckBox" Height="72" HorizontalAlignment="Left"
Margin="12,116,0,0" Name="checkBox1" VerticalAlignment="Top" />
        <Button Content="Button" Height="72" HorizontalAlignment="Left"
Margin="9,194,0,0" Name="button1" VerticalAlignment="Top" Width="160" />
        <Rectangle Height="110" HorizontalAlignment="Left" Margin="249,137,0,0"
Name="rectangle1" Stroke="Black" StrokeThickness="1" VerticalAlignment="Top"
Width="156" />
    </Grid>
</Grid>
```

Adding Code to Draw an Elliptical Shape

In addition to using the powerful visual designer to add controls to Windows Phone pages as you just did, you can add controls programmatically. The steps here show you how to do that.

1. Go to the Theming project in Solution Explorer, and open MainPage.xaml.cs (right-click MainPage.xaml and choose View Code).

2. To add a white ellipse to the page, you will use the Ellipse object available on the Windows Phone platform and manipulate its properties. Paste the following code inside the MainPage constructor:

    ```
    Ellipse e = new Ellipse();
    e.Width = 100.0;
    e.Height = 120.0;
    e.StrokeThickness = 2.0;

    e.HorizontalAlignment = HorizontalAlignment.Left;
    e.VerticalAlignment = VerticalAlignment.Top;

    Color backgroundColor = Color.FromArgb(255, 255, 255, 255);
    e.Fill = new SolidColorBrush(backgroundColor);
    ```

```
e.Margin = new Thickness(10, 300, 10, 10);

ContentPanel.Children.Add(e);
```

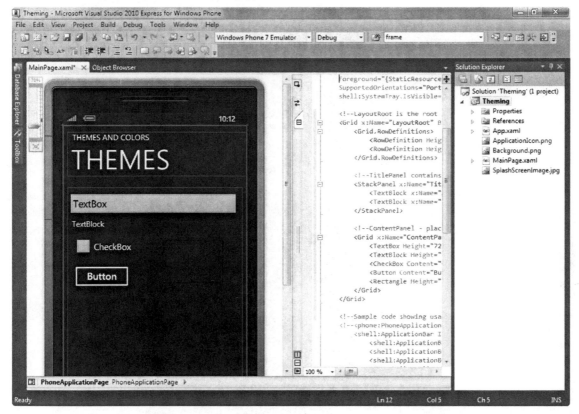

Figure 9-3. Theming application UI layout

Once you start debugging your application, the application screen should display all of the controls you've added, including a blue ellipse.

Changing the Theme

In this part of the walkthrough, you will change the emulator's theme to observe the effect it has on the theming application.

1. Click the Windows button on the emulator to bring up the Start screen. Then click the ➤ key (the arrow in the upper-right corner of the emulator screen) and select Settings ➤ Themes to bring up the Themes dialog.

2. Change the background to Light, and change the accent color to red (note that you may have to scroll to locate the red accent color).

3. Click the Windows button again to go back to the Start screen. Note that your application is no longer running (it stopped when you clicked the Windows button), so go back to Visual Studio 2010 Express and press F5 to relaunch your application.

Note that you can see the same controls as before, except the ellipse that you drew from code is nowhere to be found. Figure 9-4 shows two versions of the same application side by side, each with a different theme.

Figure 9-4. Two themes applied to the same theming application example

By now, you have probably guessed that the reason the ellipse is not visible is that the application paints it white and then displays it on a white background. But how did the other controls manage to show up on the white background when they were originally white themselves? And how can you make the ellipse behave the same way?

The answers lie in a Windows Phone concept known as *theme awareness*. By default, Windows Phone controls are theme-aware, and they adjust their appearance based on the theme selected on the device. Problems arise when the color values are hard-coded into the control, as you have done for the ellipse and the rectangle border. In the next few steps, you'll see two separate ways to correct the issue of hard-coded colors; the first with the help of a design surface and the second one via code.

1. If it's still running, stop the application. Open MainPage.xaml in design view and select the rectangular shape. Press F4 to bring up the Properties window, and then click the diamond symbol to the right of the Stroke property.

2. In the pop-up dialog, click Apply Resource. In the next dialog, double-click the PhoneAccentBrush setting to use the currently selected accent color to draw a rectangle.

3. Now adjust the color of the ellipse to the currently selected accent color. Since you drew the ellipse from code, open the MainPage.xaml.cs file and change the following line of code from

```
Color backgroundColor = Color.FromArgb(255, 255, 255, 255);
```

to

```
Color backgroundColor =
    (Color)Application.Current.Resources["PhoneAccentColor"];
```

Press F5 to run your application. You should see both the rectangle and ellipse appear in red (or the currently selected accent color).

■ **Note** Avoid using hard-coded values for color if possible. It's hard to predict what combination of themes a user will choose, so your visual elements may not show up as desired. Instead, use one of the predefined theme resources, just as you did previously, to ensure that your application is fully theme-aware in accordance with Metro design principles. The full list of available resources can be found at http://msdn.microsoft.com/en-us/library/ff769552%28VS.92%29.aspx.

■ **Note** When working with the Application Bar, as discussed in Chapter 7, it is recommended that you use a transparent background for Application Bar images. The icons themselves should be drawn in white, if possible, and the Windows Phone platform will automatically adjust the coloring of those icons on light backgrounds.

Now that you know how to ensure that your application is theme-aware, in the next section you will learn how to approach cases where you absolutely must customize your application based on the currently selected theme.

Detecting the Currently Selected Theme

Sooner or later, you'll want to customize your application depending on whether a dark or a light theme is currently active. For example, you may have a beautiful custom graphic within your application that simply does not render well when the background theme colors are changed; instead, you would like to show a different graphic depending on the currently selected theme. The following walkthrough shows you how to accomplish just that: it detects the currently selected theme and adjusts the message based on whether the current theme has a light or dark background.

1. Launch Visual Studio 2010 Express and select the Windows Phone Application template. Change the project name to DetectTheme and select OK, and Visual Studio will set up a new project.

2. Open MainPage.xaml in design mode, and add a TextBlock to the page. For this walkthrough, you will simply modify the message within this TextBlock. For real-world applications, you would probably choose to do something a bit more exotic than this, such as show a different image.

3. Open MainPage.xaml.cs (right-click MainPage.xaml in Solution Explorer and choose View Code), and add the following code to the MainPage constructor, right below the InitializeComponent() method:

```
Visibility v = (Visibility)Resources["PhoneLightThemeVisibility"];
 if (v == System.Windows.Visibility.Visible)
{
    textBlock1.Text = "Let there be light!";
}
else
{
    textBlock1.Text = "It's dark!";
}
```

Note that you are using the Visibility property to determine whether the light theme is visible and to take action accordingly.

Press F5 to run the application. If you still have a light background selected from the previous walkthrough, you will see a "Let there be light!" message. Otherwise, an "It's dark!" message will be displayed.

So far, we've touched on the basics of theming and looked at how to make your application theme-aware and customize its behavior based on the theme selected. Next, you'll look at the controls provided as part of the Windows Phone developer tools, since it's these controls that really make the Metro experience complete.

Panorama and Pivot Controls

In earlier chapters, you used several of the base controls that ship with the Windows Phone developer tools, including TextBoxes, TextBlocks, and Buttons—the kinds of controls you'd expect within any UI framework. But the Windows Phone developer tools include a number of unique controls as well, including a WebBrowser control (covered in the previous chapter) and a Bing Maps control, which will be covered in a later chapter. Two other controls are the Panorama and Pivot controls, which are integral to Metro and the Windows Phone user experience.

The Panorama and Pivot controls offer two ways to develop an application that requires page navigation. With a Panorama control, you can present the UI of an application on one horizontal canvas that extends beyond the left and right boundaries of the device screen and can be flicked to the left and right with touch gestures. With a Pivot control, you can present the UI of an application as a series of pages, much like tabbed pages, that allow the user to touch the page headers or flick through the pages. A Panorama is like a scroll; a Pivot is more like a series of cards laid out from left to right.

In the following section, you'll learn how to use a Panorama control to create some engaging UIs for an airport application that displays arrivals and departures. You'll also take a brief look at the Pivot control, whose outfitting and use is nearly identical to the Panorama control, though its effects are quite different.

Using the Panorama Control

In video ads for Windows Phone devices, the scrollable UI of the Panorama control is usually the first thing that people notice. The People hub on the Start screen of Windows Phone is implemented using this control. So is the Music + Videos hub. These interactions essentially allow scrolling horizontally far past the end of the screen. The Panorama control allows for a unique experience that is associated with the native Windows Phone look and feel.

A Panorama control can be thought of as a long, horizontal canvas. A secondary control called a PanoramaItem serves as a container that hosts content and other controls such as TextBlocks, Buttons, and Links. There are three ways to incorporate Panorama behavior into your application:

- Create a new Windows Phone project, and choose Windows Phone Panorama Application as the template to use for the application. While this is an extremely powerful approach, this type of template creates a project based on Model-View-ViewModel (MVVM), which has a significant learning curve and is quite different from the types of Windows Phone applications you have developed in most cases in this book. (For an example of an MVVM application, refer to Chapter 3.)

- Add the Panorama control to the Visual Studio toolbox (by right-clicking the toolbox and navigating to the assembly containing this control), and then drag and drop it into your application.

- Add a new page to your application that contains a Panorama control. This is perhaps the easiest way to incorporate the Panorama control into your application quickly; this is the approach you will pursue in this section.

In the following walkthrough, you will create an application to display the arrival and departures of flights at a fictional airport. In addition, you will add a search capability (or the UI elements of it) to this application. You will use the Panorama control to implement this functionality, in which the long background will give users the impression that they are inside an airport as they navigate left or right through the pages.

Your application will not contain any code, since the primary goal in this chapter is to explore the controls available for Windows Phone, and in this section you are exploring the Panorama control. As mentioned, to create a Panorama control, you will use XAML to build a new page with the Panorama control in it.

1. Launch Visual Studio 2010 Express and select the Windows Phone Application template. Change the project name to Panorama and select OK, and Visual Studio will set up a new project.

2. Right-click the project name in Solution Explorer, and select Add ➤ New Item ➤ Windows Phone Panorama Page. Accept the default name of PanoramaPage1.xaml for the file and click the OK button.

3. You now have a page with the Panorama control in it within the application, but there is no way to get to it. You could either add navigation from MainPage.xaml or simply make PanoramaPage1.xaml the main page within the application. To implement the second choice, rename the current MainPage.xaml to MainPage1.xaml and then rename PanoramaPage1.xaml to MainPage.xaml. Now the Panorama page should be the default page that comes up when the application is launched.

4. It is time to customize and add content to the Panorama control. Go ahead and change the `<controls:Panorama...` element to the following:

```
<controls:Panorama Title="airport" Foreground="Red">
```

5. To add new tabs or containers to the Panorama control, you use the `<controls:PanoramaItem...` XAML element. Add a third PanoramaItem right above the closing tag for the Panorama control `</controls:Panorama>`. This will contain a TextBox and a Button for searching for departures to a specific city. Notice that as you add the PanoramaItem, design view will reflect the changes.

```
<!--Panorama item three-->
    <controls:PanoramaItem Header="search" Foreground="{StaticResource
    PhoneAccentBrush}">
     <Grid>
       <TextBox Height="72" HorizontalAlignment="Left" Margin="-12,-2,0,0"
           Name="textBox1" Text="TextBox" VerticalAlignment="Top" Width="271" />
       <Button Content="Search" Height="72" HorizontalAlignment="Left"
           Margin="242,-4,0,0" Name="button1" VerticalAlignment="Top" Width="160"
       />
     </Grid>
    </controls:PanoramaItem>
```

■ **Note** The use of the `Foreground="{StaticResource PhoneAccentBrush}"` binding allows the foreground color of the text to be the current theme's accent color.

---

6. Make some minor adjustments to the first two PanoramaItems to bring them in line with the rest of the UI layout. Replace the top two `<controls:PanoramaItem...` elements with the following XAML:

```
    <!--Panorama item one-->
    <controls:PanoramaItem Header="arrivals" Foreground="{StaticResource
PhoneAccentBrush}">
        <Grid>
        </Grid>
    </controls:PanoramaItem>

    <!--Panorama item two-->
    <controls:PanoramaItem Header="departures" Foreground="{StaticResource
PhoneAccentBrush}">
        <Grid/>
    </controls:PanoramaItem>
```

7. Finally, add a background image to the Panorama control. The recommended size for the background image is 800 pixels high (of course, that's the standard resolution of Windows Phone devices) and 2,000 or fewer pixels wide. To specify the background image, add the following XAML tag right below the `<controls:Panorama...` tag:

```
<controls:Panorama.Background>
    <ImageBrush ImageSource="PanoramaBackground.jpg"></ImageBrush>
</controls:Panorama.Background>
```

8. Press F5 to run the application. You should see a screen that looks very similar to Figure 9-5 (minus the background image, perhaps). Flicking the Panorama control from right to left should allow you to see arrivals and departures, plus a separate tab designated for searching airport schedules.

Figure 9-5. Panorama control example

As you can see, it is pretty easy to use a Panorama control, and you can place different content within the PanoramaItem tag. Using the Panorama control, together with the Pivot control discussed in the next section, provides a very easy way to impress your users with cool designs, layouts, and coding techniques. Considering that you didn't have to hire a graphic designer to get here, this is a very powerful weapon in the Windows Phone developer arsenal.

▓ **Note** Microsoft recommends limiting the number of `PanoramaItems` to a maximum of four to ensure smooth application performance. In addition, it is considered a best practice to hide `PanoramaItems` until they have content to display.

▓ **Note** The User Experience Guidelines for Windows Phone document referenced previously contains a wealth of information on optimizing the performance of Windows Phone applications. Some of the optimization techniques refer to judicious use of the Panorama control. For example, since all of the items inside the Panorama control are loaded at the same time, it is advisable to load those items on demand and go light on animations inside the Panorama, as even when the animation is not visible to the user, it is still running and consuming valuable resources if it's loaded inside the Panorama control.

Using the Pivot Control

The Pivot control is a close cousin of the Panorama control. The basic premise of having multiple pages easily accessible is preserved; however, while the Panorama control doesn't allow the user to click the header to show the contents of a new page, the Pivot control does. Unlike in a Panorama control, though, you cannot use a long background image in a Pivot control. A screenshot of a simple Pivot control is shown in Figure 9-6. A user can tap (or click in the emulator) the word "departures" and be immediately presented with the portion of the application dealing with airport departures.

Like a Panorama control, a Pivot control can be thought of as a long, horizontal canvas. A secondary control called a `PivotItem` serves as a container that hosts content and other controls, such as TextBlocks, Buttons, and Links. Using a Pivot control is very similar to using a Panorama control; the steps to implement a Pivot control inside your application are summarized following. There are three ways to incorporate pivot behavior into your application:

- Create a new Windows Phone project, and choose Windows Phone Pivot Application as the template to use for the application. While this is an extremely powerful approach, this type of template creates an MVVM-based project, which, as mentioned previously, has a steep learning curve and differs drastically from a typical Windows Phone project. (See Chapter 3 for an example of an MVVM application.)

- Add the Pivot control to the Visual Studio toolbox (by right-clicking the toolbox and navigating to the assembly containing this control), and then drag and drop it into your application.

- Add a new page that contains a Pivot control to your application. As with the Panorama control in the previous section, this is perhaps the easiest way to incorporate the Pivot control inside your application quickly, and this is the approach you will pursue in this section.

In the following walkthrough, you will create an application to display arrivals and departures of flights at a fictional airport, this time using a Pivot control. Your application will not contain any code, since the primary goal in this chapter is to explore the controls available for Windows Phone, and in this section you are exploring the Pivot control. As mentioned, to create a Pivot control, you will use XAML to build a new page with the Pivot control in it.

1. Launch Visual Studio 2010 Express, and select the Windows Phone Application template. Change the project name to Pivot and select OK, and Visual Studio will set up a new project.

2. Right-click the project name in Solution Explorer, and select Add ➤ New Item ➤ Windows Phone Pivot Page. Accept the default name of PivotPage1.xaml for the file and click the OK button.

3. You now have a page with the Pivot control in it within the application, but there is no way to get to it. You could either add navigation from MainPage.xaml or simply make PivotPage1.xaml the main page within the application. To implement the second choice, rename the current MainPage.xaml to MainPage1.xaml and then rename PivotPage1.xaml to MainPage.xaml. Now the Pivot page should be the default page that comes up when the application is launched.

4. It is time to customize and add content to the Pivot control. Change the <controls:Pivot... element to the following:

    <controls:Panorama Title="airport">

5. To add new tabs or containers to the Pivot control, you use the <controls:PivotItem... XAML element. Add a third PivotItem to search for departures right above the closing tag for the Pivot control </controls:Pivot>.

    ```
    <!--Pivot item three-->
    <controls:PivotItem Header="search">
        <Grid/>
    </controls:PivotItem>
    ```

Press F5 to run the application. You should see a screen that looks very similar to Figure 9-6. Clicking different tabs within the Pivot control allows you to see arrivals and departures, as well as a separate container for searching airport schedules.

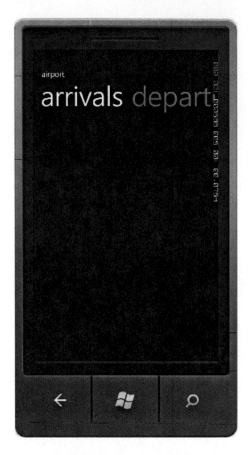

Figure 9-6. *Pivot control example*

Understanding Frame and Page Navigation

To navigate from screen to screen in a Windows Phone application, an understanding of the PhoneApplicationFrame and PhoneApplicationPage controls is important. There is only one PhoneApplicationFrame available to a Windows Phone application; this frame reserves space for the System Tray and the Application Bar, as well as the content area where PhoneApplicationPage controls live. You can create as many different pages as needed and then navigate to those pages from the frame. Refer to Figure 9-7 to see how the controls are placed on a device's screen.

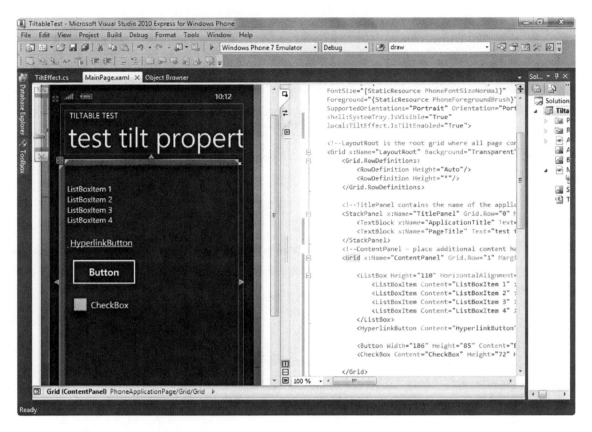

Figure 9-7. PhoneApplicationFrame and PhoneApplicationPage

To navigate from page to page within your application, you use the `NavigationService` class. This class exposes methods to navigate to pages given a URI, as well as to go back to the previous page. The following walkthrough illustrates the use of the `NavigationService` class.

Creating a UI for the NavigationTest Project

The `NavigationTest` project will contain two XAML pages (`MainPage.xaml` and `Page1.xaml`), and it will navigate between the two.

1. Launch Visual Studio 2010 Express and select the Windows Phone Application template. Change the project name to `NavigationTest` and select OK, and Visual Studio will set up a new project.

2. Right-click the project name in Solution Explorer and select Add ➤ New Item ➤ Windows Phone Portrait Page. Accept the default name of `Page1.xaml` and click OK.

3. Open MainPage.xaml in design view. From the toolbox, drag and drop the HyperlinkButton control. With that control selected, press F4 to display its properties and change the content to "Go to Page1."

4. Open Page1.xaml in design view and add a button to that page from the toolbox. Edit the content of the button to read "Go Back to Main Page."

5. Add a TextBlock underneath the button on Page1.xaml. This TextBlock will be used to show the parameters passed into this page.

In the next section, you will use NavigationService to navigate between pages.

Adding Navigation Code

When the user clicks the Go to Page 1 hyperlink, NavigationService will be used to move to page 1.

1. Open MainPage.xaml and double-click the hyperlink on that page. Implement the hyperlinkButton1_Click event handler with the following code:

```
private void hyperlinkButton1_Click(object sender, RoutedEventArgs e)
{
    NavigationService.Navigate(new Uri("/Page1.xaml", UriKind.Relative));
}
```

2. Open Page1.xaml and double-click the button on that page. Implement the button1_Click event handler with the following code:

```
private void button1_Click(object sender, RoutedEventArgs e)
{
    NavigationService.GoBack();
}
```

3. Press F5 to run the application. Now when you click the hyperlink on MainPage.xaml, you will be taken to Page1.xaml. When you click the button on Page1.xaml, you will be taken back to MainPage.xaml.

In the next section, you will enhance this application slightly to pass parameters between the pages.

Adding Code to Pass Parameters Between Pages

In the previous section, you learned how to navigate successfully from page to page. In this section, you will see how to pass parameters from one page to another.

1. Open MainPage.xaml.cs and change the hyperlinkButton1_Click event handler to the following:

```
private void hyperlinkButton1_Click(object sender, RoutedEventArgs e)
{
    NavigationService.Navigate(new Uri("/Page1.xaml?message=Hello,World",
            UriKind.Relative));
}
```

Here you are passing the hard-coded string "Hello, world" to Page1.xaml for processing.

2.   In Page1.xaml, you will try to read the query string passed from the prior pages to see if there are non-empty values. Open Page1.xaml.cs, and add the following code to that file:

```
protected override void OnNavigatedTo(System.Windows.Navigation.NavigationEventArgs
    e)
{
   base.OnNavigatedTo(e);
   string msg = "";
   if (NavigationContext.QueryString.TryGetValue("message", out msg))
     textBlock1.Text = msg;
}
```

3.   Press F5 to run the application. Now, if you click the hyperlink from MainPage.xaml, you should see the "Hello, world" message displayed on Page1.

Having talked about controls, let's close out this chapter with a neat effect you can add to your controls to increase the buzz about your application.

Adding Transition Effects

To spice up your application, you can add what is called a *tilt* effect to the visual elements. The tilt effect provides visual feedback to the user of the Windows Phone application during manipulation of visual elements within the application. So, instead of just pressed and unpressed states, elements can also have being-pressed and being-unpressed states. You can think of the being-pressed and being-unpressed states as short animations showing the UI elements going from one state (pressed) to another (unpressed). The integration of tilt is pretty straightforward, and in the end it is entirely up to you whether you include it in your application. But if you do decide to give this effect a try, follow this walkthrough.

Creating a UI

The user interface for the test application will be composed of four controls within the page: ListBox, Button, Hyperlink, and CheckBox.

1.   Launch Visual Studio 2010 Express and select the Windows Phone Application template. Change the project name to TiltableTest and select OK, and Visual Studio will set up a new project.

2.   Open MainPage.xaml in design mode, and add a ListBox with four items, a Button, a Hyperlink, and a CheckBox to the page, with the end goal of creating a UI like the one shown in Figure 9-8.

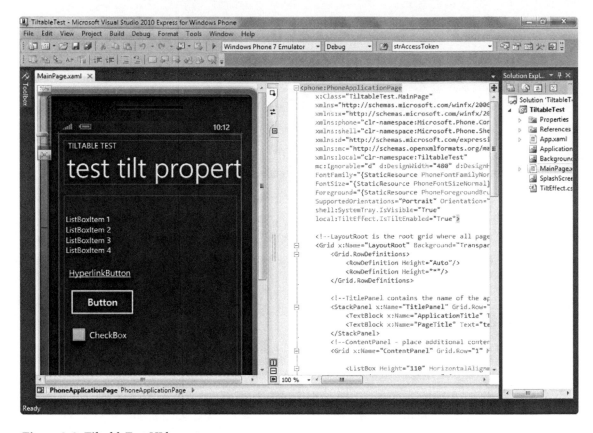

Figure 9-8. *TiltableTest UI layout*

3. You can also paste the following XAML code to get the interface depicted in
    Figure 9-8:

```
<!--ContentPanel - place additional content here-->
<Grid x:Name="ContentPanel" Grid.Row="1" Margin="12,0,12,0">

        <ListBox Height="110" HorizontalAlignment="Left" Margin="6,47,0,0"
Name="listBox1"
                VerticalAlignment="Top" Width="460" ItemsSource="{Binding}" >
                <ListBoxItem Content="ListBoxItem 1" ></ListBoxItem>
                <ListBoxItem Content="ListBoxItem 2" ></ListBoxItem>
                <ListBoxItem Content="ListBoxItem 3" ></ListBoxItem>
                <ListBoxItem Content="ListBoxItem 4" ></ListBoxItem>
        </ListBox>
        <HyperlinkButton Content="HyperlinkButton" Height="30"
                HorizontalAlignment="Left"
                Margin="-109,185,0,0" Name="hyperlinkButton1" VerticalAlignment="Top"
                Width="409" />
```

```
<Button Width="186" Height="85" Content="Button" HorizontalAlignment="Left"
  VerticalAlignment="Top" Margin="9,234,0,0" />
<CheckBox Content="CheckBox" Height="72" HorizontalAlignment="Left"
        Margin="12,325,0,0" Name="checkBox1" VerticalAlignment="Top" />
```

```
</Grid>
```

Now that you've added controls to `MainPage`, you'll add tilt effects to the controls.

Downloading TiltEffect.cs and Applying Dependency Properties

To integrate the tilt effect into your application, you will need to download `TiltEffect.cs` and properly integrate it into your project.

1. Download the Tilt Effect Control Sample from `http://go.microsoft.com/fwlink/?LinkId=200720`, and extract the contents of the ZIP file to a known location.

2. From within the `TiltableTest` project you created previously, right-click Add ► Existing Item, navigate to the location from step 1, and find the `TiltEffect.cs` file.

3. With `TiltEffect.cs` now a part of your project, double-click that file to open it. Change the statement `namespace ControlTiltEffect` to `namespace TiltableTest`. Essentially, this just changes the namespace of this file so that it now belongs to your application.

4. Now you need to add the `IsTiltEnabled` dependency property to the `MainPage.xaml` page. Open `MainPage.xaml` in a XAML view, and at the very top of the page, right below the `xmlnss:mc=...`, add the following statement:

    `xmlns:local="clr-namespace:TiltableTest"`

5. You're almost done! At the top of the page, beneath the statement `shell:System Tray.IsVisible="True"`, add the following:

    `local:TiltEffect.IsTiltEnabled="True">`

6. Right-click the project and select Build. After the project builds, you are ready to run the application.

Press F5 to run the application. Now when you click the button or the items in the ListBox, you should see an animation in which these items first contract and then expand. This is another element of interactivity that you can use to enhance the user experience of your application further.

▨ **Note** You can suppress the tilt effect on any control by adding the `local:TiltEffect.SuppressTilt="True"` attribute to that control.

Summary

In this chapter, you learned the basic concepts of Metro UI and theme support on Windows Phone devices. You learned how to detect which theme is being used, how to create theme-aware applications, and how to navigate between the pages within a Windows Phone application. You also learned how to work with Panorama, Pivot, PhoneApplicationFrame, and PhoneApplicationPage controls. Finally, you learned how to enhance user interaction further via the introduction of tilt effects in your applications. The next chapter covers the integration options available on Windows Phone.

CHAPTER 10

Integrating Applications with the Windows Phone OS

When a third-party application such as yours runs on a Windows Phone, it executes in an environment that is highly restricted. Windows Phone OS must be restrictive in order to protect unsuspecting users of mobile devices from potential malicious application behavior, which may include stealing personal data stored on the phone, dialing phone numbers without the user's knowledge, or corrupting the data stores of other applications. One of the major restrictions that Windows Phone OS places on mobile applications is limiting them to their own execution environment, or *sandbox*, and not allowing them access to other applications' space or the internals of the operating system. Sandboxing and other Windows Phone security features are covered in greater detail in Chapter 19.

Nonetheless, many applications need to access the system features of the phone: for example, to play a music file in the media library, to take a photo, or to send a text message. Windows Phone OS enables such application interactions with the device via a set of Application Programming Interface (API) tasks referred to as *launchers* and *choosers*. Some launchers and choosers may be invoked via hardware buttons on the phone, such as using a camera button to take photos. It is also relatively easy to use launchers and choosers from within your application. When one is invoked or when a user presses hardware buttons on the phone while your application is running, however, managing your application state gets a little tricky.

This chapter covers the launchers and choosers available on the Windows Phone platform, as well as the various states an application can enter when you invoke them. You also learn about integrating your applications with popular external services such as Facebook. Finally, you take a quick look at Windows Phone hubs, which bring many applications found on desktop devices and in the cloud to the palm of your hand.

Introducing Windows Phone Launchers and Choosers

When an application executes, the Windows Phone OS confines it to its own space, or sandbox. Both memory and file storage are isolated within that sandbox—one application can't access or alter another's memory or file storage. Neither can one application directly call another or access a shared data store, such as a list of contacts. There are obvious reasons for this behavior; Microsoft must ensure that the Windows Phone platform is as secure and stable as possible, and isolating applications is one giant step toward getting there.

A set of built-in APIs provides access to the most common features of Windows Phone. These APIs help you to perform tasks, such as saving a contact's e-mail address or phone number, or placing a phone call (with the mandatory prior-user authorization, of course), that require access to shared resources on the phone.

Launchers and choosers, which can be thought of as system functions provided by Windows Phone OS, provide you with the means to call into these applications. The difference between a launcher and a chooser is small but important: choosers provide a return value into the calling application, whereas launchers do not. If you think about a task of composing an e-mail message, for example, it is sufficient to "fire and forget" an e-mail application, allowing users to create and send an e-mail. A launcher is an ideal solution for this task. On the other hand, an application allowing you to select a photo from the photo library on the phone needs to pass the selected photo to your application. Windows Phone provides a chooser to perform such a task.

An important concept to remember is that launchers and choosers are separate applications. Since one of the core design principles behind Windows Phone is to maximize battery life, the application calling the launcher or chooser is suspended when the launcher or chooser activates. Depending on the circumstances, your application may enter one of several states when that happens. This chapter covers these possible states later, during the in-depth discussion of the application life cycle. In the meantime, you can familiarize yourself with the launchers and choosers available on the Windows Phone platform today. They are listed in Table 10-1 and Table 10-2. You can find all of them in the `Microsoft.Phone.Tasks` namespace; therefore, to use any of them, be sure to import that namespace into your application via the following standard directive at the very top of the code page.

Launchers

Table 10-1 lists the launchers available on the Windows Phone platform with a brief description of the functionality offered by each.

Table 10-1. Windows Phone Launchers and Their Functions

Launcher	Function
BingMapsDirectionsTask	Launch Bing maps, and show driving directions from one point to another.
BingMapsTask	Launch Bing maps, and (optionally) display the points of interest passed in.
ConnectionSettingsTask	Show the Connection Settings (such as Wi-Fi) screen to allow the user to change the properties of a connection.
EmailComposeTask	Launch the e-mail application with a new message displayed.
MarketplaceDetailTask	Launch the Windows Phone Marketplace client application, and display the details page for the specified product.
MarketplaceHubTask	Launch the Windows Phone Marketplace client application.
MarketplaceReviewTask	Launch the Windows Phone Marketplace client application, and display the review page for the specified product.
MarketplaceSearchTask	Launch the Windows Phone Marketplace client application, and display the search results from the specified search terms.

Launcher	Function
MediaPlayerLauncher	Launch the media player.
PhoneCallTask	Launch the Phone application; use this to allow users to make a phone call from your application.
SearchTask	Launch the Web Search application.
ShareLinkTask	Launch an application allowing the user to share hyperlinks on one of the social networks (whichever the user has defined on their device).
ShareStatusTask	Launch an application allowing the user to share their status on one of the social networks (whichever the user has defined on their device).
SmsComposeTask	Launch the SMS application.
WebBrowserTask	Launch the Web Browser application.

Choosers

Table 10-2 lists and describes the choosers available on the Windows Phone platform.

Table 10-2. *Windows Phone Choosers and Their Functions*

Chooser	Function
AddressChooserTask	Launch the Contacts application, and obtain the physical address of a contact selected by the user.
CameraCaptureTask	Launch the Camera application, and allow the user to take a photo from your application. (For more information and in-depth examples, please refer to Chapter 16.)
EmailAddressChooserTask	Launch the Contacts application, and obtain the e-mail address of a contact selected by the user.
GameInviteTask	Launch a game-invite screen that invites players to a multiplayer game.
PhoneNumberChooserTask	Launch the Contacts application, and obtain the phone number of a contact selected by the user.
PhotoChooserTask	Launch the Photo Chooser application, and select a photo. (Refer to Chapter 16 for more information and a detailed demo using this chooser.)

Chooser	Function
SaveContactTask	Launch the Contacts application; use this to allow the user to save new contact details, such as a name and address.
SaveEmailAddressTask	Launch the Contacts application; use this to allow the user to save an e-mail address from your application to a new or existing contact.
SavePhoneNumberTask	Launch the Contacts application; use this to allow the user to save a phone number from your application to a new or existing contact.
SaveRingtoneTask	Launch the Ringtone application, and use this chooser to save a custom audio file to a list of ringtones.

Working with Launchers and Choosers

This section explores how to work with launchers and choosers from within your application. You use PhoneNumberChooserTask and SmsComposeTask to create an application that selects a contact from the shared list of contacts on the phone and then composes a text message to that contact's phone number.

Creating the User Interface

The user interface for this sample consists of a single button. When the user clicks this button, a list of contacts is displayed, allowing the user to pick one:

1. Launch Visual Studio 2010 Express, and select the Windows Phone Application template for your new project. Change the project name to Tasks, and select OK. Visual Studio sets up a new project.

2. Open MainPage.xaml in design mode, and add a button to the page. Change the button's caption to Send SMS.

Coding Application Logic

When the user clicks the Send SMS button of your application, they should be presented with a list of contacts available on their device. Conveniently for you, even on the emulator, Microsoft has included a sample list of contacts with which you may test an application. Follow these steps:

1. Open MainPage.xaml.cs (right-click MainPage.xaml, and select View Code). At the top of the page, add the following using statement:

   ```
   using Microsoft.Phone.Tasks;
   ```

2. Declare the following module-level variable for the PhoneNumberChooserTask chooser (insert it right above the MainPage()constructor):

   ```
   private PhoneNumberChooserTask _choosePhoneNumberTask;
   ```

3. Instantiate a new PhoneNumberChooserTask object within the MainPage() constructor, and associate a method to invoke when the user selects a contact from the list. The method to call upon the chooser's return will accept the phone number selected as one of the parameters. Use the following two lines of code to accomplish that:

```
_choosePhoneNumberTask = new PhoneNumberChooserTask();
_choosePhoneNumberTask.Completed += new
        EventHandler<PhoneNumberResult>(ChoosePhoneNumberTaskCompleted);
```

4. Code the ChoosePhoneNumberTaskCompleted method that will be invoked upon selection of a contact from the list. Note the use of a SmsComposeTask launcher to create a new text message to the person you have selected from the contact list:

```
private void ChoosePhoneNumberTaskCompleted(object sender,
            PhoneNumberResult e)
{
    new SmsComposeTask() { Body = "SMS using Windows Phone Chooser", To =
            e.PhoneNumber }.Show();
}
```

5. Add code to react to the button-click event by opening the PhoneNumberChooser launcher. The easiest way to accomplish this is to double-click the button with MainPage.xaml open in design view, and make the button-click event look like the following:

```
private void button1_Click(object sender, RoutedEventArgs e)
{
    _choosePhoneNumberTask.Show();
}
```

Press F5 to run your application. Click the Send SMS button, and select Andrew R. (Andy) Hill from the list of contacts that comes up on the emulator. Immediately after selecting this contact, you should see a screen similar to Figure 10-1, where the SMS message has been composed and is ready to send to Andrew.

Figure 10-1. The SMS message is composed and ready to go to Andrew.

To summarize what you have learned so far, your application integrates with the services provided by Windows Phone OS via a set of API methods referred to as launchers and choosers. Working with launchers and choosers is very straightforward, as illustrated in the previous example. If that was all there was to application integration, it would have made for a very brief chapter. But, of course, there's more.

One major limitation of mobile platforms is their inherently short battery life. This limitation causes OS designers and phone manufacturers to come up with various techniques to balance short battery life against a positive user experience. One such technique is to allow only one application to run on the phone at any given time. You may be wondering, then, what happens when your application yields its execution to the built-in Windows Phone OS application invoked by the launcher. That brings you to the important Windows Phone concepts of *Fast Application Switching* (*FAS*) and *tombstoning,* subjects explored along with the Windows Phone application life cycle in the next section.

Working with the Windows Phone Application Life Cycle

To program responsive applications on a Windows Phone device, you must be familiar with the concepts of FAS and tombstoning on that platform. FAS is a concept introduced in the latest release of Windows Phone OS. When your application loses focus on the Windows Phone device, such as when a user invokes a launcher or a chooser or presses the hardware Start button, the application is kept in memory initially to allow the OS to fast-switch, or reload it from memory, once the user reactivates it. During this stage, an application is referred to as being *dormant*. However, if Windows Phone OS realizes that it needs to use the memory occupied by the inactive application, it remembers its state and provides developers with a means to save session-related information to a custom State dictionary object. This event of removing the application from memory is referred to as *tombstoning*. Even with tombstoning, there is always a chance that your application may never be reactivated. So, if data needs to be permanently preserved within your application, you should make provisions in the application to save the data to the isolated storage instead of the transient State object.

You get to observe both Fast Application Switching and tombstoning at work shortly, but before that, you need to examine a typical life cycle of a Windows Phone application. Table 10-3 summarizes the application events that can occur during the execution of a typical Windows Phone application. The table also describes the actions that you, as a developer, should take when each of those events occurs.

Table 10-3. *Applications Events, Triggers, and Actions*

Application Event	Occurs When	Your Actions
Application_Launching	The user taps the application icon on the installed applications screen (or taps an application tile on the Windows Phone start screen), and a new instance of an application is created.	Do not read application settings from the isolated storage, as this will slow down the loading process; do not attempt to restore the transient state. When an application launches, it should always appear as a new instance.
Application_Activated	For this event to occur, two conditions must be met: (1) the user navigates away from your application, either by using a launcher or a chooser, or by starting another application; and (2) the user then comes back to your application either by completing the launcher or chooser or using the hardware Back button. This event is *not* raised when an application is first launched.	The application should allow the user to continue the interaction as if they had never left the application. It must first check the special IsApplicationInstancePreserved flag to determine whether it was dormant or tombstoned, and then proceed accordingly. Transient state information should next be restored, but the application should not attempt to read the contents of the isolated storage, to avoid a potential slowdown.

Application_Deactivated	The user navigates away from your application either by invoking a launcher or a chooser, or by launching another application. This event is not raised when your application is closing.	You should save all transient (that is, related to the current application session) state information into the State dictionary. You should save persistent state information to an isolated storage. Applications are given ten seconds to complete this event; after ten seconds, if this event is still not completed, an application is terminated and not tombstoned.
Application_Closing	The user uses the Back key to navigate past the first page of your application.	Save all of the persistent state information into the isolated storage.

In the next section, you code and observe the conditions under which each of the events in the application life cycle is triggered.

Observing Application Life Cycle Events

To help you better understand the conditions under which tombstoning occurs and the events that are fired, let's enhance the application built previously in this chapter to trace the events raised within the application.

Enhancing the User Interface

You will enhance the application user interface by adding a text box and a button control to the design surface of MainPage.xaml to make it look similar to Figure 10-2. Launch Visual Studio 2010 Express, and open the previously created Tasks project. Double-click MainPage.xaml in Solution Explorer, and add a text box and a button to the design surface, as shown in Figure 10-2. Clear the Text property of the text box, and set the button's caption to Launch Browser.

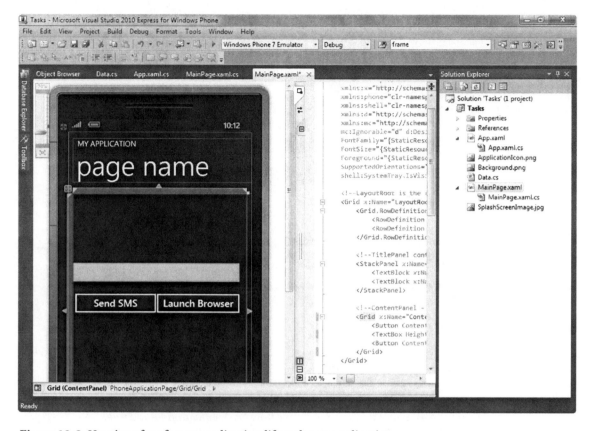

Figure 10-2. User interface for an application life cycle test application

Adding Application Logic to Invoke the WebBrowserTask Launcher and to Log Events

Now you add logic to invoke a WebBrowserTask launcher and navigate to www.windowsphone.com, as well as add messages to print in the Debug window when various application life cycle events occur:

1. Add the following using directive to the top of MainPage.xaml:

    ```
    using System.Diagnostics;
    ```

2. You launch the web browser when the user clicks the Launch Browser button.
    Double-click the Launch Browser button on MainPage.xaml, and make that
    button's Click event handler look like the following:

    ```
    private void button2_Click(object sender, RoutedEventArgs e)
    {
        WebBrowserTask webTask = new WebBrowserTask();
        webTask.Show();
    ```

```
    webTask.Uri = new Uri(http://www.windowsphone.com, UriKind.Absolute);
}
```

3. The application life cycle events discussed in the previous section are all automatically stubbed out (in other words, they contain basic method signatures without any implementation logic) in the App.xaml.cs file. Open that file so that you can modify those events by adding tracing logic to them. (One way to do it is to right-click App.xaml, and select View Code.)

4. Within the Application_Launching event, add the following line of code:

```
Debug.WriteLine("Application Launching");
```

5. Within the Application_Activated event, add the following line of code:

```
Debug.WriteLine("Application Activated");
```

6. Within the Application_Deactivated event, add the following line of code:

```
Debug.WriteLine("Application Deactivated");
```

7. Within the Application_Closing event, add the following line of code:

```
Debug.WriteLine("Application Closing");
```

Running the Application

Before running the application, make sure to bring the Visual Studio 2010 Express Output window to the forefront—in Visual Studio, select Debug ➤ Windows ➤ Output on the menu bar. Press F5 to run the application that you built in the previous steps, and observe the messages displayed in the Output window:

1. When the application first comes up, observe how an *Application Launching* message is printed in the Output window, indicating that the Application_Launching event has fired. However, the Application_Activated event has not fired upon the initial launch of an application.

2. Click the Launch Browser button to bring up Internet Explorer with the Windows Phone web site open. In the Visual Studio 2010 Express Output window, notice how the Application_Deactivated event fired as soon as the web browser was launched (see Figure 10-3), indicating that an application is being put into a dormant state and could possibly be tombstoned.

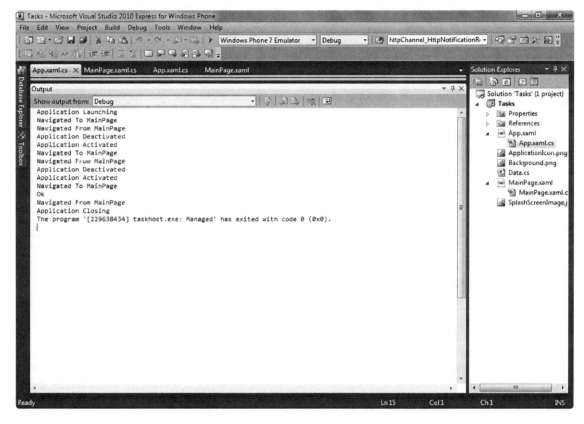

Figure 10-3. Application life cycle illustrated by switching between applications on the phone

3. Click the Back button on the emulator screen. Notice how the `Application_Activated` event fires and prints a message in the Output window.

4. Click the Start button, and observe how `Application_Deactivated` is fired again. If you click the Back button now, the `Application_Activated` event is triggered.

5. Finally, click the Back button again. Since you have navigated past the first page of the application, the application is terminated, triggering the `Application_Closing` event and printing the corresponding message in the Output window.

To summarize the previous examples, any time your application lost focus, an `Application_Deactivated` event was triggered. Any time an application gained focus (except for the initial launch), an `Application_Activated` event was triggered. These concepts are important to keep in mind as the next section discusses saving and retrieving Windows Phone application state information.

Table 10-4 summarizes the actions you took and the corresponding events that were raised in your application. You can cross-reference Tables 10-3 and 10-4 for actions to take in order to persist a state when a given event is raised in your application.

Table 10-4. Summary of Your Actions and Resulting Application Events

Your Action	Application Event
Launched the application	`Application_Launching`
Pressed the Launch Browser button to launch IE on the phone	`Application_Deactivated`
Clicked the Back button to go back to your application	`Application_Activated`
Clicked the Start button	`Application_Deactivated`
Clicked the Back button to return to your application	`Application_Activated`
Clicked the Back button to go past the first page of your application	`Application_Closing`

Managing Application State

Try the following experiment: Open the Tasks project if it's not already open in Visual Studio 2010 Express for Windows Phone. Then, go to the menu option Project ➤ Tasks Properties, and open the Debug tab. Select the "Tombstone upon deactivation while debugging" check box to force tombstoning in your test app when the user deactivates it.

Remember from the discussion in the previous section that, by default, the application remains in memory as long as Windows OS can keep it in memory to enable FAS. Tombstoning could happen at any time, however, if Windows OS removes the application from memory to give a newly active application more memory to run.

After selecting the "Tombstone upon deactivation while debugging" check box, press F5 to run your application. In the text box field that comes up, type **Hello, world**. (You can press the Page Up key to allow you to type using your keyboard in the emulator.) Click the Launch Browser button, and then press the Back button to return to your application.

Notice how the text box is blank (the "Hello, world" text is gone) once you come back to the main application screen. Now imagine if your program was a real-world application capturing many different pieces of data, and that it provided a `WebBrowserTask` to allow for quick lookup of data on the Internet. It would certainly not be acceptable to the end user to lose all the information when the `WebBrowserTask` completed. Hence, you must devise a mechanism to preserve such data when the application is being tombstoned—enter state management.

If you have done any sort of web development, the concept of state management will already be very familiar to you. However, if you haven't been exposed to state management before, it's a fairly easy concept to grasp. According to Microsoft's documentation, when an application like the Tasks application in the previous example is tombstoned, it should have a provision to save state information in case it is reactivated. The sections that follow show you how to save and retrieve state information in your application.

Managing State at the PhoneApplicationPage Level

The concept of state management at the page level applies not only to those times when an application is about to be tombstoned and the page needs to persist its state for possible future retrieval. Many times, individual pages in a Windows Phone application must save their session data to allow for navigation to other pages in that same application; if the user comes back to the original page, the application should be smart enough to retrieve data previously entered by the user.

To accomplish session persistence for both tombstoning and page-navigation scenarios, each page relies on the following three methods in the PhoneApplicationPage class:

- OnNavigatedFrom():Called when the page is no longer an active page in a frame

- OnNavigatedTo():Called when the page becomes the active page in a frame

- OnBackKeyPress():Called when the hardware Back key is pressed

In the following code demo, you use each one of these methods, as well as the State dictionary object, to persist data from the text box in the Tasks application that you built earlier in this chapter.

You not be making any changes to the user interface of the Tasks application—it will stay very basic, just as it is shown in Figure 10-2. You will, however, add code to the Tasks application to persist the information that has been entered inside the single text box in that application. Follow these steps to accomplish this task:

1. Launch Visual Studio 2010 Express, and open the previously created Tasks project if it's not already open.

2. Open MainPage.xaml.cs (one way is to right-click MainPage.xaml, and select View Code). You add code to save text entered in the text box on MainPage.xaml into the session objects if the page becomes inactive in a frame—for example, in that page's OnNavigatedFrom method. Add the following code to the MainPage.xaml.cs file:

```
protected override void
            OnNavigatedFrom(System.Windows.Navigation.NavigationEventArgs e)
{
    Debug.WriteLine("Navigated From MainPage");

    if (State.ContainsKey("TextboxText"))
    {
        State.Remove("TextboxText");
    }
    State.Add("TextboxText", textBox1.Text);
    base.OnNavigatedFrom(e);
}
```

Notice the use of the State dictionary object—it is very similar to the Session variable of ASP.NET Web-based applications and, in the previous method, you add the value from the text box into the State dictionary object.

3. You now add a provision to use FAS if it's available: for example, if an application has not been unloaded from memory. To accomplish that, you define a property inside the App class and set its value from within the Application_Activated event. First, open App.xaml.cs, and place the following property declaration inside the App class:

```
    public static bool IsFastAppSwitchingAvailable { get; private set; }
```

4. Next, make the `Application_Activated` event look like the following. (Notice how the `IsApplicationInstancePreserved` property is checked and its value is used to set the `IsFastAppSwitchingAvailable` property value.)

```
private void Application_Activated(object sender, ActivatedEventArgs e)
{
    if (e.IsApplicationInstancePreserved)
    IsFastAppSwitchingAvailable = true;

    Debug.WriteLine("Application Activated");
}
```

5. Finally, add code to retrieve values from the State dictionary object (if FAS is not available) when the user navigates to the current page. You do that inside the OnNavigatedTo method:

```
protected override void OnNavigatedTo(System.Windows.Navigation.NavigationEventArgs e)
{
    Debug.WriteLine("Navigated To MainPage");

    if (App.IsFastAppSwitchingAvailable == false)
    {
        if (State.ContainsKey("TextboxText"))
        {
            string strTextboxText = State["TextboxText"] as string;
            if (null != strTextboxText)
                textBox1.Text = strTextboxText;
        }

        base.OnNavigatedTo(e);
    }
}
```

The code you have written thus far is sufficient to save the text from the text box for the duration of the application session; even if an application is tombstoned, and the user later returns to the current page, the text will be properly preserved. Let's test this quickly:

1. Press F5 to run this application (leaving the "Tombstone upon deactivation while debugging" check box selected).

2. Enter **Hello, world** in the text box, and click the Launch Browser button.

3. Once the browser comes up, press the Back button.

You should see "Hello, world" still displayed in the text box, unlike the behavior you saw previously in this chapter where you did not handle any state information at all.

While saving information for the duration of the session is extremely important, there are many occasions when you would like to save information permanently so that even if you turn off your phone (or the battery dies), you still have access to that information. Let's expand the demo to accommodate saving text into the isolated storage on the Windows Phone so that it is available for use as long as the application's isolated storage is intact (and as long as you don't remove this information from the isolated storage). Follow these steps to accomplish this task:

1. Add the following two using directives to the top of the MainPage.xaml.cs file:

```
using System.IO.IsolatedStorage;
using System.IO;
```

2. You add code to save text into the isolated storage area of your application if the user presses the Back button past your application's first page (for example, when the user presses the Back button as soon as the application launches). If you would like to get more familiar with isolated storage, see Chapter 13. Add the following method to the MainPage.xaml.cs file:

```
protected override void OnBackKeyPress(System.ComponentModel.CancelEventArgs e)
{
    base.OnBackKeyPress(e);
    MessageBoxResult res = MessageBox.Show("Do you want to save your work before
                        leaving?", "You are exiting the application",
                        MessageBoxButton.OKCancel);

    if (res == MessageBoxResult.OK)
    {
        Debug.WriteLine("Ok");
        SaveString(textBox1.Text, "TextboxText.dat");
    }
    else
    {
        Debug.WriteLine("Cancel");
    }
}
```

Notice how the message box is used to ask the user whether to save information to the file in the isolated storage; if the user chooses Yes, the SaveString method is called, passing the value to save and the file to save it to.

3. Finally, you need to code the SaveString method that performs all the heavy lifting when saving data to the isolated storage. This method accepts the name of the file as one of the parameters, and then it creates a file with that name in the isolated storage. After the file is created, the method saves the data string passed to it inside that file.

Here is the full listing of the method to persist data to an isolated storage; make sure it is also present in your code:

■ **Note** While persisting string values inside the file is perfectly acceptable for the small application that you are building in this demo, you might consider using a different data structure for bigger production applications with lots of data to persist. Serializing data to XML would be a better alternative for such applications, as would saving data inside a dictionary or key-value collection objects.

```
private void SaveString(string strTextToSave, string fileName)
```

249

```
    {
        using (IsolatedStorageFile isf = IsolatedStorageFile.GetUserStoreForApplication())
        {
            //If user chooses to save, create a new file
            using (IsolatedStorageFileStream fs =
                                isf.CreateFile(fileName))
            {
                using (StreamWriter write = new StreamWriter(fs))
                {
                    write.WriteLine(strTextToSave);
                }
            }
        }
    }
}
```

You are now ready to run your application. Press F5 to launch it, type "Hello, world" in the text box shown, and press the Back button. Remember that pressing the Back button past the first page of an application results in termination of that application. Click Yes in the message box prompting you to save your work before leaving. Next re-launch your application. You *should* see "Hello, world" displayed in the text box, but you don't. What happened? If you guessed that you still have to retrieve the values previously stored inside the isolated storage, you are correct. You retrieve those values in the next section, together with looking at the best practices for retrieving this information.

Retrieving Application Initial State

Microsoft guidelines state that within the Application_Launching event, there should not be any isolated storage access or web service calls so that the application comes up and is available for use as quickly as possible. Instead, Microsoft recommends *asynchronously* loading values from the isolated storage of an application once the application is fully loaded. This set of restrictions forces developers to code the initialization routines using the following two guidelines:

- Invoke data initialization and retrieval on a separate thread so as to maximize the responsiveness of an application.

- Perform application initialization inside the OnNavigatedTo method of the PhoneApplicationPage class.

In this demo, you add the necessary methods to load application data properly from the isolated storage:

1. You continue modifying the Tasks project with which you have worked throughout this chapter. At the top of MainPage.xaml.cs, add the following using directive:

   using System.Threading;

2. Open MainPage.xaml.cs, and go to the OnNavigatedTo method in that code. You will make adjustments to that method to load data asynchronously (on a separate thread) from the isolated storage, if there is no data in the State dictionary. If you recall, the State dictionary object is used to hold transient application data, or data that is being saved and retrieved as the user navigates between pages in the application. Therefore, you check the State object to

determine whether transient or permanently persisted data should be retrieved. Make the OnNavigatedTo method look like the following:

```
protected override void OnNavigatedTo(System.Windows.Navigation.NavigationEventArgs e)
{
    Debug.WriteLine("Navigated To MainPage");

    if (App.IsFastAppSwitchingAvailable == false)
    {

            if (State.ContainsKey("TextboxText"))
            {
                string strTextboxText = State["TextboxText"] as string;
                if (null != strTextboxText)
                    textBox1.Text = strTextboxText;
            }
            else
            {
                LoadAppStateDataAsync();
            }
    }

    base.OnNavigatedTo(e);
}
```

3. The LoadAppStateDataAsync method is responsible for invoking a method that accesses isolated storage data on a separate thread. The full method is shown here:

```
public void LoadAppStateDataAsync
{
    Thread t = new Thread(new ThreadStart(LoadAppStateData));
    t.Start();
}
```

4. Finally, the LoadAppStateData method accesses isolated storage data looking for a particular file (hardcoded to be TextboxText.dat at the moment) and the settings in that file:

```
public void LoadAppStateData()
{
    string strData = String.Empty;

    //Try to load previously saved data from IsolatedStorage
    using (IsolatedStorageFile isf =
            IsolatedStorageFile.GetUserStoreForApplication())
    {
        //Check if file exsists
        if (isf.FileExists("TextboxText.dat"))
        {
            using (IsolatedStorageFileStream fs = isf.OpenFile("TextboxText.dat",
                    System.IO.FileMode.Open))
            {
```

```
                    using (StreamReader reader = new StreamReader(fs))
                    {
                        strData = reader.ReadToEnd();
                    }
                }
            }
        }
        Dispatcher.BeginInvoke(() => { textBox1.Text = strData; });
}
```

Notice the `Dispatcher.BeginInvoke(() => { textBox1.Text = strData; })` statement. It is used to make sure that text is updated on the application's UI thread, even though all of the processing may have occurred on some other thread. Updating the user interface from background threads is prone to cross-thread access exceptions without this code snippet.

5. Your application is now complete. It should handle FAS as well as both transient and persistent states. To test it, press F5 and enter **Hello, world** in the text box presented. Next, press the Back button and answer Yes to save your work before leaving. The application is now terminated; if you press F5 again to re-launch the application, the screen should display with "Hello, world" already populated in it.

Best Practices for Managing the Application Life Cycle on the Windows Phone OS

Microsoft provides an important set of application behavior guidelines to follow to ensure a consistent and positive user experience on a Windows Phone platform. Some of the highlights of those best practices are as follows:

- Ensure that when the user launches a new instance of an application, it is clear that it is indeed a new instance. (In other words, the last example of automatically retrieving settings from the isolated storage upon application launch may not be ideal.) At the same time, if an application is being reactivated, the user should feel that the reactivated application has returned in its previous state.

- Since the user may never return to the application once it becomes tombstoned, any data that needs to be saved to a persistent data store should be saved when either the Closing or Deactivated event fires.

You can take a look at the full list of best practices for managing the application life cycle (most of which have already been covered in this chapter) at `http://msdn.microsoft.com/en-us/library/ff817009(v=VS.92).aspx`.

Integrating with Facebook

Applications running on mobile devices, including Windows Phone devices, are ideally suited to take advantage of social networks—these devices are always on and are always with their respective owners, allowing for constant interaction with peers and colleagues. Today, integration of mobile devices into social networks is virtually assumed, so it makes a lot of sense for your application to take advantage of as many social networking features as are applicable. The next section walks through integrating with the biggest social network of them all (currently): that is, Facebook. These integration efforts will allow you to practice what you have learned so far in this chapter about tombstoning and managing application states, as well as to explore new concepts of tapping the vast marketing potential of your application through Facebook. More good news for application developers is that similar integration principles apply to other social networks as well—for example, LinkedIn uses the same protocol (OAuth, which you learn about shortly) for authorizing applications on behalf of users to retrieve and manipulate data.

■ **Note** Before the latest Windows Phone OS was released, the techniques for integrating with social networks were limited to the ones discussed in this section. Now, however, new launchers are available to assist you with sharing information on the social networks of your choice. As you have seen previously in this chapter, the ShareLinkTask and ShareStatusTask launchers are extremely simple to use and accomplish social network integration with minimal effort. However, the material presented in this chapter is still valuable for cases where more streamlined social network integration is desirable, as well as for getting acquainted with the basic principles of authorization via OAuth that you may use in the applications you build. In addition, if you want to go on to more advanced functionality in the social networks, such as traversing Facebook's social graph, you will have to learn about OAuth and other topics that are covered in this section.

A Few Words about OAuth

Facebook uses the OAuth protocol for third-party application authentication and authorization. OAuth is the authorization protocol characterized by separating resource ownership and access to the resource by third parties (referred to as *clients* in the OAuth documentation). In the context of Windows Phone development, the applications that you build that need to post to users' Facebook walls or retrieve resources from users' social graphs are clients, and Facebook users (who are also users of your application) are the resource owners. Instead of blindly giving away their username and password to your app, Facebook users instead grant your application limited time and scope to perform authorized operations on their behalf. These operations may include posting on users' walls or querying users' information. The authorization to perform these operations comes in the form of an OAuth token obtained from Facebook.

Facebook provides an excellent set of step-by-step guidelines for integrating your applications into its vast ecosystem. You can access these guidelines at http://developers.facebook.com/docs/authentication/. The guidelines state that there are essentially three steps to proper Facebook authorization via OAuth, as follows:

1. User authentication

2. Application authorization

3. Application authentication

Let's take a look at how these three steps would happen on a Windows Phone device.

In the next demo, you enhance the Tasks application that you built to this point with the ability to post simple messages to your application users' Facebook wall. In the first step (user authentication), you need to launch a web browser on the Windows Phone device and direct it to www.facebook.com, asking the user to provide authentication. (Note that you cannot simply "post" a username and password to a Facebook web page from within a XAML page in your application. Doing so would break the trust chain that OAuth was designed to protect, since your application can easily capture the username and password values.) Once the user is successfully authenticated, they will be presented with a dialog listing all of the action your application intends to take on their behalf—the second step in the OAuth implementation. This second step is necessary in order for the user to make an informed decision about whether to grant your application the necessary rights. Finally, in the third step (application authentication), your application will supply a special, unique secret key that identifies your app on Facebook to ensure that the user is giving their information to your app and not to someone else's. Let's go ahead and code these three steps.

■ **Note** Before your application is able to interact with Facebook, you must register it on Facebook and obtain the application ID and a secret key. These values are unique to your application; do not share them with anyone! To register your application, go to http://developers.facebook.com/setup and follow the step-by-step guidelines to obtain the necessary information pieces for your app.

Enhancing the User Interface for Facebook Integration

In this section, you continue working with the Tasks application and add a further option to post a message to Facebook on the main page of your application plus a separate page containing web browser control for navigating to www.facebook.com. You'll see why a separate page is needed shortly. Follow these steps:

1. Launch Visual Studio 2010 Express, and open the previously-created Tasks project. Double-click MainPage.xaml in Solution Explorer, and add a button to the design surface, somewhere underneath the other two buttons. Set the name of the button to be btnFacebook, and set the button's caption to Post to Facebook.

2. Right-click the project name (Tasks) in the Solution Explorer, choose Add ➤ New Item, and then choose Windows Phone Portrait Page. Name the page FBLogin.xaml.

3. Double-click the newly added FBLogin.xaml page in Solution Explorer, and add a web browser control to that page. Make the web browser control occupy the whole width and height of the page, since the user will be using this control to log into Facebook.

Adding Application Logic to Post to Facebook

Now, you will add logic to post to Facebook from your application. Remember the brief discussion about OAuth? Posting to Facebook is a multistep procedure, which includes (1) user authentication, (2) app authorization, and (3) app authentication. Follow these steps to implement each of these steps successfully:

1. First things first. You need to add a couple of references to the project to make the code work. Right-click the project name in Solution Explorer, and select Add Reference. Add a reference to the Microsoft.Phone.Reactive and System.Observable assemblies.

2. Add the following using directives to the top of the page:

```
using Microsoft.Phone.Reactive;
using System.IO;
using System.Diagnostics;
using System.Text;
```

3. User authentication will happen inside the newly added FBLogin.xaml page. Therefore your button click event handler should redirect the user to that page. Add the following code to the btnFacebook button click event (notice how you pass the MessageToPost parameter to the page):

```
private void btnFacebook_Click(object sender, RoutedEventArgs e)
{
    NavigationService.Navigate(new
        Uri(String.Format("/FBLogin.xaml?MessageToPost={0}", textBox1.Text),
        UriKind.Relative));
}
```

4. In the next step, you define certain constants, such as the permission types that an application needs, as well as a standard URL that Facebook gives to desktop and mobile developers to use upon successful authentication of an application (the STR_FB_SuccessUrl constant in the following code). Facebook developer documentation gives an in-depth overview of permission types available to your application; your sample application simply needs permission to post to a user's Facebook wall. Open the FBLogin.xaml.cs page (right-click FBLogin.xaml, and select View Code), and add the following constant declarations to the top of the page. (Note that you must supply your application ID and your application's secret key for the STR_FB_AppID and FB_AppSecret parameters, respectively.) Remember, you can always download all the code for this book instead of manually typing it in:

```
const string STR_FB_Permissions = "publish_stream";
const string STR_FB_SuccessUrl =
    "http://www.facebook.com/connect/login_success.html";
const string STR_FB_Login =
    "https://graph.facebook.com/oauth/authorize?display=wap
    &client_id={0}&redirect_uri={1}&scope={2}";
const string FB_GetAccessToken =
    "https://graph.facebook.com/oauth/access_token?
    client_id={0}&redirect_uri={1}&client_secret={2}&code={3}";

const string STR_Post = "POST";
const string STR_Access_token = "access_token";
const string STR_FB_AppId = "Your App ID";
const string FB_AppSecret = "Your App Secret";
const string STR_FormEncoded = "application/x-www-form-urlencoded";
```

5. In this step, you use Reactive Extensions for .NET (Rx.NET) to subscribe to the
    web browser's control Navigated event. Rx.NET is ideally suited for working
    with events, such as navigation to and from www.facebook.com and the like.
    Chapter 18 is devoted to learning about and using Rx.NET. For now, however,
    a simple understanding that you are reacting to the web browser's Navigated
    event and then creating a web request to Facebook in the following code is
    sufficient. Upon receiving the Navigated event, the following code parses out a
    session ID obtained from Facebook and then uses that session ID to compose
    a custom message to Facebook requesting an authentication token for the
    application. The actual posting of the message to the Facebook wall happens
    in step 6. Make the FBLogin() constructor look like the following code:

```
public FBLogin()
{
    InitializeComponent();

    this.Loaded += (sender, args) =>
    {
        var url = string.Format(STR_FB_Login, STR_FB_AppId,
        HttpUtility.UrlEncode(STR_FB_SuccessUrl), STR_FB_Permissions);
        IObservable<IEvent<NavigationEventArgs>> FBResponse;

        //register a subscription to FaceBook navigated event
        FBResponse = Observable.FromEvent<NavigationEventArgs>(webBrowser1,
            "Navigated");
        FBResponse.ObserveOn(Deployment.Current.Dispatcher)
            .Subscribe(evt =>
            {
                //on successful user authentication event only
                if(evt.EventArgs.Uri.ToString().StartsWith(STR_FB_SuccessUrl))
                {
                    //1. get a session ID from the query string
                    var sessionId =
                        evt.EventArgs.Uri.Query.Substring("?code=".Length);

                    //get the user and compose an authentication token request
                    string strTokenId = GetGraphToken(sessionId);
                    string strMessage = String.Empty;
                    NavigationContext.QueryString.TryGetValue("MessageToPost",
                        out strMessage);

                    //2. get OAuth authentication token and use it to update
                    //   user's Facebook wall
                    UpdateWall("POST", strTokenId, strMessage);
                    NavigationService.GoBack();
                }
            },
            ex =>
            {
                //log/process exceptions here

            }
```

```
        );

        //invoke the navigation process
        webBrowser1.Navigate(new Uri(url, UriKind.Absolute));
    };
}
```

6. Finally, you code a couple of helper methods that will create a message to
    Facebook in the format that Facebook can understand, properly parse
    Facebook responses, and redirect. The first one of those methods is the
    GetGraphToken method shown here:

```
public static string GetGraphToken(string sessionId)
{
    string strAccessTokenUrl = String.Empty;
    try
    {
        strAccessTokenUrl = string.Format(FB_GetAccessToken, STR_FB_AppId,
            STR_FB_SuccessUrl, FB_AppSecret, sessionId);
    }
    catch (Exception exc)
    {
        System.Diagnostics.Debug.WriteLine("ERROR: " + exc.Message);
        System.Diagnostics.Debug.WriteLine(exc.StackTrace);
    }

    return strAccessTokenUrl;
}
```

The final helper method performs the heavy lifting of posting to Facebook. The gist of it is to use
Rx.NET to create a POST request asynchronously to the Facebook web site, asking for a special OAuth
authentication token and, upon successfully getting it, update the user's Facebook wall. Don't feel
overwhelmed by the length of the following method—you have learned the basic flow of OAuth
authorization already, and this method simply implements the details of that flow inside a single
function that you could reuse inside the applications you build:

```
public static void UpdateWall(string method, string url, string postData)
{
    var webRequest = WebRequest.Create(url) as HttpWebRequest;
    webRequest.Method = method;

    if (method == STR_Post)
    {
        webRequest.ContentType = STR_FormEncoded;
        // request an authentication token
        Observable.FromAsyncPattern<WebResponse>(
                webRequest.BeginGetResponse,
                webRequest.EndGetResponse)()
                .Subscribe(
                wr =>
                {
                    try
                    {
```

```
                                        // upon completion of request for authentication
                                        // token, parse out access token
                                        using (var responseReader = new
                                            StreamReader(wr.GetResponseStream()))
                                        {
                                            string strOutput = responseReader.ReadToEnd();

   // use access token to compose the request to post to user's Wall

   var payload = string.Format("{0}&message={1}&caption={2}&link={3}&name={4}", strOutput, "My
       WP7 App: \n\n" + postData, "WP7 App", "http://www.windowsphone.com", "WP7 Facebook
       Integration");

   var uri = new Uri(string.Format("https://graph.facebook.com/me/feed?{0}", payload));
   var wc = new WebClient { Encoding = Encoding.UTF8 };
   Observable.FromEvent<UploadStringCompletedEventArgs>(wc, "UploadStringCompleted")
       .Subscribe(evt =>
       {
          try
          {
             if (evt.EventArgs.Result != null)
             {
                //successfully updated wall, print SUCCESS message into
                // Debug window
                Debug.WriteLine("SUCCESS!");
             }
          }
          catch (WebException ex)
          {
             StreamReader readStream = new StreamReader(ex.Response.GetResponseStream());
             Debug.WriteLine(readStream.ReadToEnd());
          }
       },
       ex =>
       {

       }
   );

   wc.UploadStringAsync(uri, null, payload);
   }
}
catch (WebException ex)
{
   StreamReader readStream = new StreamReader(ex.Response.GetResponseStream());
   //Get the error message from Facebook
   Debug.WriteLine(readStream.ReadToEnd());
   }
   });
   }
}
```

You are now ready to run the application. Press F5, type **Hello from WP7 and Rx.NET** in the text box that comes up, and then press the Post to Facebook button. You should be prompted to log in to Facebook (it's probably a good idea to create a test account on Facebook for testing your application); and, upon successful authentication, your message should appear on your Facebook wall.

This section provided you with the basics of integrating your applications with social networks using OAuth. You should be able to modify your applications relatively easily to talk to LinkedIn and other providers implementing OAuth using the previous sample code. The beauty of this implementation is the fact that the whole OAuth flow is embedded inside a single page (FBLogin.xaml), providing for modularized application development.

A final word of caution, however, and it's a very important one: even though you embedded your Facebook application ID and secret application key inside the code in the sample, you should never do this in applications that you intend to distribute to end users. As you will see in Chapter 19, it is extremely easy to gain access to an application's source code, and you don't want to be sharing your application's secrets with anybody. In a real-world solution, your Windows Phone application will request a Facebook ID and secret key from a secure web service that you provide (upon initialization, or right before the user makes a request to post to the Facebook wall, for example). This chapter has avoided showing you an implementation of this service in order not to complicate the example further; however, there are good demos on building web services throughout this book, including the one in Chapter 17 where you build a simple WCF service to help with push notifications.

■ **Note** Remember never to embed your Facebook application ID or your secret key inside your production code!

Integrating into Windows Phone Hubs

Among the many strengths of the Windows Phone platform is the extent of its integration into the rest of the .NET ecosystem developed by Microsoft, which remains one of its biggest advantages over competing phone platforms. The integrated experience comes in the form of hubs on the phone Start screen, which are essentially menu areas that collect data based on functions. The following hubs are available, and they are tightly integrated into the Windows Phone OS:

- *People hub:* Integrates feeds from Windows Live and Facebook. You can also connect other services like LinkedIn, YouTube, Flickr, WordPress, and many more to Windows Live.

- *Pictures hub:* Makes it easy to share pictures and videos with your friends via social networks.

- *Games hub:* With its first and only Xbox Live app, allows for game, avatar, achievements, and profile integration.

- *Music and Video hub:* Makes the full collection of music and videos available to Windows Phone devices. The Zune pass that allows unlimited leasing of music may be one of the best-kept secrets of Windows Phone platform!

- *Marketplace hub:* Allows users to find and install certified applications and games on the phone.

- *Office hub:* Supports Exchange and Exchange ActiveSync, Outlook (with e-mail, calendar, and contacts all available), PowerPoint, SharePoint, Word, and Excel. You can edit Office documents on your mobile device and have your changes available in real time (that is, as you edit them) to others.

The marketing campaign for the first version of Windows Phone was about allowing users to "glance and go," or to get the information or functionality they need from the phone very quickly (quicker than competing platforms, that is). Hubs play a critical role in providing this "glance and go" experience, and your application can raise that role even further by integrating with hubs directly. When you integrate with one of the hubs, your application becomes visible and available through that hub, and not just through the standard list of applications installed on the device. Of course, the functionality provided by your application must fit with the functionality a user might expect from the hub; for example, a music-discovery service that allows you to search for and find new music based on what you like and currently own would certainly conform to the goal of the Music and Video hub.

Detailed instructions for integrating with the Pictures hub are provided in Chapter 16 by using the Extras feature of that hub. The next section of this chapter briefly covers the Music and Video hub, giving you a general idea of what it would take for your application to appear in this hub and to provide users more of the "glance and go" experience. In addition, you touch on the integration features of Windows Phone platform available to users of SharePoint, a major enterprise collaboration platform from Microsoft.

Integrating Your Application with the Music and Video Hub

Integrating with the Music and Video hub is simple: once you ensure that your application makes use of the MediaHistory and MediaHistoryItem classes and provides images to display in the Music and Video hub tile, the Windows Phone application certification process (discussed in detail in Chapter 5) takes care of the rest. When the certification process detects that your application uses the MediaHistory and MediaHistoryItem classes, your application's hub is set to Music and Video, and your application shows up on the panorama panel titled Apps in that hub. The quickest way to get to the Apps tab is to swipe the panorama from left to right when you are in the Music and Video hub.

Once your application is inside the Music and Video hub, it can manipulate the tile for that hub, and it can also update the historical list of media items played or the list of newly available media items. To update the history and new media-items lists, your application instantiates a new MediaHistoryItem object, sets its properties, and calls the WriteRecentPlay and WriteAcquiredItem methods, correspondingly. The walkthrough that follows shows you how to create an item in the New Media Item list. To update the Now Playing tile on the phone, you once again create a new MediaHistoryItem object, set its properties, and then assign it to the MediaHistory.Instance.NowPlaying property.

Since the emulator does not provide any of the hubs against which to test integration, you have to deploy your application to a real device in order to test this feature. You may need to wait for your application to be certified before it is available for testing as part of the Music and Video hub. To help prevent potentially lengthy application development procedures for hub integration, Microsoft has come up with a workaround for testing Music and Video hub integration. Inside the WMAppManifest.xml file, located in the Properties folder in your Solution Explorer, make sure to set the HubType value to 1, as illustrated here:

```
<App xmlns="" ProductID="{c98b0a70-e0c1-462f-a756-5d0aff98e066}" Title="Tasks"
 RuntimeType="Silverlight" Version="1.0.0.0" Genre="apps.normal"  Author="Tasks author"
 Description="Sample description" Publisher="Tasks" HubType="1">
```

In the following walkthrough, you apply your knowledge of the integration steps to create a simple application that adds an "I ♥ (heart) Windows Phone" image to the newly available list and makes your app available in the Music and Video hub. Note, however, that testing this application is available only with a Windows Phone device, so make sure to set the Deploy target to Windows Phone Device in Visual Studio. Follow these steps:

1. Launch Visual Studio 2010 Express, and create a new `MusicHubIntegration` project.

2. You need to add an image to a project to show in the New tab of the Music and Video hub. This image must be of type JPEG and be 173 pixels wide and 173 pixels high. Rename the image iheartwp.jpg. Alternatively, you can download the source code for this chapter and copy the existing iheartwp.jpg image. Include it in the project by right-clicking the project, selecting Add Existing Item, and then navigating to the iheartwp.jpg image.

3. To test the Music and Video hub integration on the phone without going through the Marketplace certification process, set the `HubType` property to 1 in the `WMAppManifest.xml` file.

4. Open `MainPage.xaml.cs`, and add the following using references to the top of the page:

    ```
    using Microsoft.Devices;
    using System.IO;
    using System.IO.IsolatedStorage;
    using System.Windows.Resources;
    ```

5. Next you write the code to update the New tab of the Music and Video hub. Notice how the code manipulates the `MediaHistoryItem` item discussed at the beginning of this section. Make the `MainPage()` constructor look like the following:

    ```
    // Constructor
    public MainPage()
    {
        InitializeComponent();

        SaveFilesToIsoStore();
        MediaHistoryItem mediaHistoryItem = new MediaHistoryItem();
        using (var store = IsolatedStorageFile.GetUserStoreForApplication())
        {
            mediaHistoryItem.ImageStream = store.OpenFile("iheartwp.jpg",
                FileMode.Open, FileAccess.Read);
        }
        mediaHistoryItem.Source = "";
        mediaHistoryItem.Title = "NowPlaying";
        mediaHistoryItem.PlayerContext.Add("keyString", "Song Name");
        MediaHistory.Instance.WriteAcquiredItem(mediaHistoryItem);
    }
    ```

6. Finally, you add two supporting functions that write the iheartwp.jpg file to the local isolated storage on the phone. You need to do this in order to have access to that file on the device at runtime. Note that these functions are generic and flexible enough for you to use them in any other projects that

require storing files in an isolated storage. Add the following two functions to
`MainPage.xaml.cs`:

```csharp
//supporting functions saving files to the Isolated Storage
private void SaveFilesToIsoStore()
{
    //These files must match what is included in the application package,
    //or BinaryStream.Dispose below will throw an exception.
    string[] files = {
        "iheartwp.jpg"
    };

    IsolatedStorageFile isoStore =
        IsolatedStorageFile.GetUserStoreForApplication();

    foreach (string f in files)
    {
        StreamResourceInfo sr = Application.GetResourceStream(new Uri(f,
            UriKind.Relative));
        using (BinaryReader br = new BinaryReader(sr.Stream))
        {
            byte[] data = br.ReadBytes((int)sr.Stream.Length);
            SaveToIsoStore(f, data);
        }
    }
}

private void SaveToIsoStore(string fileName, byte[] data)
{
    string strBaseDir = string.Empty;
    string delimStr = "/";
    char[] delimiter = delimStr.ToCharArray();
    string[] dirsPath = fileName.Split(delimiter);

    //Get the IsoStore.
    IsolatedStorageFile isoStore =
        IsolatedStorageFile.GetUserStoreForApplication();

    //Re-create the directory structure.
    for (int i = 0; i < dirsPath.Length - 1; i++)
    {
        strBaseDir = System.IO.Path.Combine(strBaseDir, dirsPath[i]);
        isoStore.CreateDirectory(strBaseDir);
    }

    //Remove the existing file.
    if (isoStore.FileExists(fileName))
    {
        isoStore.DeleteFile(fileName);
    }

    //Write the file.
```

```
                using (BinaryWriter bw = new BinaryWriter(isoStore.CreateFile(fileName)))
                {
                    bw.Write(data);
                    bw.Close();
                }
        }
```

7. You are ready to run your application. Connect your Windows Phone device to the computer, launch the Zune software, unlock the Windows Phone screen, and make sure that deploy to "Windows Phone Device" is set in Visual Studio 2010. Then press F5 to debug your application.

You may have noticed that nothing happens when application gets deployed to the device—a blank page comes up, but no other activity is noticeable. This is because all the activity goes on inside the Music and Video hub. To verify that, disconnect your phone from the computer and tap the Music and Video hub. In the Apps tab, you should now see the `MusichubIntegration` application, listed. In the New items tab, you should see the `iheartwp.jpg` image that is part of your project.

Microsoft provides a set of guidelines for images that you must submit during the certification step, should you choose to integrate with the Music and Video hub and decide to update the tile of that hub. These guidelines are summarized here:

- Your tile images must be of type JPEG.

- You must include your application title or logo on each tile image.

- The Now Playing tile must be 358 pixels × 358 pixels in size.

- Other tiles must be 173 pixels × 173 pixels in size.

Integration with SharePoint

While Microsoft has been very explicit in its marketing materials that the first release of Windows Phone OS is targeted at consumers and not enterprise customers, the company has already started creating several critical hooks necessary for enterprises to take notice of the platform. One such hook is the fact that you can work in the enterprise SharePoint environment on your Windows Phone device. The SharePoint Workspace Mobile application comes preinstalled on every Windows Phone device, and it is located in the same spot on every device—inside the Office hub. Once you log in into a SharePoint site, you can browse all Office documents, and they appear in the same format as on any other computer capable of connecting to SharePoint. You can modify documents, and your changes, as well as potential conflicts when others modify the same document, will be detected and resolved via SharePoint integration. Another exciting feature is *Offline Documents*, which allows you to download and edit documents even if a connection to a SharePoint site is not available. You can synchronize the documents later, and you will also be guided through the process of resolving potential conflicts in the document caused by multiple people working on it.

SharePoint integration is just one example of the powerful platform integration you have on Windows Phone. As the platform continues to evolve, even broader and better integration options will be available within the vast Microsoft ecosystem.

Summary

In this chapter, you learned how applications integrate with Windows Phone OS. You learned how to use launchers and choosers to accomplish common tasks on the platform. You learned what effects launchers and choosers have on the state of the application that uses them, and you reviewed the application life cycle and managing state information in this life cycle. Finally, you got a brief overview of all the major applications already tightly integrated within Windows Phone and grouped in hubs. In the next chapter, you will learn about the Trial API, and you will build sample trial applications for submission to the Marketplace.

CHAPTER 11

Creating Trial Applications

Today many mobile software vendors maintain two versions of their application code: one for the trial version and another for purchase. The code base for the trial version typically includes some but not all of the functionality of the full version. It also includes code that urges users to upgrade to the full version of the product. The Windows Phone platform, however, eliminates the need to maintain a separate code base for trial software thanks to the handy IsTrial method. The IsTrial method of the Microsoft.Phone.Marketplace.LicenseInformation class provides the functionality you need to create a trial version. Microsoft.Phone.Marketplace.LicenseInformation is a sealed class that contains the methods you'll use to test your application. You already learned how to deploy applications to the Windows Phone Marketplace in Chapter 5. In this chapter, you will learn how to add a trial option to the applications you deploy so that potential customers have a chance to try your products before they buy them. The IsTrial method determines whether an application is running under a trial or a full license, allowing you to limit the functionality of your application based on the result that IsTrial returns.

Understanding Trial and Full Modes

If you wish to let potential buyers try your application first, you must let Microsoft know that trial functionality is allowed when you submit your application to the Windows Phone Marketplace. If you specify that trials are allowed, then Microsoft will automatically include a Free Trial button for your application in the Marketplace, as shown in Figure 11-1. An important consideration for application developers is that, at present, trials do not expire—they can be replaced by full application versions only if customers decide to purchase them. Note that while you can certainly simulate time-limited trials (discussed in the next paragraph), it's not the recommended way to use the Trial API. Time-restricted applications can be reinstalled, resulting in a mere inconvenience for the end user to continue using your application without paying you a dime.

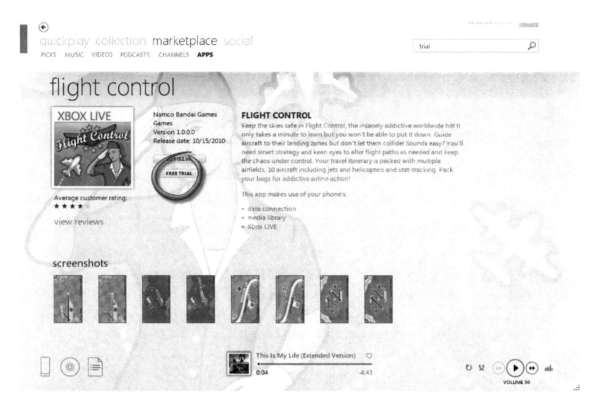

Figure 11-1. A Free Trial button is available in the Marketplace for applications that support trial mode.

Microsoft recommends that application providers prompt—that is, "nag"—users of their trial software to purchase a full version during the trial period. If a user selects the purchase option, control of the application should be programmatically transferred to the Windows Phone Marketplace, and the application details page should be displayed. Within the `Windows.Phone.Tasks` namespace, there is a set of methods that make it quick and easy to complete Marketplace tasks, including those that allow searching within the application and music categories and those that show the application details page. These methods were covered in Chapter 10 in the discussion of launchers and choosers. If, after reviewing the application details, the user decides to purchase your application, the trial license is replaced with the full license, and the execution of the `IsTrial` method will indicate that the application is no longer running in trial mode.

The implementation of trial functionality is entirely up to the application developer. The developer may choose to limit the functionality of the application and prompt the user to purchase the full version to access all application features. Alternatively, the developer may choose to prevent the trial application from running after a certain time period. The way to accomplish a time-limited trial would be either to store the date the application was first run in Isolated Storage and stop after a certain time period, or store the number of times the application has been run and disallow its execution after a certain number of runs. As we have already mentioned, however, time-limited trials are not encouraged on the Windows Phone platform.

You will now explore in detail both the `IsTrial` method and the Windows Phone Marketplace API classes that are used to make trials work.

Using the IsTrial Method

Using the IsTrial method is straightforward. This method is part of the
Microsoft.Phone.Marketplace.LicenseInformation class, and it returns true if an application is being
used on a trial basis (that is, when the user clicks the Free Trial button instead of the Buy button in the
Windows Phone Marketplace) and false if an application is running with a full license. The Windows
Phone Marketplace handles installation of trial and full licenses and determines when each is
appropriate. However, when you execute the IsTrial method while you're developing an application or
before the application user has acquired a trial or full application license, you should make provisions
for the application to execute properly when it is running under either a trial license or a full license.

The short example that follows demonstrates the use of the IsTrial method, and prints a message
to the screen showing whether the current application is running under a trial or a full license.

Creating the UI

In this section, you will be creating a very simple UI to test your IsTrial method in Visual Studio 2010
Express for Windows Phone.

1. Launch Visual Studio 2010 and create a new Windows Phone application
   project. Name it TrialSample.

2. You will now create a utility class called TrialInfo that will become the single
   point of access for the code in your application to evaluate whether your app is
   running in trial or full mode. The reason for creating this class is to allow you
   to properly test your application by simulating trial mode. To add this class,
   right-click the project name and select Add ➤ New Item, and then choose
   Class. Rename the class to TrialInfo and paste the following using statement
   to the top that file:

```
using Microsoft.Phone.Marketplace;
```

3. Make sure that the class is defined as static; that is, the definition of the class
   should be

```
public static class TrialInfo
```

4. Create the following IsTrial property definition inside that class:

```
        public static bool IsTrial
        {
            get
            {
#if DEBUG
                return true;
#else
                LicenseInformation lic = new LicenseInformation();
                return lic.IsTrial();
#endif
            }

            set
            {
```

```
            IsTrial = value;
        }
    }
```

5. Notice the use of the #if DEBUG construct in the code. The DEBUG constant is defined when an application runs in debug mode; the release versions of the application that get submitted to the Marketplace do not have this constant defined, leading to the execution the code block in the #else section of code and a call into the actual Licensing API.

6. Now add UI elements. From the toolbox, drag and drop a TextBlock onto the application design surface. Since you are only getting familiar with the IsTrial method, leave the name of the TextBlock unchanged (textBlock1) and adjust it so that it occupies the entire width of the screen.

Coding the Application Logic

Now you will populate the TextBlock with information about whether or not the current application is in trial mode in the code.

1. Open MainPage.xaml.cs (right-click MainPage.xaml and select View Code), and add the following statement to the top of the page:

    ```
    using Microsoft.Phone.Marketplace;
    ```

2. In the MainPage() constructor, add the following code right after InitializeComponent():

    ```
    bool isTrial = TrialInfo.IsTrial;
    if (isTrial == true)
    {
        textBlock1.Text = "You are running a trial version of our software!";

    }
    else
    {
            textBlock1.Text = "Thank you for using the full version of our
                    software!";
    }
    ```

3. Press F5 to run the application to see the results of the IsTrial method execution. When the application comes up, you should see a message stating whether you are running a trial version of your application (that is, the IsTrial method returned true) or the full version.

In the next section, you get to explore options that go beyond simply displaying a text message when the user is executing the trial version of your software. Namely, the Windows Phone Marketplace exposes a set of classes to help the user review the details and pay for the full license of your application.

Using the Marketplace APIs

Now that you know how to find out whether an application is running in trial mode, let's add the ability to review an application and buy it. To do that, you'll need two new classes found in the Microsoft.Phone.Tasks namespace: MarketplaceDetailTask and MarketplaceReviewTask. These classes, known as *application launchers* on the Windows Phone platform and described in detail in Chapter 10, contain all the necessary functionality for your application to switch from trial to full mode.

Both the MarketplaceDetailTask and MarketplaceReviewTask classes implement a Show method that launches the Windows Phone Marketplace application and navigates to the specified application page. For the purposes of allowing users to switch from a trial license to a full license, there is little difference between these two classes. However, for reference purposes, note that MarketplaceDetailTask allows an application developer to specify an ID for the application (in the ContentIdentifier property) to show the Windows Phone Marketplace page for a specific application. This application ID is optional—if it's not supplied to the MarketplaceDetailTask class, the details for the current application are shown in the Marketplace. The MarketplaceReviewTask class, on the other hand, does not expose any public properties, and its Show method displays the review page with an option to buy for the current application only.

■ **Note** Navigation to the Windows Phone Marketplace must be simulated in your application while you are developing it using the emulator. This is because the required licensing and Windows Phone Marketplace ID properties are not created until after your application is complete and submitted. (Refer to Chapter 5 for submitting your application to the Marketplace.) However, Microsoft provides a special "secret" code that signifies that your application can successfully execute the Show method of the MarketplaceDetailTask and MarketplaceReviewTask launchers. Error code 805a0194 specifies that the Show call successfully opened the Windows Phone Marketplace application.

Let's enhance the TrialSample application created in the previous walkthrough with an option to review and buy the application from the Windows Phone Marketplace. We will enhance the code so that if an application is executing in trial mode, it will show two buttons—one with an option to upgrade to the full version and another with an option to cancel and return to the main screen.

Enhancing the UI

In this section, you will enhance the UI to include the option for your application to allow users to upgrade from trial mode to the full version.

1. Launch Visual Studio if it is not already open, and open the TrialSample Windows Phone application project created during the previous example.

2. From the toolbox, drag and drop a button onto the design surface directly beneath the textBlock1 control, as shown in Figure 11-2. With that button selected, press F4 to bring up the button properties window, then change the button's Content property to "Upgrade to Full Version," and set the button's Visibility property to "Collapsed." Change the button's name to btnUpgrade.

3. From the toolbox, drag another button onto the design surface and drop it next to btnUpgrade, as shown in Figure 11-2. With that button selected, press F4 to bring up the button properties window, and change the button's Content property to Cancel and its Visibility property to Collapsed. Change the button's name to btnCancel. You should now end up with a design surface resembling Figure 11-2.

Next you will add code that responds to the new buttons.

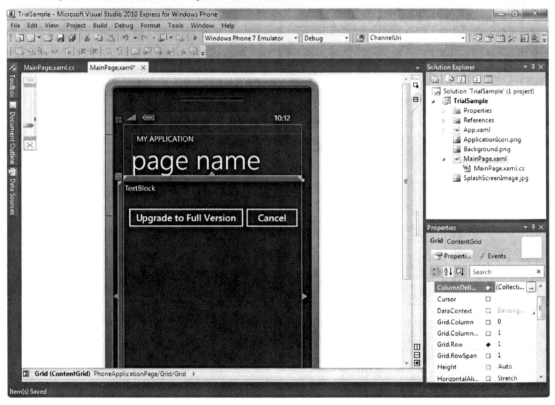

Figure 11-2. TrialSample application layout

Enhancing Application Logic

In this section, you will be using MarketplaceReviewTask to give users an option to upgrade to the full version of your application.

1. Double-click the Upgrade to Full Version button in design view, and change the btnUpgrade_Click method to the following:

```
private void btnUpgrade_Click(object sender, RoutedEventArgs e)
{
    MarketplaceReviewTask marketplaceReviewTask = new MarketplaceReviewTask();
```

```
        marketplaceReviewTask.Show();
    }
```

2. In MainPage.xaml.cs, change the MainPage() constructor to the following:

```
public MainPage()
{
    InitializeComponent();

    bool isTrial = TrialInfo.IsTrial;
    if (isTrial == true)
    {
        textBlock1.Text = "You are running a trial version of our software!";
        btnUpgrade.Visibility = Visibility.Visible;
        btnCancel.Visibility = Visibility.Visible;
    }
    else
    {
        textBlock1.Text = "Thank you for using the full version of our software!";
    }
}
```

For details on the Windows Phone Marketplace registration and application approval process, refer to Chapter 5. Let's assume here that, once the proper application registration is in place, the Windows Phone Marketplace will correctly display the application details page using the MarketplaceReviewTask class, and then swap the trial license for the full application license if the user decides to purchase the program. That still leaves you with the need to test the application using both trial and full license modes before submitting it to the Marketplace to ensure that all functionality belonging to full mode only is not available to trial users. Note that you are now in the position to easily accomplish this testing by simply manipulating the TrialInfo class and the value it returns from within the #if DEBUG block.

Building a Trial Application

The trial software application that you will build in this section is a currency converter. It calls a Web service to obtain the current exchange rate for the currencies a user specifies, and then it tells users how much of the desired currency they will receive in exchange for the currency they wish to exchange. If the application is running with a trial license, users will be able to convert currencies for free.

However, as we all know, consumers never get the official market exchange rates—various middlemen take a decent-size cut of foreign exchange transactions. Thus, to calculate the actual amount of foreign currency you can expect to receive, the full version of an application provides another screen, called the More Stuff screen. With More Stuff, users can enter the actual exchange rate quoted by an exchange broker and see how much foreign currency they will receive after they have paid a commission. This More Stuff screen will be available only to those who have paid you $0.99 and acquired the full version of your application.

Future enhancements could include maps, shared between all users of the application, that show the best places to exchange currency around town, with the commission rates as a percentage of the transaction charged by those places. If you have ever had the misfortune of exchanging currency at international airports, you will appreciate the information flow that this application provides. Power to the consumers at last!

To create this application, you will employ several Windows Phone techniques that are covered in this book. As we introduce such features, we will point to the location in the book where you can find more in-depth coverage of the material. We will also emphasize the functionality that is enabled and disabled with an application running with a trial license, and we use the approach of simulating both trial and full license modes to help ensure that your application functions correctly in both.

Now let's build and test the application.

Building the UI

The currency converter application includes three pages: one for the main application screen that performs currency conversions, one to prompt the user to upgrade to the full application license when the application is running under a trial license, and one for additional options, such as determining how much money you actually lose in a conversion. In this section, you will create each of these pages.

1. To begin, launch Visual Studio 2010 and create a new Windows Phone application project. Name it CurrencyConversion.

2. Make sure MainPage.xaml is open in design view. For MainPage.xaml, the goal is to have a screen with a layout similar to the one shown in Figure 11-3. The screen looks a little busy, so we'll go over each screen element to describe it. Element names and types will be referred to from code; hence they are important to get right. Table 11-1 summarizes the field names and types. A portion of the XAML code that creates the Amount to Convert text box, two list boxes, and the corresponding captions is shown here:

```
<TextBlock Height="30" HorizontalAlignment="Left" Margin="24,14,0,0"
Name="textBlock1" Text="Amount to Convert" VerticalAlignment="Top" />
        <TextBox Height="68" HorizontalAlignment="Left" Margin="6,36,0,0"
Name="txtAmountToConvert" Text="" VerticalAlignment="Top" Width="446" />
        <ListBox Height="93" HorizontalAlignment="Left" Margin="24,137,0,0"
Name="lstConvertFrom" VerticalAlignment="Top" Width="220" />
        <TextBlock Height="30" HorizontalAlignment="Left" Margin="24,101,0,0"
Name="textBlock2" Text="Convert from (currency)" VerticalAlignment="Top" Width="220"
/>
        <TextBlock Height="28" HorizontalAlignment="Left" Margin="262,101,0,0"
Name="textBlock3" Text="Convert to (currency)" VerticalAlignment="Top" Width="190"
/>
        <ListBox Height="93" HorizontalAlignment="Left" Margin="263,137,0,0"
Name="lstConvertTo" VerticalAlignment="Top" Width="205" />
```

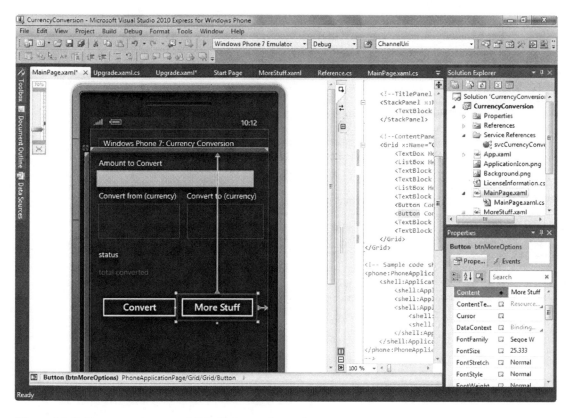

Figure 11-3. Currency converter MainPage.xaml page layout

Table 11-1. User Controls for MainPage.xaml

Application Field	Field Name	Field Type
Amount to Convert	txtAmountToConvert	TextBox
Convert from (currency)	lstConvertFrom	ListBox
Convert to (currency)	lstConvertTo	ListBox
Status	txtStatus	TextBlock
Total Converted	txtTotalConverted	TextBlock
Convert button	btnConvert	Button
More Stuff button	btnMoreOptions	Button

3. Next, add the "nag" page, or the page that will try to get users to purchase the full version of your application if they are executing it under a trial license. To do that, right-click the project name in Solution Explorer and select Add ➤ New Item ➤ Windows Phone Portrait Page. Name the page Upgrade.xaml and click OK.

4. Bring up the design surface of the Upgrade.xaml page and make it look like Figure 11-4. The page consists of a message and two buttons. The message prompts the user to upgrade. One of the buttons enables the user to purchase a full license, and the other one simply returns the user to the main application screen. Ensure that the buttons are properly named by verifying their names with Table 11-2.

Table 11-2. User Controls for Upgrade.xaml

Application Field	Field Name	Field Type
Yes, upgrade	btnUpgrade	Button
No, take me back	btnGoBack	Button

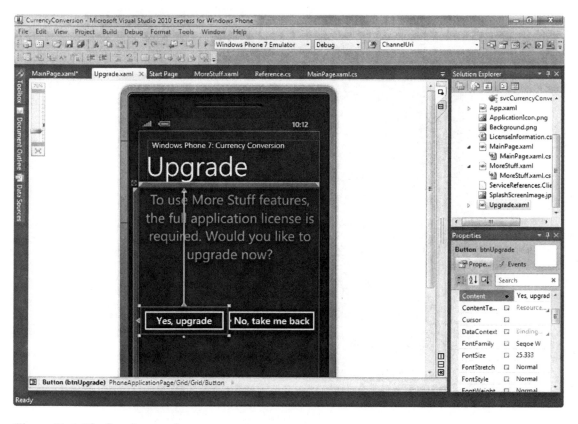

Figure 11-4. The "nag" screen layout

5. Finally, add the More Stuff page—the page that will display features available only to paid users. Sadly, the users of your application may feel cheated at this point: the only premium feature provided to them is the calculation of the money they will forego as a result of the various fees charged by currency conversion services. To add the More Stuff page, right-click the project name in Solution Explorer and select Add ➤ New Item ➤ Windows Phone Portrait Page. Name the page MoreStuff.xaml and click OK.

6. Bring up the design surface of the MoreStuff.xaml page and make it look like Figure 11-5. Refer to Table 11-3 for the field names and types.

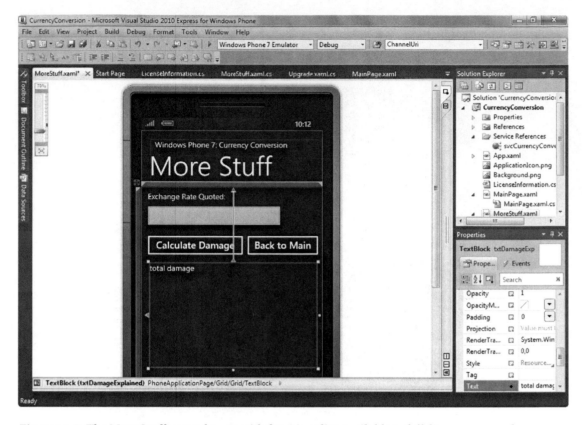

Figure 11-5. The More Stuff screen layout with functionality available to full-license users only

Table 11-3. User Controls for MoreStuff.xaml

Application Field	Field Name	Field Type
Exchange Rate Quoted	txtExchangeRateQuoted	TextBox
Calculate Damage	btnCalculateDamage	Button
Back to Main	btnBackToMain	Button
Total Damage	txtDamageExplained	TextBlock

With the design layout complete, you are now ready to add code to the application. In the next section, you will add code feature by feature, starting with a reference to the Web service that supplies currency exchange rates.

Connecting to a Web Service

To retrieve current currency exchange rates, you will be using a Web service located at
www.webservicex.net/CurrencyConvertor.asmx. While there are several ways to connect to a Web service
and retrieve data, you will be using the approach that draws on the new Microsoft Reactive Extensions
Framework, or Rx.NET. (Note that we resort to Rx.NET several times throughout this book, simply
because we are convinced that it represents the future of programming on mobile devices.) Using
Rx.NET makes it easier to follow the flow of execution by the program, since it abstracts—behind a solid
Observer pattern—the complexities of invoking a Web service asynchronously. In Chapter 18, you will
delve a bit deeper into reactive extensions for .NET.

Follow these steps to add a reference to the CurrencyConverter service and to wrap the results
returned by that service within Rx.NET:

1. With the CurrencyConversion project open, right-click Solution Explorer and
   select Add Service Reference. Paste the following URL into the Address field, as
   shown in Figure 11-6, and then click the Go button:

   www.webservicex.net/CurrencyConvertor.asmx

2. Once you click Go, Visual Studio should be able to locate the
   CurrencyConverter service.

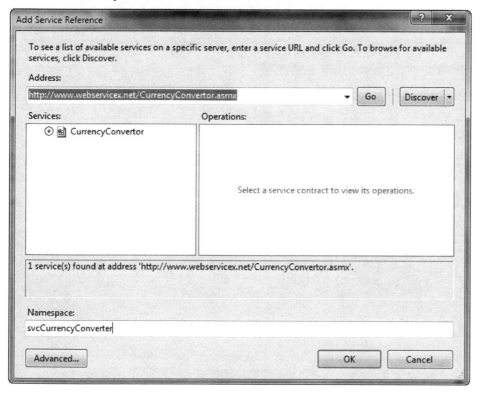

Figure 11-6. Add Service Reference dialog

3. Change the namespace in the Add Service Reference dialog to svcCurrencyConverter and click OK.

4. Next, you will need to add references to the assemblies that contain the Rx.NET modules. To accomplish this, right-click the project name in Solution Explorer, select Add Reference, and add references to the Microsoft.Phone.Reactive and System.Observable assemblies.

5. Switch to code view for MainPage.xaml (right-click MainPage.xaml and select View Code), and add the following using directive to the top of the page:

    ```
    using Microsoft.Phone.Reactive;
    ```

6. Create a class-level variable referencing the CurrencyConverter Web service. (This is a local MainPage class variable that should be initialized just above the constructor.) Also, declare and initialize a class-level rate variable.

    ```
    svcCurrencyConverter.CurrencyConvertorSoapClient currencyClient = new
            svcCurrencyConverter.CurrencyConvertorSoapClient();
    Double dblRate = 0.0;
    ```

7. Within the MainPage() constructor, create an Rx.NET subscription to the CurrencyConverter Web service by pasting the following code:

    ```
    //create subscription to the web service
    var currency =
    Observable.FromEvent<svcCurrencyConverter.ConversionRateCompletedEventArgs>(
        currencyClient, "ConversionRateCompleted");

    currency.ObserveOn(Deployment.Current.Dispatcher).Subscribe(evt =>
    {
        dblRate = evt.EventArgs.Result;
        txtStatus.Text = "The current rate is 1 " +
                lstConvertFrom.SelectedItem.ToString()  + " to " +
                evt.EventArgs.Result.ToString() +
        lstConvertTo.SelectedItem.ToString();

        if (txtAmountToConvert.Text.Length>0)
        {
            Double decTotal = evt.EventArgs.Result *
                    Convert.ToDouble(txtAmountToConvert.Text);
            txtTotalConverted.Text = txtAmountToConvert.Text + " " +
                    lstConvertFrom.SelectedItem.ToString() + " = " +
                    decTotal.ToString() + " " +
                    lstConvertTo.SelectedItem.ToString();
        }
    },
        ex => { txtStatus.Text = "Sorry, we encountered a problem: " + ex.Message; }
    );
    ```

8. This code creates a subscription to all of the results returned by the CurrencyConverter service. It processes the results and shows the conversion rates requested on the screen, including multiplying the total amount to be converted by the conversion rate.

■ **Note** If you would like to understand more about Rx.NET, skip to Chapter 18 right after you finish this chapter. Since the second part of this book is organized as a set of independent tutorials, the chapters in the second part do not have to be read sequentially and can be referred to when needed.

---

9. You are almost done establishing a connection and retrieving data from the CurrencyConverter Web service. The one piece that remains to be written is the invocation of this Web service, which, in this example, is done via the Convert button. In design view for MainPage.xaml, double-click the Convert button and change the btnConvert_Click method to the following:

```
private void btnConvert_Click(object sender, RoutedEventArgs e)
{
        currencyClient.ConversionRateAsync((svcCurrencyConverter.Currency)
                lstConvertFrom.SelectedItem, (svcCurrencyConverter.Currency)
                lstConvertTo.SelectedItem);
}
```

This code invokes the Web service asynchronously and passes it the parameters selected by the user (currency names only, in your case). Note how you have to cast the parameters to the type expected by the Web service (svcCurrencyConverter.Currency type in your case). The results of this asynchronous invocation are returned to the application, and they are processed within the subscription code just created within the MainPage() constructor code.

With the Web service wired up and the data coming back through the Rx.NET subscription to the application, the backbone of your application is complete. Now you need to introduce navigation between the different pages of the application.

Adding Page-to-Page Navigation

In the "Building the UI" section, you created three separate pages that make up the application. However, in the application's present state, only a single page (MainPage.xaml) is available during runtime. In this section, you will create navigation between pages in the currency converter application. For more in-depth coverage of this material, please refer to Chapter 2.

In this application, a separate More Stuff page should be available to users with full licenses, whereas users with trial licenses should see an Upgrade page that prompts them to upgrade. Navigating between pages in Windows Phone is similar to navigating between web pages: you can use the NavigationService.Navigate method and pass it the name of the XAML page to which to navigate within the application. This is exactly what you'll do in the currency converter application.

1. With the currency converter application open, double-click the More Stuff button and make the btnMoreOptions_Click method look like the one here:

```
private void btnMoreOptions_Click(object sender, RoutedEventArgs e)
{
    //ensure that More Stuff screen is accessible only to users with full licenses
    bool isTrial = TrialInfo.IsTrial;

    if (isTrial == true)
```

```
        {
            NavigationService.Navigate(new Uri("/Upgrade.xaml",
                UriKind.RelativeOrAbsolute));
        }
        else
        {
            NavigationService.Navigate(new Uri("/MoreStuff.xaml?rate=" +
                dblRate.ToString() + "&total=" + txtAmountToConvert.Text,
                UriKind.RelativeOrAbsolute));
        }
    }
```

2. Notice how this method uses the IsTrial API to check whether an application
    is executing under a trial or full license. Then it uses the
    NavigationService.Navigate method to display the Upgrade.xaml page if
    IsTrial returns true, and it displays the MoreStuff.xaml page if IsTrial
    returns false. Note that when you navigate to the MoreStuff.xaml page, you
    also pass two parameters to that page. One way of passing parameters on
    Windows Phone is identical to parameter passing on the Web—here, you
    include parameters for currency rate and amount as part of the URL.
    Parameters start after the name of the page (MoreStuff.xaml), are prefixed by
    the ? symbol, and are separated from each other by the & symbol.

3. Passing parameters is not enough in itself—an application must know how to
    process those parameters properly, which it usually does in the OnNavigatedTo
    method, as shown next.

4. Open MoreStuff.xaml in code view, and add the following method to receive
    parameters and assign them to global variables:

```
protected override void OnNavigatedTo(System.Windows.Navigation.NavigationEventArgs e)
{
    base.OnNavigatedTo(e);
    string strExchgRate = "";
    string strTotalToConvert = "";

    if (NavigationContext.QueryString.TryGetValue("rate", out strExchgRate))
        dblExchgRate = Convert.ToDouble(strExchgRate);

    if (NavigationContext.QueryString.TryGetValue("total", out strTotalToConvert))
        decTotalToConvert = Convert.ToDecimal(strTotalToConvert);
}
```

5. To make the previous code work, you must add the following two class-level
    variables to the MoreStuff.xaml.cs file:

```
Double dblExchgRate;
Decimal decTotalToConvert;
```

6. What's left is to add navigation to the other pages within the application. Open
    MoreStuff.xaml in design view, double-click the Back to Main button, and
    make that button click event handler look like the following:

```
private void btnBackToMain_Click(object sender, RoutedEventArgs e)
```

```
    {
        NavigationService.Navigate(new Uri("/MainPage.xaml",
            UriKind.RelativeOrAbsolute));
    }
```

7. Open Upgrade.xaml in design view, double-click the Back to Main button, and make that button click event handler look like this:

```
private void btnGoBack_Click(object sender, RoutedEventArgs e)
{
    NavigationService.GoBack();
}
```

Note the different navigation implementation in this case: you are simply using the code to go to the previous page within the application instead of navigating to the specific page.

At this point, application navigation is complete. You are ready to make sure that the trial version of the application does not allow access to the More Stuff page.

Verifying Trial and Full Modes

Creating trial applications is the central theme of this chapter, and you have spent the first part of it looking at various issues that may arise as part of trialing an application. When you allow application trials, one of your most important tasks is to ensure that certain application features are accessible to full license holders only; otherwise there would be no reason to buy the application.

For the currency converter application, you must ensure that that the MoreStuff.xaml page is visible only when the application runs with a full license. You have already seen the code that performs this check; in this section, you must verify that trial mode indeed behaves as expected. You have already learned the technique of using the TrialInfo utility class in your application, and you will use it again here.

1. With the currency converter application open, right-click the project name in Solution Explorer, select Add ➤ New Item, and then select Class from the list of available items. Name the new class TrialInfo and click OK.

2. Make the TrialInfo class look like the one here. Notice how this class is a static class.

```
public static class TrialInfo
{
    public static bool IsTrial
    {
        get
        {
#if DEBUG
            return true;
#else
            LicenseInformation lic = new LicenseInformation();
            return lic.IsTrial();
#endif
        }

        set
```

```
        {
            IsTrial = value;
        }
    }
}
```

You will test trial mode shortly, right after you put the finishing touches on your currency converter application.

Adding the Finishing Touches

You are nearly ready to test the currency converter application—just a few items remain. Before the application can become functional, it needs to know which currency to convert to which other currency. You'll create two list boxes inside the MainPage.xaml file to allow users to make their selection. To keep things simple in the first version, include only three currencies: the US dollar, the euro, and the Russian ruble. When an application loads, you need to load the list boxes with these currencies.

1. To convert values from the currency enumeration type into a list bindable to UI elements, you will need the following helper function, which uses a bit of LINQ to retrieve property values for a given Enum:

```
private object[] GetValues()
{
    var currencyEnum = typeof(svcCurrencyConverter.Currency);
    List<object> values = new List<object>();

    var fields = from field in currencyEnum.GetFields()
                    where field.IsLiteral
                    select field;

    foreach (FieldInfo field in fields)
    {
        object value = field.GetValue(currencyEnum);
        values.Add(value);
    }

    return values.ToArray();
}
```

2. Open MainPage.xaml.cs and paste the following LoadCurrencies method inside the MainPage() constructor:

```
private void LoadCurrencies()
{
  lstConvertFrom.ItemsSource = GetValues();
  lstConvertTo.ItemsSource = GetValues();
}
```

3. MoreStuff.xaml needs code to perform calculations on the currency rates passed in and entered into the application. This code belongs inside the btnCalculateDamage_Click event. In design view, double-click the Calculate Damage button and replace the btnCalculateDamage_Click event code with the following:

```
private void btnCalculateDamage_Click(object sender, RoutedEventArgs e)
{
    decimal decTotalToReceive;
    decimal decTotalAccordingToConversionRate;
    decTotalToReceive = Convert.ToDecimal(txtExchangeRateQuoted.Text) *
        decTotalToConvert;
    decTotalAccordingToConversionRate = Convert.ToDecimal(dblExchgRate) *
        decTotalToConvert;

    txtDamageExplained.Text = "With exchange rate quoted, you will receive " +
        decTotalToReceive.ToString() + "\r\n";
    txtDamageExplained.Text = txtDamageExplained.Text +  "Given market exchange
        rate, you should receive " + decTotalAccordingToConversionRate.ToString() +
        "\r\n";

    txtDamageExplained.Text = txtDamageExplained.Text + "You lose " +
        (decTotalAccordingToConversionRate - decTotalToReceive).ToString();
}
```

4. Finally, `Upgrade.xaml` needs code to bring up the Windows Phone Marketplace and load the application review page, which will enable users to purchase a full version of the application if they elect to do so. As discussed earlier in this chapter, this is the job of one of the classes within the `Microsoft.Phone.Tasks` namespace. The `Microsoft.Phone.Tasks` namespace is covered in much greater detail in the "Launchers and Choosers" section of Chapter 10. Add the following using directive to the top of the `Upgrade.xaml.cs` file:

    ```
    using Microsoft.Phone.Tasks;
    ```

5. Next, bring up the `Upgrade.xaml` page in design mode, and double-click the "Yes, upgrade" button. Make that button's click event look like the following:

    ```
    private void btnUpgrade_Click(object sender, RoutedEventArgs e)
    {
        MarketplaceReviewTask marketplaceReviewTask = new MarketplaceReviewTask();
        marketplaceReviewTask.Show();
    }
    ```

You're done writing code for the currency converter application. The application should compile and run if you press F5 now. If for some reason there are errors preventing the application from launching, it's best to compare your code to code available for download for this chapter.

Assuming your code runs, the current value of the `IsTrial` method returned by your own implementation of the `LicenseInformation` class is true. Therefore, if you run the application and click the More Stuff button, you should see a message prompting you to upgrade to the full version of the application. This is the expected behavior. Go ahead and change the value of m_fIsTrial to false. You should now see the More Stuff screen, as expected for an application with a full license.

You can also verify that the program works as expected by entering values and asking it to convert them from one currency to another. For instance, as shown in Figure 11-7, $345 is worth 267.86 euros today. To get that output, type **345** in the Amount to Convert text box, select USD from the Convert From list box, and select EUR from the Convert To list box. Then press the Convert button. Assuming that a connection to the Internet is available, you should get results that are similar.

Figure 11-7. Currency converter application converting US $345.00 to euros

While the currency converter application is functional, it can benefit from some improvements, particularly in the area of validating user input. For instance, the application throws an error if the user tries to go to the More Stuff screen without entering a value in the Amount to Convert text box. Addressing this and other similar issues, as well as enhancing the application even further, are left up to you as an exercise. Perhaps there's a multi-million-dollar market for this application out there!

Summary

In this chapter, you learned about Windows Phone trial and full-version modes. You learned that there is a single code base for both the trial and production versions of an application, and that application developers control which functionality to disable in trial mode using the IsTrial method. You also learned about simulating trial mode, an important technique when creating trial applications. Finally, you created a currency converter application that utilized several techniques discussed in this book and solidified your understanding of a number of key concepts of Windows Phone development.

In the next chapter, you will learn about internationalizing applications to make them available to many markets whose language and date/time constructs are quite different from those of the American market. That chapter will further help you with your currency converter enhancement efforts!

CHAPTER 12

Internationalization

With the latest release of Windows Phone OS, support has been added for 22 display languages, up from 5 in the first release of Windows Phone 7. Windows Phone devices now fully support the English, Chinese, Japanese, Russian, and Korea languages, among many others. This, of course, is wonderful news for Windows Phone developers—the greater the customer base, the more potential revenue and exposure for their applications. However, there is just one small gotcha when taking mobile application development to the world: the vast majority of non-English-speaking customers would like to use applications translated into their languages.

Thus, if your goal is to create an application that succeeds globally, you must ensure that it can "speak" many languages. Certainly, one way to make that happen is to create many versions of an application, one for the language spoken in each market you target. Unfortunately, that approach quickly becomes a nightmare to maintain. Imagine making a small code change to an application, such as rearranging the UI controls on its main page. That code change, of course, would then have to be propagated to each language version of the application. Fortunately, the .NET Framework and the .NET Compact Framework that power Windows Phone devices provide a set of language-culture-aware classes and a framework for implementing multilingual applications. This framework involves creating and editing resource files, which can be developed and distributed independently of your application code.

This chapter offers some simple and general steps that you can take to prepare an app for distribution in more than one language—steps that will save you time later. The topic of making a single application "speak" many languages deserves a book of its own, and indeed a few have been written already (see a list of them on Amazon's web site at `http://amzn.to/AbyEK7`). We hope that our advice in this chapter will help you avoid extra work when you are ready to share your brilliant creation with the non-English-speaking population of the world. Let's begin with a closer look at the topic of internationalization and the support for it within the Windows Phone SDK.

Understanding Internationalization

Translating your application's interface or its documentation into other languages may be the most important task you'll face when you target your application for a global audience, but it's not the only one. Languages differ in the ways they display dates, numbers, currencies, and even text. For instance, in the United States, the month is always the first part of the numeric representation of a date. In England, the month comes after the day. This could potentially create confusion—imagine payment due dates being missed because the date was not formatted according to a given culture's standards. One way to avoid misinterpretation of numeric dates is to adopt an international standard, such as ISO 8601, that specifies that all dates are to be represented from the most significant to the least significant element: year, month, day, hour, and so on.

Similarly, disagreements over cultural representations of decimal separators have the power to almost stall the development of a programming language. (See http://en.wikipedia.org/wiki/Decimal_separator.) To illustrate how such heated debates can originate, consider the following example: the number *one thousand one and one-tenth* would be written in the United States as 1,001.1, with the comma symbol used as the separator for the thousands and the period symbol used for separating the decimals. The same number would be written in continental Europe as 1.001,1, with the dot used for separating thousands and the comma used to separate the decimals.

Fortunately, the Windows Phone operating system automatically makes these locale-aware changes for you. As a developer, however, you must help the framework out a little and ensure that you use appropriate data types and appropriate formatting options for the operations you perform in your applications. For example, you should never represent dates or numbers as strings and hard-code the formatting of those strings in your application if an application is intended for more than one national market.

In addition to these variations in the way different cultures handle numbers and dates, languages also differ in the number of words they require to express an idea, with some more verbose than others. For instance, it is estimated that an average sentence in the German language is 44 percent longer than the same sentence in English. That means that a Windows Phone UI written in English—its labels, text blocks, text boxes, and so on—may need to reserve additional available whitespace when designed in the English language and later translated (dynamically, as you'll see shortly) into German or other languages.

Also, if you are targeting international markets, the design of an application should be flexible enough to allow it to display different languages properly. That means that all strings, images, and audio and video content must be placed in separate resource-only files—one for each target culture and language—to make it easy to package the application for a new locale.

■ **Note** By sticking with Unicode, with its inventory of over 95,000 characters to encode your strings content, you'll be able to display virtually any language in the world.

Another important consideration in deciding how to prepare to support your application in multiple languages is the amount of material that will need to be translated. Later in this chapter, we recommend that you use resource-only files inside Visual Studio. This technique is perfectly acceptable for smaller applications, when there are only a handful of items to translate. However, if the translation is quite extensive and requires the use of third-party translation services, you will be better served by looking at more specialized localization tools, such as Alchemy CATALYST (www.alchemysoftware.ie/products/alchemy_catalyst.html), Globalizer (www.infralution.com/globalizer.html), Lingobit Localizer (http://lingobit.com/), or Radialix (http://radialix.com/) While the use of such tools is beyond the scope of this chapter, if you ever find that editing resource files in Visual Studio becomes hard to manage, you can refer to this list to determine whether any of these products will make the task easier.

In MSDN documentation, there are usually two separate sections on internationalizing applications: globalization and localization. Roughly, *globalization* refers to ensuring that all commonly used application concepts, such as dates and currency, are properly represented and used in the system regardless of the locale of the user. *Localization*, on the other hand, refers to translating application resources, such as the text of the UI, into local representation. To muddy these concepts a little more, in the non-Microsoft world, the term *internationalization* is used to represent what Microsoft refers to as globalization. Since this is already confusing, for the purposes of this chapter, we won't make such a distinction; when we talk about "internationalizing" an application, we refer to ensuring that the application will function without problems in all countries and regions in which it was intended to work—that is, the Microsoft concepts of globalization and localization are blurred. We do this for brevity and to give you basic ideas on internationalizing your app.

.NET and the Windows Phone SDK include a number of tools to help you ready an app for international distribution. These tools include the CultureInfo class to determine the language culture in which an application is running, as well as the facility to easily manage resource files that have been custom developed for each culture. You will explore these tools next.

▩ **Note** There is a lot of material to cover when it comes to internationalization—a good place to go to for more information is the MSDN documentation of the System.Global namespace, located at http://msdn.microsoft.com/en-us/library/abeh092z.aspx.

Using Culture Settings with ToString to Display Dates, Times, and Text

To see how you can go about preparing an application for the world, you'll build a simple application that announces a new product—in this case the latest release of Windows Phone. But first you will learn how to use the CultureInfo class to ensure that dates, numbers, and text appear in the right form regardless of the culture in which the announcement is made. Then you'll see how, by using resource (.resx) files, you can easily add translated content to your app to reach new markets.

Let's jump into the code that will set the stage for discussing internationalization of Windows Phone applications.

1. Start by creating a new project inside Visual Studio and naming it InternationalizationSample. By default, the MainPage.xaml file is created in the development environment, with the designer and XAML windows open and ready to program.

2. Double-click MainPage.xaml to bring up the XAML designer window. For convenience and simplicity, you will alter the content of the TextBlocks in the TitleGrid block. Make the XAML of TitleGrid look identical to the XAML here:

```
<StackPanel x:Name="TitlePanel" Grid.Row="0" Margin="24,24,0,12">
    <TextBlock x:Name="ApplicationTitle" Text="Current Culture Setting"
Style="{StaticResource PhoneTextNormalStyle}"/>
    <TextBlock x:Name="PageTitle" Text="culture" Margin="-3,-8,0,0"
Style="{StaticResource PhoneTextTitle1Style}"/>
</StackPanel>
```

Your project should now look like Figure 12-1. So far you've simply changed the text of the default title TextBlock in the Windows Phone application.

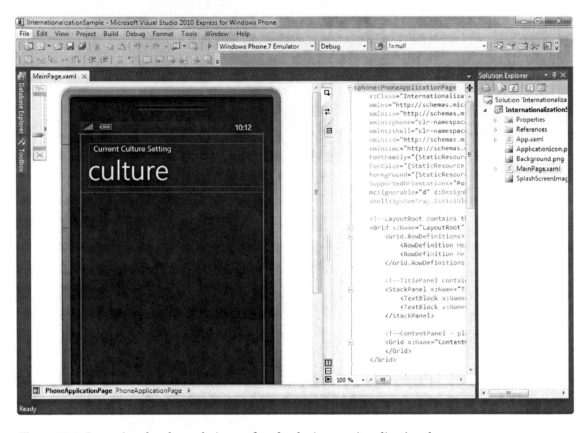

Figure 12-1. Preparing the phone design surface for the internationalization demo.

3. Next, you will dynamically populate the page title with the name of the
    device's current culture. First, double-click MainPage.xaml.cs to bring up code
    view. Alternatively, you can right-click the MainPage.xaml file and select View
    Code.

4. Add the following statement to the top of the MainPage.xaml.cs file:

    ```
    using System.Globalization;
    ```

5. Paste the following code in the MainPage() constructor:

    ```
    PageTitle.Text = CultureInfo.CurrentCulture.ToString();
    ```

6. Press F5 to run the application. You should see a phone emulator screen like
    the one in Figure 12-2.

Figure 12-2. Running the internationalization demo

Notice how the screen in Figure 12-2 reads "en-US." This caption represents two parts of the current culture setting on Windows Phone. The first part—"en"—states that the English is the current language on this Windows Phone device (or device emulator in your case), and it is a part of an ISO standard to represent the culture code associated with the language. The second part—"US"—states that the current *locale* is the United States, and it indicates that dates, currency, and other region-specific items should be shown in the format that is native to people in the United States. That part is an ISO standard as well, designed to represent a subculture code associated with a country or region.

The concept of culture in the .NET Framework refers to a set of user preferences specific to the user, such as dates, currency, and calendar format. Besides CurrentCulture, the CultureInfo class contains many properties that may be of interest to you as you internationalize your applications. You can find the full list at http://msdn.microsoft.com/en-us/library/system.globalization.cultureinfo_properties.aspx. For instance, you could use the DisplayName property to show a friendlier description of the current culture (in this case, you would get "English (United States)."

You might think that the locale setting is of minor importance, yet it is extremely important to localize your application properly. As mentioned previously, while people in England certainly speak

English, the numeric representation of dates there is *dd/mm/yyyy*, where *dd* stands for *day*, *mm* for *month*, and *yyyy* for *year*. Compare this to the United States, where the month comes first, then the date, and then the year. In other words, it would be very time-consuming to keep track of all possible localization issues and, in the end, you would very likely make mistakes. It's much easier to follow the lead of Microsoft, who has worked through many internationalization issues and has made standard libraries and functions available for you to use. Your main task then is to use those libraries properly.

Using the .NET Culture Hierarchy to Ensure Culture Neutrality

Suppose that you have built international support for only a portion of an application. What would happen if a user from a different country accessed features that haven't been internationalized? Will the application stop working, display a blank screen, and so on? The answer to this question lies in a .NET Framework concept called *culture hierarchy*.

There are three types of cultures you must be aware of as a developer: invariant, neutral, and specific. *Invariant* culture supports no culture-specific information at all—in fact, it's the same as US English, so users of an application that supports only invariant culture in Russia will get an English-language application, including dates that have the month first. Conversely, *specific* culture allows for the most granular control over culture-specific settings, and *neutral* culture is somewhere in the middle.

To summarize, these cultures are arranged in a hierarchical manner, with invariant culture being at the top of the hierarchy, neutral in the middle, and specific culture at the bottom, as illustrated in Figure 12-3. When international users access Windows Phone applications, the operating system starts at the bottom of this hierarchy and checks whether an application implements the specific culture of a given user's device. This check includes whether an application has resources, such as text for menus and labels, that have been localized for the user's location. If such localized resources are not available, the system then moves up the culture hierarchy and checks whether or not there are provisions in the application for neutral cultures. Finally, if that check fails, the application defaults to the invariant culture, which is the same as US English culture.

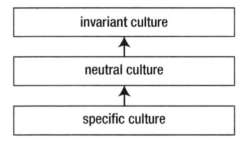

Figure 12-3. Culture hierarchy in Windows Phone

For example, if a French-speaking user from Canada accesses a Windows Phone application, the first thing the system checks is whether or not there are application resources implementing specific fr-CA culture. If that specific culture is not supported by an application, the system then checks whether the neutral fr culture is supported. If the neutral culture is not supported, then the system defaults to the invariant culture, where none of the resources are localized. In this chapter, you will learn how to create resources for specific cultures and let the .NET Framework do the heavy lifting of defaulting to neutral or invariant cultures when resources specific to users' cultures are not available.

Storing and Retrieving Current Culture Settings

On Windows Phone, the System.Globalization.CultureInfo class contains all of the necessary information about the phone's current culture settings. In this section, you will write code to retrieve basic properties of the CultureInfo class, as well as code to change the current culture of the device and react to those changes. In real-world applications, you are not likely to adjust the current culture in code, since the culture setting should be fully controlled by the user/owner of the mobile device.

In the following example, you will create a simple announcement of an upcoming event, and then, with a click of a button, adjust culture settings to display the date, time, and cost of an event properly in a different region of the world—Spain. To accomplish that, you will instantiate a new CultureInfo class and set the current thread's CurrentCulture property to this new class. Later in this chapter, you will expand upon this example and make your event advertisement speak different languages without having to change the source code.

■ **Note** You are probably wondering where and how the user would set Windows Phone culture. On both the phone and the emulator, the culture is adjusted in Settings ➤ Region & Language. Region and language settings can be accessed by clicking the small arrow to the right of the tiles on the phone screen (next to the Internet Explorer tile on the emulator). Click Region & Language, and select an international format that you'd like from the list. Notice how both the "Short date" and "Long date" properties, as well as the "First day of week" property, adjust to the new format specific to the location selected. Figure 12-4 illustrates how you can adjust regional settings on your phone.

Figure 12-4. Changing the phone's regional settings

1. Start by creating a Visual Studio project and naming it WP7AnniversaryParty.

2. Double-click MainPage.xaml in Solution Explorer to bring up the XAML designer window. For this first example, you will display the contents of just three data fields on the screen: those for the name of the event, the event's date and time, and the event cost.

3. Remove one of the two default TextBlocks automatically added to the design surface by Visual Studio. Highlight the TextBlock with the MY APPLICATION text in it (either in XAML or on the design surface) and press the Delete key.

4. Now let's add the additional six TextBlock controls that you will need. If the toolbox is not visible, either click the toolbox button on the Visual Studio Application bar or select View ➤ Other Windows ➤ Toolbox. Drag six TextBlocks to the design surface and position them two per row, one underneath the other, as shown in Figure 12-5.

5. Change the text of the three TextBlocks on the left to the following: Event Date:, Event Time:, and Event Cost:, also as shown in Figure 12-5.

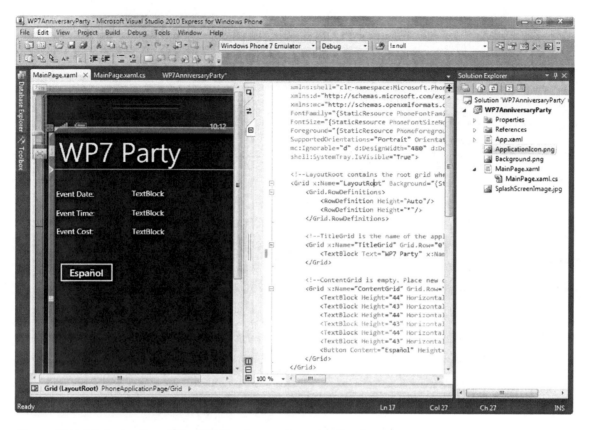

Figure 12-5. Design surface of the WP7AnniversaryParty application

6. Click each TextBlock in the right column, press F4, and change the TextBlock names to txtEventDate, txtEventTime, and txtEventCost correspondingly.

7. Finally, add a button to the design surface and name it Español. You should end up with XAML code that matches the XAML shown in Listing 12-1. (You can simply copy and paste the XAML code from the source code downloads for this chapter instead of adding elements to the design surface one by one, as you've done in the previous steps.)

Listing 12-1. WP7 Launch Party UI Code (XAML)

```
<Grid x:Name="LayoutRoot" Background="{StaticResource PhoneBackgroundBrush}">
<Grid.RowDefinitions>
    <RowDefinition Height="Auto"/>
    <RowDefinition Height="*"/>
</Grid.RowDefinitions>

<!--TitleGrid is the name of the application and page title-->
```

```
        <Grid x:Name="TitleGrid" Grid.Row="0">
            <TextBlock Text="WP7 Party" x:Name="textBlockListTitle" Style="{StaticResource
PhoneTextTitle1Style}"/>
        </Grid>

        <!--ContentGrid is empty. Place new content here-->
        <Grid x:Name="ContentGrid" Grid.Row="1">
            <TextBlock Height="44" HorizontalAlignment="Left" Margin="204,48,0,0"
Name="txtEventDate" Text="TextBlock" VerticalAlignment="Top" Width="276" />
            <TextBlock Height="43" HorizontalAlignment="Left" Margin="5,49,0,0"
Name="textBlock1" Text="Event Date:" VerticalAlignment="Top" Width="193" />
            <TextBlock Height="44" HorizontalAlignment="Left" Margin="204,98,0,0"
Name="txtEventTime" Text="TextBlock" VerticalAlignment="Top" Width="276" />
            <TextBlock Height="43" HorizontalAlignment="Left" Margin="5,99,0,0"
Name="textBlock3" Text="Event Time:" VerticalAlignment="Top" Width="193" />
            <TextBlock Height="44" HorizontalAlignment="Left" Margin="205,146,0,0"
Name="txtEventCost" Text="TextBlock" VerticalAlignment="Top" Width="276" />
            <TextBlock Height="43" HorizontalAlignment="Left" Margin="6,147,0,0"
Name="textBlock4" Text="Event Cost:" VerticalAlignment="Top" Width="193" />
        <Button Content="Español" Height="70" HorizontalAlignment="Left" Margin="6,233,0,0"
Name="button1" VerticalAlignment="Top" Width="160" Click="button1_Click" />
        </Grid>
    </Grid>
```

It is now time to add code to show the event information in different languages.

8. Double-click MainPage.xaml.cs to bring up code view. Alternatively, you can right-click the MainPage.xaml file and select View Code.

9. Add the following statements to the very top of the page (right below the last using statement):

```
using System.Globalization;
using System.Threading;
```

10. Next you will code the function that will populate the event details and the function that toggles the event locale. You will learn the internationalization concepts demonstrated in this function shortly, but for now add the code shown in Listing 12-2.

Listing 12-2. *ShowEventDetails and ToggleEventLocale Functions (C#)*

```
private void ShowEventDetails()
{
    textBlockListTitle.Text = "WP7 Party";
    //create the date of October 11, 2012 at 9:00 PM
    DateTime dtLaunchDate = new DateTime(2012, 10, 11, 21, 0, 0);
    //make the cost equal to $5
    decimal decEventCost = 5.0M;

    //ToString() can also return values in specified culture
    txtEventDate.Text = dtLaunchDate.ToString("D",
        Thread.CurrentThread.CurrentCulture);
```

```
        txtEventTime.Text = dtLaunchDate.ToString("T");

        txtEventCost.Text = decEventCost.ToString("C");
    }

    private void ToggleEventLocale()
    {
        //default to English-US culture
        String cul = "en-US";

        if (button1.Content.ToString() == "Español")
        {
            //change the culture to Spanish
            cul = "es-ES";
        }
        else
        {
            cul = "en-US";
        }

        CultureInfo newCulture = new CultureInfo(cul);
        Thread.CurrentThread.CurrentCulture = newCulture;

        ShowEventDetails();
    }
```

11. Now you will call a function to show the event details right after the application loads. Paste the call to the ShowEventDetails() function in the MainPage() constructor to show event details in English when the application is launched:

    ```
    ShowEventDetails();
    ```

12. Finally, you need to add an event handler to handle the button click, which will toggle the current culture between English and Spanish. The best way to add it is to bring up MainPage.xaml in design view and double-click the button. Add the following code:

    ```
    private void button1_Click(object sender, RoutedEventArgs e)
    {
        ToggleEventLocale();
    }
    ```

13. Press F5 to run the application. Notice how the date, time, and cost are all shown in the US format. If you press the Español button, you will see the date in Spanish, the time in the 24-hour format, and the cost in euros. The labels for Date, Time, and Cost do not change, however, since you have not made any localization provisions in your code for those. You will localize these resources in the next section of this chapter.

In the preceding example, there are a couple of interesting points worth discussing in more detail. First is how we switched from one culture to another in code. To accomplish that, we instantiated a new CultureInfo class and set the current thread's CurrentCulture property to this new class. During the instantiation of the CultureInfo class, we passed a string to its constructor representing a specific culture (es-ES for Spanish and en-US for American English). The second point is the use of standard formatting constructs in the code to make internationalizing an application easier. For example, let's put the following line of code at the end of the ShowEventDetails() function:

```
txtEventDate.Text = dtLaunchDate.ToString("MM/dd/yyyy");
```

Now when you run the application, notice how the date will be displayed as 11/10/2012 for both the Spanish and English versions of your event. This will certainly be confusing for residents of Spain, who would think that the Windows Phone anniversary date is actually on November 10, 2012. Remember to use standard formatting options for all UI elements. In the case of the date, the standard formatting used with the following line of code to show the long date representation is certainly more appropriate:

```
txtEventDate.Text = dtLaunchDate.ToString("D");
```

The final important point to notice in the previous example is the ease of switching specific cultures on Windows Phone. If you pass es-MX instead of es-ES into the CultureInfo() constructor in the ToggleEventLocale() function, you can still see the date translated into the Spanish language, but the currency and time are formatted according to the Mexican standard, not that of Spain.

Using Resource Files to Localize Content

You have now been diligently designing your application for international markets: you have allowed enough space on the UI for more verbose languages and you have used only standard formatting options for date, time, and currency values. However, you still have to perform translation of the application interface and resources to other languages. This certainly could be the most labor-intensive part of internationalizing your application.

As mentioned previously, the application should be flexible enough to function in different locales without the need for code change and recompilation. That means that all the resources required for the proper functioning of the application need to be located outside the source code of an application and loaded on demand in response to a request for culture-specific elements. The location of those resources on the Windows Phone platform are in the resource-only (or *.resx) files. In this section's example, you will enhance your WP7AnniversaryParty announcement application with the use of .resx files.

■ **Note** Large resource files may take some time to load on the Windows Phone device. However, according to the Windows Phone Application Certification Requirements document, a Windows Phone application must render its first screen within 5 seconds of launch. Make sure you always include a splash screen image within the root of your package submitted to the Marketplace. (See Chapter 19 for more details about submitting you application to the Marketplace.) This splash screen image can be any .jpg file you choose and can be named SplashScreenImage.jpg. Even with the splash screen image, however, be aware that the Microsoft Certification Requirements document further states that an application must be responsive to user input within 20 seconds after its launch. Make sure you use resource files diligently so they don't unnecessarily slow down your application.

One benefit of using .resx files is that Windows Phone will automatically find and use the resource file appropriate for the user's locale based on the current user's culture settings. Another benefit of resource files comes from the concept of culture hierarchy mentioned previously—the .NET Framework provides a default fallback mechanism (that is, going one level up in the culture hierarchy) for those resources that have not been localized. Also, .resx files can be easily parsed by external tools, since they are simply XML files. This allows easy editing of those files by third parties (such as translation services).

1. Open the WP7AnniversaryParty solution.

2. Right-click the WP7AnniversaryParty project and select Add ➤ New Item ➤ Resources File.

3. This resource file will contain the values for English-US culture. Name the resource file AppResources.resx and click Add.

■ **Note** Remember the discussion of culture hierarchies earlier in this chapter? The fact that your resource file does not contain any locale information in the file name makes this an invariant culture resource file—that is, the file that will be shown if no locale-specific resource files are found on the device.

---

4. Double-click the AppResources.resx file to bring up an empty table. Next, add four entries to that table for Event Title, Event Date, Event Time, and Event Cost, all in English, as shown in Figure 12-6.

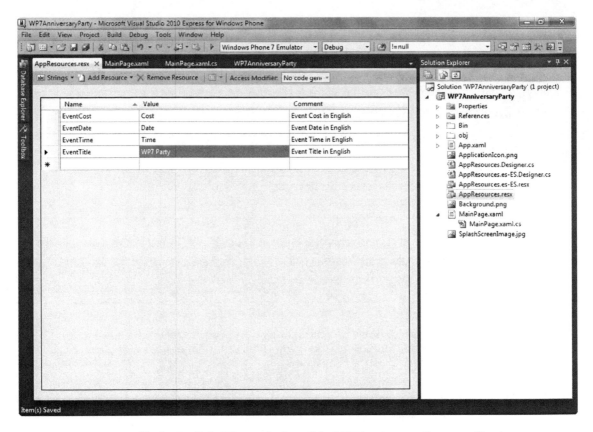

Figure 12-6. Resource file for English-US translation of the WP7AnniversaryParty application

5. Note that the contents of the first and second columns are extremely important. The first one contains the key that the code will use to reference the element, and it must be unique in this resource file. The second column contains the value, or the actual content that will be displayed on the UI at runtime. The third column is useful, but not essential: you can provide descriptive comments about each value in this column.

6. You will now add a resource file for Spanish translation of the UI elements. Right-click the WP7AnniversaryParty project and select Add ➤ New Item ➤ Resources File.

7. Name the resource file AppResources.es-ES.resx and click Add.

■ **Note** The es-ES portion of the file name is extremely important because the resource files must be named in accordance with the specific cultures they represent. In this case, you will provide Spanish (as spoken in Spain, not Latin America) translation of the UI; hence the es-ES in the resource file name. If you wanted to add German (as spoken in Germany, not Austria) translation as well, your resource file would have the name AppResource.de-DE.resx. To create a German translation of an app for Austria, you would name the resource file AppResource.de-AT.resx.

8. Add four entries, for Event Title, Event Date, Event Time, and Event Cost, all in Spanish, as shown in Figure 12-7.

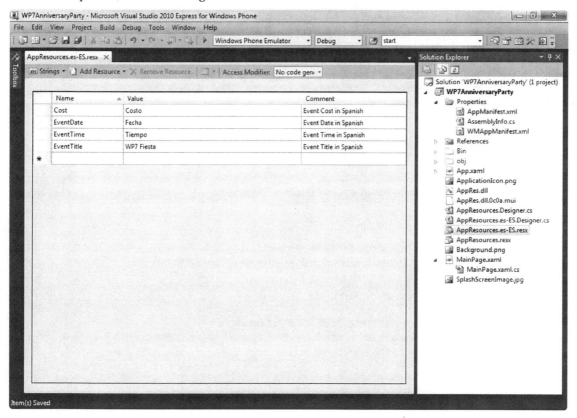

Figure 12-7. Resource file for Spanish-Spain translation of the WP7AnniversaryParty application

---

■ **Note** The translations are approximate and are used for demonstration purposes only—please forgive the authors if the translations are not 100 percent accurate.

---

9. You need to rename the TextBlocks used for captions in your application so that you can easily refer to them in code. Bring up MainPage.xaml, and change textBlock1 to txtEventDateCaption, textBlock3 to txtEventTimeCaption, and textBlock4 to txtEventCostCaption. You should end up with XAML that matches the following markup:

```
<Grid x:Name="ContentGrid" Grid.Row="1">
        <TextBlock Height="44" HorizontalAlignment="Left" Margin="204,48,0,0"
Name="txtEventDate" Text="TextBlock" VerticalAlignment="Top" Width="276" />
        <TextBlock Height="43" HorizontalAlignment="Left" Margin="5,49,0,0"
Name="txtEventDateCaption" Text="Date:" VerticalAlignment="Top" Width="193" />
        <TextBlock Height="44" HorizontalAlignment="Left" Margin="204,98,0,0"
Name="txtEventTime" Text="TextBlock" VerticalAlignment="Top" Width="276" />
        <TextBlock Height="43" HorizontalAlignment="Left" Margin="5,99,0,0"
Name="txtEventTimeCaption" Text="Time:" VerticalAlignment="Top" Width="193" />
        <TextBlock Height="44" HorizontalAlignment="Left" Margin="205,146,0,0"
Name="txtEventCost" Text="TextBlock" VerticalAlignment="Top" Width="276" />
        <TextBlock Height="43" HorizontalAlignment="Left" Margin="6,147,0,0"
Name="txtEventCostCaption" Text="Cost:" VerticalAlignment="Top" Width="193" />
        <Button Content="Español" Height="70" HorizontalAlignment="Left"
Margin="6,233,0,0" Name="button1" VerticalAlignment="Top" Width="160" Click="button1_Click" />
    </Grid>
```

10. At the top of the page, add the following two statements:

```
using System.Resources;
using System.Reflection;
```

11. In MainPage.xaml.cs, change the ShowEventDetails() function to match the code chunk shown here (note the commented-out setting of the default [English] caption):

```
private void ShowEventDetails()
{
    //textBlockListTitle.Text = "WP7 Party";
    ResourceManager rm = new ResourceManager("WP7AnniversaryParty.AppResources",
  Assembly.GetExecutingAssembly());
    textBlockListTitle.Text = rm.GetString("EventTitle");
    txtEventCostCaption.Text = rm.GetString("EventCost");
    txtEventDateCaption.Text = rm.GetString("EventDate");
    txtEventTimeCaption.Text = rm.GetString("EventTime");

    //create the date of October 11, 2012 at 9:00 PM
    DateTime dtLaunchDate = new DateTime(2012, 10, 11, 21, 0, 0);
    //make the cost equal to $5
    decimal decEventCost = 5.0M;
```

```
txtEventDate.Text = dtLaunchDate.ToString("D");
txtEventTime.Text = dtLaunchDate.ToString("T");

txtEventCost.Text = decEventCost.ToString("C");
}
```

12. Press F5 to compile and run the application. Click the button to toggle between Spanish and English. Do you see all the captions and the event title properly translated? Probably not, since you are missing one critical step: you have not indicated that your project must support different locales, and which locales it must support. You will do that in the next step.

13. It's unfortunate that at the present time you must edit a project file in a text editor (instead of Visual Studio) to indicate which locales your application supports. Open Windows Explorer and navigate to the folder where the WP7AnniversaryParty.csproj file is located. Open WP7AnniversaryParty.csproj in any text editor (Notepad is good), and find the <SupportedCultures> node. More than likely, that node will not contain any elements. Edit that node to look like the following two lines of text:

```
<SupportedCultures>es-ES;
</SupportedCultures>
```

14. If you were supporting more than one culture, you would include all of them in this node with each culture code separated by a semicolon. For example, if you were supporting German and Russian translations as well, you would put es-ES;de-DE;ru-RU; inside the <SuportedCultures> element.

15. Save WP7AnniversaryParty.csproj in the text editor. Visual Studio should detect an external change to this file and ask you if you would like to reload the project. Click Yes.

16. Add the following line of code to the ToggleEventLocale method, right below the Thread.CurrentThread.CurrentCulture = newCulture; statement:

```
Thread.CurrentThread.CurrentUICulture = newCulture;
```

17. Press F5 to run the application.

Since you have provided a non-locale-specific (invariant) file, AppResources.resx, with English (US) captions for the invitation text within it, you will see a US English interface upon launching the application. Once you click the button to toggle the application into Spanish, you should see the event title and captions translated into Spanish, as shown in Figure 12-8. The cool part about this translation is that it's completely dynamic—the string values are loaded from the resource file instead of being hard-coded!

Figure 12-8. Spanish application interface

If you examine Figure 12-8 carefully, you will notice a couple of things. First, the date of the event almost runs off the screen in Spanish—a clear mistake on our part for not allowing an extra 40 percent whitespace (by perhaps allowing text wrapping) inside that date value for languages that are more verbose than English. Second, the caption for *Cost* did not translate into Spanish—it should be *Costo* in Spanish, not *Cost*. What's going on here?

The reason for this is that in `AppResources.es-ES.resx`, there is no entry named `EventCost`. There is an entry with the name `Cost`, but that is not the name to which you are referring from code. This mistake is a good demonstration of the application's cultural fallback: there was no entry in the Spanish version for `EventCost`, so the application fell back to the default language (English-US) to represent a given caption—the very reason resource files exist!

Correct this typo by double-clicking the `AppResources.es-ES.resx` file and changing the name of the `Cost` entry to `EventCost`. Now rerun the application. You should see the proper caption, Costo, for the Spanish version of your announcement.

■ **Note** The MSDN documentation for internationalizing Windows Phone applications proposes a slightly different approach than the one we've advocated in this example. MSDN examples encourage you to add a separate class to return resources. In this example, however, we have simplified things a bit and used the `ResourceManager` class to locate resources within the resource files.

Localizing the Application Title and Tile

By now, you have learned to manage the interface of your application in different languages using resource files. You should also understand the importance of manipulating data types within an application in a culturally neutral way. But there's still a very important internationalization detail you need to address: making the application title and tile appear in the language native to the user of the mobile device. In other words, you need to internationalize the application title and tile, and that process differs from everything that we have covered so far in this chapter. Localizing the application title and tile involves creating and editing a C++ resource file, a subject that at first glance might appear intimidating. As you will see shortly, however, creating a C++ resource file is a very straightforward process once you have the right tools for the job.

■ **Note** Creating C++ resource files is very easy with Visual Studio 2010; however, you must get the right version of Visual Studio to create those files. The version that comes with the Windows Phone SDK does not support C++ projects, but you can download a free version of Visual Studio Express (not Visual Studio Express for Windows Phone) from Microsoft at `www.microsoft.com/visualstudio/en-us/products/2010-editions/express`. The version of Visual Studio 2010 that we are using in this chapter to create resource files is Visual Studio Ultimate, which, while not free, provides full integration with Windows Phone projects as well as the ability to create C++ projects, among many others.

Creating an Application Resource File

Translations of the application title and tile must live in a separate application resource DLL. The creation of this DLL is the first step toward internationalizing the application title and tile, and it is illustrated in the following walkthrough.

1. Launch Visual Studio Ultimate or Visual Studio Express (*not* the Windows Phone edition). Select File ➤ New Project ➤ Visual C++ ➤ Win32 ➤ Win32 Project.

2.   Name the project AppRes and click OK. On the wizard screen that comes up, select DLL as application type and make sure "Empty project" is checked under Additional Options, as shown in Figure 12-9. Then click Finish.

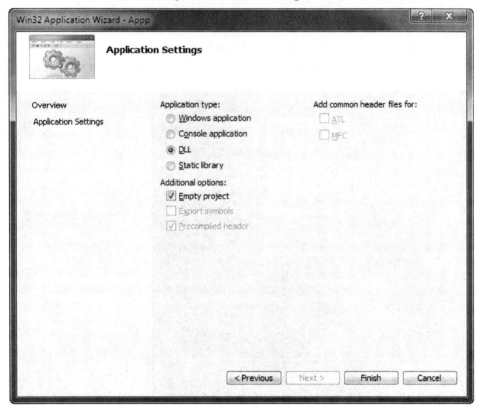

Figure 12-9. Win32 project application settings

3.   There's one setting that you will need to adjust to make this project a resource-only DLL. Right-click project name, select Properties, expand the Linker tab on the left, and click the Advanced tab. Change the No Entry Point setting to Yes (/NOENTRY), as shown in Figure 12-10.

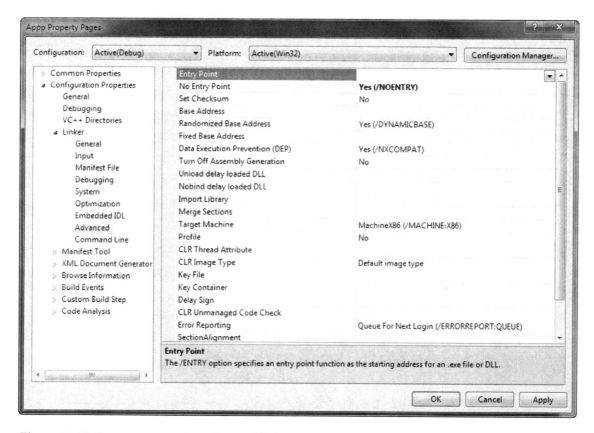

Figure 12-10. C++ resource project advanced linker settings

4.   Now you will add a string table to your project. Right-click project name, select
     Add ➤ Resource, select String Table, and click New.

5.   Edit the string table as shown in Figure 12-11. Create an entry with a ID of
     ApplicationTitle, a value of 100, and a caption of WP7Anniversary. Next,
     create an entry with ID of ApplicationTile, a value of 200, and a caption of
     WP7AnniversaryTile.

6.   Build the application DLL by right-clicking the project name and selecting
     Build.

ID	Value	Caption
ApplicationTitle	100	WP7Anniversary
ApplicationTile	200	WP7AnniversaryTile

Figure 12-11. String table for the WP7Anniversary application

With the resource DLL built, you are ready to bring that DLL over to your WP7Anniversary project and use it.

Using Resource DLL from the Windows Phone Project

In the following walkthrough, you will learn how to use the resource DLL in your Windows Phone project to internationalize the application title and tile.

1. Open the WP7AnniversaryParty solution.

2. Right-click the WP7AnniversaryParty project, select Add ➤ Existing Item, and then navigate to the AppRes.dll that was created in the previous section and select it. By default, this DLL is located in the Debug folder of the solution created in the previous section.

3. Right-click the AppRes.dll in Solution Explorer and select Properties. Set the Build action for this file to Content.

4. You will now specify that the application title and tile will come from an external resource DLL instead of being hard-coded into the WMAppManifest.xml file. Expand the Properties node in Solution Explorer, and double-click the WMAppManifest.xml file to open it in the Visual Studio text editor. Locate the <App...> XML node and change the Title property of this node to look like the following (this line specifies that AppRes.dll should be searched for the Title property, and a caption with a value of 100 should be used):

   Title="@AppRes.dll,-100"

5. Similarly, change the <Title> XML tag inside the <Tokens> section of WMAppManifest.xml to the following:

   <Title>@AppRes.dll,-200</Title>

6. Save the WMAppManifest.xml file and run the application. If you press the Windows key on the emulator now, you should notice that your application is called WP7Anniversary instead of WP7AnniversaryParty, as it was previously. WP7Anniversary is the caption from the string table inside the AppRes.dll at value 100.

The `AppRes.dll` file created in the previous section is the invariant-culture DLL. The entries from that DLL will be used when no culture-specific DLLs are available. In the next section, you will learn how to create culture-specific DLLs and translate the application title and tile into Spanish.

Creating Culture-Specific Resource DLLs

The secret to enabling Windows Phone to use culture-specific resource DLLs lies in the naming convention for those DLLs—they must have the name in the format of

`AppRes.dll.[locale id].mui`

Since we named our resource DLL `AppRes` in the previous section and used that reference in the `WMAppManifest.xml` file, we specified the `AppRes.dll` in the beginning of this naming convention. Your resource DLL could be named differently, as long as `WMAppManifest.xml` properly refers to that file name.

The full list of locale IDs is available at `http://msdn.microsoft.com/en-us/goglobal/bb964664.aspx`. From that list, we determine that the locale ID for Spain is 0c0a (hex). Armed with that knowledge, we are ready to show our application title and tile in Spanish.

1. Open the `AppRes` C++ resource project, and edit the string table values as shown in Figure 12-12, translating the captions into Spanish.

Appp.rc - String Table* ✕		
ID	Value	Caption
ApplicationTitle	100	WP7Aniversario
ApplicationTile	200	WP7AniversarioAzulejo

Figure 12-12. String table in Spanish for the WP7Anniversary application

2. Build the project by right-clicking the project name and selecting Build.

3. From the `WP7AnniversayParty` project, select Add ➤ Existing Item, and then navigate to the `AppRes.dll` that was created in the previous section—but *do not select it at this point*. Right-click that file and choose the Rename option. Give this file the name of `AppRes.dll.0c0a.mui`, which is the `AppRes.dll` for the Spanish locale. Now select the DLL to add it to the `WP7AnniversaryParty` project.

4. Make sure that the Build action for `AppRes.dll.0c0a.mui` is set to `Content` by right-clicking that file and selecting Properties.

5. You are now ready to see the results of your internationalization efforts. Change the culture of the Windows Phone emulator to Español by clicking the Windows button, selecting Settings, and then selecting Region & Language. Once you accept the changes, the emulator will restart and begin operating in the Spanish-specific culture. If you click the left arrow on the Windows Phone start screen now, you should see the name of your application shown in Spanish—namely, WP7Aniversario. If you click and hold the application title and choose the Pin to Start option, the tile of your application should show up on the Windows Phone start screen with a Spanish caption as well.

To add support for additional languages, you would need to edit the string table with translations for these new languages, build the project, name the resulting DLL in accordance with the targeted locale, and include the new DLL with the Windows Phone project.

Summary

In this chapter, you learned how to prepare an application to work in parts of the world other than the United States. You briefly explored the use of the CulturalInfo object to adjust your application for the user's language and country. You also learned how to use resource files to provide translated versions of field names and documentation. You studied the specific issues to consider when developing applications for international markets, such as dates, numbers, and currency translations between locales. You also learned how to translate application resources via Visual Studio resource files. Finally, you learned how to translate the application title and tile using resource DLLs.

In the next chapter, you will take a look at how to persist files and settings on Windows Phone via the use of local storage. You will save images, application settings, and other data, and then load them on demand from a local store on Windows Phone. You will also discover how easy it is to work with an internal Windows Phone database, which is a new feature of the Windows Phone 7.5 platform.

CHAPTER 13

Isolated Storage

In Chapter 3, you learned that Microsoft Azure provides a reliable place to store and access data, but using it requires Internet access. Sometimes it's more efficient to cache frequently accessed data on the Windows Phone device itself.

Isolated Storage is a place on a Windows Phone device where an application can save files, configuration information, and other data that you want to persist. Each application is allocated its own portion of the available space, but it can't access file systems used by the operating system itself—a limitation that prevents a rogue application from accessing system data and possibly corrupting it. The amount of storage that can be assigned to any single application depends on the phone's available space.

With Isolated Storage, a Windows Phone application can create and maintain a virtual file storage system that can contain virtual folders and files; you won't have direct access to the underlying Windows Phone file system, but Isolated Storage will provide you with APIs to work with the file system. All input and output operations can be performed only at the application's Isolated Storage level.

Support for Isolated Storage on Windows Phone is provided by the following two namespaces, whose features are depicted in Figure 13-1.

- *Isolated file storage:* `System.IO.IsolatedStorage.IsolatedStorageFile` allows you to create, use, and remove directories and files in the virtual Isolated Storage. The files can be added and retrieved through the file stream using `System.IO.IsolatedStorage.IsolatedFileStream`, which can also cache images, sounds, and files that are dynamically loaded from the Web. In the first demo, you will learn how use Isolated Storage to cache an image loaded from the Web.

- *Isolated local settings:* `System.IO.IsolatedStorage.IsolatedStorageSettings` provides APIs for storing and working with key/value pairs cached in Isolated Storage and for storing application settings and user specific settings.

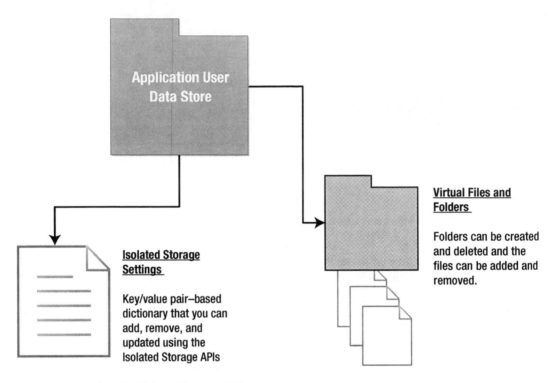

Figure 13-1. Using the Isolated Storage APIs

In this chapter, you will learn how to work with Isolated Storage. The first example will show you a technique used to cache an image downloaded from the Web into the Isolated Storage file. The second demo will show you how to save and retrieve name and value pairs using Isolated Storage settings.

Working with Isolated Directory Storage

You'll begin by building an application to work with the local storage on Windows Phone. The application, named IsolatedStorageStoreImageDemo and shown in Figure 13-2, demonstrates the basic functions available through the Isolated Storage APIs, including the following:

- Retrieving application-specific Isolated Storage
- Getting an Isolated Storage quota
- Saving and retrieving Isolated Storage files

In this demo, when the Get Image button is clicked for the first time, the application checks to see whether there is enough space available in Isolated Storage. If there is, the image will be downloaded from the web site and then saved to Isolated Storage via the Isolated Storage file stream. If the button is clicked again, the image will be loaded into an Isolated Storage file.

Figure 13–2. IsolatedStorageStoreImageDemo

You'll build the demo in three steps. First, you'll create a new Visual Studio project. Next, you'll build the project's UI. Finally, you'll finish up by adding code to respond to commands from the user.

Creating the IsolatedStorageStoreImageDemo Project

To set up the IsolatedStorageStoreImageDemo project, follow the steps you've used for previous examples in this book:

1. Open Microsoft Visual Studio 2010 Express for Windows Phone on your workstation

2. Create a new Windows Phone Application by selecting File ➤ New Project from the Visual Studio command menu. Select the Windows Phone Application template, name the application IsolatedStorageStoreImageDemo, and click OK, as shown in Figure 13-3.

Figure 13-3. Windows Phone Application template for creating IsolatedStorageStoreImageDemo

Coding the UI

You'll first code the UI, which we've chosen to implement in XAML. Sometimes it's faster to work with XAML than with managed code, especially when you're working with a simple example such as this one, which requires only a few controls. Go to Solution Explorer, open MainPage.xaml, and replace the XAML you find there with the code that appears in the following sections.

Selecting the UI Resources

Begin by adding the following XAML markup to MainPage.xaml to identify where the controls are found in the namespaces to build the application's main page:

```
<phone:PhoneApplicationPage
    x:Class="IsolatedStorageStoreImageDemo.MainPage"
    xmlns="http://schemas.microsoft.com/winfx/2006/xaml/presentation"
    xmlns:x="http://schemas.microsoft.com/winfx/2006/xaml"
    xmlns:phone="clr-namespace:Microsoft.Phone.Controls;assembly=Microsoft.Phone"
    xmlns:shell="clr-namespace:Microsoft.Phone.Shell;assembly=Microsoft.Phone"
```

```
xmlns:d="http://schemas.microsoft.com/expression/blend/2008"
xmlns:mc="http://schemas.openxmlformats.org/markup-compatibility/2006"
mc:Ignorable="d" d:DesignWidth="480" d:DesignHeight="768"
FontFamily="{StaticResource PhoneFontFamilyNormal}"
FontSize="{StaticResource PhoneFontSizeNormal}"
Foreground="{StaticResource PhoneForegroundBrush}"
SupportedOrientations="Portrait" Orientation="Portrait"
shell:SystemTray.IsVisible="True">
```

Referencing the namespace as
xmlns="http://schemas.microsoft.com/winfx/2006/xaml/presentation" allows you to use common
Windows Phone controls, such as text boxes, buttons, and list boxes, to create the main page. The code
snippet also includes a reference to the code-behind class
(x:Class="IsolatedStorageStoreImageDemo.MainPage") that will handle the main page controls' events.

Building the Main Page and Adding Components

To create the main application page and populate it with controls, add the following XAML markup to
the preceding block of code, also in MainPage.xaml:

```xml
<Grid x:Name="LayoutRoot" Background="{StaticResource PhoneBackgroundBrush}">
    <Grid.RowDefinitions>
        <RowDefinition Height="Auto"/>
        <RowDefinition Height="*"/>
    </Grid.RowDefinitions>

    <!--TitleGrid is the name of the application and page title-->
    <Grid x:Name="TitleGrid" Grid.Row="0">
        <TextBlock Text="IsolatedStorageStoreImageDemo"
                   x:Name="textBlockPageTitle"
                   Style="{StaticResource PhoneTextTitle1Style}"
                   FontSize="28" />
    </Grid>

    <!--ContentGrid is empty. Place new content here-->
    <Grid x:Name="ContentGrid" Grid.Row="1">

<Image Height="458" HorizontalAlignment="Left"
            Margin="20,134,0,0" Name="image1" Stretch="Uniform"
            VerticalAlignment="Top" Width="423" />
        <Button Content="Get Image" Height="70"
            HorizontalAlignment="Left" Margin="0,598,0,0"
            Name="btnGetImage" VerticalAlignment="Top"
            Width="443" Click="btnGetImage_Click" />
        <TextBox Height="72" HorizontalAlignment="Left"
            Margin="12,29,0,0" Name="txtImageUrl"
            Text="http://res1.newagesolution.net/Portals/0/twitter2_icon.jpg"
            VerticalAlignment="Top" Width="460" />
    </Grid>
</Grid>
```

```
</phoneNavigation:PhoneApplicationPage>
```

Once you've loaded the XAML code for the main page, you should see the layout shown in Figure 13-4. Now it's time to use the Isolated Storage APIs to add behavior to the application.

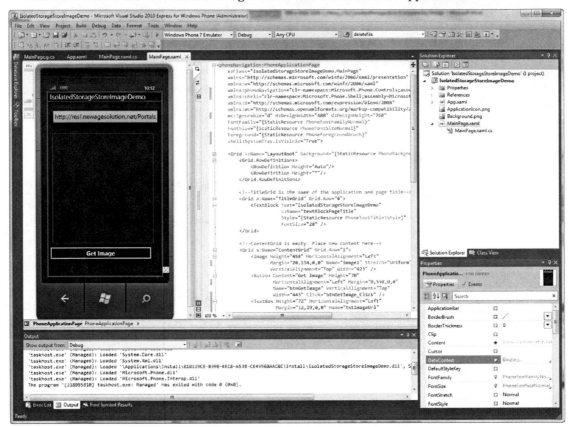

Figure 13-4. IsolatedStorageStoreImageDemo in design view

Coding the Application

In Solution Explorer, open `MainPage.xaml.cs` and replace the code there with the following C# code blocks—precisely in the order in which they are presented.

Specifying the Namespaces

Begin by specifying the namespaces the application will use. `System.IO.IsolatedStorage` and `System.IO` contain the APIs needed to work with the isolated file storage.

```
using System;
```

```
using System.Net;
using System.Windows;
using Microsoft.Phone.Controls;
using System.Windows.Media.Imaging;
using System.IO.IsolatedStorage;
using System.IO;

namespace IsolatedStorageStoreImageDemo
{
```

Initializing Variables

Now add the following block of code to MainPage.xaml.cs to initialize the application's variables:

```
public partial class MainPage : PhoneApplicationPage
{
    private string ImageFileName = null;


    WebClient _webClient; // Used for downloading the image the first time from the web
site
...
```

Initializing the Application

Now add the application's constructor, which uses the WebClient.OpenReadCompleted event to download its target image. The code contains logic to check whether enough space is available in the phone's Isolated Storage to save the downloaded image. If space is available, the image gets saved; otherwise it's loaded directly into the image control.

```
public MainPage()
{
    InitializeComponent();

    SupportedOrientations = SupportedPageOrientation.Portrait |
                SupportedPageOrientation.Landscape;

    _webClient = new WebClient();
    // Handles when the image download is completed
    _webClient.OpenReadCompleted += (s1, e1) =>
        {
            if (e1.Error == null)
            {
                try
                {
                    bool isSpaceAvailable =
                                        IsSpaceIsAvailable(e1.Result.Length);

                    if (isSpaceAvailable)
                    {
```

```
                        // Save image file to Isolated Storage
                        using (IsolatedStorageFileStream isfs =
                    new IsolatedStorageFileStream(ImageFileName,
                            FileMode.Create,
                    IsolatedStorageFile.GetUserStoreForApplication()))
                        {
                            long imgLen = e1.Result.Length;
                            byte[] b = new byte[imgLen];
                            e1.Result.Read(b, 0, b.Length);
                            isfs.Write(b, 0, b.Length);
                            isfs.Flush();
                        }

                        LoadImageFromIsolatedStorage(ImageFileName);
                    }
                    else
                    {
                        BitmapImage bmpImg = new BitmapImage();
                        bmpImg.SetSource(e1.Result);
                        image1.Source = bmpImg;
                    }
                }
                catch (Exception ex)
                {
                    MessageBox.Show(ex.Message);
                }
            }
        };
    }
```

■ **Note** In order to create a subdirectory, you must create a directory path string, such as `MyDirectory1\SubDirectory1`, and pass it to the `CreateDirectory` method. To add a file to `SubDirectory1`, you must create a string that combines the file name with its path, such as `MyDirectory1\SubDirectory1\MyFileInSubDirectory1.txt`, and then use `IsolatedStorageFileStream` to create a file. In order to add contents to the file, use `StreamWriter`.

When you use the `Remove` method in `IsolatedStorageFile`, use it with caution, as it will delete all directories and files. To avoid accidently deleting everything in Isolated Storage, create a warning prompt window to confirm with the user that it will be OK to delete everything in Isolated Storage. Another possibility is to use `IsolatedStorage.DeleteFile` or `IsolatedStorage.DeleteDirectory` to delete a specific file or directory to avoid removing all files or directories. Please refer to the MSDN documentation at `http://msdn.microsoft.com/en-us/library/kx3852wf(VS.85).aspx` for more information.

> ■ **Tip** `System.IO.Path.Combine` provides a great way to combine directory paths and files without having to worry about whether the backslashes (\) are properly added. Also, when searching files or directories, you can use a wildcard (*) when building a directory or file path.

Checking Availability of Isolated Storage Space

Now add code for the `isSpaceAvailable` helper method, which the application uses to determine whether there is enough space available in Isolated Storage to store the image.

```
// Check to make sure there is enough space available on the phone
    // to save the image that we are downloading to the phone
    private bool IsSpaceIsAvailable(long spaceReq)
    {
        using (IsolatedStorageFile store =
IsolatedStorageFile.GetUserStoreForApplication())
    {
            long spaceAvail = store.AvailableFreeSpace;
            if (spaceReq > spaceAvail)
            {
                return false;
            }
            return true;
        }
    }
```

Adding a Button Event to Retrieve the Image from Isolated Storage

When the Get Image button is clicked, it checks to see if the image exists in Isolated Storage. If the image exists, the image is loaded from Isolated Storage; otherwise the image is downloaded from the web site.

```
private void btnGetImage_Click(object sender, RoutedEventArgs e)
    {
        using (IsolatedStorageFile isf =
            IsolatedStorageFile.GetUserStoreForApplication())
        {
        bool fileExist = isf.FileExists(ImageFileName);

        if (fileExist)
        {
            LoadImageFromIsolatedStorage(ImageFileName);
        }
        else
        {
                    if (!string.IsNullOrEmpty(txtImageUrl.Text))
            {
        // Use Uri as image file name
            Uri uri = new Uri(txtImageUrl.Text);
```

```
                    ImageFileName =
uri.AbsolutePath.Substring(uri.AbsolutePath.LastIndexOf('/')+1);
                    _webClient.OpenReadAsync(new Uri(txtImageUrl.Text));
                }

            }

        }

    }
```

Adding a Method to Retrieve the Image from Isolated Storage

The image is streamed directly from Isolated Storage into the image control.

```
        private void LoadImageFromIsolatedStorage(string imageFileName)
        {
            // Load image from Isolated Storage
            using (IsolatedStorageFile isf =
IsolatedStorageFile.GetUserStoreForApplication())
            {
                using (IsolatedStorageFileStream isoStream =
isf.OpenFile(imageFileName, FileMode.Open))
                {
                    BitmapImage bmpImg = new BitmapImage();
                    bmpImg.SetSource(isoStream);
                    image1.Source = bmpImg;
                }
            }
        }

    }
}
```

Testing the Finished Application

To test the completed application, press F5 and run it.

In this brief demo, you've learned to work with Isolated Storage files by storing a downloaded image in Isolated Storage and then retrieving the image from Isolated Storage. In the next demo, you will interact with the name and value dictionary of the Isolated Storage settings.

Working with Isolated Storage Settings

In this section, you'll build an application named IsolatedStorageSettingsDemo that demonstrates the CRUD (create, read, update, and delete) operations of System.IO.IsolatedStorage.IsolatedStorageSettings. Figure 13-5 shows how its UI will appear on a Windows Phone device.

Figure 13-5. IsolatedStorageSettingsDemo

In the IsolatedStorageSettingsDemo application, when the Save button is clicked, the value in the Value text box will be added to the Isolated Storage settings using the key in the Key text box. Whenever new key/value pair data is added to the Isolated Storage settings, the key will be added to the list box of keys. When any of the keys in the list box of keys is selected, the Key text box and the Value text box will be populated with the data retrieved from the Isolated Storage settings. The Delete button will delete the selected key from the Isolated Storage settings.

To build the demo, create a new project and then add XAML markup to create a new main page and its controls. Finally, you'll add behavior to the application with C# code that makes use of Isolated Storage APIs to save and retrieve key/value pairs.

Creating a New Project

To create the new IsolatedStorageSettingsDemo project, open Microsoft Visual Studio 2010 Express for Windows Phone. Select File ➤ New Project on the Visual Studio menu, select the Windows Phone Application template from the New Project dialog, name the application IsolatedStorageSettingsDemo, and click OK, as shown in Figure 13-6.

Now you'll build the application main page.

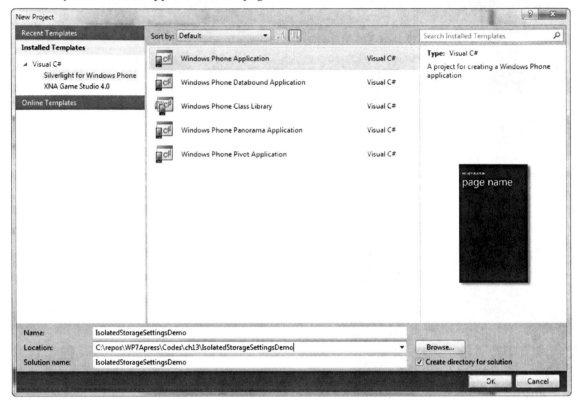

Figure 13-6. Windows Phone Application template for creating IsolatedStorageSettingsDemo

Building the Application UI (XAML)

To create the UI for IsolatedStorageSettingsDemo, go to Solution Explorer, open MainPage.xaml, and replace the XAML with the following chunks of XAML markup in the sequence shown.

Selecting the UI Resources

The following code identifies where to find the UI controls that will be used to build the main page for the application. Using the namespace xmlns="http://schemas.microsoft.com/winfx/2006/xaml/presentation" will allow you to add common Windows Phone controls such as TextBoxes, Buttons, and ListBoxes, which will be used to create the main page. Also, you are adding a reference to a code-behind class (x:Class="IsolatedStorageSettingsDemo.MainPage") that will handle the main page's controls' events.

```
<phone:PhoneApplicationPage
    x:Class="IsolatedStorageSettingsDemo.MainPage"
    xmlns="http://schemas.microsoft.com/winfx/2006/xaml/presentation"
```

```
    xmlns:x="http://schemas.microsoft.com/winfx/2006/xaml"
    xmlns:phone="clr-namespace:Microsoft.Phone.Controls;assembly=Microsoft.Phone"
    xmlns:shell="clr-namespace:Microsoft.Phone.Shell;assembly=Microsoft.Phone"
    xmlns:d="http://schemas.microsoft.com/expression/blend/2008"
    xmlns:mc="http://schemas.openxmlformats.org/markup-compatibility/2006"
    FontFamily="{StaticResource PhoneFontFamilyNormal}"
    FontSize="{StaticResource PhoneFontSizeNormal}"
    Foreground="{StaticResource PhoneForegroundBrush}"
    SupportedOrientations="Portrait" Orientation="Portrait"
    mc:Ignorable="d" d:DesignWidth="480" d:DesignHeight="768"
    shell:SystemTray.IsVisible="True">
```

Building the Main Page and Adding Controls

Now add the various controls and layouts you need to create the UI shown in Figure 13-5:

```
<Grid x:Name="LayoutRoot" Background="{StaticResource PhoneBackgroundBrush}">
    <Grid.RowDefinitions>
        <RowDefinition Height="Auto"/>
        <RowDefinition Height="*"/>
    </Grid.RowDefinitions>

    <!--TitleGrid is the name of the application and page title-->
    <Grid x:Name="TitleGrid" Grid.Row="0">
        <TextBlock Text="Isolated Storage Settings Demo"
                   x:Name="textBlockListTitle"
                   Style="{StaticResource PhoneTextTitle1Style}"
                   FontSize="30" />
    </Grid>

    <!--ContentGrid is empty. Place new content here-->
    <Grid x:Name="ContentGrid" Grid.Row="1">
        <TextBox Height="72" HorizontalAlignment="Left"
                 Margin="172,46,0,0" Name="txtKey" Text=""
                 VerticalAlignment="Top" Width="212" />
        <Button Content="Save" Height="70"
                HorizontalAlignment="Left" Margin="78,228,0,0"
                Name="btnSave" VerticalAlignment="Top" Width="160"
                Click="btnSave_Click" />

        <ListBox Height="301" HorizontalAlignment="Left" Margin="94,392,0,0"
                 Name="lstKeys" VerticalAlignment="Top" Width="290" BorderBrush="White"
                 BorderThickness="1" SelectionChanged="lstKeys_SelectionChanged" />
        <TextBlock Height="39" HorizontalAlignment="Left" Margin="94,62,0,0"
                   Name="lblKey" Text="Key" VerticalAlignment="Top" />
        <TextBox Height="74" HorizontalAlignment="Left" Margin="172,124,0,0"
                 Name="txtValue" Text="" VerticalAlignment="Top" Width="212" />
        <TextBlock Height="39" HorizontalAlignment="Left" Margin="94,140,0,0"
                   Name="lblValue" Text="Value" VerticalAlignment="Top" />
        <Button Content="Delete" Height="70" HorizontalAlignment="Left"
                Margin="224,228,0,0" Name="btnDelete" VerticalAlignment="Top"
```

```
                        Width="160" Click="btnDelete_Click" />
                <TextBlock Height="39" HorizontalAlignment="Left" Margin="94,347,0,0"
                        Name="lblListOfKeys" Text="List of Keys" VerticalAlignment="Top" />
        </Grid>
    </Grid>

</phoneNavigation:PhoneApplicationPage>
```

Once you've added the XAML markup blocks displayed in this section to MainPage.xaml, you should see the UI shown on the Visual Studio design view tab, as shown in Figure 13-7.

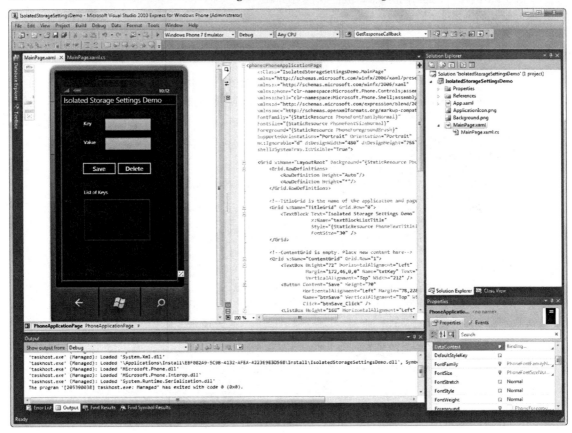

Figure 13-7. IsolatedStorageSettingsDemo in design view

Now it's time to add behavior to the application.

Coding Application Behavior (C#)

From Solution Explorer, open MainPage.xaml.cs and replace the code you find there with the following blocks of C# code.

Specifying the Namespaces

Begin by listing the namespaces that the application will use. Note that System.IO.IsolatedStorage is included to enable you to work with the Isolated Storage settings.

```
using System;
using System.Windows;
using System.Windows.Controls;
using Microsoft.Phone.Controls;
using System.IO.IsolatedStorage;
namespace IsolatedStorageSettingsDemo
{
    public partial class MainPage : PhoneApplicationPage
    {
        private IsolatedStorageSettings _appSettings;
```

Initializing the Application

Now add the next code block to the MainPage class. Notice the use of the BindKeyList() method, which will retrieve all keys from the Isolated Storage settings and bind them to the list box created in the previous section.

```
public MainPage()
        {
            InitializeComponent();
            SupportedOrientations = SupportedPageOrientation.Portrait;
            _appSettings = IsolatedStorageSettings.ApplicationSettings;
    BindKeyList();
        }
```

Adding the Save Button Event Handler

Now add an event handler for the Save button. When the Save button is clicked, the application reads the key and the value from the text boxes into the Isolated Storage settings.

```
        // Handles Create and Update
// If the key does not exist, key/value pair will be added
// ElseIf the key exists, the value will be updated
        private void btnSave_Click(object sender, RoutedEventArgs e)
        {
            if (!String.IsNullOrEmpty(txtKey.Text))
            {
                if (_appSettings.Contains(txtKey.Text))
                {
                    _appSettings[txtKey.Text] = txtValue.Text;
                }
                else
                {
                    _appSettings.Add(txtKey.Text, txtValue.Text);
                }
```

```
_appSettings.Save();
        BindKeyList();
    }
}
```

■ **Note** An Isolated Storage file will perform much better than the Isolated Storage settings, because you can stream a file into and out of the Isolated Storage file as raw data by using `StreamWriter` and `StreamReader`, whereas the storage and retrieval of data in an Isolated Storage settings key/value pair dictionary requires serialization. However, there is complexity in using Isolated Storage files: you need to use the file stream to save and retrieve the data, and you must be careful to dispose of the stream after each use. In the Isolated Storage settings, there is inherent simplicity in using the key to save and retrieve the data.

Adding the Delete Button Event Handler

Next, add an event handler for the Delete button. When the Delete button is clicked, it removes the selected key from the Isolated Storage settings and rebinds the list box.

```
private void btnDelete_Click(object sender, RoutedEventArgs e)
{
    if (lstKeys.SelectedIndex > -1)
    {
        _appSettings.Remove(lstKeys.SelectedItem.ToString());
_appSettings.Save();
        BindKeyList();
    }
}
```

Adding the ListBox Changed Event

Finally, you'll use the ListBox changed event to update the Key and Value text boxes of the application interface. When the user selects a key from the list box, the application will load the key and its associated value from the Isolated Storage settings using the selected key, and then it will populate the key and value text boxes.

```
// When key is selected, value is retrieved from the storage settings
private void lstKeys_SelectionChanged(object sender, SelectionChangedEventArgs e)
{
    if (e.AddedItems.Count > 0)
    {
        string key = e.AddedItems[0].ToString();
        if (_appSettings.Contains(key))
        {
            txtKey.Text = key;
            txtValue.Text = _appSettings[key].ToString();
        }
```

```
        }
    }

    private void BindKeyList()
    {
        lstKeys.Items.Clear();
        foreach (string key in _appSettings.Keys)
        {
            lstKeys.Items.Add(key);
        }
        txtKey.Text = "";
        txtValue.Text = "";
    }

    }
}
```

Testing the Finished Application

To test the finished application, press F5. The result should resemble the screenshot shown previously in Figure 13-5.

Summary

In this chapter, you learned how to save application data on a Windows Phone device using either an Isolated Storage file or Isolated Storage settings. From the demo applications, you learned to create, read, update, and delete Isolated Storage data.

In Chapter 14, you will learn to pinpoint the location of a device by working with Windows Phone's GPS, connected networks, and cellular telephone networks. You will also learn to interact with Microsoft's Bing Maps.

CHAPTER 14

Using Location Services

All Windows Phone devices are required to ship with a GPS receiver. As a result, you can develop applications that are *location-aware*. The GPS receiver on the Windows Phone device receives the data in the form of longitude and latitude coordinates.

There are many popular applications available for phones these days that use location data, such as restaurant-finder and navigation applications that give driving directions and plot street addresses on a map using services such as Yahoo, Google, and Microsoft Bing Maps. With the Bing Maps service, you can convert an address into GPS coordinates and plot it using the Windows Phone device's Bing Maps Silverlight control.

Also the Windows Phone GPS service offers a variety of useful functions including Windows Phone's search engines take advantage of the phone's GPS by providing relevant search results based on the location of the phone. Another interesting location-based application tracks your location while you are running and, based on the distance you travel, gives you your total calories burned.

Social networking applications such as Twitter and Facebook can also take advantage of the GPS tracking system on your phone; for example, you can tag tweets or upload photos with location information. Some applications even allow you to share your current location with your friends and family. This can be life-saving information—for instance, a kayaker lost at sea was found out because the Coast Guard was able to locate him by the GPS location that was provided by his phone.

Understanding Windows Phone Location Services Architecture

A Windows Phone device can determine its current position on the surface of the earth in one of three ways. The first approach is to use the built-in GPS receiver, which uses satellites. The is the most accurate method, but consumes the most power. The second and third approaches are to use Wi-Fi and the triangulation of the cell phone towers, which are much less accurate than using the GPS receiver, but consume less power. Fortunately, the Windows Phone location service automatically decides which option is best for the location of a device and presents its best guess of longitude and latitude through the Bing Maps location service. With a longitude and latitude reading in hand, an application can plot a location on a Bing Maps Silverlight control map. An application can also use the street address returned by the onboard location service to query the Bing Maps Web service for its corresponding GPS coordinates (longitude and latitude) and plot them on a Bing Maps map.

In upcoming sections of this chapter, you will learn how to take advantage of the Windows Phone GPS receiver to track your movements, and how to plot an address on the Bing Maps Silverlight control using the Bing Maps service.

Introducing the Windows Phone Location Service and Mapping APIs

In order to use the location service on a device, you need to reference the System.Device assembly and declare System.Device.Location in your code. Before you can take advantage of the location service, however, you must enable the location service on the phone by going to Settings ➤ Location ➤ Turn on Location Services. You can detect whether the phone's location service is enabled using the StatusChanged event of GeoCoordinateWatcher, as shown in the following code:

```
GeoCoordinateWatcher geoCoordinateWatcher;
geoCoordinateWatcher = new GeoCoordinateWatcher(GeoPositionAccuracy.High);
geoCoordinateWatcher.MovementThreshold = 100; // in meters
geoCoordinateWatcher.StatusChanged += (s, e) =>
    {
        if (e.Status == GeoPositionStatus.Disabled)
        {
            MessageBox.Show("Please enable your location service by going to Settings ->
Location -> Turn on Location Services option.");
        }
    };
```

Another way to check if the location service is enabled is to use TryStart to see if GeoCoordinateWatcher can be started:

```
if (!_geoCoordinateWatcher.TryStart(true, TimeSpan.FromSeconds(5)))
{
        MessageBox.Show("Please enable Location Service on the Phone.",
"Warning", MessageBoxButton.OK);
}
```

Next, you need to set DesiredAccuracy and provide MovementThreshold in GeoCoordinateWatcher, as shown in the preceding code block.

GeoPositionAccuracy.Default uses Wi-Fi or cell phone towers, and thus depends on the availability of these sources, while GeoPositionAccuracy.High uses the GPS receiver built into the phone device; Windows Phone will automatically choose which one to use. MovementThreshold is a very important property to set because it specifies the change in distance in meters before the PositionChanged event notifies the application that new coordinates are available; the smaller the value of MovementThreshold, the more accurately the position will be tracked, but you will pay a price in higher power consumption. Microsoft recommends that you set MovementThreshold to at least 20 meters to filter out this noise.

In the following sections, you will learn how to use the Windows Phone location service by simulating the behavior of the GPS receiver. This simulation will allow you to test location-aware applications in the emulator, which lacks a real GPS receiver.

Simulating the Location Service

In order to simulate use of the location service, you will be intercepting GeoCoordinateWatcher's PositionChanged event using an Observable object. With an Observable object, you can subscribe to an event and then stream the data received to the subscribed event delegates. For the examples in this chapter, you will subscribe to the PositionChanged event to feed GPS data to the parts of your application that consume it. The use of Observable objects is covered in more detail in Chapter 18.

Creating the GeoCoordinateWatcherDemo Project

To set up the GeoCoordinateWatcherDemo project, follow the steps from the previous examples in this book. In order to use a .NET reactive extension (Chapter 18), you will need to add a reference to Microsoft.Phone.Reactive. You'll also need to reference System.Device in order to use the location service, and more importantly, System.Observable, in order to feed GPS data to the location service.

1. Open Microsoft Visual Studio 2010 Express for Windows Phone on your workstation.

2. Create a new Windows Phone application by selecting File ➤ New Project from the Visual Studio command menu. Select the Windows Phone Application template, and name the application GeoCoordinateWatcherDemo.

3. Add a reference to Microsoft.Phone.Reactive in order to use a reactive extension. Also add a reference to System.Device in order to use the location service. In Solution Explorer, you should be able to see the added reference, as shown in Figure 14-1.

Figure 14-1. Project references to use the reactive extension and the location service

Coding the UI

You will be building the UI using the XAML in Visual Studio. For building simple controls, it's faster to work with the XAML code. Go to the solution, open MainPage.xaml, and replace the XAML you find there with the code that follows.

Declaring the UI Resources

The namespaces in the following code snippet are typically declared by default when you first create a Windows Phone project. In particular, the namespace xmlns:phone="clr-namespace:Microsoft.Phone.Controls;assembly=Microsoft.Phone" allows you to add common Windows Phone controls to the application main page.

```
<phone:PhoneApplicationPage
    x:Class="GeoCoordinateWatcherDemo.MainPage"
    xmlns="http://schemas.microsoft.com/winfx/2006/xaml/presentation"
    xmlns:x="http://schemas.microsoft.com/winfx/2006/xaml"
    xmlns:phone="clr-namespace:Microsoft.Phone.Controls;assembly=Microsoft.Phone"
    xmlns:shell="clr-namespace:Microsoft.Phone.Shell;assembly=Microsoft.Phone"
    xmlns:d="http://schemas.microsoft.com/expression/blend/2008"
    xmlns:mc="http://schemas.openxmlformats.org/markup-compatibility/2006"
```

```
mc:Ignorable="d" d:DesignWidth="480" d:DesignHeight="768"
FontFamily="{StaticResource PhoneFontFamilyNormal}"
FontSize="{StaticResource PhoneFontSizeNormal}"
Foreground="{StaticResource PhoneForegroundBrush}"
SupportedOrientations="Portrait" Orientation="Portrait"
shell:SystemTray.IsVisible="True">
```

Building the Main Page and Adding Components

Next, add two TextBlocks, txtLatitude and txtLongitude, to display the longitude and latitude that the phone location service provides:

```
<Grid x:Name="LayoutRoot" Background="Transparent">
    <Grid.RowDefinitions>
        <RowDefinition Height="Auto"/>
        <RowDefinition Height="*"/>
    </Grid.RowDefinitions>

    <StackPanel x:Name="TitlePanel" Grid.Row="0" Margin="12,17,0,28">
        <TextBlock x:Name="ApplicationTitle" Text="GeoCoordinateWatcherDemo"
Style="{StaticResource PhoneTextNormalStyle}"/>
    </StackPanel>

    <Grid x:Name="ContentPanel" Grid.Row="1" Margin="12,0,12,0">
        <TextBox Height="72" Name="txtLongitude" Text=""
                Margin="193,142,41,393" />
        <TextBox Height="72" Name="txtLatitude" Text=""
                Margin="193,236,41,299" />
        <TextBlock Height="30" HorizontalAlignment="Left"
                Margin="78,202,0,0" Name="textBlock1"
                Text="Longitude" VerticalAlignment="Top" />
        <TextBlock Height="30" HorizontalAlignment="Left"
                Margin="78,306,0,0" Name="textBlock2"
                Text="Latitude" VerticalAlignment="Top" />
    </Grid>
</Grid>
</phone:PhoneApplicationPage>
```

Once you have loaded the XAML code, you should see the layout shown in Figure 14-2. In the next section, you will add events to handle updating the UI with the GPS data received from the location service.

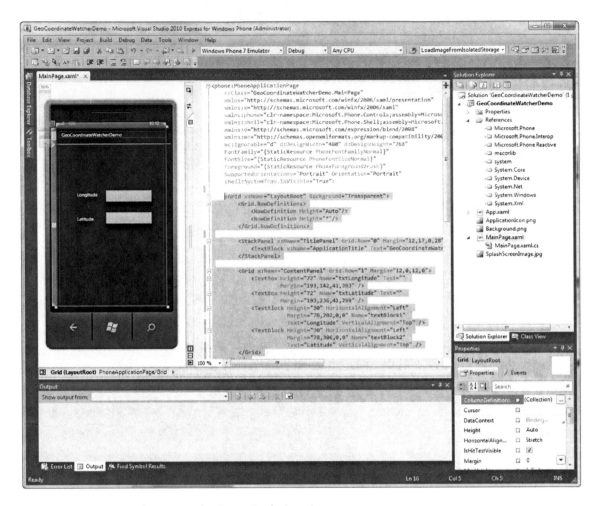

Figure 14-2. GeoCoordinateWatcherDemo in design view

Coding the Application

In Solution Explorer, open `MainPage.xaml.cs` and replace the code there with the C# code blocks that follow, which will implement the UI updates using the location service with the data received from the reactive extension.

Specifying the Namespaces

Begin by listing the namespaces that the application will use. You will need `System.Device.Location` in order to use the location service. Declare `Microsoft.Phone.Reactive` in order to use the reactive extension's `Observable` object. Also note that you will need `System.Threading` in order to feed the GPS data into the location service; you can think of the reactive extension's Observable object as if it were the satellite, Wi-Fi, or communication tower sending the GPS data.

```
using Microsoft.Phone.Controls;
using System.Threading;
using Microsoft.Phone.Reactive;
using System.Device.Location;
using System.Collections.Generic;
using System;
```

Initializing Variables

The variable _geoCoordinateWatcher is an instance of the Windows Phone location class that you'll use to access and retrieve location data. Notice in the constructor that you declared the PositionChanged event in order to receive the location service's GPS data. Also, you'll be starting the thread that will simulate the GPS data that is sent to the PositionChanged event delegate.

```
GeoCoordinateWatcher _geoCoordinateWatcher;

public MainPage()
{
    InitializeComponent();

    // initialize GeoCoordinateWatcher
    _geoCoordinateWatcher = new GeoCoordinateWatcher();

    // PositionChanged event will receive GPS data
    _geoCoordinateWatcher.PositionChanged +=
        new EventHandler<GeoPositionChangedEventArgs<GeoCoordinate>>
            (_geoCoordinateWatcher_PositionChanged);

    // simulateGpsThread will start the eactive extension
    // where EmulatePositionChangedEvents will be feeding
    // the data to PositionChanged event
    Thread simulateGpsThread = new Thread(SimulateGPS);
    simulateGpsThread.Start();
}
```

Simulating GPS Data Using the Reactive Extension's Observable Object

In the previous constructor, you initiated a thread that executes the SimulateGPS method. In the SimulateGPS method, the reactive extension's Observable object subscribes to the PositionChanged event in order to feed the GPS data. Notice that GPSPositionChangedEvents constantly sends GeoPositionChangedEventArgs every 2 seconds; this is then received by GeoCoordinateWatcher's PositionChanged event and the GPS data.

```
// Reactive extension that intercepts the _geoCoordinateWatcher_PositionChanged
// in order to feed the GPS data.
private void SimulateGPS()
{
    var position = GPSPositionChangedEvents().ToObservable();
```

```
        position.Subscribe(evt => _geoCoordinateWatcher_PositionChanged(null, evt));
    }

    private static IEnumerable<GeoPositionChangedEventArgs<GeoCoordinate>>
GPSPositionChangedEvents()
    {
        Random random = new Random();

        // feed the GPS data
        while (true)
        {
            Thread.Sleep(TimeSpan.FromSeconds(2));

            // randomly generate GPS data, latitude and longitude.
// latitude is between -90 and 90
double latitude = (random.NextDouble() * 180.0) - 90.0;
// longitude is between -180 and 180
double longitude = (random.NextDouble() * 360.0) - 180.0;
            yield return new GeoPositionChangedEventArgs<GeoCoordinate>(
                    new GeoPosition<GeoCoordinate>(DateTimeOffset.Now, new
GeoCoordinate(latitude, longitude)));
        }
    }
```

Displaying GPS Data

In this demo, the received GPS data is displayed directly to the user. Notice here that you are using
Dispatcher.BeginInvoke to execute the lambda expression of an anonymous method.

■ **Caution** Using Dispatcher.BeginInvoke to update the UI with the GPS data is absolutely necessary because
the PositionChanged event is executed in a different thread from the UI, and thus you must explicitly use
Dispatcher.Invoke to run UI-specific code.

```
    private void _geoCoordinateWatcher_PositionChanged(object sender
        , GeoPositionChangedEventArgs<GeoCoordinate> e)
    {
        this.Dispatcher.BeginInvoke(() =>
        {
            txtLatitude.Text = e.Position.Location.Latitude.ToString();
            txtLongitude.Text = e.Position.Location.Longitude.ToString();
        });
    }
```

Testing the Finished Application

To test the application, press F5. The result should resemble the screenshot shown in Figure 14-3, and you should see constantly changing longitudes and latitudes in the text boxes.

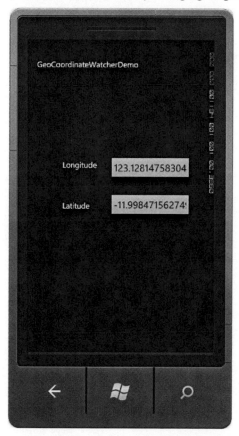

Figure 14-3. The GeoCoordinateWatcherDemo application

Using GeoCoordinateWatcher and the Bing Maps Control to Track Your Movements

You'll begin by building an application to work with the phone's location service, GeoCoordinateWatcher. The application, Bing Map Demo, is shown in Figure 14-4, and it demonstrates the basic functions available through GeoCoordinateWatcher, the location service that was introduced in the previous section. The application will display your location with a blinking icon on a map, and it will continuously update your position as you move.

In this demo, when you click the Start button, the location service will start, and it will send a notification when the device's position changes. Each time a changed-position event occurs, the Bing Maps map will be updated with the new position. You can actually start the application while you are walking and watch the position of the locator on the map (the red dot) change as you move.

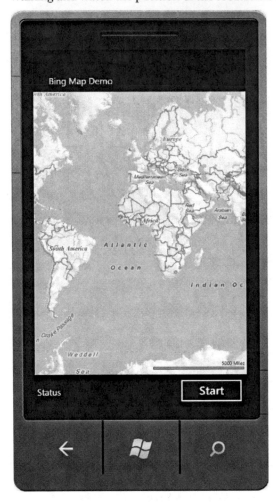

Figure 14-4. Bing Maps Demo using GeoCoordinateWatcher

You'll build the demo in four steps. First, you need to register with the Bing Maps service portal and create a new Visual Studio project. Next, you'll build the project's UI. You'll finish up by adding code to respond to commands from the user.

Registering with the Bing Maps Service Portal and Installing the Bing Maps SDK

Before you can use the Bing Maps Silverlight control and its service offerings, you must register with Bing Maps at www.bingmapsportal.com. Go to this site, and you should see something similar to Figure 14-5.

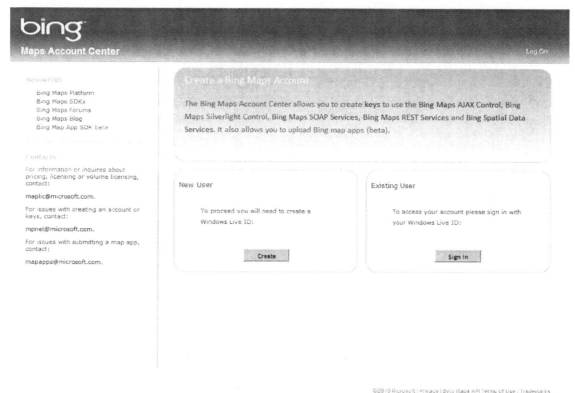

Figure 14-5. Bing Maps portal for creating a new user

4. Click the Create button, and follow the instructions provided by Microsoft.

5. Once you create a Bing Maps service user, you must create an application key so that you can use the Bing Maps control and the Bing Maps service from Windows Phone. Sign in to the Bing Maps portal and, once you are logged in, click the "Create or view keys" link shown in Figure 14-6.

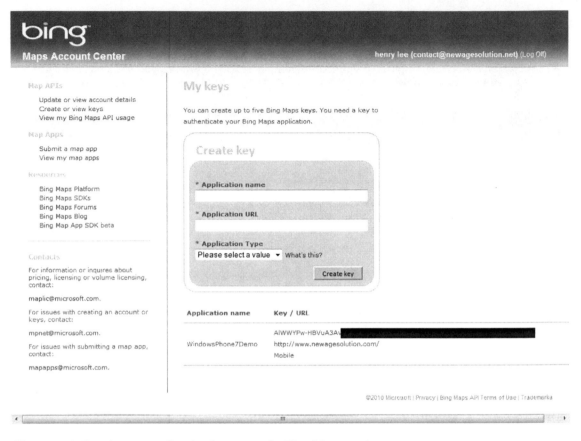

Figure 14-6. *Creating an application key to use the Bing Maps service*

Once you've created the Bing Maps application key, you must install the Windows Phone SDK, found at http://create.msdn.com/en-us/home/getting_started.

After you've successfully installed the Windows Phone SDK, the binaries (Microsoft.Phone.Controls.Maps) can be referenced from the project so that you can use the Bing Maps Silverlight control.

Creating the BingMapDemo Project

To set up the BingMapDemo project, follow the steps from the previous examples in this book:

1. Open Microsoft Visual Studio 2010 Express for Windows Phone on your workstation.

2. Create a new Windows Phone application by selecting File ➤ New Project from the Visual Studio command menu. Select the Windows Phone Application template, and name the application BingMapDemo.

3.   In order to use the Bing Maps control in Windows Phone, you must reference Microsoft.Phone.Controls.Maps, and to enable it to track your movements, you need to add a reference to System.Device, which will allow it to use the location service. Open Solution Explorer and add those references now. Check to ensure that your list of references matches the list shown in Figure 14-7.

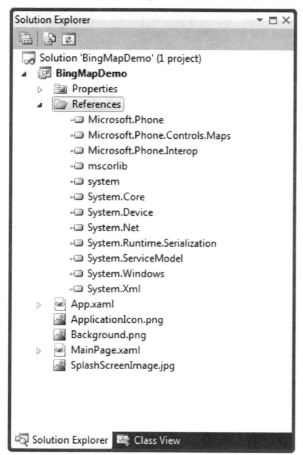

Figure 14-7. Reference assemblies needed for the Bing Maps control

Coding the UI

Now it's time to code the UI. Let's implement it in XAML. (Sometimes it's faster to work with XAML when working with a simple example that requires only a few controls.) Go to Solution Explorer, open MainPage.xaml, and replace the XAML you find there with the two blocks of code following.

Declaring the UI Resources

Most of the namespaces you see in this snippet are typically declared by default when you first create a Windows Phone project. The following namespace is unique to this application, and it allows you to add the Bing Maps control you will use to plot your location: xmlns:BingMap="clr-namespace:Microsoft.Phone.Controls.Maps;assembly=Microsoft.Phone.Controls.Maps".

```xml
<phone:PhoneApplicationPage
    x:Class="BingMapDemo.MainPage"
    xmlns="http://schemas.microsoft.com/winfx/2006/xaml/presentation"
    xmlns:x="http://schemas.microsoft.com/winfx/2006/xaml"
    xmlns:phone="clr-namespace:Microsoft.Phone.Controls;assembly=Microsoft.Phone"
    xmlns:shell="clr-namespace:Microsoft.Phone.Shell;assembly=Microsoft.Phone"
    xmlns:d="http://schemas.microsoft.com/expression/blend/2008"
    xmlns:mc="http://schemas.openxmlformats.org/markup-compatibility/2006"
    xmlns:BingMap=
"clr-namespace:Microsoft.Phone.Controls.Maps;assembly=Microsoft.Phone.Controls.Maps "
    FontFamily="{StaticResource PhoneFontFamilyNormal}"
    FontSize="{StaticResource PhoneFontSizeNormal}"
    Foreground="{StaticResource PhoneForegroundBrush}"
    SupportedOrientations="Portrait" Orientation="Portrait"
    mc:Ignorable="d" d:DesignWidth="480" d:DesignHeight="768"
    shell:SystemTray.IsVisible="True">
```

Building the Main Page and Adding a Bing Maps Control

You will add a Bing Maps control to the main page to display your position and a button to start the location service. You'll also add an animation storyboard named BlinkLocator, which will cause the locator icon to blink by changing its color. Note that inside the Bing Maps control, there is a BingMap:Pushpin named bingMapLocator. The map layer bingMapLocator contains an Ellipse control named locator, whose initial map position in latitude and longitude is (0, 0). In this application, the location service will provide changing positions in the latitude and longitude so that the locator position can be properly updated. This is a very simple but very powerful demonstration of using the location service and the Bing Maps control. You can use the same technique for Yahoo or Google Maps, as their APIs are very similar to Bing Maps.

```xml
<phone:PhoneApplicationPage.Resources>
    <Storyboard x:Name="BlinkLocator" AutoReverse="True" RepeatBehavior="Forever">
        <ColorAnimationUsingKeyFrames
Storyboard.TargetProperty="(Shape.Fill).(SolidColorBrush.Color)"
Storyboard.TargetName="locator">
            <EasingColorKeyFrame KeyTime="0" Value="Red"/>
                <EasingColorKeyFrame KeyTime="0:0:1" Value="#FFCEFF00"/>
        </ColorAnimationUsingKeyFrames>
    </Storyboard>
</phone:PhoneApplicationPage.Resources>

<Grid x:Name="LayoutRoot" Background="Transparent">
    <Grid.RowDefinitions>
        <RowDefinition Height="Auto"/>
        <RowDefinition Height="*"/>
```

```
        </Grid.RowDefinitions>

        <StackPanel x:Name="TitlePanel" Grid.Row="0" Margin="24,24,0,12">
            <TextBlock x:Name="ApplicationTitle" Text="Bing Map Demo"
                       Style="{StaticResource PhoneTextNormalStyle}"/>
        </StackPanel>

        <Grid x:Name="ContentGrid" Grid.Row="1">
            <BingMap:Map Name="bingMap" NavigationVisibility="Collapsed"
                         Margin="0,0,0,72">
                <BingMap:Pushpin Name="bingMapLocator">
                    <BingMap:Pushpin.Content>
                        <Ellipse Fill="Red" Width="20" Height="20"
                                 BingMap:MapLayer.Position="0,0"
                                 Name="locator" />
    <BingMap:Pushpin.Content>
            </BingMap: Pushpin>
             </BingMap:Map>
                <Button Content="Start" Height="72" HorizontalAlignment="Right"
Margin="0,633,0,0" Name="btnStart" VerticalAlignment="Top" Width="160"
Click="btnStart_Click" />
                <TextBlock Height="30" HorizontalAlignment="Left" Margin="6,657,0,0"
Name="txtStatus" Text="Status" VerticalAlignment="Top" Width="308" />
        </Grid>
    </Grid>

</phone:PhoneApplicationPage>
```

■ **Tip** In this code, you changed the content of the Pushpin, which is the locator that specifies where you are. You can add any type of control and change the appearance of the Pushpin. You can even include a placeholder and dynamically change the content of the Pushpin.

Once you have loaded the XAML code, you should see the layout shown in Figure 14-8. In the next section, you will add an event to consume the GPS data and plot it on the map layer of the Bing Maps Silverlight control.

Figure 14-8. BingMapDemo in design view

Coding the Application

In Solution Explorer, open `MainPage.xaml.cs` and replace the code there with the following C# code blocks, which will implement the map control functionality.

Specifying the Namespaces

Begin by listing the namespaces the application will use. Notice the inclusion of `Microsoft.Maps.Control`, which will allow you to manipulate the Bing Maps control, and `System.Device`, which will allow you to work with geoCoordinateWatcher, which will retrieve the location data from the GPS, Wi-Fi, or cellular towers.

```
using System;
using System.Windows;
using Microsoft.Phone.Controls;
using Microsoft.Maps.MapControl;
```

```
using System.Device.Location;
namespace BingMapDemo
{
    public partial class MainPage : PhoneApplicationPage
    {
```

Initializing Variables

The variable _geoCoordinateWatcher is an instance of the location service class that you'll use to access and retrieve location data. Note that you will use GeoPositionAccuracy.High, which uses the phone's GPS device. For this to work, you must use the real Windows Phone device. If you need to simulate the location service, you can refer to the previous section in this chapter or Chapter 18. You'll also set MovementThreshold to 100 meters so that the PositionChanged event fires every 100 meters, and you'll plot your current location on the Bing Maps map.

GeoCoordinateWatcher has StatusChanged and PositionChanged events that notify the application whenever the new updated position is received from the GPS.

As for bingMap, you will hide the Bing Maps logo and copyright in order to make things cleaner and make more space for the application's other controls. Finally, in order to use the map control at all, you must set ClientTokenCredentialsProvider to the value of the application key you obtained when you registered at the Bing Maps site.

```
        GeoCoordinateWatcher _geoCoordinateWatcher;


        public MainPage()
        {
            InitializeComponent();
            // Add your own BingMap Key
            bingMap.CredentialsProvider =
new ApplicationIdCredentialsProvider("ADD-YOUR-OWN-KEY");

            // Remove Bing Maps logo and copyrights in order to gain
            // extra space at the bottom of the map
            bingMap.LogoVisibility = Visibility.Collapsed;
            bingMap.CopyrightVisibility = Visibility.Collapsed;

            // Delcare GeoCoordinateWatcher with high accuracy
            // in order to use the device's GPS
            _geoCoordinateWatcher = new GeoCoordinateWatcher(GeoPositionAccuracy.High);
            _geoCoordinateWatcher.MovementThreshold = 100;

            // Subscribe to the device's status changed event
            _geoCoordinateWatcher.StatusChanged +=
                new  EventHandler<GeoPositionStatusChangedEventArgs>(
_geoCoordinateWatcher_StatusChanged);

            // Subscribe to the device's position changed event
            // to receive GPS coordinates (longitude and latitude)
            _geoCoordinateWatcher.PositionChanged +=
                New EventHandler<GeoPositionChangedEventArgs<GeoCoordinate>>(
_geoCoordinateWatcher_PositionChanged);
```

```
        }
```

Responding to StatusChanged and PositionChanged GeoCoordinateWatcher Events

In GeoCoordinateWatcher, StatusChanged fires when the GPS status changes, and PositionChanged fires when the GPS receives a new position. In StatusChanged, if the received status is Disabled, you must notify the user that the device's location service is disabled and that it must be turned on. You can enable the location service on the device by going to Settings ➤ Location and selecting "Turn on the location service."

Note here that the PositionChanged event will not fire until the position of the phone has changed by at least 100 meters, as specified by MovementThreshold. When the StatusChanged event fires, txtStatus will be updated, and when the PositionChanged event fires, the locator icon you added to the Bing Maps layer will be moved accordingly.

```csharp
        private void _geoCoordinateWatcher_PositionChanged(object sender,
GeoPositionChangedEventArgs<GeoCoordinate> e)
        {
            Deployment.Current.Dispatcher.BeginInvoke(() => ChangePosition(e));
        }

        private void ChangePosition(GeoPositionChangedEventArgs<GeoCoordinate> e)
        {
            SetLocation(e.Position.Location.Latitude,
e.Position.Location.Longitude, 10, true);
        }

        private void _geoCoordinateWatcher_StatusChanged(object sender,
GeoPositionStatusChangedEventArgs e)
        {
            Deployment.Current.Dispatcher.BeginInvoke(() => StatusChanged(e));
        }

private void StatusChanged(GeoPositionStatusChangedEventArgs e)
        {
            switch (e.Status)
            {
                case GeoPositionStatus.Disabled:
                    txtStatus.Text = "Location Service is disabled!";
                    break;
                case GeoPositionStatus.Initializing:
                    txtStatus.Text = "Initializing Location Service...";
                    break;
                case GeoPositionStatus.NoData:
                    txtStatus.Text = "Your position could not be located.";
                    break;
                case GeoPositionStatus.Ready:
                    break;
            }
        }
```

Starting the Location Service: GeoCoordinateWatcher

When the user clicks the Start button, the location service will start. TryStart will return false if the phone's location service is disabled. If the location service is disabled, a message box will be displayed to the user, instructing the user to enable the location service on the phone.

```
private void btnStart_Click(object sender, RoutedEventArgs e)
{
    if (!_geoCoordinateWatcher.TryStart(true, TimeSpan.FromSeconds(5)))
    {
        MessageBox.Show("Please enable Location Service on the Phone.",
"Warning", MessageBoxButton.OK);

    }
}
```

Plotting the Location on the Bing Maps MapLayer

BingMap has a SetView method that allows you to set the current view on the screen using the location data, latitude, and longitude received from GeoCoordinateWatcher. The zoomLevel property indicates how far into the location the map will be zoomed. BingMap also has MapLayer, which can set the position of the map layer with respect to the received location. To make things interesting, let's animate bingMapLocator with simple color blinks.

```
private void SetLocation(double latitude, double longitude,
double zoomLevel, bool showLocator)
    {
        Location location = new Location(latitude, latitude);
        bingMap.SetView(location, zoomLevel);
        MapLayer.SetPosition(locator, location);
        if (showLocator)
        {
            locator.Visibility = Visibility.Visible;
            BlinkLocator.Begin();
        }
        else
        {
            locator.Visibility = Visibility.Collapsed;
            BlinkLocator.Stop();
        }
    }
}
}
```

Testing the Finished Application

To test the application, press F5. The result should resemble Figure 14-4, shown previously. Remember that you must have a real phone device to be able to use real GPS. In the following section, you'll utilize the Bing Maps geocoding service to convert the address into a geocode of longitudes and latitudes for plotting an address on the Bing Maps Silverlight control.

Plotting an Address on a Bing Maps Map and Working with the Bing Maps Service

Microsoft provides three main services hosted on the cloud to be used by clients, including Windows Phone devices:

- GeoCodeService allows an address to be converted to longitude and latitude, and also allows geocode to be converted into an address. The Web service can be consumed by accessing the following URL: http://dev.virtualearth.net/webservices/v1/geocodeservice/geocodeservice.svc.

- RouteService includes services such as calculating the distance between two addresses, providing driving and walking directions from address to address, and step-by-step navigation. The Web service can be consumed by accessing the following URL: http://dev.virtualearth.net/webservices/v1/routeservice/routeservice.svc.

- SearchService provides location-based search results. For example, based on the submitted address, it can find restaurants within a five-mile radius. The Web service can be consumed by accessing the following URL: http://dev.virtualearth.net/webservices/v1/searchservice/searchservice.svc .

In the following section, you will be using GeoCodeService to convert an address into geocode (longitude and latitude) and plot the address on the Bing Maps Silverlight control. Through the demo, you will learn how to access the Bing Maps service using the credentials you received when you registered.

The following demo interface will contain a text box where you can enter an address to be plotted on the map and a button to invoke a method to convert the address using the Bing Maps geocode service. The geocode will be plotted on the Bing Maps Silverlight control, as shown in Figure 14-9.

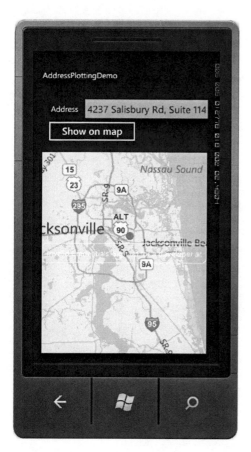

Figure 14-9. AddressPlottingDemo application

Creating the AddressPlottingDemo Application

To set up the AddressPlottingDemo project, follow the steps from the previous examples in this book:

1. Open Microsoft Visual Studio 2010 Express for Windows Phone on your workstation.

2. Create a new Windows Phone application by selecting File ➤ New Project from the Visual Studio command menu. Select the Windows Phone Application template, and name the application AddressPlottingDemo.

3. In order to use the Bing Maps control on Windows Phone, you must reference Microsoft.Phone.Controls.Maps and System.Device.

Adding a Service Reference to the Bing Maps GeoCodeService

In order to use the Bing Maps GeoCodeService, you need to add a service reference to your project.

1. In Solution Explorer, right-click the References folder and choose Add Service Reference.

2. When the Add Service Reference window pops up, enter http://dev.virtualearth.net/webservices/v1/geocodeservice/geocodeservice.svc into the Address field and click Go.

3. You'll see a list of services. In the Namespace text box, enter BingMapGeoCodeService. You should see a result similar to Figure 14-10.

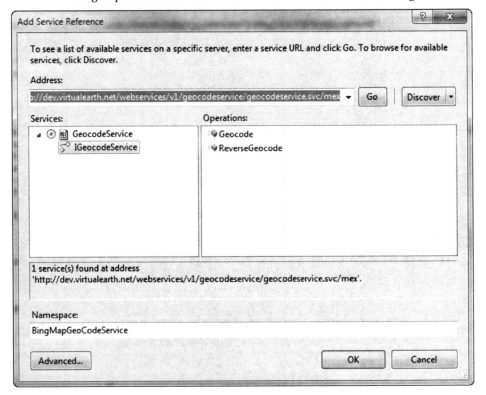

Figure 14-10. Adding a service reference

4. Click OK, and you should see BingMapGeoCodeService in Solution Explorer, as shown in Figure 14-11.

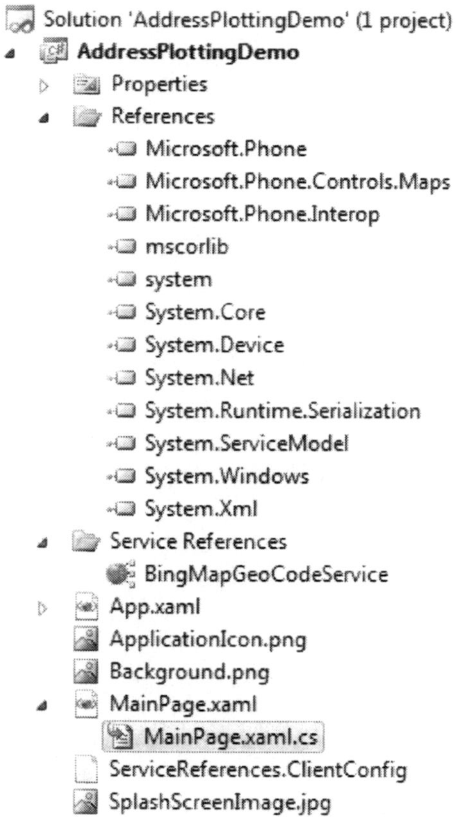

Solution 'AddressPlottingDemo' (1 project)
- AddressPlottingDemo
  - Properties
  - References
    - Microsoft.Phone
    - Microsoft.Phone.Controls.Maps
    - Microsoft.Phone.Interop
    - mscorlib
    - system
    - System.Core
    - System.Device
    - System.Net
    - System.Runtime.Serialization
    - System.ServiceModel
    - System.Windows
    - System.Xml
  - Service References
    - BingMapGeoCodeService
  - App.xaml
  - ApplicationIcon.png
  - Background.png
  - MainPage.xaml
    - MainPage.xaml.cs
  - ServiceReferences.ClientConfig
  - SplashScreenImage.jpg

Figure 14-11. Bing Maps GeoCodeService in the Service References folder

Coding the UI

AddressPlottingDemo has a very simple UI, consisting of a text block for capturing the address, a button to invoke a method for plotting the address onto the map, and the Bing Maps Silverlight control.

Declaring the UI Resources

The namespaces in the following code snippet are typically declared by default when you first create a Windows Phone project. In particular, the namespace xmlns:phone="clr-namespace:Microsoft.Phone.Controls;assembly=Microsoft.Phone" allows you to add common Windows Phone controls to the application main page.

```
<phone:PhoneApplicationPage
    x:Class="AddressPlottingDemo.MainPage"
    xmlns="http://schemas.microsoft.com/winfx/2006/xaml/presentation"
    xmlns:x="http://schemas.microsoft.com/winfx/2006/xaml"
```

```
    xmlns:phone="clr-namespace:Microsoft.Phone.Controls;assembly=Microsoft.Phone"
    xmlns:shell="clr-namespace:Microsoft.Phone.Shell;assembly=Microsoft.Phone"
    xmlns:d="http://schemas.microsoft.com/expression/blend/2008"
    xmlns:mc="http://schemas.openxmlformats.org/markup-compatibility/2006"
    xmlns:BingMap="clr-
namespace:Microsoft.Phone.Controls.Maps;assembly=Microsoft.Phone.Controls.Maps"
    mc:Ignorable="d" d:DesignWidth="480" d:DesignHeight="768"
    FontFamily="{StaticResource PhoneFontFamilyNormal}"
    FontSize="{StaticResource PhoneFontSizeNormal}"
    Foreground="{StaticResource PhoneForegroundBrush}"
    SupportedOrientations="Portrait" Orientation="Portrait"
    shell:SystemTray.IsVisible="True">
```

Creating the Main Page

The main page consists of the Bing Maps Silverlight control, a button, and an address text block to capture the user address input. Notice on the bingMap control that CopyrightVisibility and LogoVisibility are set to Collapsed, giving you much more real estate on the screen.

```
    <Grid x:Name="LayoutRoot" Background="Transparent">
        <Grid.RowDefinitions>
            <RowDefinition Height="Auto"/>
            <RowDefinition Height="*"/>
        </Grid.RowDefinitions>

        <StackPanel x:Name="TitlePanel" Grid.Row="0"
                    Margin="12,17,0,28">
            <TextBlock x:Name="ApplicationTitle"
                    Text="AddressPlottingDemo"
                    Style="{StaticResource PhoneTextNormalStyle}"/>
        </StackPanel>

        <Grid x:Name="ContentPanel" Grid.Row="1" Margin="12,0,12,0">

            <BingMap:Map Name="bingMap"
                    Width="425" Height="513"
                    Margin="0,0,19,25"
                    CopyrightVisibility="Collapsed"
                    LogoVisibility="Collapsed"
                    VerticalAlignment="Bottom" HorizontalAlignment="Right">
                <BingMap:Pushpin Name="bingMapLocator"
                            Background="Transparent">
                    <BingMap:Pushpin.Content>
                        <Ellipse Fill="Red" Width="20" Height="20"
                            Name="locator" />
                    </BingMap:Pushpin.Content>
                </BingMap:Pushpin>
            </BingMap:Map>
            <TextBox Height="72" Margin="110,10,6,0" Name="txtAddress"
                    Text="4237 Salisbury Rd, Suite 114 Jacksonville FL, 32216"
                    VerticalAlignment="Top" />
```

```
<TextBlock Height="30" HorizontalAlignment="Left"
           Margin="33,32,0,0" Name="textBlock1"
           Text="Address" VerticalAlignment="Top" />
<Button Content="Show on map" Height="72"
        Name="btnPlot" Margin="17,68,192,556"
        Click="btnPlot_Click" />
      </Grid>
   </Grid>
</phone:PhoneApplicationPage>
```

Coding the Application

One of most important things to notice in this demo application is its use of the Bing Maps geocode service to convert a street address to longitude and latitude coordinates so that it can be plotted on the map. Also, in order to use the Bing Maps geocode service, you must provide the Bing Maps credentials that you created during the registration.

Specifying the Namespaces

Once the service is referenced, you will be able to declare the namespace of the Bing Maps geocode service, AddressPlottingDemo.BingMapGeoCodeService. You are including System.Linq because you will be using LINQ to query returned GeoCodeResults with the highest confidence.

```
using System.Windows;
using Microsoft.Phone.Controls;
using AddressPlottingDemo.BingMapGeoCodeService;
using Microsoft.Phone.Controls.Maps;
using System.Collections.ObjectModel;
using System.Linq;
```

Initializing Variables

The GeocodeServiceClient variable _svc is a proxy class that lets you connect to the Bing Maps geocode service to geocode the address in order to plot it on the map. Note that you need to subscribe to the GeocodeCompleted event in order to receive results that contain longitude and latitude.

```
GeocodeServiceClient _svc;
public MainPage()
{
    InitializeComponent();

    // instantiate Bing Maps GeocodeService
    _svc = new GeocodeServiceClient("BasicHttpBinding_IGeocodeService");
    _svc.GeocodeCompleted += (s, e) =>
        {
            // sort the returned record by ascending confidence in order for
            // highest confidence to be on the top.
            // Based on the numeration, High value is
            // at 0, Medium value at 1 and Low volue at 2
```

```
                    var geoResult = (from r in e.Result.Results
                                     orderby (int)r.Confidence ascending
                                     select r).FirstOrDefault();
                    if (geoResult != null)
                    {
                        this.SetLocation(geoResult.Locations[0].Latitude,
                            geoResult.Locations[0].Longitude,
                            10,
                            true);
                    }
                };
        }
```

Handling the Button Event that Plots Address Data on the Bing Maps Map

When btnPlot is clicked, you will make a Web service request to the Bing Maps geocode service to convert txtAddress.Text to return geocoordinates in longitude and latitude. When the GeoCodeCompleted event is raised, you will receive multiple results that contain only the highest confidence level. Using GeoCodeResult, you will make a call to SetLocation, which will plot the location on the Bing Maps Silverlight control.

```
private void SetLocation(double latitude, double longitude,
double zoomLevel, bool showLocator)
        {
            // Move the pushpin to geo coordinate
            Microsoft.Phone.Controls.Maps.Platform.Location location =
new Microsoft.Phone.Controls.Maps.Platform.Location();
            location.Latitude = latitude;
            location.Longitude = longitude;
            bingMap.SetView(location, zoomLevel);
            bingMapLocator.Location = location;
            if (showLocator)
            {
                locator.Visibility = Visibility.Visible;
            }
            else
            {
                locator.Visibility = Visibility.Collapsed;
            }
        }

        private void btnPlot_Click(object sender, RoutedEventArgs e)
        {
            BingMapGeoCodeService.GeocodeRequest request =
new BingMapGeoCodeService.GeocodeRequest();

            // Only accept results with high confidence.
            request.Options = new GeocodeOptions()
            {
                Filters = new ObservableCollection<FilterBase>
                {
```

```
                  new ConfidenceFilter()
                  {
                      MinimumConfidence = Confidence.High
                  }
              }
          };


      request.Credentials = new Credentials()
      {
          ApplicationId = "Put-Your-BingMap-Credential-Id"
      };

      request.Query = txtAddress.Text;

      // Make asynchronous call to fetch the geo coordinate data.
      _svc.GeocodeAsync(request);
  }
```

Testing the Finished Application

To test the application, press F5. The result should resemble the display shown previously in Figure 14-9.
Enter an address into the Address text box and click the "Show on map" button. You should see the
pushpin move from its current position to the coordinates provided by the Bing Maps geocode service.

Summary

In this chapter, you learned how to start the location service to receive a position in latitude and
longitude. Upon receiving a position, you passed the location data into the Bing Maps control and used
the Bing Maps map layer to indicate your current GPS position. This simple but powerful concept will
help you create your own location-aware applications. Also, you learned how to utilize the Bing Maps
geocode service, which converts the address to geocoordinates so that you can plot the address location
on the map.

In Chapter 15, you will learn how to use the media elements of the phone to play video and audio, as
well as stream movies and sounds from external sites. You will also learn how media elements play a
significant role in making sound effects in a game.

CHAPTER 15

Media

In today's information age, content is everything. Think of the multitude of web sites you have visited, and reflect on those that offered high-quality content vs. those whose content you did not trust. In terms of media files, consider YouTube, which provides access to everything from wacky personal videos to substantive educational videos to the masses via the Net. Now smartphones also have the ability to play high-quality movies, music, and more, anywhere at any time. What was once possible only on a powerful desktop computer can now be done with the smartphone that you carry around with you, regardless of whether you are near a cell tower or have access to a Wi-Fi connection.

Windows Phone devices come equipped with powerful media features for developers and designers to use to create compelling applications that can play back music, audio, and video in a host of formats. A good example of such functionality can be found at the NBC Olympics web site, where the Olympic Games were streamed live and then archived, and can now be viewed again in high definition (see www.nbcolympics.com/video/index.html).

In the following sections, you will learn to use the MediaElement control to play movies and sounds. MediaElement provides more than just a simple video or sound player. Windows Phone provides users with the ability to play videos and sounds, listen to FM radio, interact with the Music + Videos hub, and purchase a variety of media from the Windows Marketplace.

In this chapter, you will learn how to embed media in your applications and customize a media player control to play videos and sounds using MediaElement. You'll also learn to use MediaPlayerLauncher, which activates the stand-alone media player application that ships with Windows Phone.

Introducing MediaElement

MediaElement is a Windows Phone control that you can add to an application to play video and sound. It first appeared with .NET, and was then ported to Silverlight and finally to Windows Phone. When the MediaElement control is placed in the Visual Studio 2010 Express or Expression Blend design view, you will see only a rectangle, which is not what you would expect of a video or audio player. The MediaElement control appears as somewhat of a blank slate in order to give designers full control over the look of the Play, Stop, Pause, Mute, and Seek buttons. For developers, MediaElement exposes APIs for full control of a player's play, stop, pause, mute, and seek behavior, as well as for stream buffering, download progress, and volume control.

You'll want to use MediaElement when you are creating an application that requires more than a simple media player, and when you want to integrate the player into your application; that is, when you do not want the user to have to exit your application to access the player. Also, MediaElement offers the built-in flexibility to customize its look and add more functionality, such as being able to share videos via

Twitter, Facebook, SMS, or e-mail. You can even allow the user to add ratings and comments on media files. You can also create a video player that offers chapters and thumbnails of each chapter.

MediaPlayerLauncher is most useful if you simply want to play video or audio files using the default Windows Phone media player. The default media player that comes with Windows Phone supports basic functions such as play, pause, move forward, move backward, and play time elapsed. Alternatively, you can completely customize MediaElement, which can support a variety of video and audio formats. See Table 15-1 for the most commonly used formats that are supported by Windows Phone; a complete list can be found at `http://msdn.microsoft.com/en-us/library/ff462087(VS.92).aspx`.

Table 15-1. Media Formats Supported on Windows Phone

Media Type	Supported Formats
Audio	WAV, MP3, WMA, MP4
Video	WMV, MP4, AVI
Images	JPEG, PNG, GIF, BMP, TIF

The first exercise in this chapter will show you a technique for streaming a video file from the Internet or playing a video file that's part of the application content using MediaElement. Then you will learn to play the same video content using MediaPlayerLauncher.

Working with Video

In this exercise, you will build a media player (for video and audio) that can play, stop, pause, mute, and seek. The latter is a media player function that lets you move the video forward or backward to any position. The UI of the media player is shown in Figure 15-1. You will learn to stream video content from the Internet as well as play content that is part of the application. (Note that you won't want to package the video as part of the phone application because video and audio files are very large.)

In the real world, you must think about the strategy of deploying media content to the Web and allowing the phone application to simply play it. In Chapter 13, you learned about caching an image download in Isolated Storage. The same technique can be used to download and cache video or music content the first time it is played.

Another approach is to store video content on a Windows IIS media server and take advantage of the HD-quality streaming technology and Microsoft digital rights management (DRM) protection that the server provides. Netflix, for example, uses DRM technology to secure the content of its streaming videos. Microsoft DRM provides a platform to protect digital materials and deliver content that can be played on any device. Also, an IIS media server can effectively distribute HD video content to low-bandwidth and low-performing computers via smooth streaming technology. If you would like to learn more about these topics, refer to `http://msdn.microsoft.com/en-us/library/cc838192(VS.95).aspx`.

Another way to store video content is in the cloud using Microsoft Azure. Please refer to Chapter 3 to learn about the Windows Azure data store.

Figure 15-1. MediaPlayerDemo application

You will build the demo application in three major steps. First you will create a Windows Phone project. Then you will build the UI of the media player. Finally, you'll finish up by wiring up the commands in the code that respond to the user.

Creating the MediaPlayerDemo Project

To create the project, follow the steps from the previous examples in this book:

1. Open Microsoft Visual Studio 2010 Express for Windows Phone on your workstation.

2. Create a new Windows Phone Application by selecting File ➤ New Project from the Visual Studio command menu. Select the Windows Phone Application template, name the application `MediaPlayerDemo`, and click OK.

Building the UI

You will build the UI in Visual Studio with XAML, which is easy to work with when building simple controls. Go to Solution Explorer, open `MainPage.xaml`, and replace the XAML you find there with the code snippets that follow.

Declaring the UI Resources

The namespaces you see in the following code snippets are typically declared by default when you first create the Windows Phone project. The namespace `xmlns:phone="clr-namespace:Microsoft.Phone.Controls;assembly=Microsoft.Phone"` allows you to add common Windows Phone controls required to build this demo: Buttons, TextBlocks, TextBoxes, ListBoxes, Sliders, and MediaElements.

```
<phone:PhoneApplicationPage
    x:Class="MediaPlayerDemo.MainPage"
    xmlns="http://schemas.microsoft.com/winfx/2006/xaml/presentation"
    xmlns:x="http://schemas.microsoft.com/winfx/2006/xaml"
    xmlns:phone="clr-namespace:Microsoft.Phone.Controls;assembly=Microsoft.Phone"
    xmlns:shell="clr-namespace:Microsoft.Phone.Shell;assembly=Microsoft.Phone"
    xmlns:d="http://schemas.microsoft.com/expression/blend/2008"
    xmlns:mc="http://schemas.openxmlformats.org/markup-compatibility/2006"
    FontFamily="{StaticResource PhoneFontFamilyNormal}"
    FontSize="{StaticResource PhoneFontSizeNormal}"
    Foreground="{StaticResource PhoneForegroundBrush}"
    SupportedOrientations="Portrait" Orientation="Portrait"
    mc:Ignorable="d" d:DesignWidth="480" d:DesignHeight="768"
    shell:SystemTray.IsVisible="True">
```

Building the Main Page and Adding Media Player Components

Next, add the code shown in Listing 15-1, which creates the common media controls the application will use: play, pause, stop, mute, and seek. Remember that you can obtain the XAML code shown in Listing 15-1 from the source code that you downloaded for this book. You will be using the Slider control to allow the user to see how much time has elapsed in the playing of the media content. Also, by clicking the Slider, the user can skip backward and forward. You will also be adding labels to track the video buffering and video downloading status using the TextBlocks. Lastly, a button called `btnMediaPlayerLauncher` will launch the default Windows Phone's media player to play the media content.

Listing 15-1. Custom Media Player Main Page and UI (XAML)

```
<phone:PhoneApplicationPage
    x:Class="MediaPlayerDemo.MainPage"
```

```
      xmlns="http://schemas.microsoft.com/winfx/2006/xaml/presentation"
      xmlns:x="http://schemas.microsoft.com/winfx/2006/xaml"
      xmlns:phone="clr-namespace:Microsoft.Phone.Controls;assembly=Microsoft.Phone"
      xmlns:shell="clr-namespace:Microsoft.Phone.Shell;assembly=Microsoft.Phone"
      xmlns:d="http://schemas.microsoft.com/expression/blend/2008"
      xmlns:mc="http://schemas.openxmlformats.org/markup-compatibility/2006"
      FontFamily="{StaticResource PhoneFontFamilyNormal}"
      FontSize="{StaticResource PhoneFontSizeNormal}"
      Foreground="{StaticResource PhoneForegroundBrush}"
      SupportedOrientations="Portrait" Orientation="Portrait"
      mc:Ignorable="d" d:DesignWidth="480" d:DesignHeight="768"
      shell:SystemTray.IsVisible="True">

<Grid x:Name="LayoutRoot" Background="Transparent">
    <Grid.RowDefinitions>
        <RowDefinition Height="Auto"/>
        <RowDefinition Height="*"/>
    </Grid.RowDefinitions>

    <StackPanel x:Name="TitlePanel" Grid.Row="0" Margin="24,24,0,12">
        <TextBlock x:Name="PageTitle" Text="MediaPlayerDemo" Margin="-3,-8,0,0"
                   Style="{StaticResource PhoneTextTitle1Style}" FontSize="48" />
    </StackPanel>

    <Grid x:Name="ContentGrid" Grid.Row="1">
        <MediaElement Height="289" HorizontalAlignment="Left"
                      Margin="26,148,0,0" x:Name="mediaPlayer"
                      VerticalAlignment="Top" Width="417"
                      AutoPlay="False"/>
        <Button Content="&gt;" Height="72"
                HorizontalAlignment="Left" Margin="13,527,0,0"
                x:Name="btnPlay" VerticalAlignment="Top" Width="87"
                Click="btnPlay_Click" />
        <Button Content="O" Height="72"
                HorizontalAlignment="Right" Margin="0,527,243,0"
                x:Name="btnStop" VerticalAlignment="Top" Width="87"
                Click="btnStop_Click" />
        <Button Content="||" Height="72" Margin="0,527,313,0"
                x:Name="btnPause" VerticalAlignment="Top"
                Click="btnPause_Click" HorizontalAlignment="Right" Width="87" />
        <Slider Height="84" HorizontalAlignment="Left"
                Margin="13,423,0,0" Name="mediaTimeline"
                VerticalAlignment="Top" Width="443"
                ValueChanged="mediaTimeline_ValueChanged"
                Maximum="1" LargeChange="0.1" />
        <TextBlock Height="30" HorizontalAlignment="Left"
                   Margin="26,472,0,0" Name="lblStatus"
                   Text="00:00" VerticalAlignment="Top" Width="88" FontSize="16" />
        <TextBlock Height="30"
                   Margin="118,472,222,0" x:Name="lblBuffering"
                   Text="Buffering" VerticalAlignment="Top" FontSize="16" />
        <TextBlock Height="30"
```

```
                    Margin="0,472,82,0" x:Name="lblDownload"
                    Text="Download" VerticalAlignment="Top" FontSize="16"
    HorizontalAlignment="Right" Width="140" />
            <Button Content="Mute" Height="72"
                    HorizontalAlignment="Left" Margin="217,527,0,0"
                    Name="btnMute" VerticalAlignment="Top" Width="89"
                    FontSize="16" Click="btnMute_Click" />
            <TextBlock Height="30" HorizontalAlignment="Left"
                    Margin="315,551,0,0" Name="lblSoundStatus"
                    Text="Sound On" VerticalAlignment="Top" Width="128" />
            <Button Content="Use MediaPlayerLauncher" FontSize="24" Height="72"
                    HorizontalAlignment="Left" Margin="13,591,0,0"
                    Name="btnMediaPlayerLauncher" VerticalAlignment="Top"
                    Width="411" Click="btnMediaPlayerLauncher_Click" />
            <TextBox x:Name="txtUrl" Height="57" Margin="91,33,8,0"
                    TextWrapping="Wrap" VerticalAlignment="Top" FontSize="16"

Text="http://ecn.channel9.msdn.com/o9/ch9/7/8/2/9/1/5/ARCastMDISilverlightGridComputing_ch9.wm
v"/>
            <TextBlock x:Name="lblUrl" HorizontalAlignment="Left" Height="25"
                    Margin="8,48,0,0" TextWrapping="Wrap" Text="Video URL:"
                    VerticalAlignment="Top" Width="83" FontSize="16"/>
            <TextBox x:Name="txtBufferingTime" Height="57" Margin="151,78,0,0"
                    TextWrapping="Wrap" VerticalAlignment="Top" FontSize="16"
    HorizontalAlignment="Left" Width="86" Text="20"/>
            <TextBlock x:Name="lblBufferingTime" HorizontalAlignment="Left"
                    Height="25" Margin="8,93,0,0" TextWrapping="Wrap"
                    Text="Buffering Time (s):" VerticalAlignment="Top"
                    Width="139" FontSize="16"/>
        </Grid>
    </Grid>

</phone:PhoneApplicationPage>
```

Once you have loaded the XAML code, you should see the layout shown in Figure 15-2. In the next section, you will add code to respond to UI events and implement MediaElement behaviors.

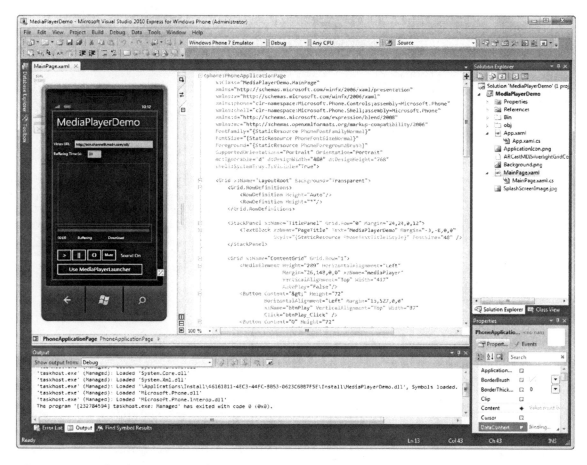

Figure 15-2. MediaPlayerDemo in design view

Coding the Application

In Solution Explorer, open `MainPage.xaml.cs` and replace the code you find there with the C# code blocks that follow to implement the media player's functions.

Specifying the Namespaces

Begin by listing the namespaces the application will use. The inclusion of `Microsoft.Phone.Tasks` will allow you to launch the Windows Phone default media player. As for MediaElement, it is declared in the XAML page, which you will simply reference here by the control's name. Also, you'll need to add a reference to `Microsoft.Xna.Framework`, which you'll be using to check whether background music is being played before playing your own video. This is necessary in order to pass the "Applications that Play Music section 6.5.1." marketplace certification. Refer to Chapter 5 for more information on how to direct users to the Windows Marketplace to buy your application.

```
using System;
using System.Windows;
using System.Windows.Media;
using Microsoft.Phone.Controls;using Microsoft.Phone.Tasks;
using Microsoft.Xna.Framework;
using Microsoft.Xna.Framework.Media;
namespace MediaPlayerDemo
{
    public partial class MainPage : PhoneApplicationPage
```

Initializing Variables

The variable_updatingMediaTimeline is an extremely important variable that stops the infinite loop in this demo. You set _updatingMediaTimeline to true while the media timeline (Slider control) is being updated during the CompositionTarget.Rendering event so that the media's backward and forward event will wait to be processed until the timeline update is complete. But the Slider control is also responsible for allowing the user to interact with the video timeline by dragging the slider forward or backward to move the media position. _updatingMediaTimeline will allow only one specific behavior to happen in the Slider control, thereby avoiding unwanted application behavior.

```
private bool _updatingMediaTimeline;

public MainPage()
{
    InitializeComponent();

    _updatingMediaTimeline = false;

    // rewinds the media player to the beginning
    mediaPlayer.Position = System.TimeSpan.FromSeconds(0);
```

Handling Video Download Progress

As the video file download progresses, you will receive the percentage of the file downloaded and will display the progress updates back to the user by updating the lblDownload.

```
// Download indicator
mediaPlayer.DownloadProgressChanged += (s, e) =>
    {
        lblDownload.Text = string.Format("Downloading {0:0.0%}",
mediaPlayer.DownloadProgress);
    };
```

Handling Video Buffering

You will set the video's BufferingTime property, and as the video buffering time progresses, you will receive a callback where you will update lblBuffering.

```
// Handle media buffering
```

```
                mediaPlayer.BufferingTime =
TimeSpan.FromSeconds(Convert.ToDouble(txtBufferingTime.Text));
            mediaPlayer.BufferingProgressChanged += (s, e) =>
                {
                    lblBuffering.Text = string.Format("Buffering {0:0.0%}",
mediaPlayer.BufferingProgress);
                };
```

Showing Time Elapsed in the Media Player

CompositionTarget.Rendering is a frame-based event that will fire once per frame, allowing you to update the media timeline (Slider control) to reflect how much of the media has been played. By default, the event will fire 60 times a second. You can verify this by checking the value of Application.Current.Host.Settings.MaxFrameRate. By using the CompositionTarget.Rendering event, you will be able to see the media player timeline changing as the media plays.

```
            // Updates the media timeline (slider control) with total time played
            // and updates the status with the time played
            CompositionTarget.Rendering += (s, e) =>
                {
                    _updatingMediaTimeline = true;
                    TimeSpan duration = mediaPlayer.NaturalDuration.TimeSpan;
                    if (duration.TotalSeconds != 0)
                    {
                        double percentComplete =
mediaPlayer.Position.TotalSeconds / duration.TotalSeconds;
                        mediaTimeline.Value = percentComplete;
                        TimeSpan mediaTime = mediaPlayer.Position;
                        string text = string.Format("{0:00}:{1:00}",
                            (mediaTime.Hours * 60) + mediaTime.Minutes, mediaTime.Seconds);

                        if (lblStatus.Text != text)
                            lblStatus.Text = text;

                        _updatingMediaTimeline = false;
                    }
                };
        }
```

■ **Tip** When defining the event handler of CompositionTarget.Rendering, you can use a lambda expression to create a delegate that contains the programming logic. For example, you can rewrite CompositionTarget.Rendering += (s, e) => { ... } by first declaring the event handler CompositionTarget.Rendering += new EventHandler(CompositionTarget_Rendering) and then creating a method void CompositionTarget_Rendering(object sender, EventArgs e) { ... }. Using the lambda expression technique makes the code much more readable and, in this demo project, gives you the ability to group the relevant code together. For more information on lambda expressions, please refer to http://msdn.microsoft.com/en-us/library/bb397687.aspx.

Implementing the Pause Button

When the Pause button is clicked, invoke MediaElement.Pause to pause the media player. Note that you are updating the status label, communicating to the user that the media is in pause mode. Occasionally, the media player may not be able to pause. You can use mediaPlayer.CanPause to make sure that you can pause; otherwise, set the status label to warn the user that the Pause button may not work.

```
private void btnPause_Click(object sender, RoutedEventArgs e)
{
    if (mediaPlayer.CanPause)
    {
        mediaPlayer.Pause();
        lblStatus.Text = "Paused";
    }
    else
    {
        lblStatus.Text = "Can not be Paused. Please try again!";
    }
}
```

Implementing the Stop Button

When the Stop button is clicked, invoke MediaElement.Stop to stop the media player and then rewind it back to the beginning and update the status label to Stopped.

```
private void btnStop_Click(object sender, RoutedEventArgs e)
{
    mediaPlayer.Stop();
    mediaPlayer.Position = System.TimeSpan.FromSeconds(0);
    lblStatus.Text = "Stopped";
}
```

Implementing the Play Button

When the Play button is clicked, invoke MediaElement.Play to play the media player. But before you can play, you must check to make sure that no background music is being played. For example, if the user is using the phone to play music and then enters your application, your application must confirm with the user that they will be playing their own video or music, which will interrupt the music that is already playing. If you don't confirm the permission to play the music with the user, your application will fail the "Applications that Play Music section 6.5.1" marketplace certification. The CanPlay method uses the XNA media framework's MediaPlayer to check if GameHasControl has been invoked to play the sound, which tells you if the user has entered your application while playing his or her own music.

```
private void btnPlay_Click(object sender, RoutedEventArgs e)
{
    if (this.CanPlay())
    {
        mediaPlayer.Play();
    }
}

private bool CanPlay()
{
    bool canPlay = false;

    FrameworkDispatcher.Update();
    if (MediaPlayer.GameHasControl)
    {
        canPlay = true;
    }
    else
    {
        if (MessageBox.Show
        ("Is it ok to stop currently playing music and play our animal sounds?"
        , "Can play our sounds?"
        , MessageBoxButton.OKCancel) == MessageBoxResult.OK)
        {
            canPlay = true;
            MediaPlayer.Pause();
            AboutViewModel.Instance.CanPlay = true;
        }
        else
        {
            canPlay = false;
            AboutViewModel.Instance.CanPlay = false;
        }
    }

    return canPlay;
}
```

Implementing the Mute Button

When the Mute button is clicked, set `MediaElement.IsMuted` to true to mute the sound, and `false` to turn on the sound.

```
private void btnMute_Click(object sender, RoutedEventArgs e)
{
    if (lblSoundStatus.Text.Equals("Sound On",
StringComparison.CurrentCultureIgnoreCase))
    {
        lblSoundStatus.Text = "Sound Off";
        mediaPlayer.IsMuted = true;
    }
    else
    {
        lblSoundStatus.Text = "Sound On";
        mediaPlayer.IsMuted = false;
    }

}
```

■ **Note** To mute the player, you can set `MediaElement.Volume` to zero instead of setting the `IsMuted` property to `true`, as shown previously.

Implementing Seek

When the Slider control, which displays the timeline of the media, is clicked or dragged, `MediaElement.Position` moves either forward or backward, depending on the user's input on the Slider control. Figure 15-3 illustrates that dragging the slider to the right will move the video timeline forward.

```
private void mediaTimeline_ValueChanged(object sender,
                                        RoutedPropertyChangedEventArgs<double> e)
{
    if (!_updatingMediaTimeline && mediaPlayer.CanSeek)
    {
        TimeSpan duration = mediaPlayer.NaturalDuration.TimeSpan;
        int newPosition = (int)(duration.TotalSeconds * mediaTimeline.Value);
        mediaPlayer.Position = new TimeSpan(0, 0, newPosition);
    }
}
```

Figure 15-3. Dragging the slider to skip around in the video

▓ **Note** Using MediaElement.Position, you can jump to any part of the media. This is very useful when you want to create chapters in a movie similar to those you see in DVD players.

Implementing MediaPlayerLauncher

When the MediaPlayerLauncher button is clicked, invoke the MediaPlayerLauncher task to launch the default Windows Phone media player.

```
        private void btnMediaPlayerLauncher_Click(object sender, RoutedEventArgs e)
        {
            MediaPlayerLauncher player = new MediaPlayerLauncher();
            player.Media = new
Uri("http://ecn.channel9.msdn.com/o9/ch9/7/8/2/9/1/5/
ARCastMDISilverlightGridComputing_ch9.wmv");
            //player.Media =
//             new Uri("ARCastMDISilverlightGridComputing_ch9.wmv",
//                                                      UriKind.Relative);
            //player.Location = MediaLocationType.Data;
            player.Show();
        }
```

■ **Note** In the commented code, where MediaPlayerLauncher plays the content that is part of the application, player.Location is set to MediaLocationType.Data, which means that it will look in Isolated Storage for a file named ARCastMDISilverlightGridComputing_ch9.wmv. Refer to Chapter 13 for the demo in which this file was downloaded and then saved into Isolated Storage for later access. If you set player.Location to MediaLocationType.Install, the media file must be added to the application as the content. Also, the media source's Uri must have UriKind.Relative, which means that the file is part of the application. The only problem with doing it this way is that the size of the application install will get much bigger.

Testing the Finished Application

To test the application, press F5. The result should resemble Figure 15-1. Try clicking each button: Play, Pause, Stop, and Mute. As the movie plays, take note of the buffering and downloading progress status. You can also drag the slider back and forth to skip around the movie's scenes. Feel free to enter your favorite movie link.

In this demo, you created a custom media player and then launched the default Windows Phone media player. Both MediaElement and MediaPlayerLauncher accessed the video content on the Web because video files are typically very big. But if you are adding simple sound effects to an application, it's not always ideal to download the contents from the Web—a better solution is to package the sound along with the application. This is especially true if you are planning to create a game where all the graphical and media assets are packaged as part of the application. In the next demo, you will learn how to add sound effects to an application.

Adding Sounds to an Application

In the first demo, you played a video, but you can also use MediaElement to play music files or create sound effects in a game or application. In this demo, you will learn how to apply a sound effect to an animated object—in this case, a flying robot. Such sound effects are essential in games. You will also learn to handle background music that users may be listening to prior to launching your application. This is done in accordance with the marketplace rules for receiving user approval to stop music that is currently playing in the background before playing the application's sound.

Figure 15-4 shows the UI of the demo application. When you click the Play button, the robot flies diagonally toward the bottom-right corner of the screen. When it reaches an edge, the robot will bounce several times while making a swooshing sound to give the animation that dash of realism it needs to satisfy gamers.

Figure 15-4. RobotSoundDemo application

You will build the RobotSoundDemo application in three steps. You'll start by creating a Windows Phone project. Then you'll build the UI and add the code to handle control events as a last step.

Creating the RobotSoundDemo Project

To create the project, follow the steps from the previous examples in this book:

    1. Open Microsoft Visual Studio 2010 Express for Windows Phone on your workstation.

2. Create a new Windows Phone application by selecting File ➤ New Project from the Visual Studio command menu. Select the Windows Phone Application template, name the application RobotSoundDemo, and click OK.

Building the UI

Before you can build the UI, you need to add the following three files to the project:

- Robot.xaml

- Robot.xaml.cs

- sound18.wma

Once you have successfully added these files to the project, you will see in Solution Explorer the list of files shown in Figure 15-5.

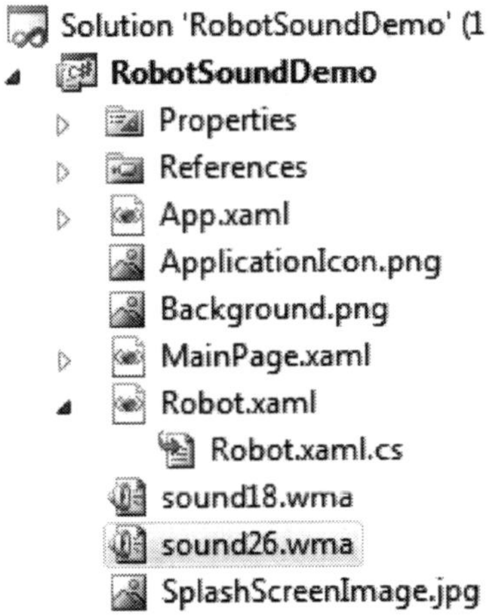

📂 Solution 'RobotSoundDemo' (1 project)
▲ 📷 **RobotSoundDemo**
   ▷ 📁 Properties
   ▷ 📁 References
   ▷ 🖼 App.xaml
     🖼 ApplicationIcon.png
     🖼 Background.png
   ▷ 🖼 MainPage.xaml
   ▲ 🖼 Robot.xaml
       🖼 Robot.xaml.cs
     🎵 sound18.wma
     🎵 sound26.wma
     🖼 SplashScreenImage.jpg

Figure 15-5. RobotSoundDemo project after adding the assets

All three files are included in the source code that is distributed with this book. The assets necessary for this demo are located in the unzipped source code directory (c:*where you unzipped*\Codes\ch15\Assets). Robot.xaml and Robot.xaml.cs are the vector graphic versions of the robot, and sound18.wma is the sound effect file to be played when the robot moves.

Selecting the UI Resources

You will add the namespace of the robot asset you just added to the project using xmlns:uc="clr-namespace:RobotSoundDemo". This namespace will allow you to add the robot user control using XAML code, in the form of <uc:Robot x:Name="ucRobot" ...>.

```
<phone:PhoneApplicationPage
    x:Class="RobotSoundDemo.MainPage"
    xmlns="http://schemas.microsoft.com/winfx/2006/xaml/presentation"
```

```
xmlns:x="http://schemas.microsoft.com/winfx/2006/xaml"
xmlns:phone="clr-namespace:Microsoft.Phone.Controls;assembly=Microsoft.Phone"
xmlns:shell="clr-namespace:Microsoft.Phone.Shell;assembly=Microsoft.Phone"
xmlns:d="http://schemas.microsoft.com/expression/blend/2008"
xmlns:mc="http://schemas.openxmlformats.org/markup-compatibility/2006"
xmlns:uc="clr-namespace:RobotSoundDemo"
FontFamily="{StaticResource PhoneFontFamilyNormal}"
FontSize="{StaticResource PhoneFontSizeNormal}"
Foreground="{StaticResource PhoneForegroundBrush}"
SupportedOrientations="Portrait" Orientation="Portrait"
mc:Ignorable="d" d:DesignWidth="480" d:DesignHeight="768"
shell:SystemTray.IsVisible="True">
```

Adding the Robot Animation to the Main Page Resource Section

In the main page resource section, add the robot storyboard animation in which the robot moves from the top-left to the bottom-right corner. The bouncing EasingFunction is added to the robot's movement, which will cause the robot to bounce toward the end of its movement.

```
<phone:PhoneApplicationPage.Resources>
<Storyboard x:Name="MoveRobot">
        <DoubleAnimationUsingKeyFrames
Storyboard.TargetProperty="(UIElement.RenderTransform).(CompositeTransform.TranslateX)"
Storyboard.TargetName="ucRobot">
            <EasingDoubleKeyFrame KeyTime="0" Value="0"/>
                <EasingDoubleKeyFrame KeyTime="0:0:0.6" Value="244">
                    <EasingDoubleKeyFrame.EasingFunction>
                        <BounceEase EasingMode="EaseOut"/>
</EasingDoubleKeyFrame.EasingFunction>
                </EasingDoubleKeyFrame>
        </DoubleAnimationUsingKeyFrames>
        <DoubleAnimationUsingKeyFrames
Storyboard.TargetProperty="(UIElement.RenderTransform).(CompositeTransform.TranslateY)"
Storyboard.TargetName="ucRobot">
                <EasingDoubleKeyFrame KeyTime="0" Value="0"/>
                <EasingDoubleKeyFrame KeyTime="0:0:0.6" Value="421">
                    <EasingDoubleKeyFrame.EasingFunction>
                        <BounceEase EasingMode="EaseOut"/>
                    </EasingDoubleKeyFrame.EasingFunction>
                </EasingDoubleKeyFrame>
        </DoubleAnimationUsingKeyFrames>
    </Storyboard>
</phone:PhoneApplicationPage.Resources>
```

Building the Main Page and Adding Components

This demo has a very simple UI that contains a Play button to animate the robot and a MediaElement to play the sound effect. Note that MediaElement.Source is set to sound18.wma, whereas in the previous demo, you set the source to the URL. This is because sound18.wma is a content type. You can verify this by right-clicking the sound18.wma file in Solution Explorer and looking at its properties, as shown in Figure 15-6.

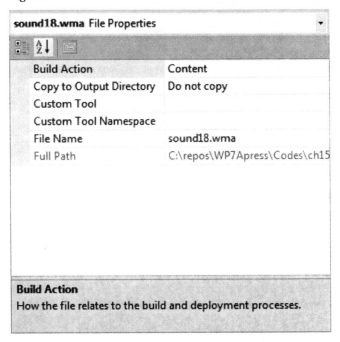

sound18.wma File Properties

Build Action	Content
Copy to Output Directory	Do not copy
Custom Tool	
Custom Tool Namespace	
File Name	sound18.wma
Full Path	C:\repos\WP7Apress\Codes\ch15

Build Action
How the file relates to the build and deployment processes.

Figure 15-6. The sound18.wma file's properties in Solution Explorer

```xml
<Grid x:Name="LayoutRoot" Background="Transparent">
    <Grid.RowDefinitions>
        <RowDefinition Height="Auto"/>
        <RowDefinition Height="*"/>
    </Grid.RowDefinitions>

    <StackPanel x:Name="TitlePanel" Grid.Row="0" Margin="24,24,0,12">

        <TextBlock x:Name="PageTitle" Text="RobotSoundDemo" Margin="-3,-8,0,0"
Style="{StaticResource PhoneTextTitle1Style}" FontSize="56" />
    </StackPanel>

    <Grid x:Name="ContentGrid" Grid.Row="1">
        <uc:Robot x:Name="ucRobot" Margin="24,27,264,442" RenderTransformOrigin="0.5,0.5"
>
                <uc:Robot.RenderTransform>
                    <CompositeTransform/>
                </uc:Robot.RenderTransform>
        </uc:Robot>
        <Button Content="Play" Height="72" HorizontalAlignment="Left"
                Margin="6,333,0,0" Name="btnPlay"
```

```
                    VerticalAlignment="Top" Width="160"
                    Click="btnPlay_Click" />
            <MediaElement x:Name="robotSound" Height="100"
                        VerticalAlignment="Bottom" Margin="176,0,204,69"
                        Source="sound18.wma" AutoPlay="False"/>
        </Grid>
    </Grid>

</phone:PhoneApplicationPage>
```

Once you've loaded the XAML code, you should see the layout shown in Figure 15-7. Now it's time to wire up the events to animate the robot and play the sound effect.

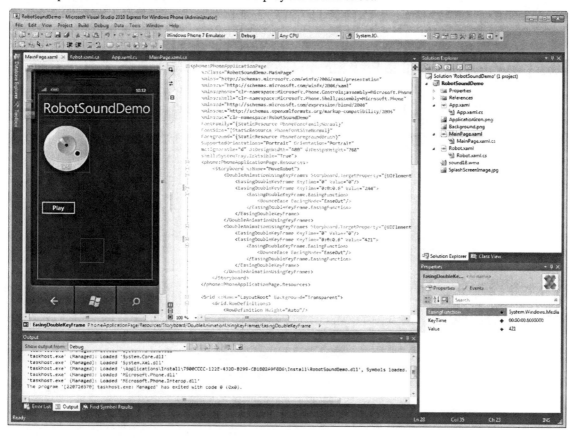

Figure 15-7. RobotSoundDemo in design view

Coding the Application

In Solution Explorer, open `MainPage.xaml.cs` and replace the code there with the following C# code blocks.

Specifying the Namespaces

Add a reference to `Microsoft.Xna.Framework` so that you can check whether background music is currently playing before starting your video.

```
using System.Windows;
using Microsoft.Phone.Controls;
using Microsoft.Xna.Framework;
using Microsoft.Xna.Framework.Media;
```

Adding an Event to Handle Play Button Clicks

When the Play button is clicked, the `MoveRobot` animation is played; at the same time, the sound effect of the robot moving will also be played. Notice in the following code that the `CanPlay` method is called to check that no background music is being played, and if it is, to let the user know that the background music application will be stopped before your application starts.

```
        private void btnPlay_Click(object sender, RoutedEventArgs e)
        {
            if (CanPlay())
            {
                MoveRobot.Begin();

                robotSound.Stop();
                robotSound.Source = new System.Uri("sound26.wma", System.UriKind.Relative);
robotSound.Play();
            }
        }

        private bool CanPlay()
        {
            bool canPlay = false;

            FrameworkDispatcher.Update();
            if (MediaPlayer.GameHasControl)
            {
                canPlay = true;
            }
            else
            {
                if (MessageBox.Show("Is it ok to stop currently playing music?", "Can stop
music?", MessageBoxButton.OKCancel) == MessageBoxResult.OK)
                {
                    canPlay = true;
                    MediaPlayer.Pause();
```

```
        }
        else
        {
            canPlay = false;
        }
    }

    return canPlay;
}
```

Testing the Finished Application

To test the finished application, press F5. The result should resemble the screenshot in Figure 15-4. Test your work by clicking the Play button, which should cause the robot to fly to the bottom-right corner of the screen, making a swooshing sound as it goes. When the robot reaches the bottom, watch it bounce several times.

Summary

This chapter showed you how to stream media content from the Web or the resource of the application, and how to play video and audio using MediaElement and MediaPlayerLauncher. You also applied basic sound effects to an animation using MediaElement. One thing that this chapter did not cover is the FMRadio API, but you can find information about it at `http://msdn.microsoft.com/en-us/library/ff769541(VS.92).aspx`.

In Chapter 16, you will learn how to interact with the Windows Phone photo application, which will allow you to create your own version of a photograph-altering application and interact with the phone's camera to capture and manipulate an image.

CHAPTER 16

Working with the Camera and Photos

Today, consumers assume that any cell phone they purchase will be able to take photos, and that the quality of those photos will be close to those of an entry-level digital camera. Furthermore, the latest mobile devices allow for the integration of their photo capabilities with the various applications that run on these devices. For instance, taking a picture with the phone, adding a caption to it, and immediately uploading the photo to a social media website are common capabilities of all smartphone platforms today.

In this chapter, you will learn how the Windows Phone platform implements yet another level of integrated user experience when it comes to the picture-taking capabilities of the phone and your application. You will learn how to build an application that takes photos, saves them, lets the user open them, and then sends them to Twitpic, a remote cloud service where they can be embedded in Twitter messages. You will also learn about accessing the live feed of the data being captured by the camera and preprocessing it before showing it to the user. This access to the buffer of live camera data is at the heart of the whole category of "augmented reality" applications, which combine and overlay real and imaginary objects onto one photo feed.

A lot of the code you will write in this chapter will have to be deployed and debugged physically on a real Windows Phone device. After all, it's not possible to take a real picture with the emulator or test many features of the pictures application. (It is, however, possible to take a "dummy" picture of a small square moving around the emulator perimeter, which proves extremely useful for testing.)

We highly recommend that, before you proceed with this chapter, you get your hands on an actual Windows Phone device. You should also install the necessary Zune software that allows debugging on that device and connect the device to your development machine. (For more information on using the Zune software to debug a photo application using a physical device, see Chapter 4.)

Introducing Windows Phone Photo Features

Before you delver into developing a Windows Phone application that snaps photos and manipulates them, it's important to understand the model for working with photos on this device. As explained in greater detail in Chapter 19, each application deployed to the device runs in its own *sandbox*, or execution environment. This execution sandbox prevents third-party applications from directly accessing common data stores on the phone, such as photos or contact lists, and prevents them from directly invoking the applications that ship with a Windows Phone device, such as the camera or messaging applications. So how can you build an application that can take pictures, manipulate them, save them to the phone, and then later access those pictures for uploading to the cloud? The answer is through *launchers* and *choosers*, which are shown in Tables 16–1 and 16–2 and are also described in greater detail in Chapter 10.

Table 16–1. *Launchers*

Launchers	Description
EmailComposeTask	Opens the default device e-mail composer.
MarketPlaceDetailTask	Opens detailed product information.
MarketPlaceDetailTask	Opens to the Marketplace within specified category.
MarketPlaceReviewTask	Opens the product review for the specified product.
MarketPlaceSearchTask	Opens the MarketPlace search result based on the search term specified.
MediaPlayerLauncher	Opens the default device MediaPlayer.
PhoneCallTask	Opens the Phone application with specified number ready to dial.
SearchTask	Opens the default search application.
SmsComposeTask	Opens the messaging application.
WebBrowserTask	Opens the default device Web browser to the specified URL.

Table 16–2. *Choosers*

Choosers	Description
CameraCaptureTask	Opens the Camera application to capture the image.
EmailAddressChooserTask	Opens the Contact application to choose an e-mail.
PhoneNumberChooserTask	Opens the Phone application to choose a phone number.
PhotoChooserTask	Opens the Photo Picker application to choose the image.
SaveEmailAddressTask	Saves the provided e-mail to the Contact list.
SavePhoneNumberTask	Saves the phone number to the Contact list.

The Windows Phone Launchers and Choosers framework is a collection of APIs you can use to access core Windows Phone applications indirectly, like the phone or contacts list, to perform a specific task. A *launcher* can launch a phone application but return no data. A chooser, such as a photo chooser on the other hand, returns data to the application that calls it. In other words, the difference between launchers and choosers lies in the fact that the former do not return results to the calling function, but the latter do return results. Tables 16–1 and 16–2 list some of the launchers and choosers that ship with the Windows Phone platform today and how each is used. (For a full list, of Launchers and Choosers, refer to Chapter 10.)

Naturally, the CameraCaptureTask is a chooser that is of particular interest. This chooser launches the built-in Windows Phone camera application, allowing a user or a third-party application to snap photos and to retrieve them for its own purposes by handling the chooser's Completed event. You will write code to capture photos shortly, but before you do that, it's important to understand one more basic concept when working with launchers and choosers—the application execution model and application tombstoning. (For a more thorough and detailed look at the Windows Phone application life cycle, refer to Chapter 10.)

Launchers and choosers are, in essence, separate applications that are launched from within your application. Because only one application can be active on the phone at any time, you must be familiar with the concepts of fast application switching and application state management to preserve your application's data properly if your goal is to provide a consistent user experience (and to pass Windows Phone Marketplace certification). If your application gathers a lot of unique data prior to a launcher or chooser call, that data must be properly preserved while the launcher or chooser is activated.

Using a Chooser to Take Photos

The first application that you will write will take photos and integrate them into your application. The first application will also lay the foundation for the rest of this chapter, since you will enhance and add features to this application as you go along. You will, therefore, create a basic navigation system in this first step for your application using an Application Bar and a standard set of icons that ship with the Windows Phone Development Tools that you downloaded and installed in Chapter 2. You'll find the icons for a 32-bit system at C:\Program Files\Microsoft SDKs\Windows Phone\v7.1\Icons and for a 64-bit system at C:\Program Files (x86)\Microsoft SDKs\Windows Phone\v7.1\Icons.

As mentioned, you will use choosers to implement the photo manipulation features on Windows Phone. To take photos, you will use the CameraCaptureTask chooser to take the photo and bring that photo into your application. Follow this demo to accomplish these tasks.

Creating a New Project and Building the User Interface

In the first part of the demo, you will create a new project and add the necessary user interface elements to allow for photo manipulation in the later sections of this chapter.

Start a new project as you learned to do in previous chapters:

1. Launch Visual Studio 2010 Express for Windows Phone, and create a new Windows Phone Application project.

2. Name your project PhotoCapture.

You will create an Application Bar with three icons. The first button of the Application Bar will be for taking photos, which is the subject of the current demo. The second button will be for opening previously-taken photos, which you will develop later. Finally, the third button will be used for saving photos to the phone. Start by creating a separate folder within your application to store Application Bar icons:

3. Right-click the name of the project within Solution Explorer, choose Add ➤ New Folder. Name that folder images.

You will use the standard Application Bar icons that came pre-installed with the Developer Tools for Windows Phone. By default, the icons are installed in the C:\Program Files\Microsoft SDKs\Windows phone\v7.1\Icons folder.

4. Within the Icons folder, go to the subfolder called dark and, using Windows Explorer, copy the following icons into the images folder within your application: appbar.feature.camera.rest.png, appbar.folder.rest.png, and appbar.save.rest.png.

5. Now you need to make the icons part of your solution. Highlight all three icons, right-click and select Property to bring up the Properties dialog. For the Build Action property, specify Content. Then, select Copy Always for the Copy to Output Directory property.

With icons ready for use in the Application Bar, you are ready to add an Application Bar to MainPage.xaml. (For an in-depth explanation of how to add and use an Application Bar within your application, refer to Chapter 7.)

6. Open MainPage.xaml, and paste the following code at the end of the XAML file just before the </phone:PhoneApplicationPage> closing tag. This XAML replaces the auto-generated template for the Application Bar:

```xml
<phone:PhoneApplicationPage.ApplicationBar>
    <shell:ApplicationBar IsVisible="True">
        <shell:ApplicationBar.Buttons>
            <shell:ApplicationBarIconButton x:Name="btnCamera" Text="Take Photo"
IconUri="images/appbar.feature.camera.rest.png" Click="btnCamera_Click"/>
            <shell:ApplicationBarIconButton Text="Open Photo"
IconUri="images/appbar.folder.rest.png"/>
            <shell:ApplicationBarIconButton Text="Save Photo"
IconUri="images/appbar.save.rest.png"/>
        </shell:ApplicationBar.Buttons>
    </shell:ApplicationBar>
</phone:PhoneApplicationPage.ApplicationBar>
```

■ **Note** The btnCamera_Click event handler will be called when the user clicks the Take Photo button. You will write code for this event handler in the next section.

Finally, you need to add an Image control to show the photos taken within your application.

7. From the Toolbox, drag and drop an Image control onto the MainPage.xaml design surface, place it in the middle, and size it to be about half of the available screen space. Name it imgPhoto.

Writing Code to Take Photos with CameraCaptureTask

Although you may lose a bit of flexibility when programming with launchers and choosers, it is hard to dispute how easy they have made working with common phone tasks, such as taking pictures. In the first release of Windows Phone OS, launchers and choosers were the only way to interact with camera tasks. However, in the current Windows Phone release, you have a lot more control over manipulating photos in your application, including access to the live preview buffer of the camera. You will get familiar with the new features of the current Windows Phone platform later on in this chapter. In the following steps, you will launch a PhotoCapture chooser and wire up a callback event to invoke when that application completes.

1. Open MainPage.xaml.cs (right-click MainPage.xaml, and select View Code). Add the following using statements to the very top of the code page:

```
using Microsoft.Phone.Tasks;
using Microsoft.Phone;
```

2. Add the following class-level variables within the MainPage class (right above the MainPage constructor):

```
private CameraCaptureTask cameraCaptureTask;
byte[] imageBits;
```

3. Add the following code for the btnCamera_Click method. This will invoke the PhotoCapture application when the user clicks the first button in the Application Bar:

```
private void btnCamera_Click(object sender, EventArgs e)
{
    cameraCaptureTask.Show();
}
```

You are now ready to write the event handler code that will be invoked when the CameraCaptureTask chooser completes its work; that is, once the user has taken a picture, and control returns to your application. When control returns to your application, the photo taken by the user is passed in as one of the arguments to the callback function; you will take that photo and show it in the imgPhoto image control that you added previously. Add the following method, which will be executed when the chooser completes, to MainPage.xaml.cs:

```
private void PhotoChooserTaskCompleted(object sender, PhotoResult e)
{
    if (e.ChosenPhoto != null)
    {
        imageBits = new byte[(int)e.ChosenPhoto.Length];
        e.ChosenPhoto.Read(imageBits, 0, imageBits.Length);
        e.ChosenPhoto.Seek(0, System.IO.SeekOrigin.Begin);

        var bitmapImage = PictureDecoder.DecodeJpeg(e.ChosenPhoto);
        this.imgPhoto.Source = bitmapImage;
    }
}
```

You need to tell your application's instance of CameraCaptureTask that the PhotoChooserTaskCompleted method must be invoked upon its completion. You will do this within the MainPage() constructor using the following two lines of code:

```
cameraCaptureTask = new CameraCaptureTask();
cameraCaptureTask.Completed += PhotoChooserTaskCompleted;
```

You are now ready to run the application. Note that, for this demo, it is not completely necessary to deploy your application to the physical device since the emulator provides limited simulated photo-taking capabilities (the aforementioned small rectangle moving around the phone area).

4. Press F5 to run the application on the emulator, and then press the camera button in the Application Bar to be presented with the Windows Phone PhotoCapture application. Press the button in the upper-right corner to simulate photo-taking within the emulator (notice how this simulation consists of a black rectangle moving around the screen's perimeter), and then press the Accept button to accept the photo. You should see a phone screen similar to the one shown in Figure 16–1 with your application displaying the captured image. Of course, if you deploy this application to an actual Windows Phone device, the photos that you take will look a bit more exciting.

Throughout the rest of this chapter, you will continue enhancing this application by wiring up the rest of the Application Bar icons, getting familiar with the Model-View-ViewModel pattern (covered in Chapter 3), and integrating your application within the Windows Phone experience, including handy image uploads to Twitter.

Figure 16–1. Results of PhotoCapture on the Windows Phone emulator

Using a Chooser to Open Photos

In the previous section, you learned how to use the CameraCaptureTask chooser to take photos with your phone. In this section, you will learn how to open previously-taken photos on your phone using the PhotoChooserTask chooser. As you have already seen, launchers and choosers make developer's lives a lot easier by simplifying and abstracting the most common tasks within the Windows Phone Application platform.

In this section, you will enhance the application you have built thus far by adding functionality to the second button of the Application Bar—Opening Photos. Windows Phone has several locations, or "folders" so to speak, where the photos are located. Those "folders" are Camera Roll, Saved Pictures, and Pictures Library. Inside Pictures Library, there are general-purpose photos provided by Microsoft that help you in your programming efforts. Since you already created a user interface for the application in the previous section, in this section you will add code to implement the photo browsing and retrieval functionality.

1. Launch Visual Studio 2010 Express for Windows Phone, and open the PhotoCapture project that you created in the previous section.

2. Open MainPage.xaml.cs, and paste the following class-level variable declaration right above the MainPage() constructor:

```
private PhotoChooserTask photoChooserTask;
```

3. You need to specify that the PhotoChooserTaskCompleted will be the callback function invoked upon completion of the PhotoChooserTask chooser. You do this via the following two lines of code inside the MainPage() constructor:

```
photoChooserTask = new PhotoChooserTask();
photoChooserTask.Completed += new EventHandler<PhotoResult>(PhotoChooserTaskCompleted);
```

4. As the final step of this demo, you will need to add the logic to launch the chooser when the user clicks the second button in the Application Bar. To accomplish this, open the MainPage.xaml file, locate the line of XAML code that starts with <shell:ApplicationBarIconButton Text="Open Photo", and indicate that btnOpenPhoto_Click must be called when that button is clicked.

```
<shell:ApplicationBarIconButton Text="Open Photo"
IconUri="images/appbar.folder.rest.png" Click="btnOpenPhoto_Click"/>
```

5. Now switch back to MainPage.xaml.cs, and paste the btnOpenPhoto_Click function definition that will launch the PhotoChooserTask chooser.

```
private void btnOpenPhoto_Click(object sender, EventArgs e)
{
        photoChooserTask.Show();
}
```

Press F5 to run application. Now, if you click the Open Photo button on the Application Bar, you should be able to browse through photos on the emulator or (better) on the phone, select a photo, and have it presented to you in the application window.

Being able to navigate to a photo on the phone and display it within an application is certainly important, but hardly a useful feature by itself. However, as you will see shortly, you can use the PhotoChooserTask chooser to select photos to upload to a cloud service, such as TwitPic, as well as for loading images inside the application in order to manipulate them (by cropping, adding shapes to them, altering their color composition, and so on) and then resaving them back onto the phone or uploading them to a social media site. Although altering photos within an application is slightly beyond the scope of this chapter, you will learn how to save photos onto the phone in the next section. Saving photos can also be used together with `CameraCaptureTask` from the first demo in this chapter to save photos taken using that chooser.

Saving Photos to the Phone

In the prior sections, you have seen how choosers can be used to make the taking and opening of photos a breeze on a Windows Phone device. Unfortunately, things become a bit more complicated when it comes to saving photos onto the device, since there are no choosers available to aid you with this task. In fact, the Windows Phone platform does not provide any mechanism you can use to get the job done. So how can you do it? Enter the Windows Phone XNA library.

In this book, we have not covered the XNA Framework on Windows Phone for a reason. The XNA Framework is a very powerful mechanism for programming graphics-intensive interfaces and, as such, is used primarily for game development, whereas Silverlight is used for the vast majority of line-of-business applications, which is the focus of this book. At times, however, you have to resort to using a mix of technologies to get things done, and saving photos onto the Windows Phone device is one example of such a situation. The `Microsoft.Xna.Framework.Media` library provides the `SavePicture` method, which saves a given array of bytes to the Saved Pictures location on the phone. The following demo shows how to add save capabilities to the `PhotoCapture` application you have built so far.

Adding a Status Message

The user interface built as part of the first demo in this chapter has an Application Bar button already defined for saving images. Therefore, you only need to make a small enhancement to the user interface to allow the user to see whether the status of the save was successful or not.

Open `MainPage.xaml`, and add a TextBlock right below the image control. Name it `txtStatus`, and clear its `Text` property. With user interface enhancements complete, you are ready to add the code that saves photos to the Media Library.

Writing Code to Save Photos with the XNA Framework

Before you can use a method from the XNA Framework, you must first add a reference to the `Xna.Framework.Media` library. To accomplish this, right-click the name of the project (PhotoCapture) in Solution Explorer, select Add Reference, and then double-click the `Microsoft.Xna.Framework` assembly. Follow these steps to implement photo-saving functionality within your application.

1. Open `MainPage.xaml.cs`, and add the following using statement to the top of that page:

   ```
   using Microsoft.Xna.Framework.Media;
   ```

2. The following method does all the work of saving a photo into the Media Library. Note specifically the `SavePicture` method, which saves the array of bytes passed into the Media Library.

   ```
   private void btnSave_Click(object sender, EventArgs e)
   {
   ```

```
    try
    {
        var library = new MediaLibrary();
        library.SavePicture("PhotoCapture Photo", imageBits);

        txtStatus.Text = "Successfully saved photo.";
    }
    catch (Exception ex)
    {
        txtStatus.Text = "Failed to save photo. Exception: " + ex.Message;
    }
}
```

3. What remains is to tie the btnSave_Click method with the click event of the Save button on the Application Bar. You will do it by editing the XAML of the MainPage.xaml file. Locate the line that starts with: `<shell:ApplicationBarIconButton Text="Save Photo"`, and change it to look like the following:

```
<shell:ApplicationBarIconButton Text="Save Photo"
        IconUri="images/appbar.save.rest.png" Click="btnSave_Click"/>
```

You are now ready to run the application on the Windows Phone emulator. Press F5 to start the application, and then press the Camera button on the Application Bar (first button) to take a picture and have it loaded into your application. Then, press the Save button on the Application Bar; you should get a status message that the image was successfully saved. Now, if you use the middle button of the Application Bar to see available photos, you should see a screen like the one shown in Figure 16–2, with three separate photo "folders," each displayed in a separate tile.

Figure 16–2. The Saved Pictures "folder" is available when at least one photo has been saved there.

Integrating Your Application with Windows Phone

So far in this chapter, you have built a stand-alone application that uses choosers and parts of the XNA Framework to manage photos snapped with a Windows Phone camera. What's unique about the Windows Phone Framework, however, is that it encourages you to have your application make use of built-in phone applications to perform certain tasks. The Photo application, for example, provides hooks to make the functionality of an application like PhotoCapture available to users without having to launch it explicitly. Those hooks are the Extras and Share commands, which are found on the context menus of each photo where the context menu is displayed when you press the photo for a few seconds.

Both Extras and Share features are best explained by observing them at work. With the real Windows Phone device in hand, click the Pictures hub, select the "folder" to view the photos from (Camera Roll, for example), and then select a specific photo from the list. Click the ellipsis (…) at the bottom of the screen. When the context menu appears, you'll see an Extras option displayed at the very bottom. This Extras option is available for you to integrate or to tie into. You will use it in the next demo to launch the

PhotoCapture application so that you can choose a picture, save it to your TwitPic, and share it with your Twitter friends.

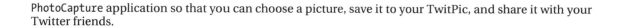 **Note** You will only see the Extras command if there's an application on the phone that implements the integration with Windows Phone Picture Viewer; as such, if you currently don't have any applications deployed to your Windows Phone device that implement the Extras functionality, you will not be able to see this menu option. You will learn how to build such integration in the next section.

The context menu that pops up when you tap the picture also includes a Share command. The Share option is also available when photos are being viewed as a list rather than one at a time. If you click the Share command, you will notice that it offers several ways to share the photo with the world. In the following section, you will learn to build an application that will use TwitPic as a cloud store for the photos on the phone and, as such, it will add TwitPic as one of the options on the Share menu.

■ **Note** Up to this point in the chapter, it has been possible (although a bit quirky) to run code against the Windows Phone emulator. The features discussed in the next two sections are not available on the emulator. To see them in action, you must deploy applications onto a Windows Phone device.

Using the Apps Link to Launch an Application

The Windows Phone platform is all about providing the best possible phone usage experience to consumers. When consumers look at a photo on the phone, they are using an application known as a *Single Photo Viewer (SPV)* that allows other applications to extend the viewer's functionality via the Apps command of the context menu.

In this section, you will further enhance the PhotoCapture application to take advantage of the Apps feature within the Photos application. The PhotoCapture application will be using PhotoChooserTask or CameraCaptureTask to allow the user to select or take a picture once it has been invoked via the Apps feature.

To integrate with SPV, an application needs the following:

1. An entry in the application manifest file (WMAppManifest.xml) declaring that the application implements the Extras functionality within the photo viewer.

2. Code to read and load or manipulate the photo selected in the Extras dialog properly.

You will implement both requirements in the next section.

Adding an Entry in WMAppManifest.xml

Adding an entry to the WMAppManifest.xml file is very straightforward. The only potential difficulty may be that the content, including the ID of the entry, has to be precise. Make sure you either copy and paste this content from the source code available for this book, or type it in very carefully.

1. Open the WMAppManifest.xml file located in the Properties node of your project.

2. Paste the following contents inside that file, which will enable the Windows Phone framework to locate those applications ready to implement the Extras functionality:

```
<Extensions>
    <Extension ExtensionName="Photos_Extra_Viewer" ConsumerID="{5B04B775-356B-4AA0-
    AAF8-6491FFEA5632}" TaskID="_default" />
</Extensions>
```

Make sure you save WMAppManifest.xml. Now you can move on to the next step.

Adding Code to Navigate to a Photo

To retrieve the photo that the user selected through the Extras feature properly, the application must override the OnNavigatedTo event in MainPage.xaml.cs. The steps here show you how to do that:

1. Open MainPage.xaml.cs, and add the following using statement to the top of the page:

```
using System.Windows.Navigation;
```

2. The reference to the Microsoft.Xna.Framework assembly should still be in the project from the prior demos. However, if you start a new project that implements the Extras functionality, make sure to add a reference to that assembly and the following using statement to refer to the Media Library properly. You will also need System.Windows.Media.Imaging to work with the image source.

```
using Microsoft.Xna.Framework.Media;
using System.Windows.Media.Imaging;
```

3. Paste the following OnNavigatedTo method. Note how the basic operation is that of reading a QueryString passed in, which determines if you have a value for the parameter token, and then trying to retrieve the photo from the Media Library by that token ID.

```
protected override void OnNavigatedTo(NavigationEventArgs e)
{
    try
    {
        IDictionary<string, string> queryStrings =
            this.NavigationContext.QueryString;
        if (queryStrings.ContainsKey("token"))
        {
```

```
                MediaLibrary library = new MediaLibrary();
                Picture picture = library.GetPictureFromToken(queryStrings["token"]);

                BitmapImage bitmap = new BitmapImage();
                bitmap.SetSource(picture.GetImage());
                WriteableBitmap picLibraryImage = new WriteableBitmap(bitmap);
                imgPhoto.Source = picLibraryImage;
            }

        }
        catch (Exception ex)
        {
            Dispatcher.BeginInvoke(() => txtStatus.Text = ex.Message);
        }
    }
```

4. Deploy the application to the phone. Then, from the phone's Start screen, select the Pictures hub, pick any picture collection, and select an individual picture of your choice. Click the ellipsis at the bottom of the screen, and select Extras. You should see the PhotoCapture application listed on the next screen that comes up. Clicking the PhotoCapture application should start the application and load the selected photo into the Image control—exactly the expected behavior.

In the next section, you will walk through the steps needed to extend the Share dialog for the photos. The concepts you use to extend the Extras and Share features are very similar; the differences, as you will see shortly, are in the details of the file name and the query string key.

Using Share to Upload PhotoCapture Snapshots to TwitPic

In this demo, you will make more changes to the PhotoCapture application to take advantage of the Share extensibility feature within the Photos application. For simplicity, the PhotoCapture application will load the selected image onto its main screen. In the next section, you will complete the circle and write the code to send the image to the TwitPic cloud service for easy reference from Twitter messages.

As with your implementation of Apps, to extend the Share option, an application needs to implement the following:

1. Add an entry to the WMAppManifest.xaml file indicating that application supports Share functionality.

2. Code to read and/or share the photo selected properly in the Share dialog.

You will implement both requirements in the next section.

Adding an Entry to the WMAppManifest.xaml

Once again, adding the entry to WMAppManifest.xaml is straightforward. The only potential difficulty may be typing it precisely as it appears below, so it's a good idea to copy and paste this snippet from the downloadable source code for this book.

1. Open the WMAppManifest.xml file located in the Properties node of your project. Then add the following entry to that file:

```
<Extensions>
<Extension ExtensionName="Photos_Extra_Share" ConsumerID="{5B04B775-356B-4AA0-AAF8-
6491FFEA5632}" TaskID="_default" />
</Extensions>
```

2. Make sure you save this XML file before moving onto the next step.

Adding Code to Navigate to the Selected Photo

To retrieve the photo that the user selected through the Extras feature properly, the application must override the OnNavigatedTo event in MainPage.xaml.cs. The steps here show you how to do that:

1. If you are continuing with the Extras demo, you already have all the necessary references and using statements in place. However, if you were to start a new project, make sure that you have a reference added to Microsoft.Xna.Framework and the following using statements are in place:

```
using System.Windows.Navigation;
using Microsoft.Xna.Framework.Media;
```

2. Paste the following OnNavigatedTo method (or add to that method if you are continuing with the Extras demo). Note how the basic operation is that of reading a query string passed in, determining whether there is a value for the Field parameter, and then trying to retrieve the photo from the Media Library by that token ID.

```
try
{
    IDictionary<string, string> queryStrings = this.NavigationContext.QueryString;
    if (queryStrings.ContainsKey("FileId"))
    {
        MediaLibrary library = new MediaLibrary();
        Picture picture = library.GetPictureFromToken(queryStrings["FileId"]);

        BitmapImage bitmap = new BitmapImage();
        bitmap.SetSource(picture.GetImage());
        WriteableBitmap picLibraryImage = new WriteableBitmap(bitmap);
        imgPhoto.Source = picLibraryImage;
    }
}
catch (Exception ex)
{
    Dispatcher.BeginInvoke(() => txtStatus.Text = ex.Message);
}
```

3. Deploy the application to the phone.

Now you're ready to test your implementation up to this point. Just as you did for your Extras integration, from the phone's Start screen, select the Pictures hub on your phone, pick any picture collection, and select an individual picture of your choice. Click the ellipsis (...) at the bottom of the screen, and select Share. You should see Upload to PhotoCapture as one of the options that come up. Clicking that option should start the application and load the selected photo into the Image control—the behavior you expect.

Now you're ready to upload the photos to TwitPic, which is the primary hosting service for photos destined for the social media network Twitter. Silverlight (in general) and Silverlight on Windows Phone (in particular) differ from other applications in that they rigorously enforce a non-blocking user interface principle: everything, including communications over the network, must happen asynchronously. The TwitPic cloud service provides a RESTful API that allows programmers to send messages to that service as long as you conform to the expected message format. In the next section, you will write code against that API to upload the photo to TwitPic.

Adding an Upload Button to the UI

On the user interface, you will need to add an additional button that will trigger the upload of the photo to TwitPic. Figure 16–3 illustrates one possible placement for this button. Name the button btnUpload, and set its caption to TwitPic.

Writing Code to Transfer an Image to TwitPic

Because network access on Windows Phone must be performed asynchronously, it takes quite a bit of code to construct the RESTful Web service request properly. Most of the code, however, is repetitive and thus all of the major points are summarized in these step-by-step instructions.

1. Right-click the project name in Solution Explorer, select Add Reference, and then select System.Xml.Linq.

2. Add the following using statements to the top of the page:

```
using System.IO;
using System.Text;
using System.Xml.Linq;
```

Open MainPage.xaml.cs, and paste the UploadPhoto function written here. This will be the only function that will be invoked when the photo upload needs to take place. This function sets the URL and the type of the request, and then it invokes the asynchronous BeginGetRequestStream, which packages the photo and the user credentials.

```
public void UploadPhoto()
{
  HttpWebRequest request =
        (HttpWebRequest)WebRequest.Create("http://twitpic.com/api/upload");
        request.ContentType = "application/x-www-form-urlencoded";
        request.Method = "POST";
        request.BeginGetRequestStream(new AsyncCallback(GetRequestStreamCallback),
            request);
}
```

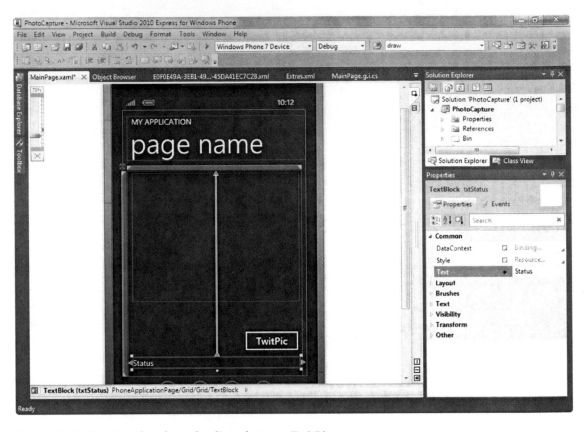

Figure 16–3. User interface for uploading photos to TwitPic

Add the following code to define the asynchronous function GetRequestStreamCallback that does all of the packaging of proper parameters. Note that the exact form of the message was dictated by TwitPic, and this method simply conforms to it:

■ **Note** The TwitPic API is sensitive to even slightly malformed messages, so be sure you copy/paste this method from the source code that comes with this book instead of manually retyping it and risk making a mistake.

```
private void GetRequestStreamCallback(IAsyncResult asynchronousResult)
{
    try
    {

        HttpWebRequest request = (HttpWebRequest)asynchronousResult.AsyncState;
        string encoding = "iso-8859-1";
```

```
            // End the operation
            Stream postStream = request.EndGetRequestStream(asynchronousResult);
            string boundary = Guid.NewGuid().ToString();
            request.ContentType = string.Format("multipart/form-data; boundary={0}",
        boundary);

            string header = string.Format("--{0}", boundary);
            string footer = string.Format("--{0}--", boundary);

            StringBuilder contents = new StringBuilder();
            contents.AppendLine(header);

    string fileHeader = String.Format("Content-Disposition: file; name=\"{0}\";
      filename=\"{1}\"; ", "media", "testpic.jpg");
            string fileData = Encoding.GetEncoding(encoding).GetString(imageBits, 0,
      imageBits.Length);

            contents.AppendLine(fileHeader);
            contents.AppendLine(String.Format("Content-Type: {0};", "image/jpeg"));
            contents.AppendLine();
            contents.AppendLine(fileData);
            contents.AppendLine(header);
            contents.AppendLine(String.Format("Content-Disposition: form-data;
    name=\"{0}\"", "username"));
            contents.AppendLine();
            contents.AppendLine("BeginningWP7");

            contents.AppendLine(header);
            contents.AppendLine(String.Format("Content-Disposition: form-data;
    name=\"{0}\"", "password"));
            contents.AppendLine();
            contents.AppendLine("windowsphone7");

            contents.AppendLine(footer);

            // Convert the string into a byte array.
            byte[] byteArray =
        Encoding.GetEncoding(encoding).GetBytes(contents.ToString());

            // Write to the request stream.
            postStream.Write(byteArray, 0, contents.ToString().Length);
            postStream.Close();

            // Start the asynchronous operation to get the response
            request.BeginGetResponse(new AsyncCallback(GetResponseCallback), request);
        }
        catch (Exception ex)
        {
            Dispatcher.BeginInvoke(() => txtStatus.Text = ex.Message);
        }
    }
```

Add the GetResponseCallback function that will asynchronously receive the results of the upload (Success or Fail) and parse that result out using LINQ to XML:

```
private void GetResponseCallback(IAsyncResult asynchronousResult)
{
    try
    {

        HttpWebRequest request = (HttpWebRequest)asynchronousResult.AsyncState;
        // End the operation
        HttpWebResponse response =
            (HttpWebResponse)request.EndGetResponse(asynchronousResult);
        Stream streamResponse = response.GetResponseStream();
        StreamReader streamRead = new StreamReader(streamResponse);
        String responseString = streamRead.ReadToEnd();

        XDocument doc = XDocument.Parse(responseString);
        XElement rsp = doc.Element("rsp");
        String status = rsp.Attribute(XName.Get("status")) != null ?
         rsp.Attribute(XName.Get("status")).Value:rsp.Attribute(XName.Get("stat")).Value;

        // Close the stream object
        streamResponse.Close();
        streamRead.Close();

        // Release the HttpWebResponse
        response.Close();

    }
    catch (Exception ex)
    {
        Dispatcher.BeginInvoke(() => txtStatus.Text = ex.Message);
    }
}
```

Now you need to call the UploadPhoto method when the user clicks the TwitPic button. Open MainPage.xaml in Design view, and double-click the TwitPic button. Inside the btnUpload_Click method, paste the following line of code:

```
UploadPhoto();
```

You are now ready to run the application. Fortunately, you can test the upload to TwitPic functionality in this demo by using Windows Phone emulator; you don't need to deploy to the actual device. Set the Windows Phone emulator as your deployment target, click F5 and, when the application comes up, click the camera button (the first button on the Application Bar). Take a picture, accept it, and then click the TwitPic button. If no errors were reported in the status TextBlock, you should see your image on TwitPic's website, with the full URL being **http://www.twitpic.com/photos/BeginningWP7**), as shown in Figure 16–4.

■ **Note** Once you successfully upload photos from your phone to TwitPic, the response XML from TwitPic contains a mediaurl node with the URL of your image. You can parse out that URL in a way that is similar to parsing out the status in the previous code. Your application can then make use of that URL by, for example, constructing an HTML page with that URL and showing it within the Web Browser control or doing anything else with it that your imagination can dream up.

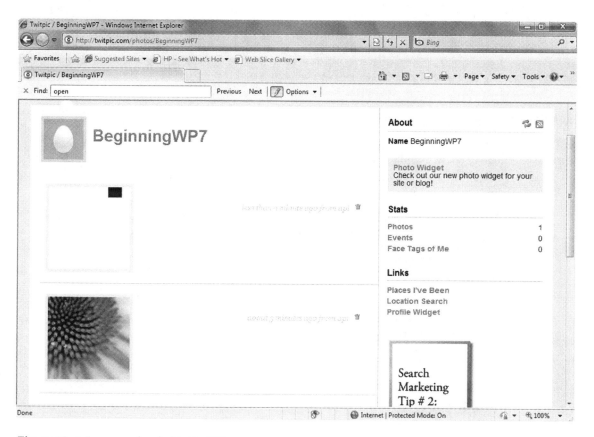

Figure 16–4. Image uploaded to TwitPic

Manipulating Live Photo Feeds

The first release of the Windows Phone OS offered just the basic functionality described above for manipulating photos. Many competing platforms were significantly ahead of this and offered many "augmented reality" features, where the locations of, for example, nearest gyms, could be superimposed on the live photo feed of the surroundings. With the latest Windows Phone release, however, Microsoft has closed the gap and gives Windows Phone developers access to raw data generated by the camera. This is done via a new simple managed PhoneCamera API.

In this section, you will get familiar with accessing raw photo data and manipulating it before presenting it to the user. Although the manipulation described in this chapter simply negates the image (flipping white to black and vice versa), this should give you a good idea of how to implement custom photo manipulations. There are many photo filter implementations (such as Sepia, for example), that have been implemented on the Windows Phone platform. You can download and easily integrate code for these filter implementations in the project you will build in this section.

Creating a New Project and Building the User Interface

As usual, in the first part of the walk-through, you will create a new project and add necessary user interface elements to allow for photo manipulation in the later sections of this chapter.

1. Launch Visual Studio 2010 Express for Windows Phone, and create a new Windows Phone Application project. Name it NegativePhoto.

2. The application will consist of a single MainPage.xaml page, and it will contain two images—one full-screen image of the current live photo feed, and a smaller version of the negated image in the center of the page. You will also add two buttons to turn the negation effect on or off, as shown in Figure 16-5. Below is the XAML for the user interface:

```
<!--LayoutRoot is the root grid where all page content is placed-->
<Grid x:Name="LayoutRoot" Background="Transparent">
    <Grid.RowDefinitions>
        <RowDefinition Height="640" />
        <RowDefinition Height="160*" />
    </Grid.RowDefinitions>

    <!--Camera viewfinder >-->
    <Rectangle Width="480" Height="640" HorizontalAlignment="Left" >
        <Rectangle.Fill>
            <VideoBrush x:Name="viewfinderBrush" />
        </Rectangle.Fill>
    </Rectangle>

    <!--Overlay for the viewfinder region to display grayscale WriteableBitmap
objects-->
    <Image x:Name="MainImage"
            Width="320" Height="240"
            HorizontalAlignment="Left" VerticalAlignment="Bottom"
            Margin="16,0,0,16"
            Stretch="Uniform"/>
```

```
        <!--Button StackPanel underneath the viewfinder>-->
        <StackPanel Grid.Row="1" >
            <Button
                Content="Negative: ON"
                Name="GrayscaleOnButton"
                Click="btnNegativeOn_Click" />
            <Button
                Content="Negative: OFF"
                Name="GrayscaleOffButton"
                Click="btnNegativeOff_Click" />
        </StackPanel>

        <!--Used for debugging >-->
        <TextBlock Height="40" HorizontalAlignment="Left" Margin="8,428,0,0"
Name="txtDebug" VerticalAlignment="Top" Width="626" FontSize="24" FontWeight="ExtraBold"
/>

    </Grid>
```

Writing Code to Activate Live Photo Feed Manipulation

The basic premise of manipulating a live photo feed is simple: as raw photo data is coming into the device, it is made available in a special buffer from which you can read and then manipulate that buffer (flip pixel colors or add objects, for example) before showing the contents of that buffer to the user. The buffer manipulation usually happens on a separate thread, so that there are no interruptions to the live photo feed. In this section, you will write code to read and manipulate the data from that buffer.

1. Before you are able to work with raw data from the photo feeds, you need to add references to the libraries used in those manipulations. Add the following using statements to the top of the page:

```
using Microsoft.Devices;
using System.Threading;
using System.Windows.Media.Imaging;
```

2. We will make use of some module-level variables, including one of the PhotoCamera and Thread types. Declare them by pasting the following code right underneath the class name:

```
PhotoCamera _camera = new PhotoCamera();
private static ManualResetEvent _pauseEvent = new ManualResetEvent(true);
private WriteableBitmap _writeableBitmap;
private Thread _ARGBFramesThread;
private bool _pumpARGBFrames;
```

3. In the OnNavigatedTo event, you will check whether camera support is available on the device, wire up camera events to fire upon initialization, and set the video source to the live feed of the camera. Below is the complete code of the OnNavigated event:

```
protected override void OnNavigatedTo(System.Windows.Navigation.NavigationEventArgs e)
{
    // Check to see if the camera is available on the device.
    if ((PhotoCamera.IsCameraTypeSupported(CameraType.Primary) == true) ||
        (PhotoCamera.IsCameraTypeSupported(CameraType.FrontFacing) == true))
    {
        // Initialize the default camera.
        _camera = new Microsoft.Devices.PhotoCamera();

        //Event is fired when the PhotoCamera object has been initialized
        _camera.Initialized += new
            EventHandler<CameraOperationCompletedEventArgs>(_cam_Initialized);

        //Set the VideoBrush source to the camera
        viewfinderBrush.SetSource(_camera);
    }
    else
    {
        // The camera is not supported on the device.
        this.Dispatcher.BeginInvoke(delegate()
        {
            // Write message.
            txtDebug.Text = "A Camera is not available on this device.";
        });

        // Disable UI.
        GrayscaleOnButton.IsEnabled = false;
        GrayscaleOffButton.IsEnabled = false;
    }
}
```

4. Next you will print the debug message once the camera initialization succeeds, and you will also add code disassociating event handlers when the user navigates away from the page. Here's the code that accomplishes that:

```
private void _cam_Initialized(object sender, CameraOperationCompletedEventArgs e)
{
    if (e.Succeeded)
    {
        this.Dispatcher.BeginInvoke(delegate()
        {
            txtDebug.Text = "Camera initialized successfully";
        });
    }
}

protected override void
    OnNavigatingFrom(System.Windows.Navigation.NavigatingCancelEventArgs e)
{
    if (_camera != null)
    {
```

```
        // Dispose of the camera to minimize power consumption and to expedite
        // shutdown.
        _camera.Dispose();

        // Release memory, ensure garbage collection.
        _camera.Initialized -= _cam_Initialized;
    }
}
```

5. With the basic housekeeping duties out of the way, you are ready to implement the core of the live photo feed manipulation. The function PumpARGBFrames, which is invoked on a separate thread, is pasted below. In the first part of this function, you declare an array of integer ARGBPx to hold pixel-by-pixel data of the photo feed. Next, while the Boolean flag to show the preview is set to True, you call the GetPreviewBufferArgb32 function of the PhotoCamera task to populate the ARGBPx array of integers with live photo data. Then you process (negate, in this particular case) each integer in the array, resulting in the color values for each pixel that are different from the original. Finally, you copy the processed array of pixels into the WriteableBitmap object that is then invalidated, or is forced to be redrawn on the screen, to update the preview image area in the middle of an application page.

```
private void PumpARGBFrames()
{
    // Create capture buffer.
    int[] ARGBPx = new int[(int)_camera.PreviewResolution.Width *
        (int)_camera.PreviewResolution.Height];

    try
    {
        PhotoCamera phCam = (PhotoCamera)_camera;

        while (_pumpARGBFrames)
        {
            _pauseEvent.WaitOne();

            // Copies the current viewfinder frame into a buffer for further
            //manipulation.
            phCam.GetPreviewBufferArgb32(ARGBPx);

            // Conversion to grayscale.
            for (int i = 0; i < ARGBPx.Length; i++)
            {
                ARGBPx[i] = ColorToNegative(ARGBPx[i]);
            }

            _pauseEvent.Reset();
            Deployment.Current.Dispatcher.BeginInvoke(delegate()
            {
                // Copy to WriteableBitmap.
                ARGBPx.CopyTo(_writeableBitmap.Pixels, 0);
```

```
                _writeableBitmap.Invalidate();

                _pauseEvent.Set();
            });
        }

    }
    catch (Exception e)
    {
        this.Dispatcher.BeginInvoke(delegate()
        {
            // Display error message.
            txtDebug.Text = e.Message;
        });
    }
}
```

6.   With the core of the system written above, some maintenance tasks remain.
     We must wire up button handlers for the events to activate and deactivate live
     photo frame processing. Those event handlers are pasted below. In the
     btnNegativeOn_Click event handler, you invoke the processing of the image
     on a separate thread and start that thread. When you click the button to stop
     photo processing, the processing preview is hidden and the flag indicating that
     photo frames need to be processed is reset.

```
private void btnNegativeOn_Click(object sender, RoutedEventArgs e)
{
    MainImage.Visibility = Visibility.Visible;
    _pumpARGBFrames = true;
    _ARGBFramesThread = new System.Threading.Thread(PumpARGBFrames);

    _writeableBitmap = new WriteableBitmap((int)_camera.PreviewResolution.Width,
        (int)_camera.PreviewResolution.Height);
    this.MainImage.Source = _writeableBitmap;

    // Start pump.
    _ARGBFramesThread.Start();
    this.Dispatcher.BeginInvoke(delegate()
    {
        txtDebug.Text = "ARGB to Negative";
    });
}

private void btnNegativeOff_Click(object sender, RoutedEventArgs e)
{
    MainImage.Visibility = Visibility.Collapsed;
    _pumpARGBFrames = false;

    this.Dispatcher.BeginInvoke(delegate()
    {
        txtDebug.Text = "";
```

```
        });
    }
```

7. Finally, the functions converting the color of individual pixels could be
    downloaded and copied either from the source code for this book, or from one
    of many locations on the Internet. This code performs bit shifting
    manipulations to arrive at the desired effect (in our case, simply obtaining the
    negative color to the one passed in, but this function can get pretty complex
    for more advance manipulations).

```
private int ColorToNegative(int color)
{
    int a, r, g, b;
    GetARGB(color, out a, out r, out g, out b);

    r = 255 - r;
    g = 255 - g;
    b = 255 - b;

    int result = GetColorFromArgb(a, r, g, b);

    return result;
}

private void GetARGB(int color, out int a, out int r, out int g, out int b)
{
    a = color >> 24;
    r = (color & 0x00ff0000) >> 16;
    g = (color & 0x0000ff00) >> 8;
    b = (color & 0x000000ff);
}

private int GetColorFromArgb(int a, int r, int g, int b)
{
    int result = ((a & 0xFF) << 24) | ((r & 0xFF) << 16) | ((g & 0xFF) << 8) | (b
                & 0xFF);
    return result;
}
```

You are now ready to compile and run the code. Press F5 to deploy it to Windows Phone emulator. If
you press the "Negative: ON" button, you will see the negative (white square on the black background)
image in the middle of the main simulated photo feed. Alternately, if you have an opportunity to test the
negative photo filter you developed in this section on a real device, you would see something similar to
Figure 16-5.

Figure 16–5. *Live Photo Feed shown without negative filter (top), then with the negative filter applied (bottom)*

Summary

In this chapter, you worked extensively with photos on a Windows Phone device. You used choosers to take pictures and loaded previously-saved pictures. You also learned a bit about the XNA Framework and how it helps you work with the Media Library. You then explored the integration options available between the Windows Phone built-in application for photos and your application. You uploaded photos that you took with your Windows Phone device to TwitPic, a photo-sharing site used extensively by Twitter. Finally, you familiarize yourself and experimented with raw photo feed data, access to which enables whole new categories of applications to be built.

In the next chapter, you will look into push notifications, a powerful mechanism for mimicking multi-tasking and providing timely notifications about important events.

CHAPTER 17

Push Notifications

One day in the somewhat distant future, smartphones and other mobile devices will ship with batteries that last for weeks without the need to recharge them. But until that day arrives, Windows Phone software developers must write applications that use energy sparingly, since a resource-intensive program, such as one that uses the built-in cellular or Wi-Fi radio continuously, can quickly drain a Windows Phone battery. To prevent this from happening, Microsoft has built a number of features into the Windows Phone application platform to ensure that the phone battery lasts as long as possible. One such feature allows applications to appear as if they are constantly running in the background, providing updates about the weather or what your friends are up to. These applications subscribe to a central notification service that keeps track of all connected devices and sends alerts and messages to those devices, such as when to buy or sell stocks or where to take cover from bad weather.

In the Windows Phone world, this service is referred to as *push notifications*, or *Windows Phone Notifications (WPN)*. In a nutshell, push notifications allow the user of an application to receive notification messages even when the application is not running.

In this chapter, you learn how notifications work on the Windows Phone, the WPN types that Microsoft provides, and the steps you need to follow to use them in an application. You build a simple phone application that can receive and process push notifications, and you create a simple service that can create and send them. The service will notify the user when the price of Microsoft stock changes (stock symbol MSFT). Without further ado, let's start experimenting with this powerful Windows Phone technology.

Understanding Push Notifications

The Windows Phone platform provides developers with three types of push notifications: *toast* notifications, *tile* notifications, and *raw* notifications. All three types of notifications follow the same basic principles of operation and processing, yet they differ in the way they display these notifications. Toast and tile notification types are used only when the application is not running, whereas raw notifications are used to receive messages continuously while the application is running in the foreground. Let's discuss each notification type in detail.

Toast Notifications

Toast notifications are displayed as overlays at the top of a phone's screen. Only a message title and a line of text can be controlled by the service or an application sending ("pushing") a toast notification. The icon that appears on the left side of a toast notification is the default icon for the application

405

deployed on the Windows Phone device. You can display toast notifications only when an application is not running; if an application is running when a toast notification is sent, it is not displayed on the phone screen.

Toast notifications are used to display information that is timely and urgent. An example of a toast notification is shown in Figure 17-1, where it appears as the "Time to buy!" text at the top of the phone screen. Here, a notification has been received about Microsoft stock becoming an attractive buy. If the user chooses to tap (or click) the toast notification, an application opens, allowing users to take additional actions in the application. In the latest release of Windows Phone OS, you can also optionally pass in arguments to your application from in a toast notification; it is up to the application to interpret and react to those arguments.

Figure 17-1. Sample toast notification

Tile Notifications

Tile notifications can alter the contents of any application tile that is pinned to the *Quick Launch* area of the phone initial screen (also referred to as the *Start Experience/ Start* screen in Microsoft documentation). Tile notifications are used to communicate information visually by displaying dark clouds with rain, for example, to represent a rapidly approaching storm. Generally, an application tile is a visual representation of an application and its contents or functionality. An application tile typically contains an icon and two strings, and tile notifications can change any of these elements as well as the background of each tile. To change a tile's background image, a tile notification must include a URI that points to the new image, which can be either local or cloud-based. The string at the bottom of an application tile is referred to as the *tile title*. The string in the middle and slightly to the right is referred to as the *tile counter*. With Windows Phone 7.5, you also have the option to change the appearance of the back of the tile, including its background and title areas. Also, since you can have multiple tiles for a single application in Windows Phone 7.5, tile notifications can specify which specific tile to update for an application.

Figure 17-2 shows the same Windows Phone Start screen seen in Figure 17-1, but with an update to the PNClient application tile, which has changed the tile's text to "MSFT +2" and set the count property to 2. By continuously updating the tile with new text and images, an application can keep a user informed without needing to launch the application.

Figure 17-2. A tile notification

Raw Notifications

The third and final type of push notification is the raw notification, which can be used to send messages or updates continuously to a Windows Phone application that is running in the foreground. Contrast this with toast and tile notifications, which are used to send updates to an application when it is not running on the Windows Phone device. Unlike toast and tile notifications, all raw notifications are dropped once an application is no longer running in the foreground on the Windows Phone device. Raw notifications are an energy-friendly alternative to polling web services for data constantly; this type of push notification also eliminates the need to keep connections to web services open for prolonged periods of time.

Each notification type has its niche or specific application development scenario types in which it is most appropriate (shown in Table 17-1). For instance, if an application receives updates only when it's actively used, such as a chat application, a raw notification is the most appropriate mechanism for transmitting these updates. If an application is ideally suited to communicate updates via the use of visual elements on an ongoing basis, such as weather updates, sports events scores, or stock prices, tile notifications are a more appropriate choice. Finally, if text-based messages are the most appropriate form of communication on an around-the-clock basis (such as e-mail receipts, Facebook friend requests, or news alerts), toast notifications would be most suitable.

Having taken a look at three available push notification types, let's look at the architecture of notification services, since knowing the architecture will help you better understand how to develop and troubleshoot push notification messages in your application.

Table 17-1. Characteristics of Windows Phone Push Notification Types

PN Type	Must Application Be Running in Foreground?	Must Application Tile Be Pinned to Start Screen?	Use
Toast	No	No	Urgent and time-sensitive data (for example, storm warning)
Tile	No	Yes	Updates (for example, count of new e-mail messages)
Raw	Yes	No	Continuous data (for example, Twitter client, stock ticker)

Introducing the Push Notifications Architecture

Windows Phone push notifications involve three players: a phone application, a Microsoft service, and a remote web-based service, as illustrated in Figure 17-3. *Microsoft Push Notification Service (MPNS)* is at the heart of push notifications. MPNS "provides a dedicated, resilient, and persistent channel for pushing a notification to a mobile device," according to the MSDN documentation. This service is hosted on Microsoft's Azure cloud operating system, and it is responsible for seamlessly establishing a channel of communication between a Windows Phone device and an application that provides notification data to that device (such as a Hurricane Center web app or stock exchange server). Typically, notifications to Windows Phone devices are provided by a web service (or a "cloud service," as is often seen in Microsoft documentation). These cloud services are generally accessible via standard web protocols, such as REST and SOAP, aside from MPNS for data retrieval and updates.

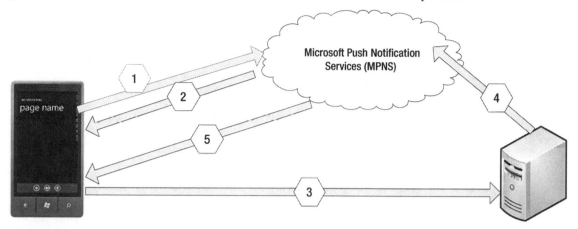

Figure 17-3. Basic push notifications architecture

Naturally, you may be wondering what happens when MPNS becomes unavailable for some technical reason. At the moment, the answer is that, should that happen, push notifications would not reach their destination; in other words, they would be simply dropped (see the Note below). Hence, push notifications should never be counted on as a reliable form of message delivery.

■ **Note** When programming push notifications, there's an additional caveat of which you should be aware: the battery level of the Windows Phone device has direct influence over the receipt of push notifications. Currently, three different values are defined for battery power in the Microsoft.Phone.Notifications namespace: Normal, Low, and CriticalLow. If the power on the device receiving push notifications drops from Normal to Low, tile and toast notifications are discontinued, and only Raw is still sent to the device. When the battery power drops to CriticalLow, all push notifications are discontinued.

The Life Cycle of a Notification

Suppose that you're building a mobile stock-trading application that consists of a central web service, which gathers and analyzes trading data, and an application running on Windows Phone devices, which displays data to users. Suppose you want the application to notify users whenever there is a significant jump in the value of Microsoft stock, which might occur right after the official launch of the next version of Windows Phone. Architecturally speaking, how would you go about doing that?

First, the application needs to take advantage of MPNS, since this will allow it to keep the user updated on market conditions even if the user is not constantly running the stock-trading app on their Windows Phone.

Second, to enable push notifications on Windows Phone, a communication channel for notifications must be created between the application and the web service that is collecting stock trading data. In the world of push notifications, a communication channel is represented by a URI that contains all of the information necessary for notifications to reach their destination. A Windows Phone client must request that this channel be created and obtain the URI associated with that communication channel.

Third, the URI of this communication channel must be communicated to the web service that will deliver, or "push," notifications about the market conditions to Windows Phone clients. Once this third step is complete, all three types of push notifications are available to the stock-trading application.

Figure 17-3 provides a detailed visual representation of how a Windows Phone client application can receive stock-trading alerts from the server using MPNS. The steps are sequentially numbered and each numbered step is described in detail here:

1. The Windows Phone application contacts MPNS and requests that a communication channel in MPNS be created.

2. MPNS responds with the URI of the communication channel, which is unique for a given Windows Phone device and an application on that device.

3. The Windows Phone application communicates the URI of the channel created in step 2 to the service providing stock quotes.

4. The stock-quotes service publishes updates to the URI communicated to it in step 3.

5. MPNS appropriately routes the updates to the proper Windows Phone device and application on that device.

When the service needs to send notifications to its clients, it contacts MPNS by making a POST request to the unique URIs created for each client (step 4). These POST requests have to conform to a predefined XML schema set by Microsoft. The type of notification sent (toast, tile, or raw) is determined by one of the header values in the POST request—namely, the X-NotificationClass header. You will see how to use this header momentarily.

The sections that follow show you how to write code for the steps that have just been described. Using the Windows Phone emulator, you'll implement an application with both toast and tile notifications.

When programming Windows Phone push notifications, perhaps the most common error that occurs is the PayloadFormat error. Generally, it means that the XML or message format received by the MPNS does not conform to the expected format. If this happens, one of the first troubleshooting steps should be to check whether an XML format expected for tile notifications is used for toast notifications or vice versa. (I certainly speak from experience!)

The Push Notification Framework

The namespace that hosts the APIs to do the push notification heavy lifting is Microsoft.Phone.Notification, and the HttpChannelNotification is its workhorse. Before a notification of any type can be sent, a notification channel must be created. The HttpChannelNotification class allows developers to create a new channel or find an existing (previously created) one using its Open and Find methods, respectively. When programming push notifications, it is a good practice to check whether the channel has been previously created using the Find operation. You will see how this is done in several upcoming demos.

Note An important note about the Open method: once the channel is open, it is not immediately active. The push notification channel becomes active when it acquires the push notification URI from the MPNS. This URI is acquired in an asynchronous manner, as you also see in the demos in this chapter.

Other important methods of the HttpChannelNotification class include BindToShellToast and BindToShellTile. These methods are responsible for associating, or binding, a particular HttpChannelNotification channel instance to toast and tile notifications. These methods have corresponding UnbindToShellToast and UnbindToShellTile methods that disassociate toast and tiles subscriptions, respectively, from a given channel. Finally, the Close method of the HttpChannelNotification class closes the channel and removes all the subscriptions associated with that channel.

Push notifications are most appropriate in situations where Windows Phone applications virtually depend on the data supplied by the server on the Web or somewhere else in the cloud. As such, to demonstrate push notifications in action, you must create two separate projects: one project is a Windows Phone application, and the other project can be a web-based application, a web service, or, for the purposes of keeping the current example simple, a Windows Forms application. To create the Windows Forms application that is used as part of the next demo, you use a version of Visual Studio that allows for the creation of Windows Forms applications: in this case Visual C# 2010 Express, since the version of Visual Studio for Windows Phone does not allow you to create Windows Forms apps. You can download a copy of Visual C# 2010 Express from www.microsoft.com/visualstudio/en-us/products/2010-editions/visual-csharp-express. Alternately, you could use any other (purchased) edition of Visual Studio 2010 to create Windows Forms applications.

Note Currently, there's a limit of 1 notification channel per application and a maximum of 30 push notification channels per device. This means that if you deploy an application to the device that already has 30 notification channels consumed by other applications, you get an InvalidOperationException ("Channel quota exceeded").

Implementing Toast Notifications

For the toast notifications demo, you implement a Windows Phone client application that creates a notification channel and a Windows Forms application that sends the notifications to the Windows Phone application via that channel. The Windows Phone client application is a single-screen application with one button and one text box, as shown in Figure 17-4.

411

Figure 17-4. Windows Phone application that creates a push notification URI and receives push notifications

The second part of the demo, the Windows Forms application, consists of the single form shown in Figure 17-5. You will follow this order of demo implementation:

1. Create the Windows Phone Notification client application. This application will establish a notification channel and print the URI of that communication channel in the Output window.

2. Create and execute the Windows Forms application that will send notifications. You will take the URI of the notification channel that you established in step 1, paste it into the Push Notifications URL field of this application, and submit the notification.

3. Verify that you are able to receive toast notifications in the Windows Phone application.

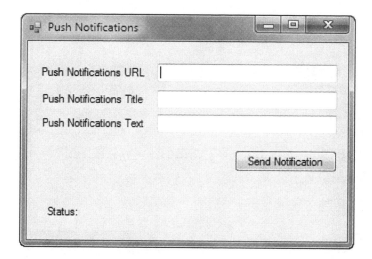

Figure 17-5. Windows Forms application that will send push notifications to a Windows Phone app

---

■ **Note** If your application implements toast notifications, per Microsoft Application Certification Requirements, you must ask the user for permission to receive those notifications and you must allow the user to disable such notifications.

Creating a Client Application

The Windows Phone Notification client application consists of a command button that creates a push notification channel and prints its URI in the Debug window. You also add a text box to the application to display the URI for visual confirmation. Follow these steps to create the application:

1. Launch Visual Studio 2010 Express for Windows Phone, and create a new Windows Phone Application project. Name it PNClient.

2. From the Toolbox, drag and drop a text box on the design surface. Rename the text box to txtURI, adjust its width to fit the full width of the screen, and adjust its height to be about a quarter of the screen's height. Set the text box's TextWrapping property to Wrap, and clear out its Text property.

3. From the Toolbox, drag and drop a button on the design surface. Rename the button to btnCreateChannel, and set the Content property to Create Channel. Your Windows Phone design surface should now look like Figure 17-6.

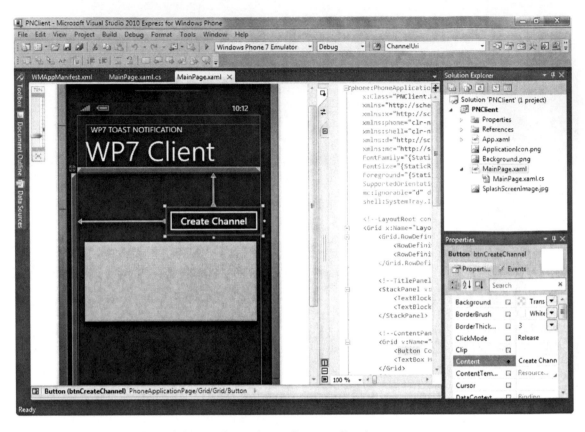

Figure 17-6. Design surface of the Windows Phone client application

4. Add the following using directives to the top of the MainPage.xaml.cs file:

```
using Microsoft.Phone.Notification;
using System.Diagnostics;
```

5. You need to add code that captures the URI of the notification channel in the Output window. At the top of the code page, right under this snippet

```
public partial class MainPage : PhoneApplicationPage
{
```

add the following code:

```
Uri channelUri;
public Uri ChannelUri
{
    get { return channelUri; }
    set
    {
        channelUri = value;
```

```
            OnChannelUriChanged(value);
        }
    }

    private void OnChannelUriChanged(Uri value)
    {
        Dispatcher.BeginInvoke(() =>
        {
            txtURI.Text = "changing uri to " + value.ToString();
        });

        Debug.WriteLine("changing uri to " + value.ToString());
    }
```

The last bit of code prints the URI of the push notification channel opened by the application in the Visual Studio Output window, which allows you to copy and paste that URI into the Windows Forms application that you build in the next section. Certainly, in a real-world application, this copy-and-paste method is not acceptable; a more robust method of exchanging that URI, such as passing it to a web service, would be more appropriate. You will build a more realistic method of exchanging this URI later on in this chapter.

6. Open MainPage.xaml in Design view (right-click MainPage.xaml in Solution Explorer, and select View Designer), double-click the Create Channel button, and make the btnCreateChannel_Click event handler look like the following:

```
private void btnCreateChannel_Click(object sender, RoutedEventArgs e)
{
    SetupChannel();
}
```

7. Paste the following SetupChannel function into the btnCreate_Click event handler. (Remember, you can always download the code available from this book's web site instead of retyping it.) Here, you use the HttpNotificationChannel class to try to find an existing push notification channel or open a new channel with a given channel name:

```
private void SetupChannel()
{
    HttpNotificationChannel httpChannel = null;
    string channelName = "DemoChannel";

    try
    {
        //if channel exists, retrieve existing channel
            httpChannel = HttpNotificationChannel.Find(channelName);
        if (httpChannel != null)
        {
            //If we cannot get Channel URI, then close the channel and reopen it
            if (httpChannel.ChannelUri == null)
            {
                httpChannel.UnbindToShellToast();
                httpChannel.Close();
```

```
                        SetupChannel();
                        return;
                    }
                    else
                    {
                        ChannelUri = httpChannel.ChannelUri;
                    }
                    BindToShell(httpChannel);
                }
                else
                {
                httpChannel = new HttpNotificationChannel(channelName);
                httpChannel.ChannelUriUpdated += new
EventHandler<NotificationChannelUriEventArgs>(httpChannel_ChannelUriUpdated);
                httpChannel.ShellToastNotificationReceived+=new
EventHandler<NotificationEventArgs>(httpChannel_ShellToastNotificationReceived);
                httpChannel.ErrorOccurred += new
EventHandler<NotificationChannelErrorEventArgs>(httpChannel_ExceptionOccurred);

                httpChannel.Open();
                BindToShell(httpChannel);
            }
        }
    catch (Exception ex)
    {
        Debug.WriteLine("An exception occurred setting up channel: " + ex.ToString());
    }
}
```

The code in the SetupChannel() function warrants an explanation, since there is quite a bit going on and it is the nucleus of creating a channel for a Windows Phone Notification client application. In the first few lines, you define a new object of type HttpNotificationChannel and give it a name. Next, you try to find the channel with a given name for the application and then bind it to receive toast notifications (via the BindToShell function shown here). If the channel is found, you use an existing channel to obtain the push notification URI, and you do not need to wire various httpChannel event handlers. If the channel is not found, you create a new one and wire up appropriate httpChannel events. Notice the ShellToastNotificationReceived event—it occurs if your application is running in the foreground when it receives a toast notification. Normally, push notifications are designed to alert the user that something is happening when the application is not running and when an application needs to receive a notification. However, occasionally your application may be running when a toast notification is received. To handle cases like this, the ShellToastNotificationReceived event handler is introduced. You code this event handler in the next step:

8. To handle toast notifications when the application is running in the foreground, add the following code for the ShellToastNotificationReceived event handler. This code reads the notification messages received and prints them in the text box on the screen:

```
void httpChannel_ShellToastNotificationReceived(object sender,
    NotificationEventArgs e)
{
    Dispatcher.BeginInvoke(() =>
    {
        txtURI.Text = "Toast Notification Message Received: ";
        if (e.Collection != null)
        {
        Dictionary<string, string> collection =
            (Dictionary<string,string>)e.Collection;
        System.Text.StringBuilder messageBuilder = new System.Text.StringBuilder();
            foreach (string elementName in collection.Keys)
            {
                txtURI.Text+= string.Format("Key: {0}, Value: {1}\r\n", elementName,
                    collection[elementName]);
            }
        }
    });
}
```

9. To bind a toast notification subscription to a given HttpNotificationChannel
    instance, you must call the BindToShellToast method of the
    HttpNotificationChannel class. Underneath the SetupChannel function, paste
    the following code to accomplish this:

```
private static void BindToShell(HttpNotificationChannel httpChannel)
{
    //This is a toast notification
    try
    {
        //toast notification binding
        if(!httpChannel.IsShellToastBound)
            httpChannel.BindToShellToast();
    }
    catch (Exception)
    {
        Debug.WriteLine("An exception occurred binding to shell " + ex.ToString());
    }
}
```

10. In the SetupChannel function, you designated that
    httpChannel_ExceptionOccurred should fire in case of an error. Add this
    function to your code as defined here:

```
void httpChannel_ExceptionOccurred(object sender,
    NotificationChannelErrorEventArgs            e)
{
    //Display Message on error
    Debug.WriteLine ( e.Message);
}
```

11. You also need to add code that fires if the ChannelUri is updated:

```
void httpChannel_ChannelUriUpdated(object sender, NotificationChannelUriEventArgs e)
```

```
{
    //You got the new Uri (or maybe it's updated)
    ChannelUri = e.ChannelUri;
}
```

At this point, you have finished building the Windows Phone client application, and you are ready to implement the Windows Forms application for sending notification messages to the mobile device.

Creating an Application to Send Notifications

In the previous section, you wrote a Windows Phone client application that creates a notification channel to the MPNS to indicate that it wishes to receive push notification messages. By creating a channel, the application has also created an MPNS endpoint to which the service application wishing to communicate with mobile devices can send POST requests. The endpoint exists on an MPNS server operated by Microsoft, and it forwards any requests it receives to the appropriate mobile device and application that the endpoint addresses.

You can create POST requests from virtually any application environment, including web sites, web services, and desktop applications, making this type of notification architecture very flexible and easy to use. In the current demo, for simplicity's sake, you create a Windows Forms application that packages POST requests to the URI generated in the previous section. This application sends requests to the MPNS, which, in turn, properly routes these requests to the mobile devices and applications.

To ensure proper message routing and successful delivery, there are two key pieces of information that any application sending push notifications to a Windows Phone device must supply to MPNS:

- *The URI of the notification channel that the service must use to communicate with a Windows Phone device:* It is up to the Windows Phone client application to request that URI and pass it to the service that will use it.

- *A proper XML message to POST to the URI:* While the format of the XML message is simple, it has to be followed precisely for the notifications to succeed.

The latest MPNS XML template for toast notifications looks like the following, where <Notification Title> and <Notification Text> are the text of the notification title and the text of the toast notification message to be sent to a Windows Phone device. Note the <wp:Param> XML node: this is new to Windows Phone with the version 7.5 release, and it an *optional* element that includes parameters to pass to your application. The use of this optional XML node in the toast notifications is explored further in this section:

```
<?xml version="1.0" encoding="utf-8"?>
<wp:Notification xmlns:wp="WPNotification">
 <wp:Toast>
  <wp:Text1>Notification Title</wp:Text1>
  <wp:Text2>Notification Text</wp:Text2>
  <wp:Param>Parameter List</wp:Param>
 </wp:Toast>
</wp:Notification>
```

Now that you know the XML template format of the expected POST request and, using cut and paste, can quickly obtain the URI of the notification channel, you're ready to create an application to dispatch notifications to the Windows Phone client app. Follow these steps:

1. Launch Visual C# 2010 Express (or another edition of Visual Studio that allows you to create Windows Forms projects), and create a new Windows Forms project. Name it PNServer.

2. Form1.cs is added by default. Double-click it to bring up the design view. From the Toolbox, drag three labels and three text boxes and make Form1.cs look like Figure 17-5. Name the text boxes txtURL, txtTitle, and txtText.

3. Add a Button control onto Form1. Change its text property to Send Notification, and change its name to btnSendNotification.

4. Add the label control to the bottom of the form, and change its name to lblStatus.

5. Right-click Form1.cs in Solution Explorer, and choose View Code. (Alternatively, you could also press F7.) Add the following using statements to the top:

```
using System.Net;
using System.IO;
```

6. After the constructor, add the following string declarations:

```
String ToastPushXML = String.Empty;
String TilePushXML = String.Empty;
```

7. To initialize the definition of the XML to be POSTed to MPNS, add the following method to PushNotifications class:

```
private void InitParams()
{
    StringBuilder builder = new StringBuilder();
    builder.Append("<?xml version=\"1.0\" encoding=\"utf-8\"?>");
    builder.Append("<wp:Notification xmlns:wp=\"WPNotification\">");
    builder.Append("    <wp:Tile>");
    builder.Append("        <wp:Count>{0}</wp:Count>");
    builder.Append("        <wp:Title>{1}</wp:Title>");
    builder.Append("    </wp:Tile>");
    builder.Append("</wp:Notification>");

    TilePushXML = builder.ToString();

    builder.Clear();
    builder.Append("<?xml version=\"1.0\" encoding=\"utf-8\"?>");
    builder.Append("<wp:Notification xmlns:wp=\"WPNotification\">");
    builder.Append("    <wp:Toast>");
    builder.Append("        <wp:Text1>{0}</wp:Text1>");
    builder.Append("        <wp:Text2>{1}</wp:Text2>");
    builder.Append("    </wp:Toast>");
    builder.Append("</wp:Notification>");

    ToastPushXML = builder.ToString();
}
```

8. Modify the PushNotifications constructor to call the `InitParams` method created in the previous step—the constructor should look like this:

```
public PushNotifications()
{
    InitializeComponent();
    InitParams();
}
```

9. Switch back to the design view on `Form1.cs` by right-clicking `Form1.cs` in Solution Explorer and choosing View Designer. Double-click the Send Notification button to bring up the `btnSendNotification_Click` event handler.

   You use the `btnSendNotification_Click` event handler, with the help of the .NET `HttpWebRequest` class, to create a POST request to the push notification URI that the Windows Phone client has obtained. The beauty of communication with MPNS is that, once this POST request is composed and sent off, MPNS takes care of the delivery of the notification from there. The critical piece of information is the URI to which to send the POST request, since that URI is what uniquely identifies both a Windows Phone device and an application where to send push notifications.

10. Make the `btnSendNotification_Click` event handler look like this:

```
private void btnSendNotification_Click(object sender, EventArgs e)
{
    if (txtURL.Text == string.Empty)
    {
        MessageBox.Show("Please enter a url");
        return;
    }

    if (txtTitle.Text == string.Empty || txtText.Text == string.Empty)
    {
        MessageBox.Show("Please enter text and title to send");
        return;
    }

    string url = txtURL.Text;

    HttpWebRequest sendNotificationRequest = (HttpWebRequest)WebRequest.Create(url);

    sendNotificationRequest.Method = "POST";
    sendNotificationRequest.Headers = new WebHeaderCollection();
    sendNotificationRequest.ContentType = "text/xml";

    sendNotificationRequest.Headers.Add("X-WindowsPhone-Target", "toast");
    sendNotificationRequest.Headers.Add("X-NotificationClass", "2");

    string str = string.Format(ToastPushXML, txtTitle.Text, txtText.Text);
    byte[] strBytes = new UTF8Encoding().GetBytes(str);
    sendNotificationRequest.ContentLength = strBytes.Length;
    using (Stream requestStream = sendNotificationRequest.GetRequestStream())
```

```
    {
        requestStream.Write(strBytes, 0, strBytes.Length);
    }

    HttpWebResponse response =
        (HttpWebResponse)sendNotificationRequest.GetResponse();
    string notificationStatus = response.Headers["X-NotificationStatus"];
    string deviceConnectionStatus = response.Headers["X-DeviceConnectionStatus"];
    lblStatus.Text = "Status: " + notificationStatus + " : " +
        deviceConnectionStatus;
}
```

The POST request includes two headers:

- The X-WindowsPhone-Target header defines the notification type. The possible values for this header are toast, token, and not defined (empty). The value toast defines the notification of toast type, while token defines a tile notification (as if it wasn't confusing enough already). If this header is not defined, then it is a raw notification.

- The X-NotificationClass header defines how soon the MPNS should deliver the notification. The value of 2 specifies that the toast notification should be delivered immediately. Table 17-2 summarizes potential values of this property for different notification types. From this table, had you specified the value of 12, for example, the MPNS would have been instructed to wait 450 seconds, or seven and a half minutes before notification delivery.

Table 17-2. Potential Values for the X-NotificationClass Property

Delivery	Tile	Toast	Raw
As soon as possible	1	2	3–10
Within 450 seconds	11	12	13–20
Within 900 seconds	21	22	23–31

Now it's time to test the application and its service.

Verifying Delivery of Push Notifications

With the Windows Phone Notification client application ready to receive notification messages and the Windows Forms application ready to send them, you are ready to verify the proper delivery of those notifications. Follow these steps to test push notification delivery:

1. First, you need to obtain the URI of the notification channel. Open the PNClient project created in the "Creating a Client Application" section. Make sure you have a connection to the Internet, and press F5 to run the project.

2. Click the Create Channel button. After a short while, you should see messages (the URI of the notification channel) printed in the text box on the screen—that's a confirmation that the notification URI is available to copy from the Output window.

3. In Visual Studio 2010 Express for Windows Phone, click the Debug Windows Output menu option to bring up the Output window. The URI should be printed together with the "changing uri to …" message, as shown in Figure 17-7. Highlight the URI, and press Ctrl+C to copy it into the buffer. Make sure to leave the application running in the Windows Phone emulator, since you will be receiving push notifications on this emulator screen.

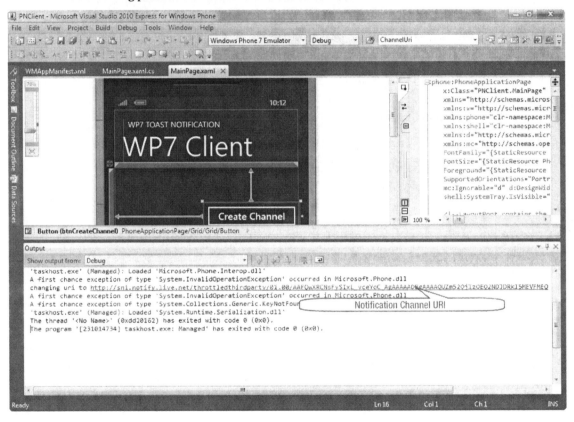

Figure 17-7. Notification channel URI printed in the Output window

4. Switch to the PNServer Windows Forms project, and press F5 to run it. In the Push Notifications URL text box, paste the URI obtained in step 3 by pressing Ctrl+V. In the Push Notifications Title and Push Notifications Text text boxes, you can enter any text—for example, **Time to buy!** and **MSFT up $2 after new WP release**. Press the Send Notification button.

Remember that push notifications appear on the phone only when the Windows Phone application associated with these notifications is not running in the foreground on the phone. Since the PNClient application is running in the foreground no notifications will appear on the phone screen when you press the Send Notification button. To enable them, do the following:

1. Press the Windows button on the emulator (the middle button on the emulator with the Windows logo on it) to switch to the Start screen of the phone, which shuts down PNClient application. In the PNServer app, press the Send Notification button again.

2. You should see a toast notification like the one shown in the very beginning of this chapter in Figure 17-1.

As you can see, creating and receiving push notifications is a somewhat involved process, with a separate Windows Phone application establishing a notification channel and receiving notifications, and a separate application sending those notifications to that Windows Phone app. Once this chapter familiarizes you with how to work with other types of notifications—namely, tile and raw—you will see how to build a service that programmatically acquires and keeps track of the connected clients. From an application development point of view, the good news is that the process of creating other notification types—tile and raw notifications—is very similar to the process of creating toast notifications described previously.

Let's enhance your notifications slightly by supplying optional parameters to the toast notifications. These parameters are passed into the application running on the Windows Phone device when the user clicks the toast notification and opens the app.

Note With Windows Phone 7.5, you now have an option to pass parameters to an application in that toast notification. The following section talks about the changes required on the server and client sides to accomplish this.

Modifying the Windows Forms Notification Server to Pass Parameters

The changes on the server side to accomplish passing parameters to the Windows Phone application are minimal: you add an XML node <wp:Param> and then, in that node, you supply parameters as you would in a query string for the web site. For example, to indicate to a Windows Phone application that a stock chart for Microsoft Corporation should be displayed upon launch, the XML string should look similar to this:

```
<wp:Param>?companyName=MSFT</wp:Param>
```

Notice the use of the ? at the beginning; this indicates that the main page of a Windows Phone application should be launched and parameters passed in to that page. Optionally, you can launch another page in the application (for example, called StockChart.xaml) and pass parameters to that. In this case, the <wp:Param> would look like this:

```
<wp:Param>/StockChart.xaml?companyName=MSFT</wp:Param>
```

Since you have only one page in the Windows Phone client application at the moment, go ahead and modify the XML string sent from the Windows Forms application with the version of the parameters for the application's main page. Namely, make the strToastPushXML string have the following definition:

```
string ToastPushXML = "<?xml version=\"1.0\" encoding=\"utf-8\"?>" +
                      "<wp:Notification xmlns:wp=\"WPNotification\">" +
                      "<wp:Toast>" +
                        "<wp:Text1>{0}</wp:Text1>" +
                                "<wp:Text2>{1}</wp:Text2>" +
                                "<wp:Param>?company=MSFT</wp:Param>" +
                      "</wp:Toast>" +
                      "</wp:Notification>";
```

Next, you modify the client application to process parameters passed in to it.

Modifying the Windows Phone Client to Receive Parameters from Toast Notifications

To process parameters in a Windows Phone application, you need to override the OnNavigated event in the application. The following code shows you how to do that. Paste this definition of the OnNavigated method in the MainPage.xaml.cs file:

```
protected override void OnNavigatedTo(System.Windows.Navigation.NavigationEventArgs e)
{
        base.OnNavigatedTo(e);
        string strCompany = string.Empty;
        string strPriceChange = string.Empty;

        if (NavigationContext.QueryString.TryGetValue("company", out strCompany))
        {
            txtURI.Text += "\n\nCompany name passed in: " + strCompany;
        }
}
```

Notice the use of the NavigationContext.QueryString.TryGetValue method. It extracts the parameter only if it was passed in.

To test the passing of parameters to your application, follow the steps from the section "Verifying Delivery of Push Notifications," except now go ahead and click the toast notifications when it comes in. Once the application launches, you should see the "Company name passed in: MSFT" string in the main text box of your application.

In the next section, you look at how to create *tile* notifications. However, instead of creating everything from scratch, you concentrate only on the changes needed to the toast notifications solution that you have just implemented.

Implementing Tile Notifications

Tile notifications can update the images and text of application tiles, as you saw in Figure 17-2. Tile notifications are ideal for applications that convey small amounts of information, especially when that information changes frequently. For example, weather reports and compass headings are both good candidates for this category.

> ■ **Note** There is currently a limitation of 500 push notifications per subscription channel per day on unauthenticated web services. Later in this chapter, you learn about overcoming this limitation by setting up authenticated web services for push notifications.

You implement the tile notifications application in the same three steps you followed to implement toast notifications in the previous section:

1. Create a Windows Phone Notification client application. This application establishes a notification channel.

2. Create and execute the Windows Forms client. You take the URI of the notification channel that you established in step 1, paste it into the Push Notifications URL text box, and submit the push notification to the application.

3. Verify that you are able to receive tile notifications in the Windows Phone application.

Creating a Client Application

Let's take the PNClient application that you created and enhance it to accept tile notifications in addition to toast notifications. You will not re-create the application; rather, this section concentrates on the changes needed to enable tile notifications:

1. Launch Visual Studio 2010 Express for Windows Phone, and open the PNClient project.

2. Locate the BindToShell function in the MainPage.xaml.cs file. Change that function to look like the one here. (Essentially, you are adding a line to bind this application to tile notifications.)

```
private static void BindToShell(HttpNotificationChannel httpChannel)
{
    try
    {
        //toast notification binding
        if(!httpChannel.IsShellToastBound)
            httpChannel.BindToShellToast();

            //tile notification binding
            if (!httpChannel.IsShellTileBound)
                httpChannel.BindToShellTile();
    }
    catch (Exception)
    {
        Debug.WriteLine("An exception occurred binding to shell " + ex.ToString());
    }
}
```

These are all the changes you need to make to the PNClient application to enable tile notifications.

Creating an Application to Send Notifications

You need to make a few changes to the code that sends push notifications to enable tile-notification processing. First, you need to use a different XML schema for tile notifications, as shown here:

```
<?xml version=\"1.0\" encoding="utf-8"?>
<wp:Notification xmlns:wp="WPNotification">
 <wp:Tile>
  <wp:BackgroundImage><URI to Image></wp:BackgroundImage>
  <wp:Count><Count Message></wp:Count>
  <wp:Title><Title Message></wp:Title>
  <wp:BackTitle><Back Tile Title></wp:BackTitle>
  <wp:BackContent><Additional content to display on the back tile></wp:BackContent>
  <wp:BackBackgroundImage><URI to Image></wp:BackBackgroundImage>
 </wp:Tile>
</wp:Notification>
```

The <URI to Image> element specifies the location, either local or remote, of the background image used to update the application tile. <Count Message> is the counter text (the one almost at the center of the tile) to set on the tile, and <Title Message> is the message text to set at the bottom of the application tile. <Back Tile Title> is the new element in Windows Phone 7.5 that allows the push notification to specify the title of the back of the tile. <Additional content to display on the back tile> is additional text that appears on the back of the tile, and you can also specify the background of the back of the tile to use in the <wp:BackBackgroundImage> element. All of the elements updating the back of the tile are new to Windows Phone with release 7.5. All of the new elements are optional—you do not have to supply values for the back tile of an application. You are also not required to include the background image URI for the front of the tile.

■ **Note** To set the background image to an image located on the Internet in the current implementation of push notifications for Windows Phone, you must specify the location of that image when creating a WPN client application. While this is certainly not very flexible—that is, you would have to know beforehand all of the images you would be using to update tiles—Microsoft generally does not encourage the use of remote images for tile updates, limiting the maximum allowed size of those images to 80KB and emphasizing in documentation that the use of remote resources leads to excessive battery drain. In addition, remote images must be downloaded in 30 seconds or less.

Follow these steps to make changes to the project to enable tile notifications:

1. Open the PNServer project, and open the code for the Form1.cs file (right-click Form1.cs in Solution Explorer, and select View Code).

2. Now you define the XML schema information in the code. Paste the following string declaration at the top of the file, right under the `string ToastPushXML` declaration:

```
string TilePushXML = "<?xml version=\"1.0\" encoding=\"utf-8\"?>" +
    "<wp:Notification xmlns:wp=\"WPNotification\">" +
        "<wp:Tile>" +
        "<wp:Count>{0}</wp:Count>" +
        "<wp:Title>{1}</wp:Title>" +
        "</wp:Tile>" +
        "</wp:Notification>";
```

3. In the `btnSendNotification_Click` event handler, change the following two lines of code

```
sendNotificationRequest.Headers.Add("X-WindowsPhone-Target", "toast");
sendNotificationRequest.Headers.Add("X-NotificationClass", "2");
```

to

```
sendNotificationRequest.Headers.Add("X-WindowsPhone-Target", "token");
sendNotificationRequest.Headers.Add("X-NotificationClass", "1"); //- tiles
```

4. Finally, you need to change the string that gets sent to the Windows Phone application. To accomplish this, change the following line of code in the `btnSendNotification_Click` event handler from

```
string str = string.Format(ToastPushXML, txtTitle.Text, txtText.Text);
```

to

```
string str = string.Format(TilePushXML, txtTitle.Text, txtText.Text);
```

These are all the changes you need to make to enable tile notifications on the Windows Phone device. You are now ready to test tile notifications on the Windows Phone emulator.

Verifying Delivery of Push Notifications

Having made changes to both the client and the server portions of the code to enable tile notifications, it's time to take them for a spin.

Just as with toast notifications, you need to obtain the URI of the notification channel:

1. Open `PNClient` project, make sure you have a connection to the Internet, and press F5 to run the project.

2. Click the Create Channel button and, after seeing the URI printed on the screen, copy it to the clipboard from the Output window.

   Remember that tile notifications appear on the phone only when a Windows Phone application associated with these notifications is not running in the foreground on the phone and (this is important!) only when the application tile is available on the Windows Phone Start screen.

3. To pin the application tile onto the Start screen, with the PNClient application running, click the phone's Windows button and then click the arrow ( ) to open the Windows Phone Options screen, as shown in Figure 17-8.

Figure 17-8. To receive tile notifications, the application tile must be pinned to the Start screen.

4. Click and hold down the left mouse button (also referred to as a *long click*) to bring up the pop-up menu shown in Figure 17-8.

5. Click the Pin to Start option. Now you should see the PNClient application tile on the Start screen, together with the Internet Explorer tile.

6. Switch to the PNServer Windows Forms project, and press F5 to run it.

7. In the Push Notifications URL text box, paste the URI obtained in step 1. In the Push Notifications Title and Push Notifications Text text boxes, enter text for the counter and tile message, respectively. For example, to get tile notification to appear as shown in Figure 17-2, enter **2** for Push Notification Title and **MSFT +2** in the Push Notification Text field.

428

Now you're ready to send and receive tile notifications. To do so, click the Push Notification button in the PNServer application. You should now see the application tile updated from default to the one containing both the counter text (2) and the message text (MSFT +2).

As you can see, processing tile notifications is only slightly different from processing toast applications. Processing raw notifications is also very similar to the previous demos; however, since raw notifications are received when an application is running in the foreground only, you need to wire up an event in the Windows Phone application to process messages received, as you see in the next section.

Implementing Raw Notifications

Raw notifications represent the third and final type of push notification available on the Windows Phone platform. Unlike tile and toast notifications, however, raw notifications are available to a Windows Phone application only if that application is running in the foreground. If the application is not running in the foreground, even if the application's icon is pinned to the phone's Start screen, raw notifications are simply dropped.

You implement raw notifications following the same three general steps as implementing toast and tile notifications:

1. Create a Windows Phone Notification client application. This application establishes a notification channel.

2. Create and execute a Windows Forms client. You take the URI of the notification channel that you established in step 1, paste it into the Push Notifications URL text box, and submit a push notification to the application.

3. Verify that you are able to receive raw notifications in your Windows Phone application.

Creating a Client Application

You create the RawNotificationPNClient application to accept raw notifications. This application is similar to the PNClient application you created in previous sections of this chapter, yet it has subtle differences from that codebase to warrant a separate project. Follow these steps:

1. Launch Visual Studio 2010 Express for Windows Phone, and create a new Windows Phone Application project. Name it RawNotificationPNClient.

2. From the Toolbox, drag and drop a text box on the design surface. Rename the text box to txtURI, adjust its width to fit the full width of the screen, and adjust its height to be about a quarter of screen's height. Set the text box's TextWrapping property to Wrap, and clear out its Text property.

3. From the Toolbox, drag and drop a button on the design surface. Rename the button to btnCreateChannel, and set the Content property to Create Channel. Once again, your Windows Phone design surface should look like Figure 17-6.

4. The Microsoft.Phone.Notification namespace contains the functionality necessary to establish a push notification channel and receive push notifications; therefore you need to add the following using directive at the top of the MainPage.xaml.cs file:

```
using Microsoft.Phone.Notification;
using System.Diagnostics;
```

5. You now program the button click event handler to create the push
    notification URL. In the Windows Phone design surface, double-click the
    Create Channel button and make that button's click event handler look like the
    following:

```
private void btnCreateChannel_Click(object sender, RoutedEventArgs e)
{
    SetupChannel();
}
```

The SetupChannel function that follows is responsible for creating a channel in
MPNS to receive updates from the server and to fire when the error occurs
during communication and when the raw notification is received. Remember
that raw notifications are available to the application only when it's running;
therefore, an event handler must be defined in code that processes raw
notifications as they come in. The code that binds the raw notification
received event to the httpChannel_HttpNotificationReceived event handler
function lives in the SetupChannel function:

```
httpChannel.HttpNotificationReceived += new
    EventHandler<HttpNotificationEventArgs>(httpChannel_HttpNotificationReceived);
```

6. Here's the complete implementation of the SetupChannel function. Add this
    code to your project:

```
private void SetupChannel()
{
    HttpNotificationChannel httpChannel = null;
    String channelName = "DemoChannel";

    try
    {
        //if channel exists, retrieve existing channel
        httpChannel = HttpNotificationChannel.Find(channelName);
        if (httpChannel != null)
        {
            //If you can't get it, then close and reopen it.
            if (httpChannel.ChannelUri == null)
            {
                httpChannel.UnbindToShellToast();
                httpChannel.Close();
                SetupChannel();
                return;
            }
            else
            {
                ChannelUri = httpChannel.ChannelUri;

                //wiring up the raw notifications event handler
                httpChannel.HttpNotificationReceived += new
EventHandler<HttpNotificationEventArgs>(httpChannel_HttpNotificationReceived);
```

```
                    }
                }
                else
                {
                    httpChannel = new HttpNotificationChannel(channelName);
                    httpChannel.ChannelUriUpdated += new
EventHandler<NotificationChannelUriEventArgs>(httpChannel_ChannelUriUpdated);
                    httpChannel.ErrorOccurred += new
EventHandler<NotificationChannelErrorEventArgs>(httpChannel_ExceptionOccurred);

                    //wiring up the raw notifications event handler
                    httpChannel.HttpNotificationReceived += new
EventHandler<HttpNotificationEventArgs>(httpChannel_HttpNotificationReceived);

                    httpChannel.Open();
                }
            }
            catch (Exception ex)
            {
Debug.WriteLine("An exception setting up channel " + ex.ToString());
            }
        }
```

What you do with received raw notifications is totally up to you: raw notifications can be simple status messages to be shown in the Windows Phone client application, or they can be directives to the application to perform a given task. In this application, you simply print a message into the text box with the text of raw notifications received.

7. To print the raw notification, add the following code:

```
void httpChannel_HttpNotificationReceived(object sender, HttpNotificationEventArgs e)
{
    if (e.Notification.Body != null && e.Notification.Headers != null)
    {
        System.IO.StreamReader reader = new
          System.IO.StreamReader(e.Notification.Body);
        Dispatcher.BeginInvoke(() =>
        {
                        txtURI.Text = "Raw Notification Message Received: " +
                                reader.ReadToEnd();
        });
    }
}
```

You are very close to completing the client application. What remains to be done is to write an error-handling function that fires when any errors occur during communication. You also write a simple event handler that fires when the push notification channel URI gets updated.

8. Add the following code to your application:

```
void httpChannel_ExceptionOccurred(object sender, NotificationChannelErrorEventArgs e)
{
```

```
        //Display Message on error
        Debug.WriteLine ( e.Message);
    }

    void httpChannel_ChannelUriUpdated(object sender, NotificationChannelUriEventArgs e)
    {
        //You get the new Uri (or maybe it's updated)
        ChannelUri = e.ChannelUri;
    }
```

9. Add the following helper code to the top of the `MainPage` class. This code prints the push notification channel URI into the Debug window; you need that URI to test the application shortly:

```
Uri channelUri;

public Uri ChannelUri
{
    get { return channelUri; }
    set
    {
        channelUri = value;
        OnChannelUriChanged(value);
    }
}

private void OnChannelUriChanged(Uri value)
{
    Dispatcher.BeginInvoke(() =>
    {
        txtURI.Text = "changing uri to " + value.ToString();
    });

    Debug.WriteLine("changing uri to " + value.ToString());
}
```

With the client application complete, press F5 to make sure the application compiles and runs. In the next section, you build a server piece to send raw notifications to this client application.

Creating an Application to Send Notifications

Sending raw notifications from the server is simpler than sending tiles or toasts: there are no XML templates for message formatting for raw notifications. You reuse the `PNServer` project created in the prior sections, and you edit the button click event handler for processing raw notifications. Follow these steps to accomplish that:

1. Open the `PNServer` project, and open the code for the `Form1.cs` file (right-click `Form1.cs` in Solution Explorer, and select View Code).

2. Replace the `btnSendNotification_Click` event handler with the following code. Note how the `X-NotificationClass` header value is 3 and how the X-

WindowsPhone-Target header value is left blank to indicate that this is a raw
notification:

```
private void btnSendNotification_Click(object sender, EventArgs e)
{
    if (txtURL.Text == string.Empty)
    {
        MessageBox.Show("Please enter a url");
        return;
    }

    if (txtTitle.Text == string.Empty || txtText.Text == string.Empty)
    {
        MessageBox.Show("Please enter text and title to send");
        return;
    }

    HttpWebRequest sendNotificationRequest =
        (HttpWebRequest)WebRequest.Create(txtURL.Text);

    sendNotificationRequest.Method = "POST";
    sendNotificationRequest.Headers = new WebHeaderCollection();
    sendNotificationRequest.ContentType = "text/xml";

    sendNotificationRequest.Headers.Add("X-WindowsPhone-Target", "");
    sendNotificationRequest.Headers.Add("X-NotificationClass", "3"); //- raw
    String str = string.Format(txtTitle.Text + "\r\n" + txtText.Text);
    byte[] strBytes = new UTF8Encoding().GetBytes(str);
    sendNotificationRequest.ContentLength = strBytes.Length;
    using (Stream requestStream = sendNotificationRequest.GetRequestStream())
    {
        requestStream.Write(strBytes, 0, strBytes.Length);
    }

    HttpWebResponse response =
        (HttpWebResponse)sendNotificationRequest.GetResponse();
    string notificationStatus = response.Headers["X-NotificationStatus"];
    string deviceConnectionStatus = response.Headers["X-DeviceConnectionStatus"];
    lblStatus.Text = "Status: " + notificationStatus + " : " + deviceConnectionStatus;
}
```

That's all the code necessary to send raw notifications to Windows Phone clients. You are now ready
to test raw notifications on the Windows Phone emulator.

Testing Delivery of Raw Notifications

Testing raw notifications is very straightforward: there are no applications to pin to the Start screen.
Simply start both the client and the server pieces of the application, make sure the push notification URI
is available to both, and fire away! This demo gives more details on testing raw notifications:

1. Just as with toast and tile notifications, you need to obtain the URI of the
    notification channel. Open the RawNotificationPNClient project, make sure

> you have a connection to the Internet, and press F5 to run the project. Click the Create Channel button and, after seeing the URI printed on the screen, copy it to the clipboard from the Output window.

2. Switch to the PNServer Windows Forms project, and press F5 to run it. In the Push Notifications URL text box, paste the URI obtained in step 1. In the Push Notifications Title and Push Notifications Text text boxes, enter **Hello** and **World**, respectively. Click the Send Notification button.

3. You should now see the message stating that the raw notification has been received and the "Hello World" message on the Windows Phone emulator screen.

As you can see, implementing raw notifications is very similar to implementing tile and toast notifications, albeit a bit simpler. Each of the notification types has its purposes; use the most appropriate notification type for your circumstances.

You may be shaking your head by now, thinking that the copy-and-paste method of communicating the push notification channel URI between the client and the server is completely unrealistic for any commercial application. I agree, and the next section shows you how to automate that communication piece.

Implementing a Cloud Service to Track Push Notifications

In the previous demos, you used a somewhat unrealistic approach to communicate push notification URLs from the Windows Phone client application to the push notification server. You copied that URL from the Debug window of the client application and pasted it into the server application, where it was used to send tiles, toasts, and raw notifications to the Windows Phone applications. To make the stock-alerts application a bit more realistic, you must automate the URL communication piece. In this section, you learn how to do that using a cloud service built with the *Microsoft Windows Communication Foundation (WCF)* stack of technologies.

Creating a WCF Service to Track Notification Recipients

This section shows you how to enhance the PNServer application built previously by adding a WCF service to it. WCF is a very powerful technology with an array of configuration options for creating and hosting cloud services. You will build what is known as a *self-hosted service*, which means it will be hosted in the Windows Forms application, and you will write code to initialize and start that service. Another important point about this service is that it is a *RESTful service*, which, for your purposes right now, means you can access operations of the service over the properly formatted URLs, as you see shortly.

Before you create a RESTful WCF service, however, you may need to make a small change in the Visual Studio environment to reference assemblies you need to create that service. The reason for this is that, by default, Visual Studio creates a lightweight profile for client applications, such as Windows Forms or *Windows Presentation Foundation (WPF)* applications. This lightweight profile omits many web-related assemblies by default because the chances of a true client application needing them are slim.

The setting that controls which assemblies are included or left out is the Target Framework setting, and it is located on your project's Properties page. You need to change this setting from .Net Framework 4 Client Profile to .Net Framework 4. To accomplish this, open the PNServer project if it's not already open, right-click the project name, and then select Properties. Locate the Target Framework setting, and set it to .Net Framework 4, as illustrated in Figure 17-9.

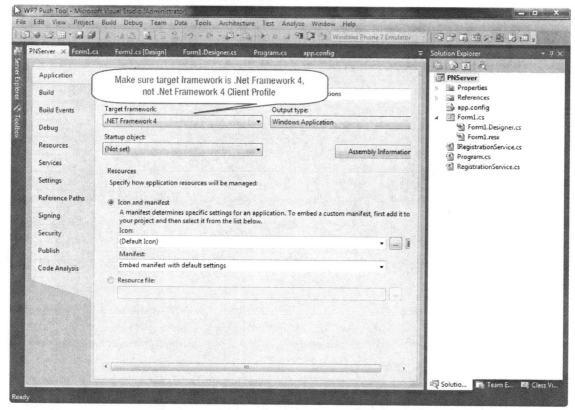

Figure 17-9. To add the RESTful WCF service to the Windows Forms application, set the application's target framework to .NET Framework 4.

Now follow these steps to complete the creation of the WCF service. Before creating the service, you need to include the System.ServiceModel.Web assembly in the PNServer project:

1. Right-click the project name, and select Add Reference. Locate the System.ServiceModel.Web assembly in the list, highlight it, and click OK.

Now you add WCF service files to the project. Adding the WCF service files consists of two parts: creating what is known as a *Service Contract*, which appears in the form of an Interface file, and defining a class that physically implements the methods defined in the Service Contract:

2. To create the Service Contract, right-click the project name, choose Add ▸ New Item, and then scroll almost all the way to the bottom and choose WCF Service. Name the service RegistrationService, and then click OK.

3. Add the following statement to the top of the IRegistrationService.cs file created:

```
using System.ServiceModel.Web;
```

4.   Add the following code to the IRegistrationService.cs file:

```
[ServiceContract]
public interface IRegistrationService
{
    [OperationContract, WebGet]
    void Register(string uri);

    [OperationContract, WebGet]
    void Unregister(string uri);
}
```

Note how you define two operations for the service to perform: register new Windows Phone clients for push notifications, and unregister them. Now it's time to add the implementation of the Register and Unregister methods:

5.   Double-click the RegistrationService.cs file that Visual Studio added to your project, and make it look like this:

```
public class RegistrationService : IRegistrationService
{
    private static List<Uri> subscribers = new List<Uri>();
    private static object obj = new object();

    public void Register(string uri)
    {
        Uri channelUri = new Uri(uri, UriKind.Absolute);
        Subscribe(channelUri);
    }

    public void Unregister(string uri)
    {
        Uri channelUri = new Uri(uri, UriKind.Absolute);
        Unsubscribe(channelUri);
    }

    private void Subscribe(Uri channelUri)
    {
        lock (obj)
        {
            if (!subscribers.Exists((u) => u == channelUri))
            {
                subscribers.Add(channelUri);
            }
        }
    }

    public static void Unsubscribe(Uri channelUri)
    {
        lock (obj)
        {
            subscribers.Remove(channelUri);
```

```
        }
    }

    public static List<Uri> GetSubscribers()
    {
        return subscribers;
    }
}
```

Take a closer look at the code that you just added to the
RegistrationService.cs file. Notice that the RegistrationService class
implements the IRegistrationService interface on the very first line—this is
important! Aside from that, the code is pretty straightforward: a collection of
push notification URIs is maintained in the static subscribers' variable, and
every client that calls the Register method of the service is added to that list of
subscribers. The lock function is used to prevent multiple clients from
changing the same data at the same exact moment in time, possibly resulting
in incomplete and unpredictable data.

The beginning of this section said that a WCF service hosted by a Windows
Forms application needs initialization code to start up. One of the places this
initialization code can go is in the load event of Form1.

6. Here's the code you need to start up the service. Copy it to the load event of
    Form1:

```
ServiceHost host;
host = new ServiceHost(typeof(RegistrationService));
host.Open();
```

7. You're almost done—you only need to provide some configuration parameters
    for the WCF service to run. Open the app.config file, and add the following
    configuration parameters to the <system.ServiceModel> element. (You should
    already have configuration settings defined in <system.ServiceModel>, but now
    you need to make sure those settings match precisely what is pasted here.)

```
<system.serviceModel>
  <behaviors>
    <endpointBehaviors>
     <behavior name="EndpointPNServerServiceBehavior">
        <webHttp />
     </behavior>
    </endpointBehaviors>
    <serviceBehaviors>
     <behavior name="">
        <serviceDebug includeExceptionDetailInFaults="true" />
     </behavior>
    </serviceBehaviors>
  </behaviors>
  <services>
    <service name="PNServer.RegistrationService">
      <endpoint address="http://localhost/RegistrationService"
          behaviorConfiguration="EndpointPNServerServiceBehavior"
          binding="webHttpBinding"
```

```
                    contract="WP7_Push_Notifications.IRegistrationService">
              </endpoint>
          </service>
       </services>
    </system.serviceModel>
```

In a nutshell, with these settings you have configured your service to listen at the following address: http://localhost/RegistrationService. You have also specified that the requests to this service will be coming over the HTTP protocol.

Finally, you modify the main application form (Form1) and add a Broadcast button that sends a push notification to all subscribed clients. Once clicked, the button click handler gets a list of all clients subscribed and sends each one of them a push notification (toast notification in the following code). Here's how to do this:

1. Open Form1.cs in Design view, and add a button to that form underneath the Send Notification button.

2. Change the button's text to Broadcast, as shown in Figure 17-10.

3. Change the button's name to btnBroadcast, double-click it, and make sure the button's Click event contains the following code:

```
private void btnBroadcast_Click(object sender, EventArgs e)
{
    if (txtTitle.Text == string.Empty || txtText.Text == string.Empty)
    {
        MessageBox.Show("Please enter text and title to send");
        return;
    }

    List<Uri> allSubscribersUri = RegistrationService.GetSubscribers();
    foreach (Uri subscriberUri in allSubscribersUri)
    {
        sendPushNotificationToClient(subscriberUri.ToString());
    }
}
```

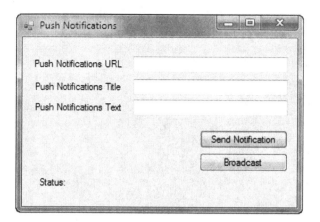

Figure 17-10. Main application form with a Broadcast button

4.   Add the following code to the sendPushNotificationToClient function:

```
private void sendPushNotificationToClient(string url)
{
  HttpWebRequest sendNotificationRequest = (HttpWebRequest)WebRequest.Create(url);

  sendNotificationRequest.Method = "POST";
  sendNotificationRequest.Headers = new WebHeaderCollection();
  sendNotificationRequest.ContentType = "text/xml";

  sendNotificationRequest.Headers.Add("X-WindowsPhone-Target", "toast");
  sendNotificationRequest.Headers.Add("X-NotificationClass", "2");

  string str = string.Format(TilePushXML, txtTitle.Text, txtText.Text);
  byte[] strBytes = new UTF8Encoding().GetBytes(str);
  sendNotificationRequest.ContentLength = strBytes.Length;
  using (Stream requestStream = sendNotificationRequest.GetRequestStream())
  {
     requestStream.Write(strBytes, 0, strBytes.Length);
  }

  try
  {
     HttpWebResponse response =
        (HttpWebResponse)sendNotificationRequest.GetResponse();
     string notificationStatus = response.Headers["X-NotificationStatus"];
     string deviceConnectionStatus = response.Headers["X-DeviceConnectionStatus"];
lblStatus.Text = "Status: " + notificationStatus + " : " + deviceConnectionStatus;
  }
  catch (Exception ex)
  {
     //handle 404 (URI not found) and other exceptions that may occur
     lblStatus.Text = "Failed to connect, exception detail: " + ex.Message;
  }
```

439

Note that the TilePushXML variable was previously defined in the discussion of tile notifications, specifically in the "Creating an Application to Send Notifications" section. With the WCF service tracking subscribed clients and with sending push notifications complete, it's now time to enhance the client application to call the web service with its push notification URL.

Modifying the Client to Call the WCF Service

The Windows Phone push notification client application needs to be modified to call the newly implemented web service with the push notification URL. Previously, you learned that the convenience of creating a RESTful WCF service lies in the fact that the operations of that web service can be accessed as URLs. For instance, the URL http://localhost/RegistrationService/Register?uri={0} accesses the Register function of the web service created in the previous section; the uri parameter is supplied on the QueryString. With that in mind, you can complete the Windows Phone push notification client implementation by creating the functions that register/unregister a Windows Phone client with the server:

1. Launch Visual Studio 2010 Express for Windows Phone, and open the PNClient project.

2. Locate the ChannelUri property getter and setter, and change them to the following. (Notice the use of two new functions, RegisterUriWithServer and UnregisterUriFromServer.)

    ```
    public Uri ChannelUri
    {
        get { return channelUri; }
        set
        {
            //unregister the old URI from the server
            if (channelUri!=null)
                UnregisterUriFromServer(channelUri);

            //register the new URI with the server
            RegisterUriWithServer(value);

            channelUri = value;
            OnChannelUriChanged(value);
        }
    }
    ```

3. Add the following two functions to invoke the WCF service you have created. (Note that when it comes time to release your service to production, you will most likely deploy this service somewhere in the cloud.)

    ```
    private void RegisterUriWithServer(Uri newChannelUri)
    {
        //Hardcode for solution - need to be updated in case the REST WCF
        //         service address changes
        string baseUri = "http://localhost/RegistrationService/Register?uri={0}";
        string theUri = String.Format(baseUri, newChannelUri.ToString());
        WebClient client = new WebClient();
        client.DownloadStringCompleted += (s, e) =>
    ```

```
        {
            if (e.Error == null)
                Dispatcher.BeginInvoke(() => {
                            txtURI.Text = "changing uri to " + newChannelUri.ToString();
                });
            else
                Dispatcher.BeginInvoke(() =>
                {
                    txtURI.Text = "registration failed " + e.Error.Message;
                });
    };
    client.DownloadStringAsync(new Uri(theUri));

}

private void UnregisterUriFromServer(Uri oldChannelUri)
{
    //Hardcode for solution - need to be updated in case the REST WCF service
    //address changes
    string baseUri = "http://localhost/RegistrationService/Unregister?uri={0}";
    string theUri = String.Format(baseUri, oldChannelUri.ToString());
    WebClient client = new WebClient();
    client.DownloadStringCompleted += (s, e) =>
    {
        if (e.Error == null)
            Dispatcher.BeginInvoke(() =>
            {
                txtURI.Text = "unregistered uri " + oldChannelUri.ToString();
            });
        else
            Dispatcher.BeginInvoke(() =>
            {
                txtURI.Text = "registration delete failed " + e.Error.Message;
            });
    };
    client.DownloadStringAsync(new Uri(theUri));
}
```

In the preceding code, notice that the URL of the cloud service is hardcoded—this URL must match the URL that you have specified in the configuration file (app.config) for the WCF service. Notice also how the event handlers (client.DownloadStringCompleted) are wired up. Those event handlers provide the status updates on whether the registration/unregistration succeeded or failed.

At this point, you have completed writing both the server and the client pieces for automated push notification. It is now time to verify that the server is able to keep track and notify its clients appropriately, without the need to copy and paste the push notification URL manually.

Verifying Automated Push Notification Subscriber Tracking

To test automated push notification tracking, the first thing you have to do is make sure the WCF service starts up appropriately and that it is able to process requests coming in. Here's how:

1. WCF Services are designed with security in mind, so there are numerous security configuration options for those services. To bypass security configuration options so they don't distract from the main points of this chapter, and to allow you to test the service you have built, you need to run the WCF service project as Administrator. The quickest way to accomplish this is to exit Visual Studio, right-click the shortcut to Visual Studio, and choose the Run as Administrator option. When Visual Studio comes up, open the PNServer solution. You are now set to run PNServer as Administrator.

2. To verify that the WCF service is ready to accept client connections, set a breakpoint at the first line of the Register function of the RegistrationService class, and then press F5 to start the PNServer application.

3. If the application is running, and the Windows form in Figure 17-10 is displayed, fire up Internet Explorer (or any other browser) and go to the following URL:

```
http://localhost/RegistrationService/Register?uri=http://www.microsoft.com
```

If the breakpoint is hit after you access this URL, this means the service is running and is ready for clients to connect.

If the breakpoint is not hit, and you see a message that the page cannot be displayed, verify that the content in the <system.ServiceModel> section of your app.config file in the PNServer project matches the content of that file described in the section on creating a WCF service. Most likely, some sort of configuration issue is preventing you from properly launching the service.

Once you've confirmed that the service is running, you can observe the automated push notification subscriber tracking in action by following these steps:

1. Launch the PNClient application, and click the Create Channel button. If you still have the breakpoint set in the Register function of the WCF service, that breakpoint should be hit. Press F5 to continue executing the debugger.

2. To be able to see toast notifications on the phone, you need to pin the application icon to the Start screen. To accomplish this, click the phone's Windows button, and then click the arrow ( ) to open the Windows Phone Options screen, as shown in Figure 17-8. Click and hold the left mouse button to bring up the pop-up menu shown in Figure 17-8, and then click the Pin to Start option.

3. With the application icon pinned onto the Start screen, you are ready to receive notifications on the phone. In the PNServer application window, enter the title and the text of the notification message to send, and press the Broadcast button. A second or two later, you should see the push notification coming through to the phone.

With clients and a cloud service dynamically exchanging push notification URLs and clients accepting push notifications, this is a good point to conclude the push notifications demos. The next sections give you a perspective on using push notifications in the real world and summarize what you have learned in this chapter.

The solution that you have built in this chapter provides the full life cycle implementation of push notifications; however, it has a set o limitations you should consider before deploying it to production. Windows Phone client applications that go down don't unregister themselves from the server; therefore, the server tries to send notifications to non-existent channels. The server application that you have created lacks persistence—all of the connected client addresses are kept in memory, which means they all will be lost if the service is shut down accidentally or on purpose. Finally, as currently implemented, the server lacks centralized scheduling or an event-based mechanism for distributing notifications: you have to push the button on the Windows Forms application to distribute the notifications. In the real world, the notifications will most likely be distributed in response to some external events (such as Microsoft stock rising rapidly), and the service has to be smart about handling those.

Using Push Notifications in the Real World

Push notifications provide a scalable framework for Windows Phone applications that lets them receive important messages without the need to run continuously in the background. This approach preserves device resources (processor, Internet connection) and extends battery life. There are many potential uses for push notifications—from Twitter updates to severe weather alerts to stock market notifications. This chapter demonstrated how you can send push notifications to Windows Phone devices using a Windows Forms application. It could just as easily be a web-based or a cloud-based application that sends those updates. In this chapter, you built a web service to keep track of and send notifications programmatically to the connected clients. This same web service could be further enhanced to send out push notifications on a schedule.

Currently, there is a limit on how many free push notifications can be sent to a single notification channel URI. That limit is 500 notifications per 24 hours per URI. That means you can send 500 messages per app per device for free every 24 hours. This limitation is in place to prevent abuse or malicious attacks and possibly spam through a notification channel. To get past the limit of 500 messages per channel in the 24-hour window, follow the guidelines in the next section, "Setting Up Secure Web Services for Push Notifications." While the communication channel between Windows Phone and the Microsoft Push Notification Service is secure, customers also have an option (for a fee) to secure the channel between their web service and MPNS, as described next.

Setting Up Secure Web Services for Push Notifications

In a nutshell, to set up secure web services for push notifications, you must acquire an SSL certificate from one of the trusted root Certificate Authorities. (A full list can be found at http://msdn.microsoft.com/en-us/library/gg521150(v=VS.92).aspx; it includes companies like VeriSign and RSA Security, among others.) Once you acquire that certificate, submit it to the Windows Phone Marketplace at the time of application certification. This will allow you to process unlimited push notification messages per secure channel.

Of course, as a prudent developer, you will want to test the secure communication channel between your Windows Phone application, MPNS, and your web service before you reach the application-certification step. Microsoft allows you to do so by letting you upload a certificate purchased from a trusted CA to the Windows Phone Marketplace ahead of the certification process. When the certificate is uploaded, you have four months to test secure communication between your Windows Phone application and your cloud service via push notifications. After your application passes certification, the four-month time limit is removed, and you gain access to unlimited push notifications via secure communication channel—truly the best practice for utilizing Microsoft push notifications.

Summary

This chapter provided you with background on and demonstrated the use of push notification services. You gained an understanding of various push notification types as well as the general architecture of push notifications. You implemented all three forms of push notifications: toast, tile, and raw. Finally, you completed the push notifications life cycle by creating a simple yet realistic WCF service to keep track of all Windows Phone clients connecting to it and to broadcast messages to all subscribed clients.

In the next chapter, you look at simplifying and abstracting asynchronous and event-based programming with Reactive Extensions for .Net, also referred to as Rx.Net. With Rx.Net, the implementation of concurrent asynchronous and events-based applications becomes easy and manageable. After reading the next chapter, you could perhaps start thinking about implementing the server portion of push notifications using Rx.NET, with notifications broadcasting messages using Rx.NET techniques in response to a given event, such as severe weather alert or a stock price alert.

CHAPTER 18

Reactive Extensions for .NET

For developers, the computing world of today demands the adoption of concurrent approaches to programming, much more so than just a few short years ago. Computer users expect ever-increasing computational power from their electronic gadgets, including their mobile devices. Unfortunately, it seems that the only way manufacturers will be able to increase computational speed in the near future is through adding extra processors (instead of making a single processor faster, as had been the case over the last few decades). In the case of processors on personal computers, the industry may soon be hitting a proverbial brick wall, with the maximum computational capacity available on a single processing unit close to being exhausted. An average personal computer today already comes with two or more processing units, and the number is likely to increase in the future.

Mobile devices still have some processing speed to grow into before they max out the processing power of a single CPU. However, the average smartphone will soon have several processing units as well, and some multiprocessor mobile phones have already started to appear on the market. In addition, uninterrupted Internet access on the phone is assumed—resources needed for proper functioning of an application may be spread around the world (in the cloud), but the user is rarely aware of that. A smartphone application should have the ability to access those resources seamlessly as needed; that is, it should accept all input from the user while these resources are accessed. In other words, it should obtain these resources asynchronously. Thus, the future for personal computers and mobile devices is both concurrent and asynchronous.

How do you approach concurrent and asynchronous programming on Windows Phone? The answer certainly is "with great caution," since it's not that easy. To help tame that complexity, a powerful framework emerged on the .NET scene at the end of 2009. That framework, called the *Reactive Extensions for .NET* (also known as *Rx.NET*), is now available for Windows Phone, and it provides sophisticated mechanisms to make event processing and asynchronous programming more intuitive. In this chapter, you learn the concepts behind Reactive Extensions for .NET and build two simple applications using the Rx.NET framework. The first searches and retrieves images on Flickr asynchronously. The second displays the current weather after accepting a city name as input from the user. An entire book could be written on the subject of Reactive Extensions alone, and there is a version of Reactive Extensions for JavaScript available as well.

In this chapter, you learn the basics of Rx.NET and leave with a basic understanding of and appreciation for this technology. However, to leverage the power of Rx.NET, you need a solid understanding of LINQ. Although the examples in this chapter should be relatively easy to follow for the novice C# programmer, even without an in-depth knowledge of LINQ, for expert coverage of the topic I recommend the excellent book *Pro LINQ: Language Integrated Query in C#2008* by Joseph C. Rattz (Apress, 2008). Another good resource is "101 LINQ Samples," available for free online at http://msdn.microsoft.com/en-us/vcsharp/aa336746.aspx. Rx.NET also relies heavily on general object-oriented principles; if you are not familiar with the concept of interfaces, it may be a good idea to understand those first before reading this chapter. Finally, Rx.NET constructs make extensive use of the newer features of the.NET Framework, such as lambda expressions and extension methods. While it's possible to follow examples in this book without in-depth understanding of either of those concepts, to use the power of Rx.NET on your own, you have to know these features of the .NET Framework.

The power of Reactive Extensions can be applied to deal with a wide range of computational issues. This chapter focuses on the way the framework deals with a problem that is probably as old as the personal computer: how do you provide a responsive user interface (UI) while utilizing the full computational resources available, and how can you do so in a manner that makes the code readable and easy to manage and maintain?

▪ **Note** The initial release of Rx.NET libraries comes preinstalled on the operating system of every Windows Phone device. However, just like any other technology, the Reactive Extensions library is constantly being enhanced to deliver ever more power to developers. As a Windows Phone developer, you are not stuck having to use the version of Rx.NET that comes preinstalled on the devices—you can always go to the Microsoft Data Developer Center (http://msdn.microsoft.com/en-us/data/gg577609) and download the latest libraries available for the phone. Once you reference and use them, they will be distributed together with your application, slightly increasing its footprint, but otherwise coexisting with the default version of Rx.NET that comes embedded on the device.

Introducing Reactive Programming

Rx.NET aims to revolutionize *reactive programming* in the .NET Framework. In reactive programming, you register an interest in something and have items of interest handed over, or pushed to the attention of the application asynchronously, or reactively, as they become available. A classic example of an application that relies heavily on the reactive programming model is the spreadsheet, where an update to a single cell triggers cascading updates to every cell that references that cell. The concept of having things pushed down as they become available is particularly well suited to applications that use constantly changing data sources, such as the weather application that you build in this chapter.

Reactive programming is often contrasted with interactive programming. In interactive programming, the user asks for something and then waits until it is delivered. To help differentiate these concepts further, let's take a look at a car shopping analogy. Usually, when shopping for a car, you go to a car dealership (or do research online) and look at different car makes and models. You pick the ones you like and test-drive them at the dealership. This arrangement is an example of an interactive transaction, where you requested a car and it was delivered in return. In a reactive approach to the car shopping experience, you would send a note to a dealership expressing interest in a certain make and model, and then you would continue with your daily routine. The dealer would then locate the cars that might be of interest and notify you when they became available.

Let's see if this analogy carries over to event processing on Windows Phone. For the sample application you build in this chapter, you want to read the contents of a text box once it is determined that no keystroke has occurred for half a second. In the sample app, this indicates that the user has finished typing, and that they're ready for the application to respond. If you were using an interactive approach, you would implement this by wiring up the KeyDown event for the text box and then checking a timer to see whether ample time had elapsed between keystrokes. In a reactive approach, as you see shortly, things are much simpler: you express interest in being notified of KeyDown events only after a half-second has elapsed between a user's keystrokes. When you're notified of such an event, you take action—searching for photos online, in this case. Before you learn how to search for photos in a reactive manner, you walk through several short examples to get a feeling for how Reactive Extensions implement the core *Observer* pattern that forms the basis of the Reactive Framework and is described in detail in the sidebar.

Rx.NET Subscription Pipeline

To use Rx.NET, you have to follow four basic steps to designate observables and to create observers:

1. Build or define an *Observable* (or Subject, as it is called in the Observer pattern described in the sidebar).

2. Subscribe to that Observable (or create an Observer if you follow along with the Observer pattern in the sidebar).

3. Receive data, and act on it for as long as the Subject continues to notify the Observer.

4. When there are no more notifications from the Subject to process, the Observer unsubscribes from the Subject by calling the Dispose method.

Rx.NET defines two new interfaces to accommodate this subscription pipeline: IObservable and IObserver. You learn how to use these interfaces in the next few sections.

THE OBSERVER PATTERN

The Observer pattern is a commonly used technique in the world of object-oriented software development. At its core, it has a Subject object that keeps track of all the objects (referred to as *Observers*) that want to be notified about changes to the Subject's state. All Observers are automatically notified of any changes to the Subject. The power of this pattern comes from not having to query the Subject for specific changes to its state—the Subject promptly lets Observers know when it gets modified. For a detailed description of the Observer pattern, you can refer *to Design Patterns: Elements of Reusable Object-Oriented Software* by Gamma et. Al. (Addison-Wesley, 1994) or you can read about it on Wikipedia at http://en.wikipedia.org/wiki/Observer_pattern.

According to Microsoft DevLabs, where the Reactive Extensions library was developed, the objective of Rx.NET is to enable the composition of asynchronous and event-driven programs. Rx.NET uses *Observable collections* to enable such composition. In Rx.NET, Observable collections perform the role of the Subject in the Observer pattern. Observable collections gather data associated with a given event or an asynchronous method call and notify everyone who has subscribed to these collections of the changes as they occur. This might sound a bit confusing, so let's jump into code that will allow you to start using key features of Rx.NET right away to build awesome Windows Phone applications.

Implementing the Observer Pattern with Rx.NET

Before you create an application that asynchronously searches photos on Flickr, let's take a short detour to understand the basics of Rx.NET. In the project that follows, you generate a simple Observable collection using Reactive Extensions for .NET. You read values from this collection as they are pushed down to you. Follow these step-by-step instructions.

Creating a Windows Phone Project

First, you create a new Windows Phone project and add the framework elements necessary to make it work on the mobile platform:

1. Launch Visual Studio 2010 Express for Windows Phone, and create a new Windows Phone Application project. Name it RxSample. In this project, you observe the messages generated by the Reactive Extensions framework in the text box on the phone screen.

2. From the Toolbox, select the textblock and drop it on the design surface. Since you are just getting your feet wet with Rx.NET, leave the name of the textblock (textBlock1) unchanged, and adjust its height and width to occupy the full area of the screen. Highlight the textblock, press F4 to bring up its Properties window, and set the TextWrapping property to Wrap.

3. On Windows Phone, the Rx.Net implementation is contained within two separate assemblies–`Microsoft.Phone.Reactive` and `System.Observable`. Add a reference to the `Microsoft.Phone.Reactive` and `System.Observable` assemblies by right-clicking the project name in the Solution Explorer and selecting Add Reference.

Adding Code to Create and Read Observable Collections

You now add code to create an Observable collection, subscribe to it, and read values from it:

1. Import the Rx.NET libraries into the current code. To do that, open `MainPage.xaml.cs` (right-click `MainPage.xaml`, and select View Code), and add the following statement to the top of the page:

   ```
   using Microsoft.Phone.Reactive;
   ```

   Remember how an Observable collection performs the role of the Subject in the Observer pattern? In Rx.NET, the `IObservable<T>` interface acts as that Subject. You now create an Observable collection that will consist of a range of integer values:

2. In the `MainPage()` constructor, add the following code right after the `InitializeComponent()` statement:

   ```
   IObservable<int> source = Observable.Range(5, 3);
   ```

3. Examine the use of the `Observable.Range` method—this method will create an Observable collection that will consist of a range of integers from 5 to 7, inclusive (the Range method created three sequential values, from 5 to 7 inclusive).

   You now create an Observer for the source Subject created in step 2. This Observer object will be notified of any changes to the source—in this case, every time a new integer is generated, or "pushed down" to the application. Notice that the Observer object implements the `IDisposable` interface as well:

4. Add the following code to create the Observer:

   ```
   IDisposable subscription = source.Subscribe(x =>
       textBlock1.Text += String.Format(" OnNext: {0}", x),
       ex => textBlock1.Text += String.Format(" OnError: {0}", ex.Message),
       () => textBlock1.Text += " OnCompleted");
   ```

5. The `Subscribe` method of `IObservable<T>` has several overloads. The one you use here accepts three *lambda expressions* (see the "Lambda Expressions" sidebar) as its parameters. The first lambda expression contains the logic to invoke when another element becomes available to the Observer (`OnNext`), the second has logic to invoke if there is an exception in the Observer (`OnError`), and the last one contains logic that is executed when the Subject completes its useful life (`OnCompleted`). The "completion of useful life" condition varies from Subject to Subject, but generally it means there are no more elements to receive from the Subject. If you're not familiar with lambda expressions, the sidebar contains a brief introduction to this new feature of the .NET Framework.

6. Tell the Observer to discontinue its interest in the Subject's state by issuing a call to the `Dispose()` method:

   ```
   subscription.Dispose();
   ```

7. Press F5 to run the application. The Windows Phone emulator screen appears, showing messages OnNext: 5, OnNext: 6, OnNext: 7, and OnCompleted, as shown in Figure 18-1. The Observable object generated three integer values, pushed them down to Observers, and called it quits.

LAMBDA EXPRESSIONS

With the release of C# 3.0, Microsoft borrowed a number of features from the family of functional programming languages. Among these features is the ability to define functions inline known to C# programmers by the intimidating term *lambda expression*. At a basic level, lambda expressions are simply functions that differ from "normal" C# functions in their syntax. In the example, `x =>textBlock1.Text += String.Format(" OnNext: {0}", x)` is a lambda expression that defines a function that accepts `x` as a parameter and infers its type from context. The `textBlock1.Text += String.Format(" OnNext: {0}", x)` statement is the body of the function. Note that if you see the `()=>` syntax in the lambda expression, as in the last parameter to the `Subscribe` function (step 3), it means no parameters are being passed in to the lambda expression. For more information about lambda expressions, visit `http://msdn.microsoft.com/en-us/library/bb397687.aspx`.

Figure 18-1. Reactive Extensions for .NET first steps

In the previous code, notice how subscription does not implement the IObserver<T> interface. That is because the Microsoft.Phone.Reactive assembly contains a set of extension methods that overload the Subscribe() method of IObservable. These overloaded methods accept OnNext, OnError, and OnComplete handlers defined by the IObserver<T> interface as lambda expressions, as described in the previous paragraphs. Hence, in your experiments and samples with Rx.NET in this chapter, you don't have to implement the IObserver<T> interface physically.

The output of your first Rx.NET application (shown in Figure 18-1) is certainly nothing spectacular. But you are just barely skimming the Rx.NET surface here. Imagine subscribing to events, such as keystrokes or data emitted by the location service. Then think about having the ability to react to those events only if certain conditions are met: for instance, filtering out location values so that the event is raised only when the location specifies a certain predefined area. In the next section, you build a small application that uses this filtering approach to make an asynchronous web service call to Flickr once the user has stopped typing text for half a second.

Using Rx.NET Event Handling to Search for Flickr Photographs

In this section, you build an application that searches Flickr photos asynchronously using Rx.NET. In particular, you learn how to create Observable data sources from events as well as how to subscribe to them. The version of Flickr search you'll create is shown in Figure 18-2. The search technique is basic and uses a WebBrowser control to display images; however, this example allows you to concentrate on learning the Rx.NET techniques for processing events on Windows Phone. In the next example, you will build a Weather Service application that demonstrates asynchronous programming with Rx.NET. Let's get started.

Figure 18-2. Flickr Search with Rx.NET

Creating a Windows Phone Project

First, create a new Windows Phone project for the Flickr image search:

1. Launch Visual Studio 2010 Express for Windows Phone, and create a new
    Windows Phone Application project. Name it FlickrRx.

2. Change the name of the application to Flickr Search, and change the page title
    to Rx at Work. To accomplish this, highlight the application name, press F4,
    edit the Text property, and then do the same for the page title.

3. Add a reference by right-clicking the project name in the Solution Explorer and
    selecting Add Reference to the Microsoft.Phone.Reactive and
    System.Observable assemblies.

Adding a User Interface

Now it's time to add UI elements to the project. The UI consists of a text box, a label, and a WebBrowser
control, as shown in Figure 18-3. Here are the steps:

1. From the Toolbox, select a text box, and drop it on the design surface. Rename
    the text box to txtSearchTerms. Make the width of the text box equal the width
    of the screen, and clear the Text property. Next select a textblock, drop it
    underneath the text box, rename it lblSearchingFor, and resize it to be the
    width of the screen.

2. From the Toolbox, select the WebBrowser control, and drop it on the design
    surface underneath the textblock. Rename the WebBrowser control
    webResults, and make it the width of the screen.

You should now have something similar to Figure 18-3.

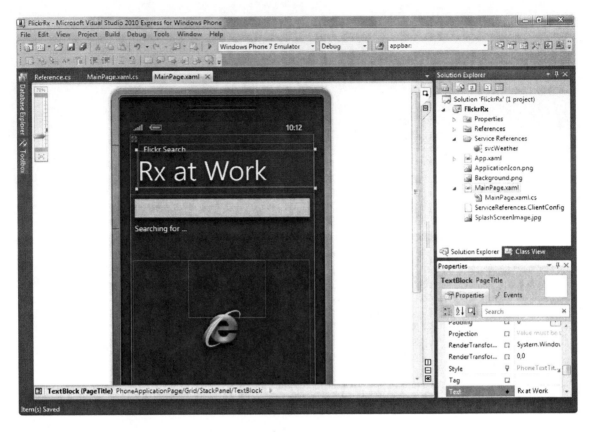

Figure 18-3. Flickr Search using Rx.NET screen layout

Adding Logic to Search Flickr for Images

The next step is to add logic to populate the WebBrowser controls with the results of a Flickr image search:

1. Open MainPage.xaml.cs (right-click MainPage.xaml and select View Code), and paste the following using statement at the top of the page:

    ```
    using Microsoft.Phone.Reactive;
    ```

Now you need to write code to capture the KeyUp events of the text box. To accomplish this, you use the FromEvent method of the Rx.NET library, which accepts the name of the object for which to capture events as well as name of the event on that object.

2. Paste the following code immediately following the InitializeComponent() statement in the MainPage() constructor:

    ```
    var keys = Observable.FromEvent<KeyEventArgs>(txtSearchTerms, "KeyUp");
    ```

```
keys.Subscribe(evt =>
{
    lblSearchingFor.Text = "Searching for ..." + txtSearchTerms.Text;
    webResults.Navigate(new Uri("http://www.flickr.com/search/?q="
    + txtSearchTerms.Text));
});
```

The first statement creates an Observable data source, keys, which consists of all KeyUp events of the txtSearchTerms text box. The second statement is a lambda expression that creates an Observer on this collection and attempts to update the lblSearchingFor textblock with the text entered into the text box. It shows the web page representing the results of searching Flickr with the text supplied in the text box.

■ **Note** The { symbol in a lambda expression is used to define an expression whose body has more than one statement within it, as your code does in the previous example.

---

3. Press F5 to run the application. As you type the first character, you should see the WebBrowser control attempting to navigate to the Flickr search page, specifying the only character entered as its search criteria. Notice how there is very little visual indication that there's some search or navigation being performed behind the scenes. You improve on that in the sections that follow, where you create an animation to play while the WebBrowser control is loading with the results of an image search.

Enhancing a Flickr Search with Throttling

At this point, you must certainly be wondering what Rx.NET has added to your toolbox besides the complexities of the Observer pattern. Couldn't you do pretty much everything you have done so far using the standard event-handling procedures available to Microsoft developers since the earliest days of Visual Basic (even before there was VB.NET)? The answer is: Rx.NET has added nothing up until now, and yes, you could have done everything with VB. The power of Reactive Extensions for .NET starts to come through in the next few steps of the example.

First, modify the application as follows:

1. Change the code line declaring an Observable collection from

```
var keys = Observable.FromEvent<KeyEventArgs>(txtSearchTerms, "KeyUp");
```

2. to

```
var keys = Observable.FromEvent<KeyEventArgs>(txtSearchTerms,
    "KeyUp").Throttle(TimeSpan.FromSeconds(.5));
```

3. Change the code block declaring an Observer from

```
keys.Subscribe(evt =>
{
    lblSearchingFor.Text = "Searching for ..." + txtSearchTerms.Text;
        webResults.Navigate(new Uri("http://www.flickr.com/search/?q="
```

```
                            + txtSearchTerms.Text));
        });
```

4. to

```
    keys.ObserveOn(Deployment.Current.Dispatcher).Subscribe(evt =>
        {
            if (txtSearchTerms.Text.Length>0)
            {
                lblSearchingFor.Text = "Searching for ..." + txtSearchTerms.Text;
                webResults.Navigate(new Uri("http://www.flickr.com/search/?q=" +
                    txtSearchTerms.Text));
            }
        });
```

5. Press F5 to run the application. Click the text box, enter the search terms for photo lookup in Flickr (for example, type in **Barcelona**), and watch the WebBrowser control retrieve the images of that beautiful European city from Flickr.

Let's examine the code that you just added. You created an Observable collection that consists of all the KeyUp events generated on the txtSearchTerms text box. When you added the Throttle(.5) statement, you effectively told Rx.NET that you wanted to observe only KeyUp events that occur more than half a second apart (0.5 seconds). Assuming that an average user will press the keys on the keyboard less than half a second apart, a half-second pause between key presses tells the application that the user is ready for the Flickr search to launch, and they're ready to "observe" the results of its execution.

In step 2, you enhanced the application in two ways. First you added logic not to invoke image search if nothing is entered in the text box (this could happen if the user erased the content with the Backspace key). Second, notice the ObserveOn(Deployment.Current.Dispatcher) construct that was used to help create an Observer. To understand its reason for being and to allow you to peek under the hood of Rx.NET, remove it. As a result, your code for step 2 will look like the following snippet:

```
keys.Subscribe(evt =>
            {
                if (txtSearchTerms.Text.Length > 0)
                {
                    lblSearchingFor.Text = "Searching for ..." + txtSearchTerms.Text;
                    webResults.Navigate(new Uri("http://www.flickr.com/search/?q=" +
txtSearchTerms.Text));
                }
            });
```

6. Press F5 to run the application now, and you see the screen shown in Figure 18-4, where Visual Studio displays an "Invalid cross-thread access" message.

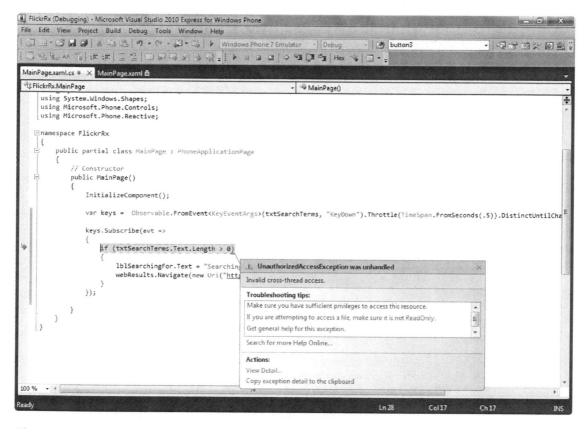

Figure 18-4. *An invalid cross-access thread exception is generated when trying to update UI directly from the background thread.*

As readers familiar with programming a UI on the .NET platform know, what is occurring is that updating the UI from a thread other than a UI thread is a tricky proposition. Under the hood, Reactive Extensions for .NET has created a separate background thread, and it will push notifications of changes from the Observable data source to the Observers from that thread. This background thread can't modify the UI thread directly.

Fortunately, the creators of Rx.NET have provided a solution to this problem by giving us the ObserveOn() extension method in the Microsoft.Phone.Reactive assembly. This extension method has several overloads, and one of them accepts a Dispatcher object. In the .NET Framework, a Dispatcher object maintains a prioritized queue of work items on a specific thread, and here it provides a way for you to observe an Observable data source on the UI thread. In the preceding example, you pass the Deployment.Current.Dispatcher property to the ObserveOn() method to get thread-safe access to the current Dispatcher and use it to update visual elements on the phone. The use of a single ObserveOn() method is significantly easier than dealing with the Dispatcher's Invoke method, which is a common way to update the UI in multithreaded Silverlight and WPF applications.

Adding an Animation that Plays as Flickr Images Load

You can further enhance the Flickr image search application by adding a simple animation that plays while the web pages with the results of your image search are loading. To do that, you create an animation in Expression Blend for Windows Phone, subscribe to the Navigated event of the WebBrowser control, and play the animation in code. Follow these steps to add this feature to your project:

1. Still in Visual Studio for Windows Phone, add a textblock to the phone's design surface, and place it between the "Searching for" textblock and the WebBrowser control. Name that textblock lblLoading, set the caption to Loading Images, and set its Visibility property to Collapsed.

Microsoft Expression Blend for Windows Phone is a powerful application for creating and editing graphics and animations for Windows Phone devices. You used it in the first part of this book to style controls and for other graphical tasks.

2. To launch Expression Blend and load it with the Flickr project, right-click MainPage.xaml in Visual Studio and select Open in Expression Blend. Microsoft Expression Blend launches with your solution open and ready to edit.

Your animation will be a progress bar in the form of a rectangle that will grow in width as time elapses. This animation will loop indefinitely so that when it reaches maximum allowable size, the rectangle will go back to its beginning and the animation will be repeated.

3. In Expression Blend, select a Rectangle from the Toolbox, draw a very narrow (almost invisible) rectangle right next to the Loading Images textblock, and set its Fill color to red.

Now you create what is called a *timeline animation* in Expression Blend. Timeline animations are created with the use of the storyboards, so you create a new storyboard in this step.

4. In the Objects and Timeline window, click the New button (shown in Figure 18-5), name the storyboard loadingImages, and click OK.

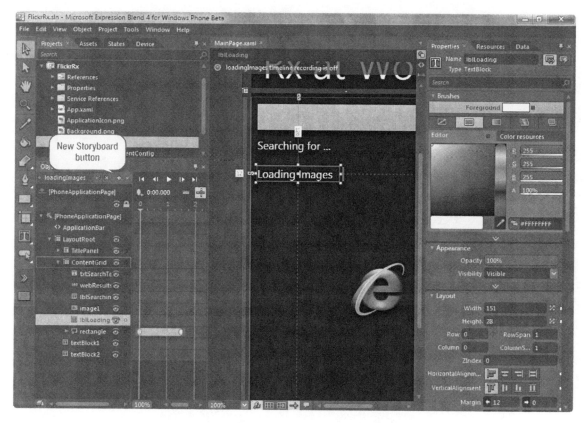

Figure 18-5. Creating a new storyboard animation in Expression Blend

The Objects and Timeline panel changes to display a timeline, and Blend is ready to record your animation.

5. Select the rectangle that you placed on the Windows Phone design surface, and click the Record Keyframe button as shown in Figure 18-6.

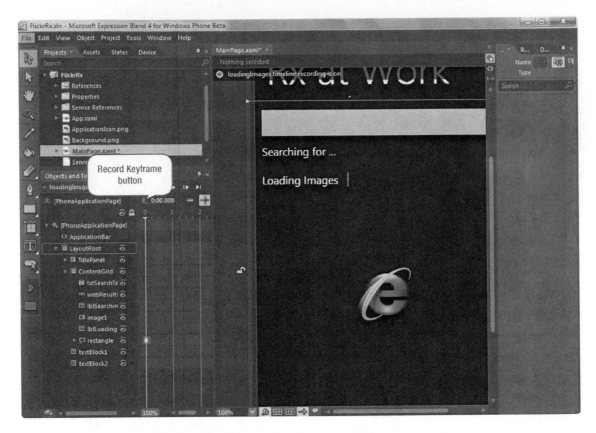

Figure 18-6. Beginning of the Loading Images timeline animation

6. Move the Animation Play head (the yellow vertical line in the Timeline) to about 1.5 seconds, as shown in Figure 18-7. Click the Record Keyframe button again, and then resize the rectangle to be close to the full phone screen width.

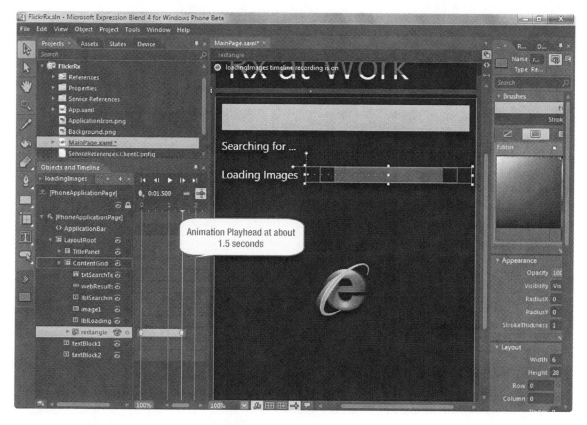

Figure 18-7. End of the Loading Images timeline animation

Now you set the animation to loop as long as it is active.

7. In Objects and Timeline, click and select the loadingImages storyboard name.
Common Properties for the Storyboard dialog appears. Select Forever in the
Repeat Behavior property of this storyboard.

With the animation complete, you are ready to show it when the user performs a search for Flickr
images.

8. Save everything in Expression Blend (File ➤ Save All), and switch back to Visual
Studio.

Now you add code first to show the animation when the search for images is initiated and then stop
the animation once that search is complete.

9. To start the animation when the user initiates a search for Flickr images, you
call the Begin method of the loadingImages animation. In MainPage.xaml.cs,
change the code that creates an Observer for the KeyUp event to the following:

```
keys.ObserveOn(Deployment.Current.Dispatcher).Subscribe(evt =>
```

461

```
        {
            if (txtSearchTerms.Text.Length > 0)
            {
                lblSearchingFor.Text = "Searching for ..." + txtSearchTerms.Text;
                lblLoading.Visibility=System.Windows.Visibility.Visible;
                loadingImages.Begin();

                    webResults.Navigate(new Uri("http://www.flickr.com/search/?q=" +
                            txtSearchTerms.Text));
            }
        });
```

Once the images load in the WebBrowser control, you stop the animation by calling the Stop method of the loadingImages animation. To accomplish this, you use Rx.NET to subscribe to the web browser's Navigated event. When this subscription receives data, you stop the animation.

10. Paste the following code at the end of the MainPage constructor:

```
var browser =
    Observable.FromEvent<System.Windows.Navigation.NavigationEventArgs>(webResults,
    "Navigated");

browser.ObserveOn(Deployment.Current.Dispatcher).Subscribe(evt =>
{
    loadingImages.Stop();
    lblLoading.Visibility = System.Windows.Visibility.Collapsed;
});
```

You are now ready to run the application.

11. Press F5, type a keyword into the text box, and observe the animation while the images are being loaded into the browser.

You're still only scratching the surface of Rx.NET and its applications, but you can already see the power of this framework. Using Rx.NET, you can think of any event as an observable data source, whether it's a location service that generates coordinate values (which you can think of as an observable set of position values), accelerometer data, key press events, or web browser events, such as those already demonstrated. Now that you have seen how to create Observable data sources from events using the FromEvent<T> method and how to subscribe to those events, let's expand on this knowledge. In the next section, you use Rx.NET to build a small real-time weather application that uses a publicly available web service to retrieve current weather asynchronously and shows a small picture representing current weather for the city name provided. Before you build this application, however, you learn about the general design guidelines for using Rx.NET from the Rx.NET Development team.

Rx.NET Design Guidelines

As a sign of a maturing platform, Rx.NET has received its own set of design guidelines (available at http://go.microsoft.com/fwlink/?LinkID=205219) to help developers make the best decisions when using the library. Some of the recommendations in that document have already been covered in this chapter: for instance, the general guideline to use Rx.NET for asynchronous and event-based computations. In the next few sections, you get familiar with few more useful strategies for creating robust Windows Phone applications with the help of Rx.NET.

Consider Drawing a Marble Diagram

If you research Rx.NET on the Microsoft web site (specifically, Channel 9), chances are that you will encounter references to what is known as *Marble Diagrams*. An example of a Marble Diagram is shown in Figure 18-8, where it depicts the use of the TakeUntil() operator in Rx.NET. In Marble Diagrams, you have input sequences of event-based and asynchronous data that you know about. The Marble Diagram helps you understand what would happen to those input sequences as a result of the application of a given Rx.NET operator.

Figure 18-8 represents a real-world example of receiving geolocation positions on the phone. It assumes that data about the phone user's location is being gathered until the user types in a new location of interest to search for (such as searching for a Starbucks in the immediate neighborhood). Initially, the top data sequence (geoLocationReading) receives data points (each data point is indicated by a small circle, or marble, on the line corresponding to the geoLocationReading in Figure 18-8). Then, a newLocation sequence starts receiving data, and the marbles are drawn on the line corresponding to the newLocation sequence. Notice how, as a result of the application of the TakeUntil() operator, the resulting sequence (result) gets only the data points (marbles on the line corresponding to the result sequence) of geoLocationReading until the marbles on the newLocation sequence start coming in. Regardless of how many data points (marbles) appear on either the geoLocationReading or newLocation sequences after that fact (indicated by an X in Figure 18-8), the result sequence does not get any additional data points (or marbles) after then.

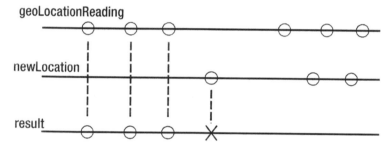

Figure 18-8. Marble Diagram for the TakeUntil Rx.NET operator

As with the TakeUntil operator, you can analyze all the Rx.NET operators by visualizing them on a Marble Diagram and understanding the resulting sequences they produce. Rx.NET design guidelines hint at another area where Marble Diagrams may be helpful: draw a marble diagram of the sequence you would like to create, and then you can determine which Rx.NET operators you need to use to achieve that Marble Diagram.

Consider Passing a Specific Scheduler to Concurrency-Introducing Operators

Earlier, this chapter stated that Rx.NET has the power to make concurrent programming easier. It does so by abstracting away many issues of threading and concurrency and handling concurrency in a declarative way. (There is no need to explicitly create threads, for example.) However, even with this concurrency abstraction, you have some control over how the execution of Rx.NET should proceed and the context of how the Rx.NET notifications should be processed. This brings us to a discussion of *schedulers.*

In Rx.NET, it is possible to schedule two things: how (or in what thread context) the subscription will execute and how (in what thread context) the notification will be published. This context is controlled by the SubscribeOn()and ObserveOn()extension methods of the IObservable<T> interface. Both of those extension methods can accept a property of the static Scheduler class, and the properties available for you to pass in are described next:

- Scheduler.Dispatcher forces the execution on the Dispatcher, which is a class that owns the application thread and internally maintains a queue of work items.

- Scheduler.NewThread schedules all actions onto a new thread.

- Scheduler.ThreadPool schedules all actions onto the thread pool.

- Scheduler.Immediate ensures that the action is executed immediately.

- Scheduler.CurrentThread ensures that the actions are performed on the thread that made the original call. This is not the same as Scheduler.Immediate, since actions scheduled on the current thread may be queued for later execution.

The following code is an example of how you would use the schedulers with subscriptions in Rx.NET. Notice how you subscribe on a new thread and observe the results of the subscription on the dispatcher:

```
Observable.FromAsyncPattern<WebResponse>(
        webRequest.BeginGetResponse,
        webRequest.EndGetResponse)()
    .SubscribeOn(Scheduler.NewThread)
    .ObserveOn(Scheduler.Dispatcher)
    .Subscribe(
```

The Rx design guidelines deem it a best practice to pass in the scheduler wherever appropriate so that concurrency is created in the right place to begin with. Now you know how to accomplish that.

This section has touched on a couple of guidelines from the *Rx Design Guidelines* document. This document includes many other suggestions for building robust, high-performing Rx.NET constructs, so you are encouraged to study it in greater detail. In the next section, you continue practicing using Rx.NET by building a simple weather application, which also introduces you to concepts such as error recovery in Rx.NET.

Using Rx.NET with Web Services to Retrieve Weather Data Asynchronously

In this section, you use a publicly available weather web service located at www.webservicex.net/WS/WSDetails.aspx?CATID=12&WSID=56 to retrieve and display the current weather for a given city in the United States. In addition to weather services, many other useful web services are available at this location, including ZIP code validation and currency conversion. As an exercise in using Rx.NET, you are encouraged to build useful, functional applications that take advantage of these services.

From the development point of view, the weather application will consist of asynchronously capturing user input (city name) and asynchronously calling the web service and then displaying the current weather for that city. Let's go ahead and create the application.

Creating a Windows Phone Project

First you create a new project, import all the libraries, and create the service references necessary to make the weather application work:

1. Launch Visual Studio 2010 Express for Windows Phone, and create a new Windows Phone Application project. Name it WeatherRx.

2. In MainPage.xaml, change the name of the application to WeatherRx and change the page title to Weather App. (You are also certainly welcome to name the application and the page according to your preference.)

3. Since you're using Rx.NET to build this application, add a reference to the Microsoft.Phone.Reactive and System.Observable assemblies by right-clicking Project Name in the Solution Explorer and selecting Add Reference.

You need to add a service reference to the weather service already mentioned. The weather service is an .asmx web service hosted at www.webservicex.net:

4. To add a reference to this service, right-click the Project Name, and select Add Service Reference. In the dialog that comes up, enter the following value in the Address Textbox: **http://www.webservicex.net/ globalweather.asmx**. Click the Go button.

5. The GlobalWeather service should appear on the left. Click the arrow next to it, make sure you select the GlobalWeatherSoap service, and then rename the namespace to svcWeather.

6. Your final Add Service Reference screen should look like Figure 18-9.

7. Click the OK button.

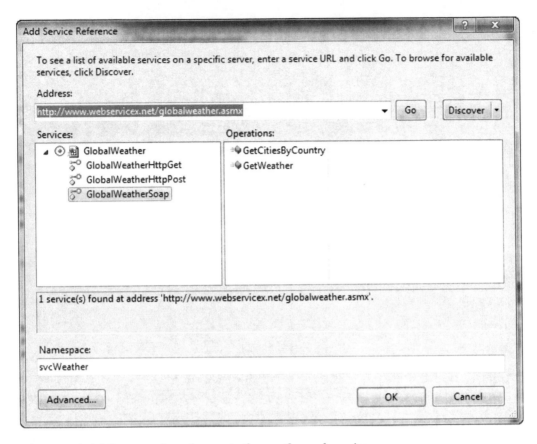

Figure 18-9. Adding a service reference to the weather web service

Creating a User Interface

For the application, your goal is to create a screen that looks like the one shown in Figure 18-10. To assist in achieving that objective, the XAML for visual elements that appear after the page title is shown here. You can also copy and paste this XAML from the sample code available in the download section for this chapter:

```
<!--ContentPanel - place additional content here-->
<Grid x:Name="ContentGrid" Grid.Row="1">
    <TextBox Height="72" HorizontalAlignment="Left" Margin="0,51,0,0" Name="txtCityName"
    Text="" VerticalAlignment="Top" Width="480" />
    <TextBlock Height="53" HorizontalAlignment="Left" Margin="6,13,0,0" Name="lblLegend"
    Text="Enter U.S. City Name below for current Weather" VerticalAlignment="Top"
    Width="462" />
    <TextBlock Height="30" HorizontalAlignment="Left" Margin="6,129,0,0"
    Name="lblTemperature" Text="Current Temperature" VerticalAlignment="Top"
    Width="435" />
```

```xml
    <Image Height="150" HorizontalAlignment="Left" Margin="241,213,0,0"
     Name="imgWeather" Stretch="Fill" VerticalAlignment="Top" Width="200" />
    <TextBlock Height="30" HorizontalAlignment="Left" Margin="6,162,0,0" Name="lblWind"
     Text="Current Wind Conditions" VerticalAlignment="Top" Width="435" />
    <TextBlock Height="30" Margin="6,379,39,0" Name="lblStatus" Text=""
     VerticalAlignment="Top" />
    <Button Content="Retry" Height="72" HorizontalAlignment="Left" Margin="69,429,0,0"
     Name="btnRetry" VerticalAlignment="Top" Width="160" Visibility="Collapsed"
     Click="btnRetry_Click" />
    <Button Content="Quit" Height="72" HorizontalAlignment="Right" Margin="0,429,79,0"
     Name="btnQuit" VerticalAlignment="Top" Width="160" Visibility="Collapsed"
     Click="btnQuit_Click" />
  </Grid>
</Grid>
```

Notice that the last `</Grid>` statement closes the LayoutGrid element, not shown in the preceding fragment.

Figure 18-10. WeatherRx design layout

Adding Logic to Get Weather Information

With design elements and proper references in place, you are ready to add code to the application. This example splits the code into multiple functions for enhanced readability:

1. Right-click the project name, select Add Reference, and choose the `System.Xml.Linq` assembly from the list. You need a couple of LINQ-to-XML functions to parse the return string from the web service.

2. Open `MainPage.xaml.cs` by clicking `MainPage.xaml` and selecting View Code, and add the following using statements to the top of the page:

    ```
    using Microsoft.Phone.Reactive;
    using System.Xml.Linq;
    ```

3. Add the following module-level variable declarations right above the `MainPage()` constructor:

    ```
    svcWeather.GlobalWeatherSoapClient weatherClient = new
        svcWeather.GlobalWeatherSoapClient();
    IObservable<IEvent<GetWeatherCompletedEventArgs>> _weather;
    const string conCountry = "United States";
    ```

4. Notice how you specify a constant "United States" always to be passed in as a second argument to the web service. You could also enhance your application by making the country selection dynamic.

5. Add the following code after the `InitializeComponent()` statement of the `MainPage()` constructor:

    ```
    WireUpWeatherEvents();
    WireUpKeyEvents();
    ```

6. Here you are wiring up web service and keystroke events in separate functions—a technique that will be very useful in subsequent sections of this chapter when you deal with error recovery.

7. Create the `WireUpWeatherEvents` function and its supporting `GetWeatherSubject` function by pasting in the following code. Note how you create a separate function (`GetWeatherSubject`) to return an Observable collection from the weather web service event:

    ```
    private void WireUpWeatherEvents()
    {
        GetWeatherSubject();
        _weather.ObserveOn(Deployment.Current.Dispatcher)
            .Subscribe(evt =>
            {
                if (evt.EventArgs.Result!= null)
                {
                    string strXMLResult = evt.EventArgs.Result;
                    XElement weatherElements = XElement.Parse(strXMLResult);
                    string strTemperature =
                        weatherElements.Element("Temperature").Value;
                    string strWind = weatherElements.Element("Wind").Value;
    ```

```
                            lblTemperature.Text = "Current Temperature: "+ strTemperature;
                            lblWind.Text = "Current Wind: " + strWind;
                        }
                    }

                );
            }

            private void GetWeatherSubject()
            {
                if (_weather == null)
                {
                    _weather =
Observable.FromEvent<svcWeather.GetWeatherCompletedEventArgs>(weatherClient,
"GetWeatherCompleted");
                }
            }
```

8. Create the `WireUpKeyEvents` function that defines an Observable collection from the KeyUp events, and create a subscription to that collection by adding the following code:

```
            private void WireUpKeyEvents()
            {
                var keys = Observable.FromEvent<KeyEventArgs>(txtCityName,
                    "KeyUp").Throttle(TimeSpan.FromSeconds(1)).DistinctUntilChanged();
                keys.ObserveOn(Deployment.Current.Dispatcher).Subscribe(evt =>
                {
                    if (txtCityName.Text.Length >= 5)
                    {
                        WireUpWeatherEvents();
                        weatherClient.GetWeatherAsync(txtCityName.Text, conCountry);
                    }
                });
            }
```

9. Press F5 to run the application. You should see a screen prompting you to enter a name of the U.S. city for which you'd like to retrieve the current weather. If you enter your city name, you should get a reasonable estimate of your current weather and wind conditions. Figure 18-11 shows sample output for the New York area.

Figure 18-11. Sample output of the WeatherRx application for New York City

Let's spend some more time dissecting the tools you used to build this application. First you used Rx.NET to create an Observable collection from the asynchronous responses to the weather web service calls. You used the following statement to create that collection:

```
_weather = Observable.FromEvent<svcWeather.GetWeatherCompletedEventArgs>(weatherClient,
    "GetWeatherCompleted");
```

You then defined an Observer for this data source, so that when the data is pushed from the web service to Observers, you take action by displaying that data in the UI.

Next you created an Observable collection of the KeyUp events in the txtCityName text box and created an Observer for that collection. As a result, whenever users pause their typing for one second, the Observer on the keys data source validates whether five or more letters have been entered in the City Name field. Then it goes ahead and calls the function GetWeatherAsync, which in turn invokes an asynchronous request to the weather web service.

It's important to note the asynchronous nature of all these calls—if you had other functionality built into the application, you could continue using it while all the asynchronous requests complete. As stated several times in this chapter, *asynchronous processing* is an area that Rx.NET was specifically designed to address.

If you have done some form of asynchronous programming prior to Rx.NET, you can certainly appreciate the single line of code just shown. Prior to Rx.NET, two methods were provided for the implementation of an asynchronous method design pattern in .NET. The first method started the computation, and the second method acquired the results of the computation. If there was more than one asynchronous operation, even just the simple ones illustrated in the weather example, managing those multiple methods quickly became a headache. The fact that Rx.NET also attempts to parallelize asynchronous requests across all available cores is a hefty bonus to an already generous benefit package of clarity and powerful querying of Observers.

Handling Errors in Rx.NET

In the world of asynchronous programming, and especially in the world of distributed asynchronous programming, errors are a fact of life and should be expected. Rx.NET Observers provide a separate OnError event handler to deal with any unforeseen errors that may arise. For instance, to make the WeatherRx application more robust, let's add an OnError handler to the weather.Subscribe call. The resulting code looks like this:

```
_weather.ObserveOn(Deployment.Current.Dispatcher)
        .Subscribe(evt =>
        {
            if (evt.EventArgs.Result!= null)
            {
                string strXMLResult = evt.EventArgs.Result;
                XElement weatherElements = XElement.Parse(strXMLResult);
                string strTemperature = weatherElements.Element("Temperature").Value;
                string strWind = weatherElements.Element("Wind").Value;

                lblTemperature.Text = "Current Temperature: " + strTemperature;
                lblWind.Text = "Current Wind: " + strWind;
            }
        },
        ex =>
        {
            Deployment.Current.Dispatcher.BeginInvoke(() => lblStatus.Text = ex.Message);
        }
    );
}
```

Note the somewhat cryptic use of the Deployment.Current.Dispatcher.BeginInvoke statement to get around cross-thread access issues discussed previously (it's a lambda expression, and it uses a lambda expression within its own body). In the preceding code, the OnError handler simply displays the exception text, but there is nothing stopping you from dissecting an error thoroughly and providing a possible corrective action. For instance, if the web service is not available at the address specified, you may retry your call to a different location of the web service. Rx.NET also has the exception-handling operators Catch, Finally, OnErrorResumeNext, and Retry, which aid in recovering from errors. You explore some of these operators in the next section as you examine potential ways of handling intermittently available data connections on phones.

Handling Data-Connection Issues with Rx.NET

On a phone, slow or lost data connections are a fact of everyday life. Ideally, phone applications should detect such issues and provide a recovery mechanism to deal with them.

Two potential ways to deal with slow or lost connectivity on the phone are to let the user decide whether the application should retry what it was doing before the connection timed out or was lost, and to provide an automated retry mechanism.

Rx.NET can aid in both scenarios. Furthermore, Rx.NET includes a special Timeout operation that generates a timeout error if it does not receive data, such as a web service callback, from its Observable in a user-specified interval. Let's look at the Timeout operation in action. Let's change the WireUpWeatherEvents function to time out if it does not get any data for two seconds:

1. Replace the WireUpEvents() function of the WeatherRx application with the following code:

```
private void WireUpWeatherEvents()
{
    GetWeatherSubject();
    _weather.ObserveOn(Deployment.Current.Dispatcher)
        .Timeout(TimeSpan.FromSeconds(2))
        .Subscribe(evt =>
        {
            if (evt.EventArgs.Result!= null)
            {
                string strXMLResult = evt.EventArgs.Result;
                XElement weatherElements = XElement.Parse(strXMLResult);
                string strTemperature =
                    weatherElements.Element("Temperature").Value;
                string strWind = weatherElements.Element("Wind").Value;

                lblTemperature.Text = "Current Temperature: " +
                    strTemperature;
                lblWind.Text = "Current Wind: " + strWind;
            }
        },
        ex =>
        {
            Deployment.Current.Dispatcher.BeginInvoke(() => lblStatus.Text =
                ex.Message);
        }
    );
}
```

Run the application, and notice how, after two seconds, it immediately times out and displays the timeout exception text on the emulator. What happened? You did not even get a chance to specify the city name!

Your code needs a little *refactoring*, or changing around. In the code so far, you subscribed to the web service's events immediately on application launch; since you did not get any data two seconds after the launch of the application, that subscription timed out. The change you need to make is to subscribe to the web service's events right before you invoke that web service. However, you have to be careful to create this subscription just once.

2. Remove the call to WireUpWeatherEvents from the MainPage constructor, and place it in the WireUpKeyEvents function, like so:

```
private void WireUpKeyEvents()
{
    var keys = Observable.FromEvent<KeyEventArgs>(txtCityName,
      "KeyUp").Throttle(TimeSpan.FromSeconds(1)).DistinctUntilChanged();
    keys.ObserveOn(Deployment.Current.Dispatcher).Subscribe(evt =>
    {
        if (txtCityName.Text.Length >= 5)
        {
            WireUpWeatherEvents();
            weatherClient.GetWeatherAsync(txtCityName.Text, conCountry);
        }
    });
}
```

Now the timeout feature should work properly. Notice, however, that it will most likely take slightly more than two seconds to return a valid response from the Weather service. (In fact, due to the load on that service, you may need to increase the timeout value to as high as 300 seconds.)

Rx.NET also provides a Retry method that optionally takes a parameter for the number of times to retry to resubscribe to the Observable collection. If you don't specify that parameter, Rx.NET tries to resubscribe to the Observable collection indefinitely. One way to deal with an absent or slow connection is to retry the subscription two or three times and then, if unsuccessful, give the user the option to either retry once more or cancel. You see how to give the user this option in the next section.

Revising WeatherRx to Manage Slow Data Connections

To modify the WeatherRx application, you first add buttons to the UI to allow the user either to retry the failed connection or to exit gracefully. Then you add code to the application to react to the events on these new User Interface elements.

To add the new elements to the WeatherRx UI, do the following:

1. Open MainPage.xaml, and add two buttons right below the lblStatus textblock, as shown in Figure 18-12. Name the first button btnRetry, and set its Content property to Retry. Name the second button btnQuit, and set its Content property to Quit. Set the Visibility of both buttons to Collapsed.

Figure 18-12. Weather application with error-recovery elements

On retry, you re-create the Observable connection to the weather web service, if it's needed, and then invoke the web service again.

2. Double-click the Retry button, and add the following handler code to the btnRetry_Click function:

```
private void btnRetry_Click(object sender, RoutedEventArgs e)
{
    btnQuit.Visibility = System.Windows.Visibility.Collapsed;
    btnRetry.Visibility = System.Windows.Visibility.Collapsed;
    lblStatus.Text = "";

    WireUpWeatherEvents();
    weatherClient.GetWeatherAsync(txtCityName.Text, conCountry);
}
```

If the user selects Quit, let's simply hide the buttons and the exception text.

3. Double-click the Quit button, and add the following code to the btnQuit_Click function:

```
private void btnQuit_Click(object sender, RoutedEventArgs e)
{
    btnQuit.Visibility = System.Windows.Visibility.Collapsed;
    btnRetry.Visibility = System.Windows.Visibility.Collapsed;
    lblStatus.Text = "";
}
```

Finally, you need to ensure that there is only one subscription to the weather web service at any given time.

4. Change the WireUpWeatherEvents method to look like the following listing. Notice how the timeout value is now set to a more reasonable 30 seconds.

```
private void WireUpWeatherEvents()
{
  GetWeatherSubject();
  _weather.ObserveOn(Deployment.Current.Dispatcher)
      .Timeout(TimeSpan.FromSeconds(30))
      .Subscribe(evt =>
      {
          if (evt.EventArgs.Result!= null)
          {
              string strXMLResult = evt.EventArgs.Result;
              XElement weatherElements = XElement.Parse(strXMLResult);
              string strTemperature =weatherElements.Element("Temperature").Value;
              string strWind = weatherElements.Element("Wind").Value;

              lblTemperature.Text = "Current Temperature: " + strTemperature;
              lblWind.Text = "Current Wind: " + strWind;
          }
      },
      ex =>
      {
          Deployment.Current.Dispatcher.BeginInvoke(() => lblStatus.Text =
              ex.Message);
          Deployment.Current.Dispatcher.BeginInvoke(() =>
              btnQuit.Visibility=System.Windows.Visibility.Visible);
          Deployment.Current.Dispatcher.BeginInvoke(() => btnRetry.Visibility =
              System.Windows.Visibility.Visible);
      }
  );
}
```

This example illustrates one approach to handling connection issues on Windows Phone devices: you specify a timeout period and, if you don't get a response in that period, you prompt the user to retry or to quit.

Handling Multiple Concurrent Requests with Rx.NET

So far, the weather application that you created is sending as many requests for weather data as the user types in city names. However, the order in which the data comes back from the weather web service is not guaranteed. For example, if the user first types in **New York** and then types in **Boston**, the weather results for New York City may come in behind Boston, yet the user would not realize that they're seeing New York's weather when the search term *Boston* remains on the screen. It would be great if a solution gave the application the power to cancel out all weather requests that occurred prior to the latest one. In this case, for example, a request for New York weather would be canceled as soon as the request for Boston weather was made.

Rx.NET provides such a solution. Two operators in Rx.NET—TakeUntil() and Switch—allow for cancellation of operations that occur prior to the latest operation and are still *in flight*, or are still pending the return values. Through the use of an elegant LINQ query, these operators tie together Observable collections, as you see shortly. But first there is some bad news: in the current implementation of .NET Framework on Windows Phone, it is impossible to link the beginning of the asynchronous SOAP web service invocation to the end of that invocation. The root of the problem is the exclusion of the CreateChannel method implementation in the Windows Communication Foundation libraries on Windows Phone. Microsoft had to slim down and optimize the .NET Framework on the Windows Phone, and the loss of this method for now seems to be due to those optimization efforts.

Nevertheless, the technique for canceling in-flight requests still applies to the clients with the full .NET Framework installed (Windows Forms and WPF applications) and to the Silverlight platform. Perhaps in the not-too-distant future, this technique will also be available on Windows Phone; therefore, it is useful to learn its basics in this last section of this chapter.

For the weather application, you fake the technique of canceling those requests by creating a new Observable collection for the weather service each time a user types in a new city name. Note, however, that the Observable subscriptions that you create listen for any completed weather service requests, and not the specific ones. In other words, your implementation of canceling in-flight requests on Windows Phone is currently incomplete and not reliable due to the aforementioned limitation in the current implementation of the Windows Phone framework—at present, you can't link the beginning of the SOAP web service call to the end of that service call on this platform.

To make the cancellation of operations on the Observable collections possible while those operations are in flight, you change the code around to expose Observable collections to LINQ queries. Follow these steps to make operation cancellation possible:

1. At the top of the MainPage class (right above the constructor), paste in the following code to declare a module-level Observable collection for the KeyUp events of the City Name text box:

    ```
    IObservable<IEvent<KeyEventArgs>> _keys;
    ```

2. Expose the Observables for both the KeyUp event of the City Name text box and the web service callback by adding the following two methods to your code:

    ```
    private IObservable<IEvent<GetWeatherCompletedEventArgs>> GetWeatherSubject()
    {
        return
                Observable.FromEvent<svcWeather.GetWeatherCompletedEventArgs>
                (weatherClient, "GetWeatherCompleted");
    }

    private void GetKeys()
    {
     if (_keys == null)
     {
         _keys = Observable.FromEvent<KeyEventArgs>(txtCityName,
                 "KeyUp").Throttle(TimeSpan.FromSeconds(1)).DistinctUntilChanged();
     }
    ```

```
    }
```

The magic that makes the cancellations work appears in the next code snippet. Pay particularly close attention to the LINQ query; it establishes the relationship between the Observable collection for the KeyUp events and the Observable collection for the web service callbacks. Note that, had Windows Phone framework supported what is referred to as the Asynchronous pattern for web service calls (with the use of BeginXXX/EndXXX methods), you could have established a direct relationship between key sequences and web service invocations. However, with the following code, you have only a loose or indirect relationship between those two, since each subscription listens for any and all responses from the weather web service and not just for specific ones. Right after the LINQ statement, a Switch() operator instructs the application to dispose of the old subscription to the weather web service once there is a new key sequence awaiting in the keys Observable collection.

3. Add the following code to the application:

```
private void WireUpWeatherEvents()
{
    GetKeys();
    var latestWeather = (from term in _keys
            select GetWeatherSubject()
                .Finally(() =>
                {
                    Deployment.Current.Dispatcher.BeginInvoke(() =>
                        Debug.WriteLine("Disposed of prior subscription"));
                })
    ).Switch();

    latestWeather.ObserveOnDispatcher()
        .Subscribe(evt =>
        {
            if (evt.EventArgs.Result!= null)
            {
                string strXMLResult = evt.EventArgs.Result;
                XElement weatherElements = XElement.Parse(strXMLResult);
                string strTemperature =weatherElements.Element("Temperature").Value;
                string strWind = weatherElements.Element("Wind").Value;

                lblTemperature.Text = "Current Temperature: " + strTemperature;
                lblWind.Text = "Current Wind: " + strWind;
            }
        },
        ex => {
                Deployment.Current.Dispatcher.BeginInvoke(() =>lblStatus.Text =
                    ex.Message);
            }
    );
}
```

Notice the .Finally statement in the code. Its purpose is to print a "Disposed of prior subscription" message into the Output windows when one Observable collection is being removed and replaced with the newer one. This occurs when there is a new event in the _keys module-level Observable collection.

Finally, you need to make some minor changes to the `WireUpKeyEvents` function: namely, the Observable sequence generation for the `KeyUp` event on the city name moves into a separate `GetKeys` method.

4. Replace the `WiredUpKeyEvents()` function with the following code:

```
private void WireUpKeyEvents()
{
    GetKeys();
    keys.ObserveOn(Deployment.Current.Dispatcher).Subscribe(evt =>
    {
        if (txtCityName.Text.Length >= 5)
        {
            weatherClient.GetWeatherAsync(txtCityName.Text, conCountry);
        }
    });
}
```

You are now ready to run the application.

5. Press F5, and observe that the application behavior is virtually unchanged from the previous examples: you still type in the city name and receive weather information for that city. However, behind the scenes, notice the messages printed in the Output window indicating that Observable sequences are being disposed of in accordance with the new data (new city names typed in) available in the key sequence Observable collection.

Perhaps in the very near future you will see a `CreateChannel` method available on the Windows Phone platform. Once that happens, you could very easily enhance the previous example with the code linking the beginning and end of an asynchronous web service call through the `Observable.FromAsyncPattern` method. For now, however, you can still take advantage of this extremely powerful feature of Rx.NET in Silverlight (on the desktop client) or on clients running the full version of .NET Framework (unlike Windows Phone, which runs a portion of it, or .NET Compact Framework).

Summary

This chapter provided a general overview of Reactive Extensions for .NET and its implementation of the Observer pattern. You built two applications that demonstrated the features of Rx.NET, including event representations as Observable data sources and seamless concurrent asynchronous processing and error handling. You learned about Marble Diagrams and some of the main design guidelines for building Rx.NET applications. You observed techniques for managing unreliable data links and the principles of cancelling in-flight operations using the Rx.NET framework.

As concurrent asynchronous programming becomes the norm, Rx.NET provides a powerful framework for programming that norm, including programming for the cloud. This chapter has touched lightly on the subject of Rx.NET, but you should have gained an appreciation for this technology and, ideally, will take the initiative to learn (and, most important, practice) Rx.NET development techniques on your own.

In the next and final chapter of this book, you learn how to make your Windows Phone applications more secure. You learn about the common threats to mobile devices and the steps you must take to protect yourself and your customers from unwanted and potentially harmful attention.

CHAPTER 19

Security

Because everything about the design and operation of Windows Phone targets consumers, it is only natural that Microsoft has carefully thought through the ways to protect Windows Phone users from both intentional and unintentional harm. Windows Phone ships with a compelling set of built-in security features that strive to accomplish that goal.

The capabilities of the Windows Phone platform allow data to be protected both in transit and on the device. Because of the centralized application certification process, consumers gain confidence that no malicious applications will be downloaded and installed on their devices. Moreover, should the phone be lost or stolen, each device comes with a free web-based tool that allows the user to control the Windows Phone device remotely, including locking and wiping all data on that phone.

In this chapter, you will learn how the Windows Phone Marketplace certification process acts as a gatekeeper, allowing only legitimate applications to be present on the device. Then you'll look at the ways you can ensure that your Windows Phone application can receive, transmit, and store sensitive data in a secure manner. Finally, you'll take a look at the free support for remote lock and data wipe that Microsoft provides to protect lost or stolen Windows Phone devices.

We will lead you through an analysis of Windows Phone security features in the following four domains: application security, network security, data security, and device security. Also, you will learn how to use the tools the Windows Phone platform has to address the specific security concerns associated with each domain.

Understanding Application Security

In an ideal world, all Windows Phone applications would come from legitimate sources and behave like good citizens. However, experience shows us that many applications break the rules and that safeguards must be put in place to prevent malicious behavior. On the application security front, the Windows Phone platform includes safeguards to verify the identity of the author of the application and sandboxes the execution of each mobile application. In the next few sections, you will explore these safeguards in detail.

The Windows Phone Marketplace

For a moment, let's travel a couple of decades back in time. The early years of Windows XP were not happy ones at Microsoft. The whole world was upset with the company for allowing its operating system to be exploited by multiple malicious programs. Even though Windows XP shipped with safeguards that could prevent these problems, the activation of the safeguards was left up to the user, and that activation rarely happened. What Microsoft quickly learned from that experience was that it must take on the responsibility to protect its user base from both known and potential harm.

Because mobile devices contain huge amounts of personal information and, by their nature, are frequently lost or misplaced, application monitoring is all the more necessary. For Microsoft to assume this responsibility for Windows Phone applications, it must have as much control as possible over the applications built and deployed onto its platform, while still encouraging developer creativity as much as possible. To facilitate this dual goal of simultaneously being autocratic and democratic, Microsoft created the Windows Phone Marketplace. The Windows Phone Marketplace is the single online distribution point for all Windows Phone applications. The objectives of the Windows Phone Marketplace and the way it achieves those objectives are described in the following sections.

Non-Repudiation: Proof of the Integrity and Origin of Data

The first objective of the Windows Phone Marketplace is to confirm the identity of an application's author. In the Internet era, attempts to benefit from a false identity are extremely common—every day, millions of e-mails claim to come from legitimate sources, when in fact they do not. In a similar fashion, without a centralized approval mechanism, any malicious Windows Phone application could claim to be genuine and capture the user's personal information. In terms of software security, the concept of *non-repudiation* refers to the guarantee that the application indeed comes from the source it claims to have come from.

On the Windows Phone platform, the origin and safety of applications are confirmed during application certification, a required step for all Windows Phone applications. (Note that the application certification process is covered in an earlier chapter of this book.) However, since application certification is very important, we are deliberately repeating that information here to save you the effort of flipping back and forth. During application certification, the developer submits his or her application to the Windows Phone Marketplace and pays a fee, at which point Microsoft runs a series of automated and manual tests to confirm the application's safety and, to some extent, its reliability.

Currently, no application can be loaded onto the phone without going through the certification process. As we discuss later in the chapter, it is possible to have an application that is not visible in the Windows Phone Marketplace (via a feature of Windows Phone called *deep linking*); however, that application still has to pass all the rigors of the certification process. In the future, this policy may be revisited to allow enterprise customers to bypass the Windows Phone Marketplace in favor of their own custom enterprise application store. However, at the time of this writing, this is only a possibility.

All Windows Phone developers must sign up for the marketplace and provide legitimate proof of their identity before any of the applications they create are available for installation on users' phones. Once their identity is verified, application developers receive a code-signing certificate. This digital certificate verifies that the application was created by the specified company or individual, fulfilling the concept of non-repudiation mentioned previously.

Intellectual Property Protection

Software piracy is a huge problem affecting both the giants of software development, such as Microsoft, and small shops trying to build mobile applications. To help safeguard applications from piracy, Microsoft requires that a valid application license issued by the Windows Phone Marketplace be present on the Windows Phone device before it allows the execution of an application. This means that, even if somebody figures out how to load an application onto the device without going through the Windows Phone Marketplace, the application will not run since the license key for that application will not be available.

Safe Application Behavior

The Windows Phone Marketplace application approval process includes a suite of certification tests to prohibit risky applications from being loaded onto users' phones. Risky applications may contain malware or viruses themselves, or they may contain code constructs that could allow malicious code execution.

All applications submitted to the Windows Phone Marketplace will be subject to malicious software screening, which will attempt to confirm that applications are free from viruses and malware. After successful completion of those tests, additional tests are performed to confirm that the application was written using only type-safe Microsoft Intermediate Language (MSIL) code. Writing applications in MSIL avoids public enemy #1: *software buffer overruns,* as described in *Writing Secure Code,* by Michael Howard and David LeBlanc (Microsoft Press, 2001). In addition, an application must not implement any security-critical code (the Windows Phone application platform prohibits an application from running security-critical code). We will revisit MSIL and briefly discuss security-critical code on mobile devices at the end of this chapter.

To get a better idea of how the Windows Phone Marketplace submission process helps improve the security of a user's device, let's walk through the steps involved in submitting an application to the Marketplace.

Submitting an Application to the Windows Phone Marketplace

In this example, you will prepare a package to submit your application to the Windows Phone Marketplace and learn the steps involved in successfully publishing an application to the Marketplace, beginning with the creation of a XAP file. Let's get started.

Generating a XAP Submission File

The submission file that the Windows Phone Marketplace requires is a XAP file that gets generated when the Windows Phone application is built. A XAP file is a zipped file containing all the elements an application needs to run. To generate a XAP file, you must first build your application, as described in the following steps:

1. Open your Windows Phone application project inside Visual Studio Express for Windows Phone.

2. Set the Solution Configuration option to Release, as shown in Figure 19-1.

3. In Solution Explorer, right-click the name of the solution and select Build. At this point, if the build succeeds, Visual Studio will create the `ProjectName.xap` file, where `ProjectName` is the name of your solution.

4. Locate the `ProjectName.xap` file you created in step 3. Open Windows Explorer and navigate to the project's directory and the `bin/Release/` folder. You should find a file there named `ProjectName.xap`. This is the file that you will upload to the marketplace.

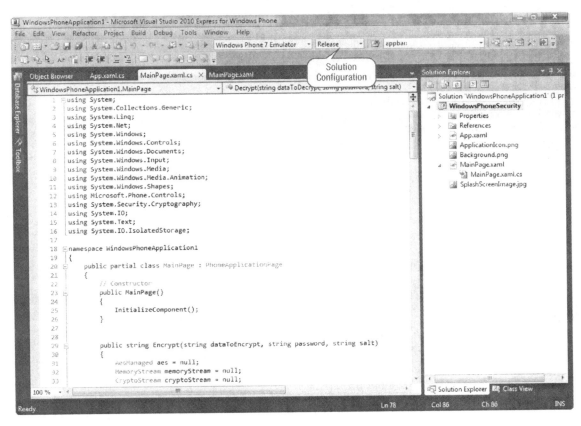

Figure 19-1. Before deploying your application, make sure to set Solution Configuration to Release.

The next step is to log in to the Windows Phone Marketplace and submit the XAP file you just created.

Uploading the XAP File to the Marketplace

Before uploading files to the Windows Phone Marketplace, you must create Windows Phone Marketplace login credentials at http://create.msdn.com/. To do this, once you open the Marketplace web site, click the "Join to submit your apps & games" link and follow the wizard to create your username and password for the Marketplace. With your login credentials created, follow the step-by-step guide listed here to submit your application to the Marketplace:

1. Log in to the Windows Phone Marketplace (http://create.msdn.com/) and create a new application submission.

2. When prompted, locate the XAP file that you created in the previous section (remember, it's in the bin/Release/ folder of the project's directory) and follow the instructions to upload it to the Marketplace.

3. Enter a description for your application, select its category, and upload an icon for it.

4. Next, choose the countries in which you would like your application to be available and set the pricing.

5. While you are busy entering application details (description, category, and pricing), the Marketplace is at work validating the XAP file and confirming that it can be passed on for further testing of its reliability and security.

6. If the basic XAP file validation fails, you will get a failure notification and you will have to start the process over.

7. If the validation succeeds, you will be presented with a screen that lets you make your application available to customers right away once it passes certification, or wait until you decide it's time to publish.

8. The automated process within the Windows Phone Marketplace opens up the submitted XAP file and updates the application manifest file (WMAppManifest.xml) with a unique product identifier and to which hub on the Windows Phone device (for example, the Media + Video hub) this application belongs. In addition, a header file, WMAppPRHeader.xml, is created. It will be used to protect the digital rights to your application. Finally, an additional update to the application manifest file listing all of the security capabilities of the application is performed, and the application is repackaged into a new XAP file. This new XAP file is then deployed to the actual Windows Phone device at the Marketplace for certification testing.

Certification testing consists of both manual and automated verification that the application complies with the rules set by Microsoft regarding the content, security, performance, and reliability of Windows Phone applications. One of the rules states that the application must use only well-documented Windows Phone API methods, further ensuring that an application will not exhibit malicious behavior. If an application violates any of these provisions, it will not be published, and you will get a failure report with the details of the problem-causing behavior.

If the application successfully passes the certification tests, the XAP file will be signed and it will become available for installation from the Windows Phone Marketplace according to the option you selected in step 5.

■ **Note** When you update your application, you will have to go through the same certification steps as you did for the original application. Review Chapter 5 for more information.

Sandboxed Execution and the Execution Manager

Sandboxed execution refers to the concept that each application runs in its own isolated environment, or sandbox, so that it has no access to applications running in different sandboxes on the same device. The Windows Phone platform implements this concept of sandboxed execution. Applications running on the same Windows Phone device are isolated from each other and must communicate with services provided by the Windows Phone platform by using a well-defined, standard mechanism. System files and resources are shielded from user applications. To store and retrieve application-specific configuration data, applications must use Isolated Storage, which is designed to be protected from access by any application other than the currently running one. For in-depth information on working with Isolated Storage, please refer to Chapter 13 of this book.

To ensure security and responsiveness of the Windows Phone platform further, Microsoft built in additional safety provisions. These provisions include the use of the Execution Manager, as well as granting only the rights an application absolutely requires to function.

The *Execution Manager* monitors application resource usage in accordance with certain defined conventions. For instance, the Execution Manager may terminate an application in the background if it deems that an application in the foreground is not responsive. Similarly, the Execution Manager may dismiss an application if it makes an excessive number of requests for phone resources.

The Windows Phone application platform also tries to minimize the number of privileges granted to an application. For instance, if an application does not require the use of the location services library, Windows Phone will create a custom execution environment for the application that does not include the rights to that library. This way, the number of potential exploits (or *attack surfaces*, as they are referred to in the computer security industry) against the application is minimized.

Private Application Distribution Options

With the release of Windows Phone 7.5, developers gained the ability not to list their applications in the Marketplace but rather to make them available to a set of beta users within a given organization. The way this is accomplished is via a deep-linking process, where an application can only be downloaded by using a unique URL obtained during the application certification process. The application is not discoverable via searches in the Marketplace. This protection from public distribution is not enough in itself, since anybody who obtains the URL would be able to install the application on their device. In addition to deep-linking, as a best practice, applications that are not intended for public distribution should programmatically implement security mechanisms that restrict access to a certain group of people.

Implementing Network Security

If your application accesses sensitive data over a network, it is critical that this data be encrypted during transit from the remote location to the Windows Phone device. Similarly, if an application you are trying to access on Windows Phone requires authentication, it is important to implement a secure authentication mechanism between the mobile device and that application. The Windows Phone platform allows you to accomplish both of these objectives. Any time you have to transmit sensitive data from a remote location, you should use the *Secure Sockets Layer (SSL)* protocol, an industry standard for encrypting data. If your environment requires secure authentication, it is possible to use digital certificates on a Windows Phone device for that authentication, eliminating the need for usernames and passwords.

In the next sections, you will walk through establishing SSL connections and configuring a certificate for secure authentication on a Windows Phone device.

Securing Connections with SSL

SSL protocol is a sophisticated way of securing connections between the client (Windows Phone device) and the cloud service, and it utilizes the concepts of asymmetric cryptography and certification authority (CA) hierarchies. When a Windows Phone device initiates a secure connection to the remote service, it requests that service's certificate. That certificate is checked, and the CA that issued the certificate is determined. Once the CA of the certificate is known, the Windows Phone client then checks its own installed list of certification authorities. If it finds a CA in its list, that implies that a trust relationship between the Windows Phone device and the CA has been previously established and that a secure connection between the phone and the remote server can be created.

Windows Phone devices come with several CAs preinstalled. This means that, most of the time, establishing an SSL connection will be a seamless experience. As long as the remote service obtained its certificate from a very well-known CA (such as VeriSign, for example), SSL connections can be created both from Internet Explorer on the phone and from your application code. The following example demonstrates how to test if you can establish a secure connection to the remote server (PayPal) that has a certificate issued by a well-known CA (VeriSign).

Testing and Opening an SSL Connection

In this brief example, you will test if you can establish a secure connection to a remote server, and then you will write a small Windows Phone application that programmatically loads secure content from the PayPal web site.

1. The quickest way to test whether a connection to a secure web site can be established is to open up Internet Explorer in the Windows Phone emulator or on a Windows Phone device, and type the URL of a secure remote server. Launch the Windows Phone emulator by clicking Start ➤ All Programs ➤ Windows Phone Developer Tools ➤ Windows Phone Emulator. Once the emulator loads, click the Internet Explorer icon and type in `https://www.paypal.com` to go to the secure PayPal site. You should see the main screen of the PayPal web site.

■ **Tip** It may get quite tiresome having to press all of the keyboard buttons in the emulator. To enable the use of the computer keyboard in the emulator window, you can press the PgUp key once the emulator loads. To discontinue using the keyboard in the emulator, press the PgDn key.

---

2. Now you will create a small Windows Phone application that will access the PayPal site via a secure connection. You could access any secure remote service in a similar manner, but only if that service has a certificate issued by a CA that the Windows Phone device trusts. In the next section of this chapter, you will go through creating, exporting, and installing the self-signed certificates, which is a bit more involved. As usual, launch Visual Studio 2010 Express for Windows Phone and create a new Windows Phone application project. Name that project `SSLConnection` and click OK. `MainPage.xaml` is presented in the designer.

3. From the toolbox, drag and drop the WebBrowser control onto the design surface. Make the width and height of that control the full width and height of the available design surface on `MainPage.xaml`.

4. Switch to code view (right-click `MainPage.xaml` and select View Code) and add the following code to the `MainPage()` constructor This code will create an `HttpWebRequest` object, register the callback function for that object (which you will write in the next section), and create a request to retrieve the contents of `www.paypal.com` securely.

```
string pageURL = "https://www.paypal.com";
HttpWebRequest request = (HttpWebRequest)WebRequest.Create(pageURL);
request.Method = "GET";
request.BeginGetResponse(HandleResponse, request);
```

5. Write the `HandleResponse` callback function for the request. This function will display the contents of whatever was returned as a result of the previous request to `https://www.paypal.com`. Note the use of the WebBrowser control, which was discussed in detail in previous chapters of this book. Several other concepts, such as the use of the `Dispatcher.BeginInvoke` function to get to the UI thread, were illustrated previously as well. The following code focuses on how to access a secure site.

```
void HandleResponse(IAsyncResult result)
{
    StreamReader reader = null;
    HttpWebResponse httpResponse =
        (HttpWebResponse)(((HttpWebRequest)result.AsyncState).EndGetResponse(result));
    reader = new StreamReader(httpResponse.GetResponseStream(), Encoding.UTF8);

    string pageResponse = reader.ReadToEnd();
    Dispatcher.BeginInvoke(() => webBrowser1.NavigateToString(pageResponse));
}
```

6. Press F5 to run the application. You should see the PayPal page displayed in the web browser window.

As you can see from the previous example, establishing a secure connection to the remote service is fairly straightforward if a remote service has a certificate issued by a major CA with whom Windows Phone has an existing trust relationship. Just remember to use the `https` protocol instead of `http` when accessing a remote Web service securely. But certificates issued by a major CA can be expensive and may not be necessary if all users of the remote service trust that the service is legitimate. In addition, you may want to experiment or test your secure service without spending a lot of money on the certificates. Self-signed SSL certificates offer the same degree of data protection in transit (data is encrypted using SSL), without the expense of using the CA. There is a slight administrative overhead in issuing and installing those certificates, but you will easily tackle it in a few steps in the next example.

Creating a Self-Signed Certificate

There are three steps to enabling the use of self-signed certificates on a Windows Phone device:

1. You have to create a self-signed certificate.

2. You have to export that certificate for installation on the mobile device.

3. You have to install that certificate on the Windows Phone device.

Creating and exporting the self-signed certificate occur on the server where the secure service resides. Installing the certificate, of course, happens on each device that will need to establish a secure connection to the service using a self-signed certificate.

Internet Information Services (IIS) is the web server software written by Microsoft. IIS has evolved significantly over the years, and the current version as of this writing is IIS 7.5. With IIS 7.5, creating self-signed certificates and enabling SSL by using those certificates is much easier than with previous versions of IIS. IIS 7.5 comes with Windows 7 by default, but you may still need to configure or install it via Control Panel ➤ Programs and Features ➤ Turn Windows Features On or Off. The following example assumes that you are using IIS 7.5 on a Windows 7 machine. The example also assumes that both the server and the Windows Phone client (the emulator) reside on the same machine.

4. Open the IIS Manager by clicking Start ➤ Control Panel ➤ Administrative Tools ➤ Internet Information Services (IIS) Manager.

5. Create a new web site by right-clicking the Sites node on the left and choosing Add Web Site. Name the site WP7Server, and fill in the rest of the web site properties, as shown in Figure 19-2.

■ **Note** The physical path setting for the new site on your computer may certainly be something other than what is shown in Figure 19-2, but be sure to make the Port setting something other than the default 80 (note how it is set to 8888 in the figure); otherwise IIS might complain that port 80 is already taken.

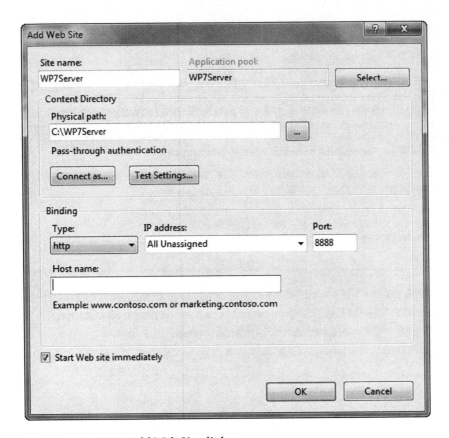

Figure 19-2. IIS 7.5 Add Web Site dialog

6. Next, you will issue a self-signed certificate. Click the root machine node on the left, and then click the Server Certificates node, as shown in Figure 19-3. This should bring up a dialog listing all of the certificates currently registered on the machine.

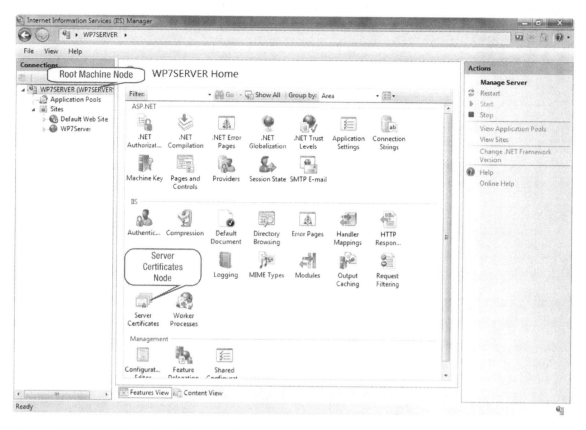

Figure 19-3. *IIS 7.5 Server Certificates node*

7. Click the Create Self-Signed Certificate link on the right-hand side of the dialog. Then specify a name for that certificate when prompted—for example, wp7cert.

8. Next you will enable SSL on the new web site that you created. To do this, you will need to create a binding of that web site to the https protocol. In the list of sites, click WP7Server and then click Bindings on the right-hand side, as illustrated in Figure 19-4.

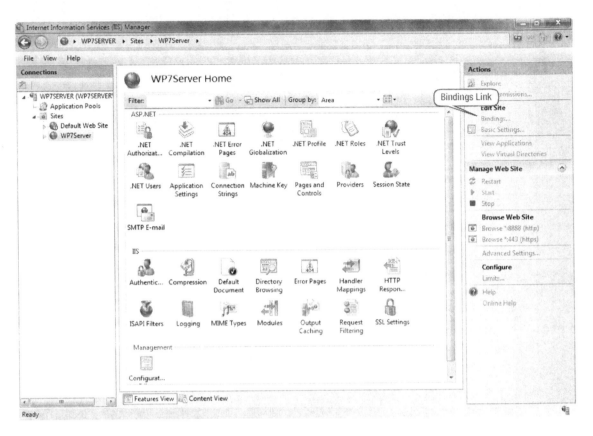

Figure 19-4. Web site bindings link

9. To create an https binding for the site so that traffic to and from the site can be
    encrypted using SSL, click Add Binding. When the dialog shown in Figure 19-5
    comes up, select the https-type binding and select the wp7cert certificate from
    the certificates list. This certificate will be used to encrypt traffic between the
    web site and your Windows Phone client application.

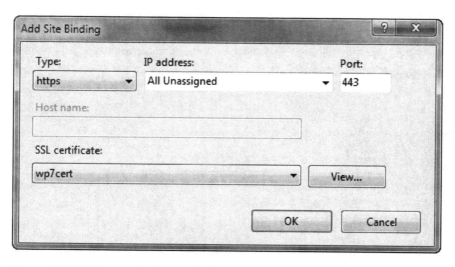

Figure 19-5. Adding an https site binding

10. Finally, you need to create some content to browse on the secure web site. In the real world, this would most likely be done by having the service return some sort of sensitive data, such as financial or security information. However, for this example, you will simply create an HTML file and save it to the server. Open Notepad and paste the following HTML into it:

```
<html>
<h1>Hello, Windows Phone</h1>
</html>
```

11. Save the HTML file you created to the physical path for the web site that you specified in step 2 (referenced in Figure 19-2), and name the file index.html. For example, if you kept your Physical Path setting as C:\WP7Server\ in step 2, then you will save the HTML file as C:\WP7Server\index.html.

■ **Note** You may get a "Permission Denied" error when you try to save the HTML file (we did). If so, make sure that the currently logged-in user has permission to write to that folder and try again.

---

12. You are now ready to test out your self-signed certificate. On your computer, open Internet Explorer and navigate to https:/*machinename*/, where *machinename* is the name of your computer (for example, wp7server). You should see the "Hello, Windows Phone" message in the browser.

13. Now let's test whether you can access secure data from your Windows Phone application. From your Windows Phone emulator, open Internet Explorer and navigate to https:/*machinename*/. The very first time you start up the emulator, you will see a screen like the one shown in Figure 19-6, minus the trust relationship error message. If you click Continue, however, you will be able to establish SSL connections to the web server from both the browser on the Windows Phone device and the application.

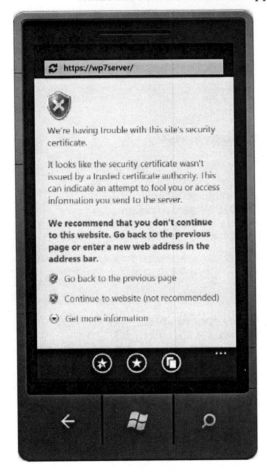

Figure 19-6. Certificate authority error on the Windows Phone emulator

Exporting a Self-Signed Certificate

It is possible to establish secure connections between mobile applications executing on the Windows Phone device and remote services, such as Microsoft Exchange, using self-signed certificates.

The first step in establishing a secure connection with the use of a self-signed certificate between the client and the server is to export the certificate from the server. The next example shows you how to do this; it assumes that you are using Internet Explorer 9 to export certificates, and that you have created a self-signed certificate using the steps in the previous section.

1. On the server, open Internet Explorer and click Tools ➤ Internet Options. If the menu bar with the Tools menu option is not visible, press the Alt key.

2. In the window that comes up, click the Content tab, and then click the Certificates button. In the Certificates dialog that comes up, select the Trusted Root Certification Authorities tab. The self-signed certificate that you created should be listed in this tab. You can scan the Friendly Name column and look for wp7cert, as shown in Figure 19-7.

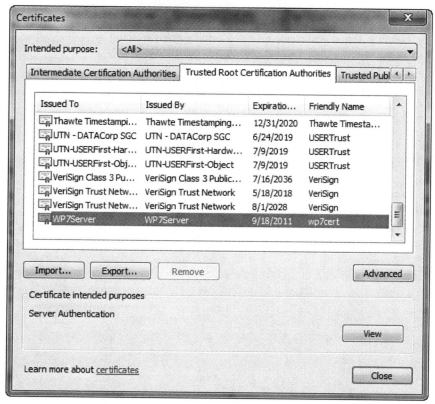

Figure 19-7. List of trusted root CAs, with the self-signed certificate highlighted

3. Click the Export button, and then click Next. On the next screen, select "No, do not export the private key" (the default option), and click Next.

4. On the next screen, choose the DER Encoded binary X.509 format (the default option), and click Next. Finally, select the folder into which to export the certificate, name the file wp7cert.cer, put it somewhere that makes it easy to find later, click Next, and then click Finish. You should get a message notifying you that the export was successful.

With the certificate exported, you are now ready to finalize the trust relationship between the Windows Phone device and the server secured by a self-signed certificate. You will do that in the next section.

Installing a Self-Signed Certificate on Windows Phone

The easiest way to install a self-signed certificate on a Windows Phone device or emulator is simply to e-mail the exported certificate file to yourself as an attachment. Then let the built-in Windows Phone features recognize the certificate file and properly install it on the device. The next few steps will guide you through this process.

1. Open or navigate to your e-mail program; for example, if you use Hotmail as your default e-mail service, log in and create an e-mail message to yourself. In that e-mail, add an attachment—the exported self-signed certificate in the wp7cert.cer file you created in the previous example. Send the e-mail to yourself.

2. From the Windows Phone device or emulator, access the e-mail message you just sent. Once you click the wp7cert.cer attachment, Windows Phone should prompt you to open the certificate file. Go ahead and click (or tap) the screen to get the "Install certificate?" prompt shown in Figure 19-8. Then click the Install Certificate button. After the installation, click OK.

3. Finally, from your Windows Phone emulator, open Internet Explorer and navigate to https://machinename/. You should now be able to access the requested web site without being warned that the certificate is invalid.

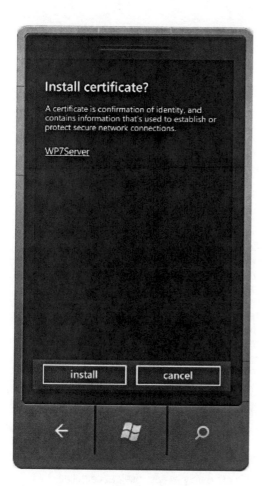

Figure 19-8. Installing certificates via e-mail

You are now familiar with how to secure data in transit from a remote service to a Windows Phone device. You have seen how to use SSL with both trusted third-party certificates from established CAs and self-signed certificates. In the next section, you will take a look at securely storing data on your Windows Phone device by encrypting it.

Implementing Data Security

In this section, you will learn how to secure data that gets stored on a Windows Phone device. While the data in Isolated Storage is sandboxed for each application—that is, an application cannot access the contents of the Isolated Storage of another application—it is still important to encrypt sensitive data stored on the device. Encrypting data makes it impossible for anybody other than the data owner to read that data—something that is especially critical for enterprise users. Windows Phone provides a powerful subset of .NET encryption classes that make data encryption not only possible, but extremely easy on Windows Phone devices. The following data encryption algorithms are supported on Windows Phone:

- AES

- HMACSHA1

- HMACSHA256

- Rfc2898DeriveBytes

- SHA1

- SHA256

As you will see in the next example, many of these algorithms complement each other to provide a robust data encryption strategy for Windows Phone devices. But first let's briefly review the purpose of each of the supported encryption algorithms.

AES (Advanced Encryption Standard) is a symmetric encryption algorithm, which means that it uses the same key (password) to encrypt and decrypt data. Since the key used to encrypt/decrypt data could be easily guessed by iterating through words in a dictionary in an automated manner, an additional secret key is added during the encryption process.

This additional key is called *salt,* and it is usually a random set of bits, such as an employee identification number, that is used to make the AES-encrypted message harder for intruders to decrypt.

HMACSHA1 and *HMACSHA256* algorithms both generate a unique *message authentication code (MAC)* from the data and password supplied. Both algorithms use the same approach to generating a MAC: they take the data and hash it with the secret key using a standard hash function; HMACSHA1 uses SHA1 and HMACSHA256 uses SHA256. The difference between HMACSHA1 and HMACSHA256 lies in the strength of the message generated: HMACSHA1 output is 160 bits long while HMACSHA256 generates results that are 256 bits in length.

Finally, *Rfc2898DeriveBytes* is an algorithm that relies on the HMACSHA1 function to generate a strong key, using the password and salt values supplied, to encrypt and decrypt data.

■ **Note** Do not store password or salt values in application code. It is extremely easy to peek at compiled .NET code using tools such as Ildasm.exe, Red Gate Reflector, or even a simple text editor, and retrieve the value of the password/salt. At the end of this chapter, you will learn how to protect your application code from possible decompilation by obfuscating it; however, even with obfuscation, the password and salt values should never be stored inside application code. Instead, obtain those secret values during an application's runtime, implementing a Web service that communicates with the Windows Phone device and supplies passwords and salt values.

In the first data security example, you will experiment with the HMACSHA1 and HMACSHA256 algorithms to observe the keys that those algorithms generate from the input and password/salt values supplied. In the second example, you will encrypt and decrypt data on the device using the AES algorithm.

Using HMACSHA1 and HMACHSHA256

Both the HMACSHA1 and HMACSHA256 functions are one-way. Once the MAC is generated using either of those functions, it is impossible to recreate the original message from the generated MAC. This makes those functions ideal for storing values of security codes. The only way to produce a match of the MAC on those values is to supply a valid password and security code. The following example demonstrates how to generate HMACSHA1 and HMACSHA256 messages.

Creating a UI

Your application interface will consist of text boxes to accept a message and a password from which to create a MAC, and it will show the MAC generated using both the HMACSHA1 and HMACSHA256 algorithms.

1. Open Visual Studio Express for Windows Phone and create a new project called HMACTest.

2. Make MainPage.xaml look like Figure 19-9. For reference, the XAML of this page is pasted here. (Remember that you can also download the code samples from this book's web site):

```xml
<!--LayoutRoot contains the root grid where all other page content is placed-->
<Grid x:Name="LayoutRoot" Background="Transparent">
 <Grid.RowDefinitions>
     <RowDefinition Height="Auto"/>
     <RowDefinition Height="*"/>
 </Grid.RowDefinitions>

 <!--TitlePanel contains the name of the application and page title-->
 <StackPanel x:Name="TitlePanel" Grid.Row="0" Margin="24,24,0,12">
     <TextBlock x:Name="ApplicationTitle" Text="MY APPLICATION"
      Style="{StaticResource PhoneTextNormalStyle}"/>
     <TextBlock x:Name="PageTitle" Text="HMAC Test" Margin="-3,-8,0,0"
      Style="{StaticResource PhoneTextTitle1Style}"/>
 </StackPanel>

 <!--ContentPanel - place additional content here-->
 <Grid x:Name="ContentGrid" Grid.Row="1">
     <Button Content="Generate" Height="72" HorizontalAlignment="Left"
Margin="149,437,0,0" Name="button1" VerticalAlignment="Top" Width="160" Click="button1_Click"
/>
         <TextBox Height="72" HorizontalAlignment="Left" Margin="149,23,0,0"
          Name="txtMessage" Text="" VerticalAlignment="Top" Width="317" />
         <TextBlock Height="99" HorizontalAlignment="Left" Margin="21,216,0,0"
          Name="textBlock1" Text="TextBlock" VerticalAlignment="Top" Width="445"
          TextWrapping="Wrap" />
         <TextBlock Height="114" HorizontalAlignment="Left" Margin="24,321,0,0"
          Name="textBlock2" Text="TextBlock" VerticalAlignment="Top" Width="442"
          TextWrapping="Wrap" />
         <TextBlock Height="30" HorizontalAlignment="Left" Margin="21,44,0,0"
          Name="textBlock3" Text="Message:" VerticalAlignment="Top" Width="122" />
```

```
            <TextBlock Height="30" HorizontalAlignment="Left" Margin="21,129,0,0"
             Name="textBlock4" Text="Key:" VerticalAlignment="Top" />
            <TextBox Height="72" HorizontalAlignment="Left" Margin="149,101,0,0" Name="txtKey"
             Text="" VerticalAlignment="Top" Width="246" />
        </Grid>
    </Grid>
```

Coding the Application Logic

The next step is to add logic that takes advantage of the cryptography classes on Windows Phone to show MACs.

1. Add the following using directive to the top of the page:

    ```
    using System.Security.Cryptography;
    ```

2. Because you want all of the encryption logic to happen on the button click, add an event handler to the click event of the Generate button. To do that, double-click the Generate button and paste the following code inside the handler. Note how after declaring the HMACSHA1 and HMACSHA256 classes, all of the magic happens in the ComputeHash function, which returns an array of bytes that you convert to the hexadecimal string.

    ```
    string message = txtMessage.Text;
    string key = txtKey.Text;

    System.Text.UTF8Encoding encoding = new System.Text.UTF8Encoding();
    byte[] keyByte = encoding.GetBytes(key);

    HMACSHA1 hmacsha1 = new HMACSHA1(keyByte);
    HMACSHA256 hmacsha256 = new HMACSHA256(keyByte);

    byte[] messageBytes = encoding.GetBytes(message);
    byte[] hashmessage = hmacsha1.ComputeHash(messageBytes);
    textBlock1.Text = ConvertToString(hashmessage);

    hashmessage = hmacsha256.ComputeHash(messageBytes);
    textBlock2.Text = ConvertToString(hashmessage);
    ```

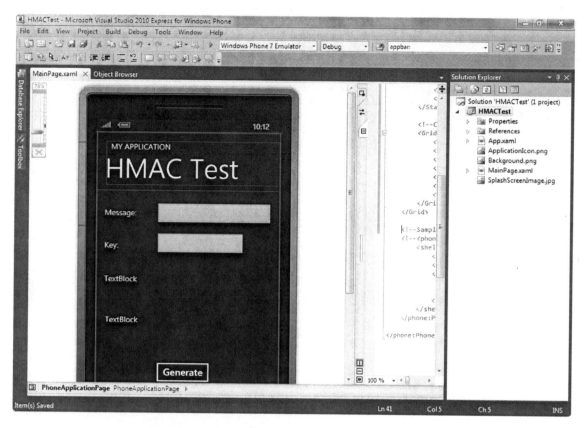

Figure 19-9. UI for the HMACTest application

3. Finally, paste the contents of the ConvertToString helper function, which converts a byte array passed into the hexadecimal string.

```
public static string ConvertToString(byte[] buff)
{
    string sbinary = "";

    for (int i = 0; i < buff.Length; i++)
    {
        //hex-formatted
        sbinary += buff[i].ToString("X2");
    }
    return (sbinary);
}
```

Press F5 to run the application. Enter some message text (for example, "Hello, World") and key (for example, "test"), and observe the MAC values generated using the HMACSHA1 algorithm (the top TextBlock) and the HMACSHA256 algorithm (the bottom TextBlock). Notice that, not only does the length of the MACs differ, but the MACs themselves are completely different from each other.

In the next example, you will encrypt and decrypt data using AES.

Using Rfc2898DeriveBytes and AES to Encrypt Data

To encrypt data from prying eyes on a Windows Phone device, you need a strong encryption mechanism that in turn relies on a strong key to make encryption withstand all of the known attempts to break it. The Rfc2898DeriveBytes algorithm, available on Windows Phone, creates a very strong key for use in AES encryption from the password and salt values passed in. This example demonstrates how to use both of these algorithms in combination on a Windows Phone device.

Creating a UI

The interface will prompt the user for data to encrypt and for a password and salt to use for that encryption. The interface will also have two buttons—one for encryption and the other one for decryption of data.

1. Open Visual Studio Express for Windows Phone and create a new project called AESEncryption.

2. Make the MainPage.xaml page look like the one shown in Figure 19-10. For convenience, the XAML of this page is pasted here:

```xml
<!--LayoutRoot contains the root grid where all other page content is placed-->
<Grid x:Name="LayoutRoot" Background="Transparent">
    <Grid.RowDefinitions>
        <RowDefinition Height="Auto"/>
        <RowDefinition Height="*"/>
    </Grid.RowDefinitions>

    <!--TitlePanel contains the name of the application and page title-->
    <StackPanel x:Name="TitlePanel" Grid.Row="0" Margin="24,24,0,12">
        <TextBlock x:Name="ApplicationTitle" Text="CLASSIFIED" Style="{StaticResource
        PhoneTextNormalStyle}"/>
        <TextBlock x:Name="PageTitle" Text="AES Encryption" Margin="-3,-8,0,0"
        Style="{StaticResource PhoneTextTitle1Style}"/>
    </StackPanel>

    <!--ContentPanel - place additional content here-->
    <Grid x:Name="ContentGrid" Grid.Row="1">
        <TextBox Height="65" HorizontalAlignment="Left" Margin="6,41,0,0"
        Name="txtDataToEncrypt" Text="" VerticalAlignment="Top" Width="462" />
        <TextBlock Height="30" HorizontalAlignment="Left" Margin="20,21,0,0"
        Name="textBlock1" Text="Data to encrypt" VerticalAlignment="Top" Width="419" />
        <TextBox Height="72" HorizontalAlignment="Left" Margin="6,334,0,0"
        Name="txtPassword" Text="" VerticalAlignment="Top" Width="462" />
        <TextBlock Height="30" HorizontalAlignment="Left" Margin="20,310,0,0"
        Name="textBlock2" Text="Password" VerticalAlignment="Top" Width="346" />
        <TextBox Height="72" HorizontalAlignment="Left" Margin="6,426,0,0" Name="txtSalt"
        Text="" VerticalAlignment="Top" Width="462" />
        <TextBlock Height="36" HorizontalAlignment="Left" Margin="21,403,0,0"
        Name="textBlock3" Text="Salt" VerticalAlignment="Top" Width="304" />
```

```
        <Button Content="Encrypt" Height="72" HorizontalAlignment="Left"
         Margin="20,504,0,0" Name="button1" VerticalAlignment="Top" Width="160"
         Click="button1_Click" />
        <Button Content="Decrypt" Height="72" HorizontalAlignment="Left"
         Margin="296,504,0,0" Name="button2" VerticalAlignment="Top" Width="160"
         Click="button2_Click" />
        <TextBlock Height="30" HorizontalAlignment="Left" Margin="24,101,0,0"
         Name="textBlock4" Text="Encrypted Data" VerticalAlignment="Top" Width="432" />
        <TextBox Height="72" HorizontalAlignment="Left" Margin="8,123,0,0"
         Name="txtEncryptedData" Text="" VerticalAlignment="Top" Width="460" />
        <TextBlock Height="27" HorizontalAlignment="Left" Margin="21,197,0,0"
         Name="textBlock5" Text="Decrypted Data" VerticalAlignment="Top" Width="435" />
        <TextBox Height="72" HorizontalAlignment="Left" Margin="13,221,0,0"
         Name="txtDecryptedData" Text="" VerticalAlignment="Top" Width="460" />
    </Grid>
</Grid>
```

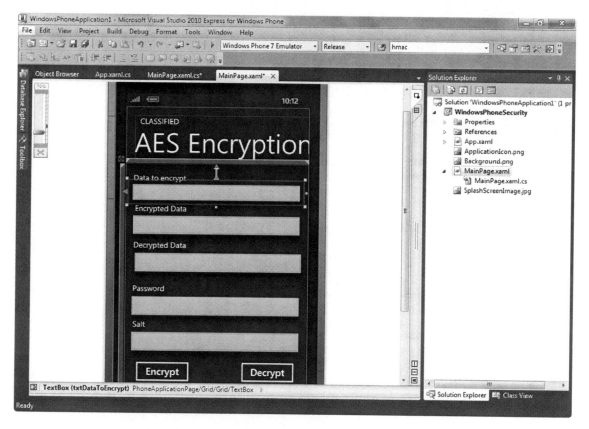

Figure 19-10. UI for the AESEncryption application

Coding the Application Logic

AES encryption in the .NET Framework is implemented via a class called AesManaged. The following code uses this class, together with the Rfc2898DeriveBytes class, to encrypt the data.

1. Add the following using directive to the top of the page:

```
using System.Security.Cryptography;
using System.IO;
using System.Text;
```

2. Code the Encrypt method. The Encrypt method takes data to encrypt and a password and salt as parameters, and it returns a string. Notice how the Encrypt method creates the Rfc2898DerivedBytes class and uses it to generate a strong key from the password and salt combination. That key is later used by the AesManaged class to encrypt data.

```
public string Encrypt(string dataToEncrypt, string password, string salt)
{
    AesManaged aes = null;
    MemoryStream memStream = null;
    CryptoStream crStream = null;

    try
    {
        //Generate a key based on a password and salt
        Rfc2898DeriveBytes rfc2898 = new Rfc2898DeriveBytes(password,
            Encoding.UTF8.GetBytes(salt));

        //Create AES algorithm with 256-bit key and 128-bit block size
        aes = new AesManaged();
        aes.Key = rfc2898.GetBytes(aes.KeySize / 8);
        aes.IV = rfc2898.GetBytes(aes.BlockSize / 8);

        memStream = new MemoryStream();
        crStream = new CryptoStream(memStream, aes.CreateEncryptor(),
            CryptoStreamMode.Write);

        byte[] data = Encoding.UTF8.GetBytes(dataToEncrypt);
        crStream.Write(data, 0, data.Length);
        crStream.FlushFinalBlock();

        //Return base-64 string
        return Convert.ToBase64String(memStream.ToArray());
    }
    finally
    {
        //cleanup
        if (crStream != null)
            crStream.Close();

        if (memStream != null)
            memStream.Close();
```

```
            if (aes != null)
                aes.Clear();
        }
    }
```

3. Code the Decrypt method. The Decrypt method is the inverse of Encrypt: it
    takes data to decrypt and a password and salt as parameters, and it returns an
    input string. Since AES is a symmetric algorithm, the same password and salt
    values must be used to decrypt data as were used to encrypt it. The Decrypt
    method initializes the Rfc2898Bytes key and uses it to create a Decryptor for
    data.

```
public string Decrypt(string dataToDecrypt, string password, string salt)
{
    AesManaged aes = null;
    MemoryStream memStream = null;
    CryptoStream crStream = null;

    try
    {
        Rfc2898DeriveBytes rfc2898 = new Rfc2898DeriveBytes(password,
            Encoding.UTF8.GetBytes(salt));
        aes = new AesManaged();
        aes.Key = rfc2898.GetBytes(aes.KeySize / 8);
        aes.IV = rfc2898.GetBytes(aes.BlockSize / 8);

        memStream = new MemoryStream();
        crStream = new CryptoStream(memStream, aes.CreateDecryptor(),
            CryptoStreamMode.Write);
        byte[] data = Convert.FromBase64String(dataToDecrypt);
        crStream.Write(data, 0, data.Length);
        crStream.FlushFinalBlock();

        byte[] decryptBytes = memStream.ToArray();
        return Encoding.UTF8.GetString(decryptBytes, 0, decryptBytes.Length);
    }
    finally
    {
        if (crStream != null)
            crStream.Close();

        if (memStream != null)
            memStream.Close();

        if (aes != null)
            aes.Clear();
    }
}
```

4. Add code to call the Encrypt method when the user clicks the Encrypt button.
    Double-click the Encrypt button in MainPage.xaml and add the following code
    to the click event handler:

```
txtEncryptedData.Text = Encrypt(txtDataToEncrypt.Text, txtPassword.Text,
    txtSalt.Text);
```

5. Finally, add code to call the Decrypt method when the user clicks the Decrypt button. Double-click the Decrypt button in MainPage.xaml, and add the following code to the click event handler:

```
txtDecryptedData.Text = Decrypt(txtEncryptedData.Text, txtPassword.Text,
    txtSalt.Text);
```

Press F5 to run the application. Enter some data (for example, "Classified Information"), a password (for example, "test"), and a salt (note that it must be at least eight characters long; otherwise AES classes will throw an exception), and observe the values being encrypted in the Encrypted Data text box. Click Decrypt and you should see the original text in the Decrypted Data field. Note that if you enter password or salt values that are different between encryption and decryption, the application will raise an exception.

Now that you understand a bit about the cryptography framework on Windows Phone, it's time to take a look at the physical security of the device.

Information Rights Management

In addition to encrypting data, Windows Phone version 7.5also implements a feature of Microsoft Office known as *Information Rights Management (IRM)*. With IRM, policies can be set on documents, such as e-mails or Excel spreadsheets, so that the documents cannot be edited or forwarded. When an IRM-enabled document is received by Windows Phone, the platform fully enforces the rights specified for that document. This feature of Windows Phone is very appealing to enterprise users, especially since other competing platforms do not implement IRM.

Understanding Device Physical Security

With Windows Phone 7, customers rarely have to worry about sensitive data ending up in malicious hands if the device is lost or stolen. This is because several standard features that come with the phone allow you to feel confident about the security of the device. In this section, you will walk through the Windows Phone physical security safeguards that Microsoft provides. All of these features are accessible at http://windowsphone.live.com. You will need to create a Microsoft Live ID if you don't have one already and properly associate it with your Windows Phone device. Following are the features that the web portal offers for easy phone management. (They are all accessible via the Find this Phone link.)

- *Map It*: Using this feature, Windows Phone users are able to see the location of their phones using Bing Maps.

- *Ring It*: Using this option, you can instruct the phone to ring for 60 seconds using a special ringtone, even if the ring tone has been turned off.

- *Lock It and Display a Message*: You can also lock the phone from the web site and display a custom message to instruct people who may have found your phone about how to get in touch with you.

- *Erase It*: Finally, if all is lost and there is no hope of recovering the phone, you can remotely wipe all of the data from the phone and reset it to factory settings.

As you can see, the Windows Phone security story is very compelling, especially considering the short amount of time Windows Phone has been on the market. You can expect this story to become better and more feature-rich in the very near future. Certainly, more and more features from the full .NET Framework will find their way onto Windows Phone devices, which should further contribute to their security.

■ **Note** The ability to access hidden Wi-Fi networks is another security feature that is available on Windows Phone devices. Windows Phone can connect to hidden Wi-Fi networks; that is, ones with IDs that are not being broadcast publicly. To connect to a hidden Wi-Fi network, you must know the network's ID when establishing your Wi-Fi connection. Even though hiding Wi-Fi networks is frequently referred to as "security by obscurity," and it is criticized for not being a very effective security strategy, access to hidden Wi-Fi networks is an often-requested feature for mobile devices, and it is available on Windows Phone.

Meeting Certification Requirements

Microsoft documentation on the security built into Windows Phone lists explicit requirements regarding application code. In this section, you will gain an understanding of what types of application behavior are not tolerated by Microsoft.

Applications Must Implement MSIL Code

Microsoft imposes a requirement on Windows Phone application developers to use managed code to construct their applications. The strong typing, bounds checking, and memory management features of managed code help minimize the most common types of attacks (also referred to in the security community as *attack vectors*) on both the application and the Windows Phone application platform.

Generally, if you use C# with its default settings, you will be in compliance with this restriction. Problems will arise, however, if you venture into unsafe C# code territory, which can be enabled by using the unsafe keyword in a method signature. In addition to using the unsafe keyword, applications with unsafe code must be compiled with a special switch, as shown in Figure 19-11. As an example of unsafe code, consider the following code, which uses a simple SquarePtrParam function to accept a pointer variable (non-MSIL code) and perform pointer arithmetic on it:

```
public partial class MainPage : PhoneApplicationPage
{
    unsafe public MainPage()
    {
        int i=5;
        InitializeComponent();
        SquarePtrParam(&i);
        PageTitle.Text = i.ToString();
    }

    // Unsafe method, using a pointer to square the number
    unsafe static void SquarePtrParam(int* p)
```

```
        {
            *p *= *p;
        }
    }
```

The good news for Windows Phone developers is that, while the previous code is perfectly valid .NET code, the Windows Phone templates in Visual Studio disable the option to compile unsafe code. This option is generally found under Project ➤ Properties ➤ Build, and the Allow Unsafe Code check box is grayed out on Windows Phone templates, making the option of writing an unsafe application for Windows Phone a challenging exercise. Even though it is possible to work around this limitation by modifying the project file (.csproj) using a text editor and specifying the <AllowUnsafeCode> attribute, it is certainly not worth the trouble because the Windows Phone Marketplace will reject the application anyway.

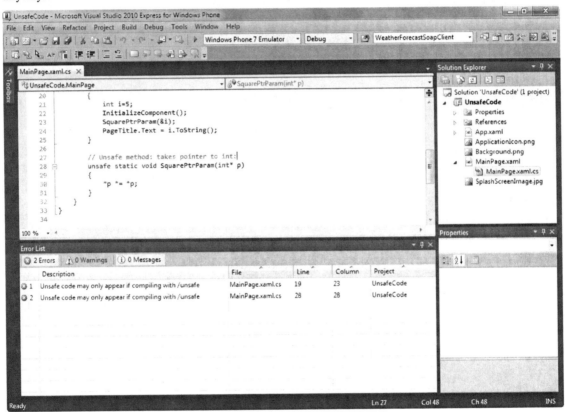

Figure 19-11. Applications that implement unsafe code must be compiled with a special switch.

Applications Must Not Implement Any Security-Critical Code

With .NET version 4.0, Microsoft has moved away from the complexities of its *Code Access Security (CAS)* model and toward a simpler model, which it calls *Transparent Security*. The first transparency rule set was initially introduced in .NET 2.0 and was expanded to transparency level 2 in .NET 4.0. With transparency level 2, code is segregated into three types: transparent code, security-safe-critical code, and security-critical code. These types are discussed in the following sections.

Transparent Code

In the transparent category are applications that run in a sandbox, which are pretty much all of the Windows Phone applications that you will ever write. These applications have a limited permission set granted by the sandbox. That means that, as a developer, you don't have to be concerned about checking security policies when you write your applications, as long as you don't try to perform any operation deemed not accessible by the transparent code policy. For reference purposes, here is the list of tasks that transparent applications are not permitted to perform:

- Directly calling critical code

- Performing an Assert operation or elevation of privilege

- Containing unsafe or unverifiable code

- Calling native code or code that has the SuppressUnmanagedCodeSecurityAttribute attribute

- Calling a member that is protected by a LinkDemand

- Inheriting from critical types

Security-Safe-Critical Code

In the security-safe-critical category is code that is fully trusted but is still callable by transparent code. It exposes a limited surface area of full-trust code. Correctness and security verifications happen in security-safe-critical code.

Security-Critical Code

This category of code can't be called by transparent code. This code typically implements system-level functionality and has unlimited access to Windows Phone resources, making it a perfect place to embed malicious behavior. Therefore, Microsoft disallows this type of code. To pass the Windows Phone Marketplace certification criteria successfully, applications must not implement any security-critical code. In addition, applications must not invoke native code via PInvoke or COM Interoperability.

You will most likely never have to worry about the ins and outs of the Transparent Security model when you program for Windows Phone. But in case you decide to try to implement unsafe or security-critical code in your application, remember that Marketplace certification tests will quickly uncover this type of behavior and deny entry to your application.

Capability List

To protect users' privacy and enforce developer accountability, the Windows Phone Marketplace fully discloses to the user whether an application is relying on any of the following services for proper operation:

- Gamer services

- Location services

- Media libraries

- Microphones

- Networking

- Placing phone calls

- Push notifications

- Sensors

- Web browsers

These capabilities are requested on a Windows Phone device when an application developer submits her application for certification. Only the requested capabilities are granted, protecting device users from unexpected behavior of potentially privacy-intruding applications.

Obfuscating Your Application Code

The clarity and speed of writing your application in a managed .NET language (C# or Visual Basic .NET), and the ability to avoid unsafe code constructs are very appealing features of the Windows Phone platform. Unfortunately, from a security and intellectual-property perspective, managed languages have one significant drawback: they can easily be decompiled or reverse-engineered using tools such as ildasm.exe or Red Gate Reflector, potentially exposing your application source code to anybody who has access to your application's XAP file. This means that the programming logic that you may have spent days or weeks tweaking could be easily copied by your competition or eavesdropped upon for a possible attack on your application.

To illustrate how easy it is to peek inside your compiled application, let's use the Red Gate Reflector tool and open up one of the compiled assemblies created earlier in this chapter.

■ **Note** Reflector was a free tool for a long time; however, Red Gate has started charging for its use recently. You can still download a 14-day evaluation trial of this tool at http://reflector.red-gate.com/download.aspx.

Launch Reflector by double-clicking Reflector.exe from the location you downloaded it to, and click File ➤ Open Assembly. Navigate to AESEncryption.dll, which should be located inside the Bin/Debug/ folder of the AESEncryption project created in the previous section (AESEncyrption.dll is created automatically for you in the Debug folder when you run the application inside the emulator). Once you open that assembly, expand the AESEncryption ➤ AESEncyrption.dll ➤ AESEncryption ➤ MainPage node and click the Encrypt method. You should see something similar to Figure 19-12, with virtually all of your code for the Encrypt method exposed in the right pane.

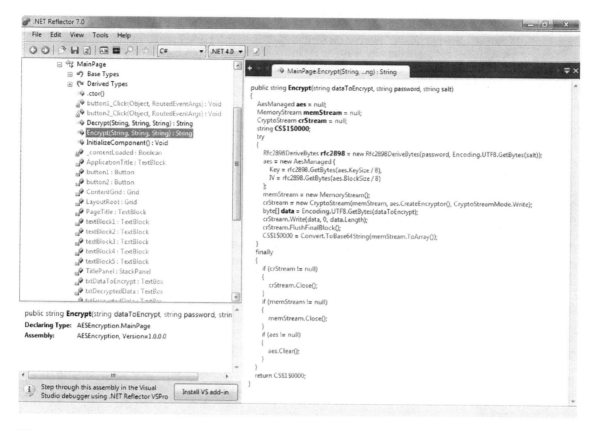

Figure 19-12. The Encrypt method of the AESEncryption project in Reflector

Obfuscation serves to protect intellectual property in your code from the prying eyes of Reflector and other such tools. There are several .NET obfuscation products on the market, including Dotfuscator, DeepSea, and Crypto. The one you will be using in this chapter is Dotfuscator because the full version of Dotfuscator for Windows Phone is freely available for you to try out first before making a decision to buy. However, the basic principles of hiding code should be applicable to all of the products mentioned.

■ **Note** You can download a copy of Dotfuscator for Windows Phone from the PreEmptive Solutions web site, at www.preemptive.com/know-more/windows-phone-7.

Follow the steps in this example to obfuscate the code from the AESEncryption project.

1. Start by launching Dotfuscator from Start ➤ All Programs ➤ Dotfuscator.

2. When the Select Project Type dialog comes up, select Create New Project. On the Input Files menu bar, select Add New Input (the folder icon) and navigate to the AESEncryption.xap file. Note how Dotfuscator understands that Windows Phone applications consist of XAP files, while we had to navigate to the DLL file when we used Reflector, since it is not currently customized to work with Windows Phone applications. Make a mental note of it for now—you will come back to this minor difference in the way these two programs function shortly.

3. By default, Dotfuscator is not set to obfuscate anything in the assembly. You must tell the application that you want the assembly obfuscated and variables hidden. To do so, go to the Settings tab. Set Disable Control Flow and Disable String Encryption to No, as shown in Figure 19-13.

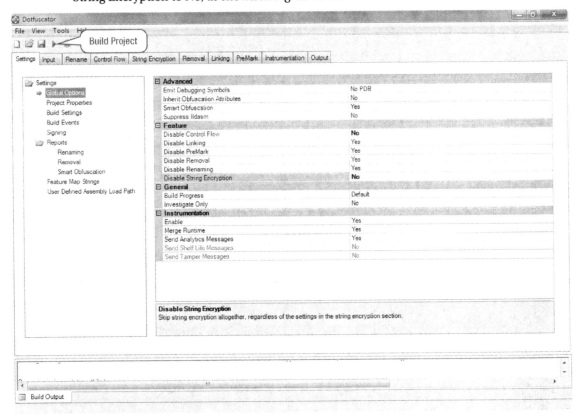

Figure 19-13. Enabling Dotfuscator settings for code obfuscation

4. Still on the Settings tab, click the Build Settings node and make sure to set the destination directory to a folder that you can easily locate on your computer, such as C:\Projects\Dotfuscated\.

5. You are now ready to create an obfuscated version of your XAP file. To do that, click the Build button in Dotfuscator, as shown in Figure 19-13. Once the Build completes, you should have a new XAP file generated in the output directory that you configured in step 4.

6. You are now ready to peek inside the obfuscated file to determine whether the code has indeed been made unreadable to Reflector. Reflector can only understand DLL assemblies, not XAP files generated for Windows Phone applications. Recall how a XAP file is simply a renamed ZIP file containing several files, including application resource files and a DLL assembly within it. Rename the obfuscated XAP file to have a .zip extension and peek inside that file.

7. Extract the AESEncryption.dll assembly from the obfuscated XAP file generated in step 5. From within Reflector, navigate to that assembly and open it.

8. Expand the AESEncryption ➤ AESEncyrption.dll ➤ AESEncryption ➤ MainPage node, and click the Encrypt method. Instead of code in the right pane, you should now see something similar to Figure 19-14, in which the logic of the method is unreachable to tools like Reflector and ildasm.exe.

This example should give you the basic idea on obfuscating managed .NET code. You can tweak settings inside Dotfuscator to ensure that your application's intellectual property is properly secured. Note, however, that you should always deploy your obfuscated code to your (unlocked) Windows Phone device for testing. Sometimes, the obfuscator tools get a bit ambitious and scramble the information that is expected to be in a certain format by the Windows Phone platform, which results in application failing to load and launch properly. Always test your XAP file before submitting it to the Marketplace for certification!

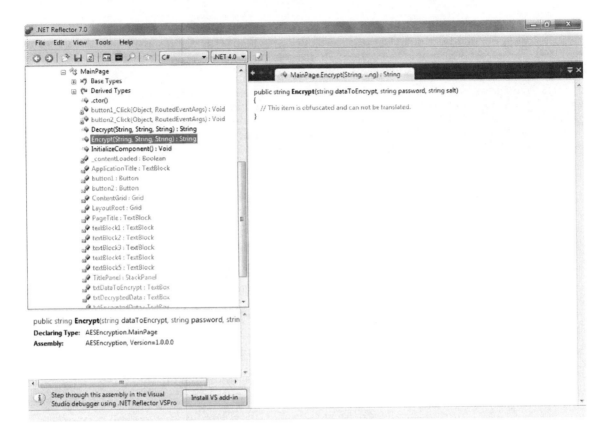

Figure 19-14. Obfuscated Encrypt method

Summary

In this last chapter of the book, you learned about the facilities that the Windows Phone platform provides to secure data in transit and on devices, as well as how Windows Phone imposes a set of rigorous tests to confirm the identity of the application developer and ensure that the applications in the Windows Phone Marketplace don't contain malicious code. You also looked at making your code unreadable, or obfuscated, to tools like `ildasm.exe` and Reflector. Windows Phone also provides security for the device itself, giving users the ability to find or call the phone remotely, and erase all data from the phone remotely. Windows Phone has already implemented a strong set of security features, and those features will only get more and more comprehensive as time passes.

Index

■ A

Accelerometer
  coding application
    capturing and displaying data, 161–162
    namespaces specification, 160, 161
    start and stop,implementation, 162–163
    testing, 163
    variables intializing, 161
  data retrieval
    CaptureAccelerometerData demo, 156
    design view,CaptureAccelerometerData
      demo, 160
    Microsoft.Devices.Sensors, 157
    start and stop, 158–159
    UI resources, 158
    Windows Phone, 157
    x, y, and z directions, 156
  distance calculation, 154
  Move a Ball
    application,MoveBallDemo, 163
    applying captured data, 168
    components,start and stop, 165–166
    creation, 164
    demo design view, 166
    Demo UI,MoveBall, 164
    handling captured data, 168
    namespaces specification, 167
    start and stop button events, 169
    testing, 169
    UI resources, 165
    variables initializing, 167
  orientation and movement, 151–153
  pitch, roll, and yaw calculation, 154–155
  SDK support, 155
Advanced Encryption Standard (AES), 496
Application Bar
  add button events
    btnAdd_Click function, 187
    collapse button, 184, 185
    expand button, 185, 186

    MainPage.xaml,location, 184
    text box, 186, 187
    TextBlock, 187
    visibility property, 186
  add, save and delete, 173
  built-in functionality, 174
  event handlers, 189–190
  fixed height, 174
  Foursquare and Graphic.ly,shortcuts, 172
  glue code, 183, 184
  glue XAML and managed code, 190
  graphics requirements, 175
  menu events, 188–189
  menu items, 174
  save button events, 188
  windows phone application
    ApplicationBarSample project, 176
    C# code, 182, 183
    close-up, 180
    copy to output directory, 176
    debugging, 182
    IsMenuEnabled properties, 181
    MainPage code, 181
    managed code, 175
    Microsoft.Phone.Shell.ApplicationBar,
      181
    opacity property, 180
    shell:ApplicationBar.MenuItems element,
      179
    strings Menu Item, 182
    text property, 181
    Visual Studio 2010, 176
    XAML, 175 (see also XAML)
    XAML code implementation, 180, 181
  Windows Phone menu system, 171
  worker function, 183
Application_UnhandledException, 107–109
Azure (Microsoft), 38, 39

■ B

Bing Maps service, 11

■ C

CalculatorService Exception, 114–115
Cameras and photos
    augmented reality applications, 379
    cell phone, 379
    Windows Phone photo features
        accept button, 384
        auto-generated template, 382
        btnCamera_Click event handler, 382
        btnCamera_Click method, 383
        btnOpenPhoto_Click, 385
        btnUpload, 393
        CameraCaptureTask, 381, 383
        choosers, 380
        emulator application, 384
        extras and share features, 388
        extras demo, 392
        image control, 382
        image transfer,TwitPic (*see* TwitPic)
        imgPhoto image control, 383
        launch an application, 389
        launchers, 380
        Model-View-ViewModel pattern, 384
        navigation, 390–391
        OnNavigatedTo event, 392
        OnNavigatedTo method, 392
        open photo button,click, 385
        phone Start screen, 392
        PhotoCapture, 381
        PhotoChooserTaskCompleted, 385
        Pictures Library, 385
        properties dialog, 382
        sandbox, 379
        saving photos, 386
        share option, 389
        standard Application Bar icons, 382
        status message, 386
        take photos, 381
        TwitPic, 392
        Upload PhotoCapture Snapshots (*see* TwitPic)
        Windows Phone emulator, 384
        WMAppManifest.xaml, 391
        WMAppManifest.xml, 389, 390
        XNA framework,coding, 386–388
    Zune software, 379
Catching and debugging errors
    exception
        Application_UnhandledException method, 109
        breakpoint,RootFrame_NavigationFailed, 108
        debugging, 107
        ErrorHandlingDemo application, 103, 104
        FormatException, 104, 107
        NavigationFailedEventArgs.Uri, 108
        querying, 105, 106
        Visual Studio,raised format, 105
        Windows Phone system, 105
    handling device exception
        AccelerometerFailedException, 121
        CatchDeviceException UI, 122
        CatchDeviceExceptionDemo project, 121, 122
        Microsoft.Devices.Sensors, 122, 123
        user interface (UI) (*see* User interface)
    web service exception
        CalculatorService, 110, 114–115
        debug CalculatorService, 111
        e.Result,exception, 114
        e.Result.ToString(), 113
        ErrorHandlingDemo solution, 110
        InvalidCastException error, 112, 113
        multiple project startup option, 110
        Reference.cs, 113
        txtDeviceManufacturer, 115
        txtDeviceName, 115
        WCF test client, 112
    windows phone device
        access denied message, 120
        debugging, 120
        detail page, 118
        developer registration, 118, 119
        error message, 121
        my windows phone page, 120
        phone icon, 117
        video and audio playing, 117
        Zune software, 116
Cloud database
    entity framework, 40
    SQL Azure database (*see* SQL Azure database)
Code Access Security (CAS), 506

■ D

Data security
  AES, 496, 500
  data encryption algorithms, 495
  HMACSHA1 and HMACHSHA256
    AESEncryption application, 500, 501
    AesManaged, 502
    Algorithms, 496
    cryptography classes, 498
    decrypt method, 503, 504
    Decryptor creation, 503
    encrypt and decrypt data, 499
    encrypt button, 503
    HMACTest, 497
    IRM, 504
    MainPage.xaml, 497
    Rfc2898DeriveBytes, 500
    security.cryptography, 498
    UI application, 499
Digital rights management (DRM), 358

■ E

Expression Blend, 8–9
Extensible Application Markup Language
  (XAML), 6
  application exception, 178
  application resources section, 177
  IconUri properties, 179
  PhoneApplicationPage.ApplicationBar
    element, 178
  PhoneNavigation element, 178
  <phone:PhoneApplicationPage> node, 177
  shell:ApplicationBar element, 178
  shell:ApplicationBarIconButton, 179
  Solution Explorer, 177

■ F

Facebook
  OAuth
    application authentication, 253
    application authorization, 253
    authorization protocol, 253
    FBLogin() constructor, 256, 257
    GetGraphToken method, 257
    Rx.NET, 257, 258
    step-by-step guidelines, 253

    STR_FB_SuccessUrl constant, 255
    user authentication, 253, 255
    user interface enhancement, 254
  ShareLinkTask and ShareStatusTask
    launchers, 253
Fast application switching (FAS), 240, 241
Flickr photographs
  images search, 454, 455
  playing animation
    beginning,timeline animation, 460
    end,timeline animation, 461
    FromEvent<T> method, 462
    image loading, 458
    loadingImages animation, 461
    MainPage constructor, 462
    MainPage.xaml in Visual Studio, 458
    Record Keyframe button, 459
    storyboard animation, 459
    storyboard loadingImages, 458
    timeline animation,Expression Blend, 458
    WebBrowser control, 458
  screen layout, 454
  throttling, 455–457
  user interface(UI), 453
  WebBrowser control, 452
  Windows Phone project, 452, 453
Frame and page navigation, 228–231

■ G

GeoCoordinateWatcherDemo Project, 331, 332

■ H

Handling an Exception error fixing, 109

■ I, J, K

Information Rights Management (IRM), 504
Internationalization
  application title and tile localization
    application resource file creation, 305–
      308
    C++ resource file, 305
    resource DLL, 308–310
  content localization
    AppResource.de-AT.resx resource file, 301
    AppResources.resx resource file, 299
    fallback mechanism, 299
    .resx files, 298

Internationalization, content localization (*cont.*)
  ShowEventDetails() function, 302
  Spanish application interface, 304
  SplashScreenImage.jpg, 298
  ToggleEventLocale method, 303
  translation services, 299
  WP7AnniversaryParty.csproj file, 303
CultureInfo class, 289
culture settings, 289–292
  CultureInfo class, 293, 297
  CultureInfo() constructor, 298
  CurrentCulture property, 293, 297
  Event Date:, Event Time:, and Event Cost:, 294
  MY APPLICATION text, 294
  regional settings, 294
  ShowEventDetails and
    ToggleEventLocale Functions, 296
  ShowEventDetails() function, 297, 298
  standard formatting options, 298
  System.Globalization, 296
  System.Globalization.CultureInfo class, 293
  System.Threading, 296
  TextBlock controls, 294
  ToggleEventLocale() function, 298
  WP7 Launch Party UI Code, 295, 296
  WP7AnniversaryParty, 294, 295
  XAML designer window, 294
globalization, 288
ISO 8601, 287
localization, 288
MSDN documentation, 305
.NET culture hierarchy, 292
Unicode, 288
Internet Explorer 9, 193
Internet Information Services (IIS), 487
ISO culture codes, 291
Isolated storage
  API, 311, 312
  application coding
    completed application testing, 320
    CreateDirectory method, 318
    directory path string, 318
    image retrieval, 319, 320
    IsolatedStorage.DeleteFile, 318
    IsolatedStorageFileStream, 318
    Isolated Storage Space, 319
    namespaces specifying, 316
    Remove method, 318
    variables initializing, 317

  WebClient.OpenReadCompleted event, 317
  functions, 312
  IsolatedStorageStoreImageDemo, 312–314
  namespaces, 311
  settings
    BindKeyList() method, 325
    coding application behavior, 324
    delete button event handler, 326
    finished application testing, 327
    IsolatedStorageSettingsDemo, 320–322
    Key text box, 321
    ListBox changed event, 326, 327
    main page creation, 323, 324
    namespaces, 325
    save button event handler, 325, 326
    StreamWriter and StreamReader, 326
    System.IO.IsolatedStorage.IsolatedStorageSettings, 320
    UI resources selection, 322, 323
  System.IO.IsolatedStorage.IsolatedFileStream, 311
  System.IO.IsolatedStorage.IsolatedStorageFile, 311
  System.IO.IsolatedStorage.IsolatedStorageSettings, 311
  user interface coding
    main page creation, 315, 316
    resources selection, 314
    solution explorer, 314
  virtual file storage system, 311

■ L

Language-culture-aware classes, 287
LoadAppStateData method, 251
LoadAppStateDataAsync method, 251
Location services, 133
  application coding
    C# code, 334
    Dispatcher.BeginInvoke, 335
    geoCoordinateWatcher variable, 334
    GeoCoordinateWatcher's
      PositionChanged event, 335
    namespaces listing, 334
    PositionChanged event, 334, 335
    SimulateGPS method, 335
  Bing Maps Service
    AddressPlottingDemo application, 348

AddressPlottingDemo.BingMapGeoCode
Service, 352
application testing, 354
button event handling, 353, 354
GeoCodeService, 347
GeocodeServiceClient variable_svc, 352
RouteService, 347
SearchService, 347
service reference adding, 348, 350
UI coding, 350–352
built-in GPS receiver, 329
GeoCoordinateWatcherDemo application,
336
GeoCoordinateWatcherDemo Project, 331–
333
mapping API, 330
movements tracking
application testing, 347
Bing Map Demo, 337
bing maps service portal and SDK
installation, 338, 339
BingMapDemo project creation, 339, 340
bingMapLocator, 346
main page creation, 341, 343
Microsoft.Maps.Control, 343
StatusChanged and PositionChanged
GeoCoordinateWatcher events, 345, 346
TryStart, 346
UI resources declaration, 341
variables initialization, 344, 345
triangulation, 329
Wi-Fi, 329

M

Media files
MediaElement, 357–358
smartphones, 357
sound application
assests, RobotSoundDemo project, 372
design video, RobotSoundDemo, 375
MediaElement, 370
namespaces specification, 376
play button clicks, 376–377
properties, sound18.wma file, 374
Robot animation, 373
RobotSoundDemo application, 371
RobotSoundDemo project, 371
Robot.xaml, 372
Robot.xaml.cs, 372
sound18.wma, 372, 373
testing, 377
UI resources, 372
vector graphic versions, 372
XAML code, 375
video (see Video)
Windows Phone devices, 357
YouTube, 357
Metro design system
graphic design, 213
screen orientations, 216
Segoe WP, 214
visual elements, 214
Windows Phone chrome, 214–216
Microsoft Azure, 38
Microsoft Push Notification Service (MPNS), 408
Microsoft SQL Server Management Studio, 51–53
Model-View-ViewModel (MVVM) design pattern,
38

N

NavigationService.Navigate method, 279
Network security
IIS
access secure data, 491
add web site dialog, 488
certificate authority error, 492
error message, 491
https site binding, 491
physical path setting, 487
server certificates node, 489
testing, 491
web server software, 487
web site bindings link, 490
Windows Phone client application, 490
self-signed certificate, 487
e-mail program, 494
installing certificates, 495
Internet Explorer and navigate, 494
message notifying, 493
Microsoft Exchange, 492
trusted root CAs, 493
Windows Phone device or emulator, 494
SSL
securing connections, 484
testing and opening, 485–486
Notepad phone application
BoolToVisibilityConvert, 79–81
cloud database (see also Cloud database)

Notepad phone application (*cont.*)
  object model, 57–63
  Windows Azure project, 56–57
  MainPage
    AddNew Button Event, 78
    code constructor, 77
    Delete Button Event, 78
    namespaces, 77
    Save Button Event, 77
    View/Edit Button Event, 78
  Microsoft Azure
    runtime framework, 39
    services, 39
  MVVM pattern, 38
  Notepad Service, adding reference, 81
  NotepadViewModel, 82
    adding constructor, 85–86
    AddUser method, 86
    DeleteNote method, 86
    event handlers, 87–88
    INotifyPropertyChanged, 82–83
    INotifyPropertyChanged interface, 88
    SaveNote method, 86
    variables, 83–85
  n-tier architecture, 38
  SQL Azure (*see* SQL Azure database)
  testing, 89–90
  user interface of, 70, 71
    BoolToVisibilityConvert, 71–73
    MainPage, 75
    NeedUserId property, 76
    NoteListUserControl, 74–75
    resource declaration, 75
    ShowNoteList property, 76
    UserRegistrationUserControl, 71–73
  Web service, 38
  Windows Azure, deploying to (*see* Windows
    Azure)
  Windows Phone client, 38
  Windows Phone Project, 70

■ O

OAuth
  application authentication, 253
  application authorization, 253
  authorization protocol, 253
  FBLogin() constructor, 256, 257
  GetGraphToken method, 257
  Rx.NET, 257, 258

  step-by-step guidelines, 253
  STR_FB_SuccessUrl constant, 255
  user authentication, 253, 255
  user interface enhancement, 254
Obfuscating
  AESEncryption project, 508
  AESEncryption.xap file, 510
  Dotfuscator, 509, 510
  encrypt method, 509, 511, 512
  intellectual property, 509
  Red Gate Reflector tool, 508
  reflector, 511
  settings, 510
  testing,Windows Phone device, 511
Object model, Cloud database
  Connection Properties window, 61
  Data Source window, 60
  database objects, 62
  Entity Data Model Wizard, 58
  Entity Framework, 57
  Entity model Notepad.edmx, 63
OnNavigatedTo method, 251

■ P, Q

Panorama control, 223–225
Physical Security
  capability list, 507
  erase, 504
  lock, 504
  map, 504
  meeting certification requirements
    MSIL code, 505–506
    security-critical code, 507
    security-safe-critical code, 507
    transparent code, 507
  ring, 504
Pivot control, 226–228
Publishing life cycle, 129–131
Push notification service (PNS), 133
Push notifications
  architecture
    life cycle, 409–410
    MPNS, 408, 409
    push notification framework, 410–411
  raw notifications, 407 (*see also* Raw
    notifications)
  real world, 442
  secure web services, 443

tile notifications, 406 (*see also* Tile notifications)
toast notifications, 405–406 (*see also* Toast notifications)

■ R

Raw notifications
  characteristics, 408
  client application
    btnCreateChannel_Click() function, 430
    debug window, 432
    error-handling function, 431
    httpChannel_HttpNotificationReceived event handler function, 430
    MainPage.xaml.cs file, 429
    RawNotificationPNClient,creation, 429
    send notifications, 432–433
    testing delivery, 433
    TextWrapping property, 429
    Windows Phone client application, 431
  send messages or updates, 407
RootFrame_NavigationFailed
  handling exception, 109
  unhandled exception, 107–109
Rx.NET
  create and read observable collections, 449–451
  data-connection issues handling, 472–473
  design guidelines
    marble diagram drawing, 463
    scheduler to concurrency, 463
  error handling, 471
  flickr photographs (*see* Flickr Photographs)
  multiple concurrent requests
    BeginXXX/EndXXX methods, 477
    CreateChannel method, 476, 478
    operation cancellation, 476
    Windows Phone framework, 476
    WiredUpKeyEvents() function, 478
    WireUpWeatherEvents() function, 477
  observer pattern, 448
  reactive extensions library, 448
  reactive programming, 446, 447
  subscription pipeline, 447
  weather web service
    adding service reference, 466
    .asmx web service, 465
    asynchronous processing, 471
    design layout, WeatherRx, 467

GetWeatherAsync function, 470
GetWeatherSubject function, 468
GlobalWeather service, 465
InitializeComponent() statement, 468
LINQ-to-XML functions, 468
Microsoft.Phone.Reactive and System.Observable assemblies, 465
user interface(UI), 466–467
WeatherRx application, 465, 470
WireUpKeyEvents function, 469
WireUpWeatherEvents function, 468
WeatherRx revising, 473–475
Windows Phone project, 448

■ S

Scalable vector graphics (SVG), 208
Secure Sockets Layer (SSL), 484
Security
  web-based tool, 479
  Windows Phone Marketplace
    execution manager, 484
    intellectual property protection, 480
    multiple malicious programs, 479
    non-repudiation, 480
    private application distribution, 484
    safe application behavior, 481
    sandboxed execution, 483, 484
    solution configuration, 482
    XAP file submission, 481, 482
    XAP file uploading, 482, 483
Segoe WP, 214
SQL Azure
  account, logging in to, 41
  account, signing up, 40
  create server page, 43
  database (*see* SQL Azure database)
  SQL Server Management Studio (Microsoft), 51–53
SQL Azure database, 39
  create database screen, 48
  database server, 47
  database tables
    NotepadDB database schema, 54
    NotepadDB tables, 55
  entering IP address, 45
  firewall configuration, 43
  firewall rule screen, 46
  service access, 44
  subscription information, 49

SQL Azure database (*cont.*)
    testing, 49–51
    username/password for, 42
    WCF service
        AddNote method, 66
        AddUser method, 66
        contract, 64–65
        data contract, 65–66
        DeleteNote method, 67
        GetNote method, 68
        testing, 69–70
        UpdateNote method, 67
SQL Server Management Studio, 51–53
Storage area networks (SAN) networks, 38

■ T

Tile notifications
    btnSendNotification_Click event handler, 427
    client application, 425
    images and text updation, 424
    push notifications,verification, 427–429
    Quick Launch area, 406
    receive notification, 425
    start screen, 407
    string ToastPushXML declaration, 426
    Windows Forms client execution, 425
    Windows Phone Notification client application creation, 425
    WPN client application, 426
    XML schema, 425
Tilt effect, 231, 233
Toast notifications
    btnSendNotification, 419
    btnSendNotification_Click event handler, 420
    builder.ToString() function, 419
    client application
        BindToShell function, 416
        btnCreate_Click event handler, 415, 416
        design surface, 414
        hellToastNotificationReceived() function, 417
        httpChannel_ExceptionOccurred, 417
        HttpNotificationChannel, 416
        MainPage.xaml.cs file, 414
        PhoneApplicationPage, 414
        SetupChannel() function, 416
        TextWrapping property, 413

Visual Studio Output window, 415
Windows Phone application, 413
HttpWebRequest sendNotificationRequest, 420
POSTed to MPNS, XML, 419
push notification
    messages, 418
    verification, 421–423
sample, 406
server to pass parameters, 423, 424
single-screen application, 411
string declarations, 419
URI notification, 418
Windows Forms application, 412, 413
Windows Forms project, 418
Windows Phone application, 412
Windows Phone client to receive parameters, 424
XML message, 418
X-NotificationClass header, 421
X-NotificationClass property, 421
X-WindowsPhone-Target header, 421
Tombstoning, 240, 241
Track push notifications
    app.config file, 437
    automated push notification subscriber, 441–442
    broadcast button, 438
    IRegistrationService, 436, 437
    PNServer application, 434
    RegistrationService.cs file, 436
    RESTful WCF service, 435, 439
    sendPushNotificationToClient function, 439
    System.ServiceModel.Web assembly, 435
    URL cloud service, 441
    WCF service, 440
    Windows Forms application, 437
    Windows Phone client, 439
    WPF application, 434
Transition effects, 231–233
Trial applications
    currency converter, 271, 284
        btnCalculateDamage_Click event, 282
        full application license, 272
        LINQ, 282
        LoadCurrencies method, 282
        main application screen, 272
        MainPage.xaml page layout, 272, 273
        Microsoft.Phone.Tasks namespace, 283
        MoreStuff.xaml page, 275, 276, 281
        "nag" page, 274

page-to-page navigation, 279–281
TrialInfo class, 281
Upgrade.xaml page, 274, 275
web service, 277–279
XAML code, 272
free trial button, 265, 266
IsTrial method, 267–268
marketplace API, 269–271
More Stuff screen, 271
time-restricted applications, 265
Windows.Phone.Tasks namespace, 266
TwitPic
activating code, live photo
ARGBPx array, 401
btnNegativeOff_Click, 402
btnNegativeOn_Click event handler, 402
ColorToNegative() method, 403
debug message, 400, 401
GetARGB () method, 403
libraries, 399
module-level variables, 399
negative image, 403, 404
OnNavigatedTo event, 399
PumpARGBFrames function, 401
GetRequestStreamCallback, 394–395
LINQ to XML, 396
live photo feeds, 398
mediaurl node, 396
RESTful Web service, 393
selected photo navigation, 392
System.Xml.Linq, 393
Upload PhotoCapture Snapshots, 391
uploaded image, 397
UploadPhoto function, 393
UploadPhoto method, 396
user interface, 394, 398–399
Windows Phone emulator, 396
WMAppManifest.xaml, 391

Notepad phone application
BoolToVisibilityConvert, 71–73
MainPage, 75
NeedUserId property, 76
NoteListUserControl, 74–75
resource declaration, 75
ShowNoteList property, 76
UserRegistrationUserControl, 71–73
resources, 123
TwitPic, 394, 398–399

■ V

Video
coding application
buffering, 364
MediaPlayerLauncher, 369
mute button, 368
namespaces specification, 363–364
pause button, 366
play button, 367
slider to skip control, 368, 369
stop button, 366
testing, 370
time elapsed, 365, 366
variables initializing, 364
video download progress, 364
DRM protection, 358
IIS media server,HD video content, 358
MediaPlayerDemo application, 359
MediaPlayerDemo project, 359, 360
Microsoft Azure, 358
stop, pause, mute, and seek, 358
UI
btnMediaPlayerLauncher, 360
custom media player main page and UI,
360–362
MediaPlayerDemo, 363
resources declaration, 360
TextBlocks, 360
Windows IIS media server, 358
Visual Studio 2010 Express Output window, 244

■ W

WebBrowser control
Bing image search, 196
cars online, image browsing, 194
display and security settings, 204
dynamic content display, 200–201

■ U

User interface(UI)
accelerometer start and stop components,
124
application
accelerometer start and stop behavior,
126–127
namespaces specifying, 125
variables initializing, 126
CatchDeviceExceptionDemo design, 125

WebBrowser control (*cont.*)
HorizontalAlignment and VerticalAlignment
properties, 195
HTML5 features, 194
canvas, 208
canvas drawing, 211, 212
geolocation, 207
geolocation API testing, 208, 209
IsGeolocationEnabled property, 208
IsScriptEnabled property, 208
media playback, 207
media playback testing, 209, 210
NavigateToString method, 208
new form fields, 207
SVG, 208
HTML-formatted content, 193
local HTML content display, 198–200
MainPage.xaml.cs file, 195
My Car Browser application, 196
saving web pages, 201–204
Uri object, 196
viewport, 204–206
webBrowser1_Loaded() function, 196
Windows Phone, 193
Windows Azure, 39
AppFabric, 39
Notepad service
account signing up, 91
compile and publish, 94
create and configure, 92
NotepadService.cspkg and
ServiceConfiguration.cscfg, 95
registration process, 91
testing, 99
Windows Azure Cloud Service project, 56
Windows Communication Foundation (WCF),
434
service, 55
Service Web Role, 57
Windows phone
application development life cycle, 12–13
applications, 2–4
chrome, 214–216
cloud services, 11
code writing, 22–23
customization, 25–28
developer tools, 15
hardware specifications, 4–6
marketplace, 1–2
Metro design, 11
project creation

HelloWorld, 17–18
new project, 17
Visual Studio 2010 Express, 16
Silverlight, 6
Silverlight controls, 18
MY APPLICATION TextBlock, 18–19
TextBox control, 20–22
Visual Studio 2010 Express toolbox, 19–20
smartphone features, 4
styling, 28–33
theme
accent colors, 217
background settings, 217
code snippet, 217
current theme detection, 221, 222
custom themes, 216
elliptical shape drawing, 218, 219
Resources.MergedDictionaries, 216
theme changing, 219–221
UI creation, 217, 218
tools
documentation and support, 10
Expression Blend, 8–9
visual studio, 7–8
Windows Phone emulator, 9–10
user experience guidelines, 213
Windows Phone emulator, 23–25
XNA, 7
Windows Phone 7.5, 193
Windows Phone applications, 103
certification requirement
content policies, 133
GPS, 133
malicious software, 131
must do, 132
must not do, 132
performance and resource management,
135
phone functionality, 131, 136
PNS, 133
reliability, 131, 135
resource,efficient use, 131
security, 136
technical support information, 136
XAP file, 132
submission validation
code requirements, 134
language validation, 134
marketplace images, 135
packaging requirements, 134
phone features, 134

Windows Phone Marketplace (*see* Windows Phone Marketplace)
Windows Phone hubs
  "glance and go" experience, 260
  games hub, 259
  marketplace hub, 259
  music and video hub, 259
    guidelines, 263
    I ♥ (heart) Windows Phone" image, 260–263
    MediaHistory and MediaHistoryItem classes, 260
    MusichubIntegration application, 263
    SharePoint, 263
    WMAppManifest.xml file, 260
    WriteRecentPlay and WriteAcquiredItem methods, 260
  office hub, 260
  people hub, 259
  pictures hub, 259
Windows Phone Marketplace
  finding, 148–149
  packaging
    Notepad project, 137
    phone application, 137
    project path, 138
    Solution Explorer, 136
    Visual Studio, 136
  submittion
    App name,Hub field, 140
    Artwork section, 141
    confirmation, 145
    description page, 142
    keywords, 141
    My Apps page, 138, 139
    my dashboard menu, 145
    pricing page, 143
    progress status,testing, 146
    submit page, 144
    upload page, 140
  updation, 146–148
Windows Phone Notifications (WPN). *See* Push notifications
Windows Phone OS
  application life cycle, 245
    application behavior guidelines, 252
    application events, triggers and actions, 241, 242
    Application Launching message, 244
    Application_Activated event, 245

Application_Closing event, 245
Application_Deactivated event, 244
dormant, 241
FAS, 241
initial state retrieval, 250–252
page level, state management, 247–250
tombstoning, 241
user interface enhancement, 242, 243
WebBrowserTask, 246
WebBrowserTask Launcher, 243, 244
facebook (*see* Facebook)
launchers and choosers
  AddressChooserTask chooser, 237
  application logic coding, 238–240
  BingMapsDirectionsTask launcher, 236
  BingMapsTask launcher, 236
  built-in API, 235
  CameraCaptureTask chooser, 237
  ConnectionSettingsTask launcher, 236
  core design principles, 236
  e-mail application, 236
  EmailAddressChooserTask chooser, 237
  EmailComposeTask launcher, 236
  GameInviteTask chooser, 237
  MarketplaceDetailTask launcher, 236
  MarketplaceHubTask launcher, 236
  MarketplaceReviewTask launcher, 236
  MarketplaceSearchTask launcher, 236
  MediaPlayerLauncher, 236
  Microsoft.Phone.Tasks namespace, 236
  PhoneCallTask launcher, 237
  PhoneNumberChooserTask chooser, 237
  PhotoChooserTask chooser, 237
  SaveContactTask chooser, 237
  SaveEmailAddressTask chooser, 238
  SavePhoneNumberTask chooser, 238
  SaveRingtoneTask chooser, 238
  SearchTask launcher, 237
  ShareLinkTask launcher, 237
  ShareStatusTask launcher, 237
  SmsComposeTask launcher, 237
  user interface creation, 238
  WebBrowserTask launcher, 237
Windows Phone Hubs (*see* Windows Phone hubs)
Windows Presentation Foundation (WPF), 434
Wireless Markup Language (WML), 193

■ X, Y

XAML. *See* Extensible Application Markup
   Language
XAP file, 132

■ Z

Zune software, 4

access denied error message, 121
application, 121
developer registration, 118, 119
device detail page, 118
ID and password, 119
my windows phone page, 120
phone icon, 117
USB cable,connect, 117
welcome page, 116
Windows Phone account, 116

CPSIA information can be obtained at www.ICGtesting.com
Printed in the USA
LVOW050908070312

271952LV00005BA/1/P